"useful for ideas about at-home jobs as well as job leads"
—*Good Housekeeping*

"excellent"—*Parents* Magazine

"perfect prelude to a telecommuting job search . . . [a] comprehensive classic"—*Home Office Computing*

"one of the best books on the market on this subject"—*Small Press Reviews*

"an excellent reference to getting a job that lets you work at home"—*The Secretary* Magazine

"eye-opening, I'd even say inspiring"—*Whole Earth Review*

"a wealth of information . . . very practical advice . . . Besides being a tremendous financial resource, this book is just plain fun to read"—*Welcome Home*

" a neat package" —*The Salt Lake Tribune*

"an invaluable source of information to anyone who wants to find a job working at home" —*Northwest Arkansas Times*

" I recommend it most enthusiastically; compliments to author Lynie Arden for a job well done" —R.H. Hoffman, WNWK

"Packed with solid information on how to make home-working work for you... " —*Looks at Books*

The Work-at-Home Sourcebook has been selected as one of the "Best of the Best" education and career information print materials by members of the National Education and Information Center Advisory Committee.

The Work-at-Home Sourcebook

Ninth Edition

Lynie Arden

Live Oak Publications
Boulder, Colorado

Distributed by Publishers Group West

Publisher's Cataloging-in-Publication
(Provided by Quality Books Inc.)

Arden, Lynie, 1949-
    The work-at-home sourcebook / Lynie Arden. --9th ed.
    p. cm.
    Includes index.
    ISBN 0-911781-19-6

    1. Home labor--United States--Directories.
    2. Home-based enterprises--United States--Directories.
    3. Business enterprises--United States--Directories.
    I. Title.

HD2336.U5A73 2005   338.7'4'02573
                    QBI05-200003

Live Oak Publications
P.O. Box 339
Boulder, CO 80306

Disclaimer

Every attempt has been made to make this book as accurate and complete as possible. There may be mistakes of content or typography, however, and the author and publisher make no guarantees, warranties, or representations of any kind. This book is designed as a general guide to the subject. The reader is urged to investigate and verify information and its applicability under any particular situation or circumstances.

The author and publisher shall have no liability or responsibility to anyone with respect to contacts, negotiations, or agreements that may result from information in this book, or for any loss or damage caused or alleged to have been caused directly or indirectly by such information. If legal advice or other expert assistance is required, the services of a competent professional person should be sought.

Table of Contents

WORKING AT HOME

How To Go To Work From Your Home

"This is our lifestyle; it's called freedom."
—Janice Katz, Sacramento Professional Typist's Network

Personnel manager Pat Mahy wasn't looking for a job at home, but when Escrow Overload asked her to give it a try, she said okay.

"Starting out I had my doubts. I couldn't imagine being without the stimulation of other people at work. It had some appeal, though. I figured my time might be better spent if I wasn't wasting it commuting. Well, I was thrilled within a week!"

Pat is one of the 65 million Americans who currently work at home, a number that is currently growing by a whopping 600,000 a year. Some government studies have indicated that as much as 75% of the work done in this country will be moved home by 2010.

Not everyone would be happy working at home, of course, and many people are simply not interested in moving their work home. Still, more and more people are having the same experience as Pat Mahy, who says "I'm still finding more hidden benefits to working at home the longer I do it."

Using This Book

If you want to give working at home at try, this book can be a good place to start. It won't teach you how to start a home business from scratch and it won't duplicate certain other work-at-home topics that are well covered in other books. As far as we know, though, nowhere else can you find as many specific opportunities for working at home—involving so many diverse options— already assembled for you into one neat package.

A Wide Range of Possibilities

You'll quickly notice that there are a variety of work styles represented in this book. Once you leave the confines of the traditional nine-to-five centralized work mode, a colorful rainbow of employment options appear. There is freelancing, independent contracting, working on commission, salaried positions, co-oping, and various combinations of these and other ways of working. You can get paid by the hour, by the piece, by the sale, by the project, or by the year.

You'll want to consider your needs carefully. Do you need the security of a salary? If so, freelancing is not for you. Have you always wished you could get paid for what you produce because you do it faster and better than almost everybody else? Then you may be able to boost your income by opting for piece rates. Alternately, you might want to be able to depend on a set salary, yet have lots of opportunities for earning more than the base rate by earning commissions, bonuses or other incentives. Telemarketing and market research positions, for example, often offer this type of compensation package.

One other point needs to be made about salaries. In comparing the salaries (and other forms of compensation) offered for working at home to those of conventional employment, be sure to take into consideration the many savings you'll enjoy by working at home. The money you'll save on clothing, commuting, parking, lunches and other items may make it worthwhile for you to take a home-based job that, on the surface at least, offers less money than you would make going into an office every day.

Opportunities Everywhere

You'll find over 1,000 companies in this book, which have work-at-home arrangements, but it's important to keep in mind that these listings represent only a small sample of the work-at-home opportunities actually available today. This book will be most valuable to you if you use it as an idea generator.

Suppose, for example, that in skimming through the company listings you notice there are a number of medical billing jobs at home. You had a job doing the billing for a GP for several years and feel confident you could do the work, but for one reason or another none of the specific jobs in the listings are exactly right for your situation.

By all means don't be discouraged. Study the job listings carefully, noting the names of the companies, their pay structure, how many home workers they employ and other pertinent information. Then go talk to hospitals, clinics, and doctors in your town. They may never have considered hiring home workers before but if you can explain how other medical groups have organized their home work programs—and the benefits they are getting from their programs— you'll have a good chance at getting exactly the work you want.

Some of the benefits you'll want to mention are the following (and they're not limited to medical groups):

Increased Productivity

A 20% increase in productivity is average, with some employers reporting substantially more than that. Some dedicated telecommuters have reported up to an 80% increase over their office-bound counterparts.

Lower Turnover

Once settled into a home-based job, would you give it up? Turnover among home-working employees is so low, some companies have waiting lists up to a year long for new applicants.

Near Zero Absenteeism

Flexiplace usually means flexitime, too. Work schedules can be manipulated to accommodate child-care needs, fevers and sniffles, and yes, an occasional case of playing hooky on a beautiful spring day. As long as the work gets done within the overall time limits of the job, everyone's happy.

Improved Recruiting

In areas with low unemployment, flexiplace is often used as an added inducement to potential employees. This is especially true for fields like computer programming where demand for highly qualified workers often exceeds supply. Several years ago, Continental Illinois Bank had a problem finding qualified secretaries in the Chicago area. They reasoned that many competent women were at home with children and were therefore unable to participate in the job market. The bank started Project HomeWork to solve the problem.

Lower Costs

Many companies start homework programs when they run out of room for expansion and don't want to tie up additional capital in office space. Insurance, utilities, training, maintenance and other costs often go down when workers go home.

HOME WORK AND THE LAW

There are two areas of the law that directly affect home workers; labor laws and zoning ordinances.

Labor Laws

Only a handful of states have labor laws specifically regarding working at home. In each case, their purpose is to govern "industrial home work" (work which would normally be done in a factory such as product assembly). Industrial homework is usually low skilled, low pay work in which there has been a history of worker exploitation. The purpose of the state labor laws is to insure worker safety and insure that minimum wage requirements are met. States without labor laws specifically relating to homework fall under the jurisdiction of the U.S. Dept. of Labor and its Fair Labor Standards Act of 1938 (FLSA).

The FLSA initially prohibited seven industries from using home workers. In 1938, this was a good idea since sweatshop conditions were the established norm. In December, 1984, after years of see-sawing through the courts, the ban on knitted outerwear was lifted. The remaining prohibited industries were: gloves and mittens, belts and buckles, jewelry, women's apparel, embroidery, and handkerchiefs.

Senator Orrin Hatch introduced the Freedom of the Workplace bill (S.665) soon after the ban on knitted outerwear was lifted. It calls for the complete reversal of the FLSA restrictions on homework. As written, workers' rights would be protected by the same certification process that is required for home knitters.

Congresswoman Olympia Snowe of Maine introduced a similar bill, the Home Employment Enterprise Act (HR2815) in the House of Representatives. It was virtually the House twin of Hatch's bill. Congresswoman Snowe told the House, "Cottage industries play a vital role in the economy of the state of Maine, large parts of New England, and other areas of the nation. The independent nature of homework and the unavailability of alternative employment opportunities make working at home ideal. It is time to safeguard the freedom to choose to work at home."

Before either bill came up for a vote, prohibitions on industrial homework in five of the six industries were lifted by the U.S. Dept. of Labor, effective January 9, 1989. New, tougher enforcement requirements went into effect at the same time.

Ann McLaughlin, Secretary of Labor, said "Workforce flexibility is a critical element of our effort to create jobs, enhance the quality of worklife for American workers and improve our competitive edge in world markets. The changing workforce demographics demand that we provide employment opportunities that allow workers the freedom to choose flexible alternatives including the ability to work in one's own home. Women, for example, have entered the workforce by the millions; homework adds a measure of worker flexibility and economic freedom.

" At a time when flexibility is an operational imperative to our competitive advantage, government should enhance, not impede, workers' choices," McLaughlin added.

There is only one industry the FLSA still prohibits from using home workers - women's apparel. This omission was apparently an attempt on behalf of the DOL to avoid direct confrontation with its most active opponent in this action, The International Ladies Garment Workers Union. Aside from the prohibition mentioned here, there are no other occupations covered by labor laws. Furthermore, these laws only pertain to employees, not independent contractors, independent business people, or otherwise self-employed workers.

Zoning

Before working at home in any capacity, you should find out what your local zoning ordinance has to say about it. If you live in a rural area, chances are good that you have nothing to worry about. In populated areas, however, there are often specific provisions in the zoning laws pertaining to home occupations.

Zoning laws tend to focus on the impact of a given activity. Sometimes called "nuisance laws," they are designed to protect neighborhoods from disruptive noise, traffic, odors, etc.

Chicago is an extreme example. Up until recently, within the city limits, it was illegal to use electrical equipment in a home occupation. That meant no calculators, no typewriters, no computers. The laws were outdated in Chicago and are still too often outdated elsewhere around the country. It took public pressure to get the city council in Chicago to adopt a new ordinance that would be more accommodating to homework, and it's possible for you to initiate zoning changes in your city, too.

Zoning boards are made up of your neighbors and local business people, and it is likely they are unaware of problems caused by outdated zoning ordinances. If you are frustrated by your city's zoning code, get to know these people, attend some meetings, and propose that the laws be changed.

Independent Contractor Status and Tax Savings

More often than not, home workers are paid as independent contractors. In essence, this means you are totally responsible for your own work. While different government agencies don't necessarily agree on the definition of independent contractor, generally speaking, there are two major factors affecting how home workers are classified. They are the "degree of control which the employer exercises over the manner in which the work is performed," and "opportunities for profit and loss."

It should be noted that no government agency will take you on your word that you are an independent contractor. Even if you have a written contract with a company declaring that you both agree to an employer/independent contractor relationship, the legitimacy of that relationship must be proven.

The issue here is not whether being an employee is better or worse than being an independent contractor. There are advantages and disadvantages in each situation. Rather, the issue is whether the term "independent contractor" is being applied consistently and correctly. If you meet all I.R.S. criteria for independent contractor status, you'll be responsible for your own taxes, most notably Social Security tax, renamed "Self-Employment Tax" for this purpose.

Business expenses will help you at tax time, so you need to keep records right from the start of any and all expenditures. Business expenses generally fall into two categories: direct and indirect.

Direct expenses are those that occur in the day-to-day operation of your business. Costs for office supplies, phone service, advertising, bookkeeping, equipment, books, trade publications and seminars related to your work, and insurance are all examples of direct, fully deductible expenses.

You shouldn't forget the more subtle types of deductions, either. Entertainment in the course of your work, whether in your own home or not, is ordinarily deductible (at least a certain percentage of it anyway) if you discuss or conduct business while you're entertaining and keep a record of what went on and with whom.

The same thing is true for vacations. You can generally write off a portion of your vacation expenses if you spend some time along the way looking for new business. Remember, the government expects you to try to expand your business.

Indirect expenses are those that are a part of your usual domestic bills-utilities, rent or mortgage payments, maintenance and housecleaning, property insurance, etc. Indirect expenses come under the heading of the Home Office Deduction.

The Home Office Deduction is the most common and significant way for home workers to reduce their federal tax. In order to claim the deduction, you must show that your homework space is used regularly and exclusively as your principal place of business and meeting place. (If you are a salaried employee, you may also be eligible if you can prove that your employer requires you to keep a home office as a condition of employment. In this case, you should consult an expert to determine if you meet the requirements.)

Home office expenses are deductible at the rate of whatever percentage of square footage your workspace takes up. If your home is 1,000 square feet and you use 200 square feet exclusively for workspace, you can normally deduct 20% of those receipts. A word of caution: if you use your workspace for any other purpose than work, you cannot deduct any of these expenses. Therefore, working on the kitchen table is a bad idea unless you really don't have any choice.

At last count, there were some 23 possible deductions for a home office. To make sure you don't miss any, get a copy of I.R.S. Publication 587, "Business Use of the Home." It is available free from any I.R.S. office and is updated annually.

Making the Most of Working at Home

If you persevere in your efforts to land a home job, in time you're likely to succeed. Your home work space is where you will be spending a large portion of your life-in fact, you will most likely spend more time there than any other place. The consideration you give to its design could have a tremendous impact on the success of your homework experience.

Wouldn't it be wonderful to have a work place all your own, some private space free from distractions? A beautiful office maybe, with a separate entrance, big windows facing out onto a garden, with elegant furniture and the latest equipment modern technology has to offer. Fortunately, dreaming is free.

You may have to start out on the kitchen table or in a corner of the living room. Millions have started the same way and that's okay-for a while. To make the most out of working at home, though, you'll need to begin planning ways to make your working space more comfortable, efficient and permanent.

Five elements directly affect mental attitude and productivity in every workspace: light, sound, furniture, air quality, and color.

Proper lighting is essential to the good health of any worker. It has been conclusively demonstrated that improper or inadequate light has varying degrees of negative effects on people. At the very least, it can cause significant decreases in productivity. Some people have more serious reactions, including long-term bouts with depression.

Adequate overall lighting is not necessarily optimal lighting. Care should be taken to reduce glare from both direct and indirect sources. Whether light is reflected from a bright window or from a computer monitor, glare can cause eyestrain and headaches. You can usually solve glare problems by moving your furniture around, changing the type and strength of your light bulbs, or installing screens over windows and monitors.

Sound doesn't usually have the same impact on the work place as light, but it is an important factor to consider. Noise can come from traffic, children and lawnmowers outside and appliances, children, pets and your own work equipment inside, causing distraction and lower productivity. You can install sound absorbing material to reduce noise or you can attempt to mask the noise with neutral sounds (white noise) or with music. Most electronics stores sell white noise generators.

The right furniture can also make a difference in your work performance and satisfaction. The type of work surface you need depends on the type of work you're doing, but in any case it doesn't have to be fancy or expensive. What is important is that the surface be large enough to suit the task, that the height is right for you, and that it is sturdy enough to hold your equipment without wobbling.

A good chair is definitely worth the investment. It should provide ample back support, thereby reducing fatigue and backaches. Features such as adjustable back tension, an easily adjusted height mechanism and rollers will make your life easier, too. If you work with a keyboard, even for short periods of time, don't get a chair with armrests. Armrests can prevent you from getting close enough to the edge, with resulting aches and pains in your back, neck and shoulders.

Air quality and temperature can also have a major impact on your physical comfort. Ideally, you want fresh, clean air no warmer than 75 degrees or cooler than 68 degrees. Indoor pollution can be caused by lack of ventilation, especially with highly weatherized homes. Pollution sources include carpets, upholstery, stoves, aerosols and cleaning fluids, to name only a few. In addition, there are few jobs that don't involve their own polluting substances. Correction fluid, hobby and craft supplies, paint, glue and lint are examples.

The best way to clean up your indoor air is with ventilation. Plants help, too. Certain common houseplants, such as Spider Plants, gobble up indoor toxins. Electric air filters can help, too. They cost more than plants, but require less care. Negative ion generators are especially helpful in the presence of electronic equipment such as computers.

Color is the final factor, which you should consider. It can set the overall tone of your workspace and make it a place you want to be-or a place you'd rather avoid.

White and very light colors aren't stimulating, but do reflect the most light, making a space appear larger than it is. Blacks, browns, and grays make a space appear smaller than it is, absorbing light and creating feelings of fatigue. Blues and greens are relaxing, feel cool, and reduce blood pressure. Reds, oranges, and yellows are bright, stimulating, cheerful and warm. In too strong a contrast, however, they can cause irritability and increased blood pressure.

Carefully choosing the color scheme and other aspects of your workspace can make a big difference in your productivity as well as how you feel about your work. It's usually not necessary to spend a lot of money to make your work place pleasant; just use some imagination and take the time to think through how you can make the most of the space that's available to you.

HOME BUSINESS OPPORTUNITIES

BUSINESS OWNERSHIP:
THE FINAL STEP TO INDEPENDENCE

It wasn't long ago that starting a new business was beyond the reach of many. Starting a business from scratch required a large investment, usually over $100,000 for a storefront operation. Keeping the business going with the high overhead took a great deal of time and effort. For those of us interested in adding more freedom and flexibility to our lives, business ownership was a fate worse than a job.

Times change. There are now a growing number of ways to go into business without the heavy burdens of the past. You can start a business at home without the huge investment and with much of the risk removed. By buying into a proven business system, you can take advantage of the knowledge and experience of a successful business. For as little as a few hundred dollars, you can have independence and security - an unbeatable combination.

This section is not about starting a business on your own. Instead, it contains over 400 opportunities to buy into a proven business system. Some are franchises; some are not. All offer some level of training and support and all give you a better chance of success than going it alone.

A franchise is a successful business formula that essentially sells a clone of itself to a franchisee for a license fee, and then collects royalties on the revenues. Franchising is a preferred way for a business to expand its operations. The franchisee gets a business plan, financial planning and marketing strategies, a trademark, advertising help, training and ongoing technical and business support. The franchisee has the satisfaction of running his/her own business, but still has the security and support of being associated with a large organization. There is a price to be paid for the security-in the form of royalties and also in being obligated to do things according to the company's policies and guidelines.

For those with more independent leanings, there are many stand-alone business systems that offer a basic package similar to a franchise, but without the ongoing obligations. You can buy a turnkey system that provides you with everything you need to get started-from a business plan to paperclips. But an independent turnkey business system is generally less expensive than a franchise because they don't offer ongoing support, use of the company name, or national advertising. And, while franchises often grant territorial exclusivity, independent business opportunities generally offer no such protection against local competition. But-in addition to lower upfront costs-they don't charge ongoing royalties or advertising fees. Some independent business systems do offer ongoing support or consultation services for a set period of time, usually a year, so there is plenty of time to get valuable answers to questions about your new business.

Not all independent business systems are turnkey. You'll see, as you read through some of the listings, that there is a wide range of services offered. With many, you can decide for yourself how complete your package should be. You may want, for example, to obtain training at home through the use of videotapes if you can't afford to get away for a week to attend training classes at company headquarters. With many companies, you have that choice. Other options might include office equipment, a computer system and/or software, a start-up tool kit, advertising materials, or consulting services.

No matter which type of business opportunity you opt for, you are to be congratulated for having the courage to take the final step to independence. In addition to having more control over your life, business ownership is a great way to insure yourself of optimal income potential. For anyone who is serious about making money at home, the listings in this section offer a real opportunity for success.

AUTOMOTIVE

Automotive services, particularly in the after-market, have always comprised a huge industry. That hasn't changed. What has changed is the need to have all automotive services performed at centralized locations. More and more opportunities are opening up to home-based entrepreneurs, mostly through mobile services.

In this section you will find a variety of opportunities to make a good income taking care of cars. Auto detailing, one of the most popular business opportunities, is now a $2.5 billion industry. Its popularity among new entrepreneurs is based on the assumption that anyone can clean a car, even if this is the ultimate car wash. And it's true. Furthermore, it's a business that can be started for under $1,000 and profits can go into six figures annually.

The next step up from detailing is restoration. Restoration services include paint chip repair; paintless dent repair; and the repair and recoloring of vinyl, leather, and plastic parts.

A long, long time ago we were able to get our car oil changed at our friendly neighborhood service station. The word "service" was changed to "gas" and quick lube shops took over the oil and lube responsibilities. Today, you don't even have to leave home to get an oil change. Mobile services will come to you, wherever you are, so all you have to do is make a phone call. This business is more expensive to get into because there is the need for a properly outfitted van, but there is a tremendous opportunity for repeat business that's very appealing.

And finally, glass repair is still growing fast, saving customers time and money over the replacement alternative.

AIRBAG TECHNOLOGY, INC., 9675 SE 36th Street, Suite 100 Mercer Island, WA; www.airbagservice.com. (425) 391-9664.
Franchise: Yes.
Description: Mobile airbag replacement and repair servicing the body shop and automotive collision industry.
Requirements: You should have some mechanical experience or aptitude at the least. The standard franchise fee is $25,000. You will also need about $35,000 for van, tools, computer, etc.
Provisions: The fee covers an exclusive territory, three weeks technical training course, proprietary software, live technical support, established business system, national and local marketing and advertising support.

AMERICAN GOLD PLATING EQUIPMENT & SUPPLY, 217 East Lincoln, Reading, MI 49274; www.americangoldplating.com. (800)245-7450.
Franchise: No.
Description: Providing gold plating to individuals wanting to dress up their vehicles and other items with 24K gold. The work is easy to do and quite profitable.
Requirements: The startup cost for the complete system is under $1,000. The only other requirement is the ability to be outgoing and demonstrate the service.
Provisions: The investment covers all of the equipment and supplies that go into the gold plating business, a detailed manual, a quick-start guide and telephone support.

AMSOIL, INC., 925 Tower Ave., Superior, WI 54880; (800)777-8491.

www.amsoil.com.
Franchise: No.
Description: AMSOIL manufactures synthetic lubricants and automotive performance products for a wide range of applications including cars, RVs, trucks, ATVs, boats, snowmobiles and other equipment. This is an opportunity for a dealership.
Requirements: There are no inventory requirements or capital investment in office or warehouse space. The startup costs range from $50 to $250.
Provisions: Strong support network and company support, marketing and promo materials, and leads. No territory restrictions.

APPEARANCE PLUS, INC., 170 E. Hillsboro Blvd., Deerfield Beach, FL 33441; www.appearance-plus.com. (800)408-5020/(954)596-2112
Franchise: No.
Description: Auto detailing, mobile washing, and waxing of cars, boats, aircraft and RVs.
Requirements: Start as low as $2,000 or go as high as $25,000.
Provisions: Products, equipment, marketing material, the right to use the name as an authorized dealer, ongoing company support, and full training program at the corporate office.
Profit Potential: $50,000 to $100,000 per year.

AUTOPLUS WINDOW STICKERS, 12750 Yacht Club Cir., Ft. Myers, FL 33919; www.autoplusnet.com. (800) 825-4838.
Franchise: No.
Description: Produce window stickers for used car sales and provide window sticker service to new and used car dealerships.
Requirements: The new introductory software package is $195 and the standard distributor package is $995. For another $1,000, they'll throw in a digital camera and Palm computer in the Express package.
Provisions: Distributors get training, technical support, software, tools, and supplies.

CHIPS AWAY, 1536 Saw Mill Run Blvd., Pittsburgh, PA 15210; www.chipsaway.com. (800) 837-CHIP.
Franchise: No.
Description: A mobile service that provides scratch, scuff, and paint chip repair quickly and easily. Since the Patent Pending process only adheres to primer paint, no masking is necessary. Paint colors are easily matched exactly for a flawless finish. Send for video if you're interested in this opportunity.
Requirements: The system starts at $6,995 and can go as high as $14,000. There is financing available for up to 48 months.
Provisions: The fee buys complete training and all tools, equipment, and supplies necessary to start the business.
Profit Potential: It is possible to make a six-figure income.

CUSTOM AUTO RESTORATION SYSTEMS, INC., 479 Interstate Ct., Sarasota, FL 34240; (800) 736-1307.
Franchise: No.
Description: Company offers a full business start-up for mobile paint touch-up, velour and vinyl repair, paintless dent repair, windshield repair, and odor removal systems.
Requirements: Prices range from $500 to $8,000.
Provisions: Depending on the size of your investment, you can receive equipment,

supplies, training (business and technical), and hands-on training at headquarters.
Profit Potential: $100,000 per year.

DETAIL PLUS, P.O. Box 20755, Portland, OR 97294; www.detailplus.com. (800)284-0123.
Franchise: No.
Description: All phases of auto detailing and cosmetic car care including windshield repair, paint touch-up, paintless dent repair, 24K gold plating, and vinyl and leather repair.
Requirements: Each service system is sold separately from $500 to $5,000. With start-up expenses, costs can go much higher. There is financing available.

FIBRENEW, Box 33, Site 16, RR8, Calgary, Alberta, Canada T2J 2T9; www.fibrenew.com. (603)278-7818.
Franchise: Yes.
Description: A service that specializes in repairing plastics and leather in the aviation, automobile, commercial marine and residential markets.
Requirements: The total investment ranges between $30,000 and $50,000. Must also have a good vehicle because this is a mobile service.
Provisions: The cost covers airfare to Canada, 18 nights accommodations, training, and complete product, equipment and office package. Ongoing support.

FITZGERALD'S, 221 North American St., Stockton, CA 95202; www.fitzgeraldsrestoration.com. (800) 441-3326.
Franchise: No.
Description: Automotive interior restoration including the repair and recoloring of vinyl, leather, velour, and plastic parts on the side of vehicles. The typical job takes less then an hour and the work is done on-site right out of the licensee's vehicle.
Requirements: $500 for one subject and $3,000 for complete package of all four subjects (vinyl, leather, velour, and plastic).
Provisions: All licensees receive all of the necessary equipment and chemicals, plus marketing help and sales leads. Five days of training is followed up by a bi-monthly newsletter and unlimited consultation.
Profit Potential: Approximately $1,000 per week or more.
Comments: Fitzgerald's has over 1,500 home-based licensees.

4 CAR CARE, 198 Union Blvd., #200, Lakewood, CO 80228. (800)422-7227.
Franchise: Yes.
Description: Automotive repair referral service begun by a former racecar driver. Repair shops pay to be inspected on-site and certified before being listed with 4 Car Care. The franchisee then makes referrals to consumers within their protected territory.
Requirements: The minimum total investment is about $25,000 and there is financing available.

GLASS MECHANIX, INC., 4881 W. Hacienda Ave., #6 Las Vegas, NV 89118; www.glassmechanix.com. (800)826-8523.
Franchise: No.
Description: Windshield repair service.
Requirements: $1,900; financing is available.
Provisions: The fee covers training, machines, and enough materials to repair 500 windshields.

Profit Potential: A windshield takes about 15 minutes to repair, and the average charge is $35. The cost is about 50 cents so it is possible to earn up to $300 a day in this business.

Comments: This company was started in a two-bedroom condominium in 1982 and now has over 3,000 licensees.

GLASS TECHNOLOGY, INC., 434 Turner Drive, Durango, CO 81301; www.gtglass.com. (800)441-4527.
Franchise: No.
Description: Windshield repair.
Requirements: Total cost ranges from $1,500 to $5,000.
Provisions: Glass Technology offers a complete windshield repair business including everything needed to get started: equipment, supplies, training, and ongoing support. Training covers not only the technical aspects of the business, but business management as well.
Profit Potential: Profit per repair is about $34 for 15 minutes of work. Performing nine repairs per day would yield $80,000 per year.
Comments: This can be a good business if you take advantage of the market by approaching insurance companies, fleet accounts, and car dealers. How to get these accounts is included in the training.

GLAS-WELD SYSTEMS, 20578 Empire Blvd., Bend, OR 97701; www.glasweld.com. (800)321-2597/(541) 388-1156.
Franchise: No.
Description: Glass repair service.
Requirements: $1,695 to $3,300.
Provisions: The investment includes equipment and enough materials to make 125 repairs and earn over $4,000 in revenue. A set of six training tapes is also included. Training topics include business start-up, generating sales, expansion, customer relations, advertising and promotion, and time management. Video training and field training are available options.
Profit Potential: Up to $75,000 a year. Glas-Weld currently has over 2,000 licensees.

HI-TECH INDUSTRIES, 236 S. Rainbow Blvd., #151, Las Vegas, NV 89145; www.hi-techind.com. (702) 878-4948.
Franchise: No.
Description: Recycle antifreeze for the industries such as auto, construction, fleet, farm, mining, logging, government, etc. All services are performed on customer's site.
Requirements: Areas available starting at $9,850. Financing is available.
Provisions: You get all the equipment, supplies, chemicals, ad proofs, support, training needed to perform the service plus an assigned marketing area.
Profit Potential: Up to $150,000 a year.

LIQUID RESINS INTERNATIONAL, 4295 N. Holly Rd., Olney, IL 62450; www.liquidresins.com. (800) 458-2098.
Franchise: No.
Description: Glass repair is one of the fastest growing parts of the automotive industry. Most mobile windshield repair technicians travel from one business location to another, show samples of the work that can be done and request permission to inspect the business vehicles on a regular basis. Upon finding breaks in the windshield a repair is quickly performed and the bill is sent to the owner's insurance company, which in turn normally

pays for the total cost of the repair.

Requirements: $500 for Mobile Repair Kit and training, which varies in price depending on the method, you choose.

Provisions: The entrepreneur receives a complete repair kit with all the tools necessary to perform repairs on any type of break or crack. There are enough resins in the kit to provide the purchaser with $8,000 to $12,000 income. The average price per repair, across the country, is $40. The purchaser can have his/her choice of manual, video, classroom or on-the-job training, which is priced separately.

Profit Potential: Three repairs per day at $40 each equals $31,200 per year; nine repairs per day at $40 each equals $93,600 per year.

LOCATIONLUBE, P.O. Box 700, E. Sandwich, MA 02537; www.locationlube.com. (508)888-5000.

Franchise: No.

Description: Mobile oil change van-servicing vehicles at customer's location.

Requirements: The total investment is $11,500. Financing is available with $1,000 to $5,000 down.

Provisions: Equipment and training.

MATCO TOOLS, 4403 Allen Rd., Stow, OH 44224; www.matcotools.com. (888) 696-2826.

Franchise: Yes.

Description: Distributor of professional hand tools and equipment. This company has been in business since 1979 and is well known for its quality mechanics'. tools and service equipment from toolboxes to shop equipment. There are now over 1,200 franchisees.

Requirements: The total investment ranges from $60,000 to $152,000 with financing available through the franchisor. The franchisor also has financing available for accounts receivable.

Provisions: Extensive training, equipment, and inventory

NATIONAL DETAIL SYSTEMS, 2510-G N. Las Posas Rd., #450, Camarillo, CA 93010; www.nationaldetail.com. (800)356-9485/(805)384-9349.

Franchise: No.

Description: Mobile auto detailing service.

Requirements: No experience is necessary. The package starts at $2,400.

Provisions: All dealers are given complete instructions from start to finish through our exclusive step-by-step training and operations manuals, full color 90-minute videotape and companion audiocassette training tapes. You can work part-time with extremely flexible business hours. Included is an initial supply of products enough to complete 30 to 40 vehicles. You will also receive upscale promotional material and camera-ready artwork for business cards, gift certificates, referral cards, business forms, brochures, yellow page and newspaper ads, direct mail coupons and much more.

Profit Potential: The company claims that you will earn approximately $30 to $60 per hour. Your typical cost of cleaning/polishing products to complete an average detail is only $3.50. You should be able to generate approximately $3,000 worth of business from your initial order of supplies. National Detail currently has over 900 licensees.

NOVUS, 10425 Hampshire Ave., South, Minneapolis, MN   55438; www.novusglass.com. (800) 944-6811.

Franchise: Yes.

Description: NOVUS offers a windshield repair and scratch removal business.
Requirements: The franchise fee starts at $10,000, plus there are additional costs for training, equipment, supplies, and materials that add up to around $35,000.

NVS CORPORATION, 271 Western Ave., Lynn, MA 01904; (781) 595-6224.
Franchise: No.
Description: Windshield repair.
Requirements: The cost of a complete system is $1,999.
Provisions: The system includes equipment, enough materials to make 1,000 repairs, and detailed illustrated instructions.
Profit Potential: Up to $80,000 a year.

RAMP SOLUTIONS, 115 W. Canon Perdido, Santa Barbara, CA 93101; www.GatorRamps.com. (800) 969-RAMP.
Franchise: No.
Description: Distributorship for new type of pick-up truck ramp.
Requirements: $499.
Provisions: The fee covers a protected territory and start-up package.

SNAP-ON TOOLS, 2801 80th St., P.O. Box 1410, Kenosha, WI 53141; www.snapon.com. (800)776-3344.
Franchise: Yes.
Description: Professional tools and equipment sales to mechanics at their place of business.
Requirements: The franchise fee is only $5,000, but you will need at least another $10,000 for inventory and that could go much higher to be properly outfitted. The franchisor does, however, make financing available for inventory, accounts receivable and even payroll. The monthly royalty fee is $50.
Provisions: Training, inventory, and exclusive territory.

SUPER CLEAN YACHT SERVICE, 910 W. Coast Hwy., Newport Beach, CA 92663; www.supercleanyachtservice.com. (949)646-2990.
Franchise: Yes.
Description: Detailing for pleasure boats and yachts, which includes exterior and interior cleaning. The company offers proprietary cleaning products that are environmentally safe.
Requirements: The franchise fee ranges from $7,500 to $25,000 with financing available through the franchisor. You will need an addition startup investment of at least $5,000. The cash liquidity requirement, however, is only $2,500.
Provisions: Equipment plus training based on 20 years marine experience.

ULTRA BOND, 2458 I-70 Business Loop B-1, Grand Junction, CO 81501; www.ultrabond.com. (800)347-2820.
Franchise: No.
Description: Glass repair service.
Requirements: The combination repair kit costs $1,750. To buy exclusive rights to a protected territory, the initial total is $3,250 plus a $100 monthly supply order is required.
Provisions: Your investment covers all equipment and supplies, two days of training in California, a training video, monthly newsletter, business start-up assistance, and ongoing support.
Profit Potential: Over $50 an hour.

BUSINESS SERVICES

Business services include any business whose customers are business owners and/or managers. This area covers quite a range, and so this section will describe opportunities in advertising, payroll services, business consulting, bookkeeping and accounting, tax preparation, management training, financial management, various office support services, business products, pre-employment screening, and an assortment of miscellaneous services that cater to niche markets.

As you can see by viewing these services as a group, an incredible number of dollars is being spent by businesses. There are twenty million companies that require bookkeeping, accounting, and tax preparation services. These businesses also spend $150+ billion annually on business products such as office supplies, furniture, printing, and business forms. That amount alone comprises over 3% of the GNP. Advertising takes a minimum 5% of any company's budget. The cooperative direct mail industry, although its growth has slowed somewhat with the advent of the Internet, still stands at $20 billion a year business. Corporations, more concerned than ever about how productivity is affecting the bottom line, spend $30 billion on management training each year.

Clearly, there is a lot of money to be made in business services. This is not, however, safe ground for amateurs. It is quite different from dealing with the public. Whereas a consumer may be willing to take a chance on an unknown product or an unfamiliar company, a business owner will not be so willing to take chances when it may affect the health of the business. Business owners are also more knowledgeable than the general public about the products and services they need. They trust only those who understand their business needs and who are willing to take the time to nurture a lasting business relationship. This takes time, but those with patience will be rewarded.

Those most likely to succeed in business services have assertive personalities and business experience. They are used to dealing with business owners and have some contacts within the business community. Working from a home office need not be a hindrance, but it is especially important to project a professional image.

ACCU-RATE, 2805 Rocky Ridge Dr., El Paso, TX 79904; www.increaseyourincome.com. (915)757-7819.
Franchise: No.
Description: Accu-Rate reviews hospital bills and identifies billing errors for corporations, unions, schools, and local government agencies. Most hospital bills are inaccurate and/or have hidden fees that would rival the overcharges of the Defense Department. Clients pay a percentage of the savings only after savings have been recovered.
Requirements: There are two levels; $995 and $4,995. Must have a computer with MS

Office, printer, fax, and answering machine.
Provisions: Three days of training, training manual, list of prospective clients, daily update of organizations requiring Accu-Rate services, telephone support, and promotional material.

ACCUTRAK INVENTORY SPECIALISTS, 1818C Hwy. 17 N., #320 Surfside Beach, SC 29575; www.accutrakinventory.com. (843) 293-8274.
Franchise: Yes.
Description: AccuTrak Inventory Specialists is an inventory auditing and consulting franchise that conducts inventories and offers inventory control and loss prevention consulting. Franchisees help businesses of all sizes to control inventory, reduce shrink, improve employee performance, identify additional profit opportunities and protect their bottom line.
Requirements: The franchise fee is $22,500 and total startup costs will range from $30,000 to $50,000. There is an ongoing royalty fee of 7%.
Provisions: Specialized inventory software, in-depth training for one week at corporate headquarters and an additional week at the franchisee's location, continued support and immediate income.

ACTION INTERNATIONAL, 5670 Wynn Rd., #C, Las Vegas, NV 89118; www.action-international.com. (888)483-2828.
Franchise: Yes.
Description: Franchisees act as business coaches and mentors. They work with employees and owners of small to medium-sized businesses, to find the right balance between company performance and personal lifestyle.
Requirements: The franchise fee starts at $25,000 and the total startup costs are around $60,000. Third party financing is available. The ongoing royalty is a flat $1,500 per month. A solid background in business and marketing skills are also necessary.
Provisions: The 10-day training program is provided at company headquarters or arrangements can be made for onsite training at the franchisee's location.
Profit Potential: Not available.

AIR BROOK LIMOUSINE, P.O. Box 123, Rochelle Park, NJ 07662; www.airbrook.com. (800)800-1990/ (201) 587-8385.
Franchise: Yes.
Description: Limousine service to transport business owners and managers between office and airport.
Requirements: The franchise fee ranges from $7,500 to $12,500. A refundable deposit of $2,000 is required for start-up. Royalties range from 35% to 40%.
Provisions: The fee buys a 10-year franchise license and training. Financing is available from the company with no interest.
Profit Potential: Not available.
Comments: This company has been around since 1969 and has over 125 franchise operators.

AMERICAN INSTITUTE OF SMALL BUSINESS, 7515 Wayzata Blvd., Suite 201, Minneapolis, MN 55426; http://studybiz.com. (612)545-7001.
Franchise: Yes.
Description: AISB is a publisher of training manuals and courses on the subject of small business. All services are based on a two-volume publication titled "How to Set Up a Small Business." The U.S. Small business Administration, Dun and Bradstreet,

and many local Chambers of Commerce have endorsed this publication. Franchisees market the materials primarily through seminars. Includes educational materials on financing, business plan writing, Windows 95 and 98, computer programs, how to write a business plan software package and many other business subjects and offers workshops on small business subjects.

Requirements: There is no franchise fee or royalties. Training costs $1,000. Company's profits come from sales of the training manuals and other materials.

Provisions: AISB promises to provide referrals from national advertising and other promotions to local franchisees. Investors receive all materials at cost, which is list price less 50%; also receive scripts, overhead transparencies, etc. for the Training Programs.

AMERICAN INSTITUTE, American Institute Bldg., First Floor, 7326 S.W. 48th Street, Miami, FL 33155; www.hiddenmoney.com. (800)US-AUDIT.
Franchise: No.
Description: Business services including utility bill auditing. This business teaches you how to audit electric bills, catch overcharges, and save your clients money. It can even be run like a mail order business. All you need is a telephone answering machine and calculator.
Requirements: Fees range from $100.
Provisions: Complete training to set up a home business immediately.
Profit Potential: $80,000 from home.

AT-HOME PROFESSIONS, 2001 Lowe Street, Fort Collins, CO 80525; (800) 347-7899.
Franchise: No.
Description: At-Home Professions is a unique institution established in 1981. It develops and provides career education specifically for the types of jobs that are commonly performed at home. The courses utilize home study methods and can be done at the student's own pace. Courses include medical transcription, medical coding, medical claims and billing, massage, legal transcription, bookkeeping, paralegal, wedding/ event planning, accounting, veterinary assisting, day care and introduction to computers.
Requirements: Admission standards vary somewhat for each course, but generally an applicant must be a high school graduate, hold a GED, or pass an admissions test. Tuition also varies and can be paid as-you-go with no interest.
Provisions: In addition to providing top quality training programs and course materials, this organization also includes great follow-up services. At-Home Professions provides placement services, promotion of graduates through advertising and events such as trade shows, continuing employment instruction and advice, and personal counseling in job-search techniques. At-Home Professions is accredited by the Accrediting Commission of the Distance Education and Training Council.

BANKS, BENTLEY & CROSS, 5015 Birch St., #121, Newport Beach, CA 92660; (949)786-0161.
Franchise: No.
Description: This professional business debt management service provides business arbitration, debt negotiation and other financial consultation services for businesses.
Requirements: $995.
Provisions: Complete business plan, training, turnkey marketing program, and consultation.
Profit Potential: Six figures annually.

BEVINCO BAR SYSTEMS LTD., 510-505 Consumers Rd., Toronto, Ontario, Canada M2J 4V8; www.bevinco.com. (888)238-4626.
Franchise: Yes.
Description: Liquor inventory control service involving weekly onsite audits of liquor use. The service is computerized and well received by bar and restaurant owners because they can save a lot of money. This is a very lucrative business that is the largest of its kind in the world.
Requirements: Startup costs will be about $40,000 and there is an ongoing fee of $12 per audit performed.
Provisions: The heart of the program is the proprietary software program. In addition, there is two weeks of hands-on training, ongoing toll-free support from a Master franchisee in your area, and a protected territory that has at least 250 licensed establishments.

BUSINESS ROUND TABLE, 37 Chandler Crescent, Moncton, New Brunswick, Canada E1E 3W6; www.business-round-table.com. (506)857-8177.
Franchise: Yes.
Description: Mentoring services designed to help entrepreneurs succeed not only in their businesses, but in their personal lives as well. The groups meet once a month and franchisees act as facilitators.
Requirements: In addition to a cash investment of about $20,000 (including franchise fee), you should be a good facilitator and teacher, have experience as an entrepreneur, and ideally have some experience as a trainer or consultant to small business owners.
Provisions: Complete hands-on training is provided at the franchisee's location.
The typical territory is a community with a population over 500,000 people.

BUTLER LEARNING SYSTEMS, 1325 West Dorothy Lane, Dayton, OH 45409; (937)298-7462.
Franchise: Yes.
Description: This company produces and publishes management training programs in the areas of human resources development and sales marketing.
Requirements: There are no franchise fees, but there is a contractual agreement that states the consultants will market and use the Butler products in the way they were intended to be used. The materials are then purchased wholesale, and the consultants make a profit from the markup.
Provisions: Complete training is provided.

CARDSENDERS, 47 Oxbow Creek, Laguna Hills, CA 92653 www.cardsenders.com. (800)843-6055.
Franchise: No.
Description: Provide personalized mailing services for businesses and professionals in your community. Help businesses create good will and loyalty by sending highly creative greeting cards to their customers and employees, plus provide greeting card services to friends and family. Part-time or full-time opportunity, working a flexible schedule.
Requirements: Home-Study License, for complete business package is $6,900.
Provisions: License package includes comprehensive written reference materials, greeting card presentation portfolio, proprietary CardSenders system, software, marketing materials, toll-free telephone and Web-based support, plus available training classes.

CLOSEUP: CardSenders

In today's high-tech atmosphere, it is even more important for businesses to keep in personal touch with their customers. Sending personalized greeting cards is an inexpensive, reliable means of doing just that. Amidst the hastily written e-mails and impersonal faxes, it's a greeting card that stands out.

Sharon Valdes of El Paso was a corporate manager who got tired of commuting two hours a day. She spent about a year looking for a home-based business so she could spend those two hours each day with her children. When she found CardSenders, she immediately fell in love with the concept.

"This was the most positive, uplifting thing out there," Sharon says. "I had to believe in what I was going to do. What I do is help companies foster loyalty by using greeting cards. Loyalty is so important in business. It is much cheaper to keep a customer than to get one. If you can get customers to perceive that they are wanted and their satisfaction is number one, then they will stay with you. I do that with thank you notes, anniversary and birthday cards." Sharon mostly sends birthday cards, not just to customers but to employees as well. "With employees it boosts morale and productivity."

Sharon says her business practically started itself. "I did everything CardSenders told me to do. It was not a hard thing to sell. I got my first customer when I went to get a rider on my insurance policy for my computer. I told my agent what I did and he said, 'Gee, I have to do that.' It's not like you have to sell something like screws or even an insurance policy. People understand the value of this intuitively. A lot of companies are already doing it for themselves so, for them, I don't even have to explain the concept. I just point out why I am less expensive and more efficient."

There are two elements that make the CardSenders system work: the great selection of cards and the proprietary software. Signatures and business logos are actually reproduced inside the cards, often using hand-written samples from the sender. The result looks amazingly real.

The software is used to address and maintain customer lists. Sharon says she can take small or big customers and give them the same cost effectiveness. "The value is so great, my customers love it."

"I will never ever work for somebody else again," Sharon insists. "For the price you can't beat this opportunity. But best of all is the time I get to spend with my kids. You can't put a price on that."

CLIENT CONNECTION, INC., 1780 S. Bellaire St., Suite 608, Denver, CO 80222; www.clientconnectioninc.com. (800)331-4097.
Franchise: No.
Description: Greeting card mailing service that provides professionals with customized

greeting cards to their current and prospective client base to help them build repeat and referral business.

Requirements: $8.995.

Provisions: Comprehensive training, airfare and accommodations in Denver, six months of mentoring, office supplies, sales presentation videos, and six months of software tech support.

COST CONTAINMENT SOLUTIONS, INC., 9921 Fringe Tree Ct., Louisville, KY 40241; www.costcontain.com. (800)872-3709.

Franchise: No.

Description: Business to business expense reduction service for the small to mid market in most industries.

Requirements: Notebook computer, proficiency in MS Office, plus a licensing fee. Total startup costs are around $30,000.

Provisions: Initial and ongoing training, access to system and trademark, Web site listing, ongoing support, and joint advertising opportunities.

CRESTCOM, INT'L, INC., 6900 E. Belleview Ave., Greenwood Village, CO 80111; www.crestcom.com. (303)267-8200.

Franchise: Yes.

Description: Franchisees provide training for management, sales, and office personnel.

Requirements: General business experience and marketing expertise is necessary. The franchise fee starts at $39,500 and there is financing available.

Provisions: Training is provided at company headquarters.

Comments: Absentee ownership is allowed.

EMPIRE BUSINESS BROKERS, INC., 4040 Clinton St., Buffalo, NY 14224; http://www.empirebb.com. (716)674-2015.

Franchise: Yes.

Description: Selling of existing businesses for the owners and also representing franchisers in the sale of their franchises. Franchise development and financial brokerage services are also offered.

Requirements: $9,900 training fee with additional start-up costs around $2,000.

Provisions: You get five days of training, on-going support, free home page, and access to over 4,000 listings of businesses for sale.

ENERGY AUTOMATION SYSTEMS, INC., 145 Anderson Ln., Hendersonville, TN 37075; www.energyautomation.com. (888)608-7737.

Franchise: No.

Description: Dealers sell energy automations systems to businesses. Customers receive a detailed energy survey and comprehensive analysis of electrical usage, a set of recommendations to reduce the electrical bill, a projection and a guarantee of savings, and a return on investment higher then 50% a year. Products include occupancy sensors, fluorescent light controllers, transient surge protectors, etc. The company produces the actual report for you and local contractors of your choice perform installations.

Requirements: A startup dealership costs from $29,500 to $39,500. There are no ongoing fees. You can attend a free, one-day orientation in Nashville with no obligation.

Provisions: Complete training.

Profit Potential: The average gross profit for each sale is between $15,000 and $20,000.

ENTREPRENEUR'S SOURCE, 900 Main St. S., Bldg. 2, Southbury, CT 06488;

www.theesource.com. (800)289-0086.
Franchise: Yes.
Description: This is a franchise consulting firm that's been around for 20 years. The clients are people who are looking for a franchise opportunity. Franchisees match them up with the best franchise for them. The clients pay nothing for the service. The profit is paid by the franchisor when a successful match is completed.
Requirements: The franchisee fee is $45,000 and there is no financing offered.
Provisions: Training starts with a week at company headquarters and there is plenty of ongoing training and support.
Profit Potential: Not available.
Comments: 100% of franchisees are owner/operators.

EXPENSE REDUCTION CONSULTING, INC., 6920 Annapolis Ct., Parkland, FL 33067; www.ercinc.com. (954)255-2511.
Franchise: No.
Description: Providing expense-reduction consulting services to businesses.
Requirements: The startup investment is about $16,000 and the company offers financing.
Provisions: Training is conducted at corporation headquarters and at the operator's location. Also provided are advertising and marketing training and support, newsletters, technical support, operations manuals, phone support, and sales leads.

FIDUCIAL, 10480 Little Patuxent Pkwy., 3rd Fl., Columbia, MD 21044; www.fiducial.com. (866)434-3824.
Franchise: Yes.
Description: Triple Check offers support services to independently owned and operated offices offering tax services, business services and/or accounting services. Everyone is part of tax operation; business services and financial services and optional add-ons.
Requirements: There is no initial franchise fee. Royalties are based on increased fee income. Start-up costs start at $25,000.
Provisions: Licensees are offered a full range of support services, including research and technical support, marketing programs, and public relations programs plus a variety of operating systems.

FILTAFRY, 5401 S. Kirkman Rd., #310, Orlando, FL 32819; www.filtafry.com. (407)926-0255.
Franchise: Yes.
Description: FiltaFry provides a mobile on-site service for the micro-filtration of cooking oil, the vacuum based cleaning of deep fryers, and full fryer management. Customers include restaurants of all kinds. The service is welcomed because it saves money, improves food quality, and reduces health and safety risks.
Requirements: General business experience is only required for those who want multi-unit franchises. The franchise fee is $15,000. There is financing available, but only for the startup costs.
Provisions: Training is thorough and extensive. Two weeks are spent at company headquarters and 2-3 weeks are at the franchisee's location.
Comments: This a fairly new franchise that has grown to 28 franchisees in just two years.

GREEN CONCEPTS, 3960 S. Higuera St., San Luis Obispo, CA 93401. (805)782-0128; www.green-concepts.com.

Franchise: No.
Description: Interior plant rentals and maintenance programs. Rent plants to banks, hotels, restaurants, offices, and private homes.
Requirements: The startup cost is very low at only $500 including licensing fee and there is financing available from the company.
Provisions: Complete training is provided at company headquarters and on-site. The licensee also receives a training manual, portfolio, and video. There is plenty of ongoing support as well as advertising and marketing materials and the company will even help get accounts.

GREETINGS, P.O. Box 25623, Lexington, KY 40524; (859)272-5624.
Franchise: Yes.
Description: Advertising business utilizing hot air balloons.
Requirements: The franchise fee is $15,000. In addition to the franchise fee, you will need approximately $11,950 for supplies, equipment, working capital, etc. All franchisees are required to attend training in Lexington at their own expense. There is a 5% royalty based on gross sales.
Provisions: The fee covers training, operating system, promotional programs, a record keeping system, customer references, and ongoing support.

THE GROWTH COACH, 10700 Montgomery Rd., #300, Cincinnati, OH 45242; www.thegrowthcoach.com. (888)292-7992.
Franchise: Yes.
Description: Provides business coaching and mentoring for small business owners and self-employed individuals. Coaching can be arranged on a regular basis or for special projects only.
Requirements: The franchise fee is $17,500 and there is financing available for that. The additional startup costs are low at only $3,000. General business experience is required.
Provisions: Initial training is conducted at company headquarters. After that, it is ongoing over the phone whenever necessary. There is plenty of marketing support including tools, ad slicks, and strategies.

IMPACT, 205-8475 Ontario St., Vancouver, B.C. Canada V5X 3E8; (604)324-6600.
Franchise: No.
Description: Impact's basic service is an advertising display called Tel-Ad. It is a case that holds as many as 100 professional advertising photos. The photos are identified with stick-on numbers that coincide with a push button pad located in the counter top for direct access to the advertiser's business premises. The heart of the display is a programmable logic board that is capable of storing up to 100 numbers in its memory. Once a patron has selected a service to contact, they would simply pick up the handset and press the number of the advertiser shown on the photo. Independent business operators place the Tel-Ad displays wherever tourists traffic such as hotel lobbies.
Requirements: The purchase price is $5,000.
Provisions: The price covers the price of a complete display plus supplies and four manuals. The manuals include installation instructions, business start-up procedures, complete instructions on how to work with hotels, signs, contracts, ads, phone scripts, and everything needed to make this a viable business.
Profit Potential: One system should generate from $20,000 to $45,000 a year.
Comments: Impact has more than 75 operators.

IMPACT DESIGNS, 675 Fairview Dr., Ste 246, Carson City, NV 89701; www.impactdesigns.net. (888)203-5886.
Franchise: No.
Description: Consult with businesses that advertise in the Yellow Pages, helping them to increase their Yellow Pages response while reducing their costs.
Requirements: Training fee of $9,900, 40% financed.
Provisions: Full training, all forms necessary to conduct the business, telemarketing support, and ongoing support.

IMPRESSIONS ON HOLD INTERNATIONAL, 4880 S. Lewis Ave #200, Tulsa, OK 74105; www.impressionsonhold.com. (800) 580-4653.
Franchise: Yes.
Description: Selling on-hold advertising to businesses. Once the sale is made, it is the home office's job to produce and administer the work.
Requirements: $47,000 investment. Need strong outside sales and marketing experience.
Provisions: You get a protected territory, ownership of accounts sold, training and equipment for presenting the service.

KUSTOM CARDS INTERNATIONAL, INC., 1018 E. Willow Grove Ave., Wyndmoor, PA 19038; www.kustomcards.com. (800)207-1678.
Franchise: No.
Description: Kustom Cards designs and manufactures photographic business cards and magnets.
Requirements: The cost of getting into this dealership ranges from $50 to $350. Readers of this book receive a 50% discount.
Provisions: The fee buys a complete sales manual with samples, order forms, and on-going phone support.

LEADERSHIP MANAGEMENT, INC., 4567 Lake Shore Dr., Waco, TX 76710; www.lmi-bus.com. (800)568-1241.
Franchise: Yes.
Description: This company has been providing management training and consulting since 1965.
Requirements: The franchise fee is $30,000 and there is financing available. There is very little additional capital needed for startup.
Provisions: All the necessary materials and training.
Comments: LMI programs are distributed in 23 languages and 60 countries.

MR. PLANT, 1106 2nd St., Encinitas, CA 92024; www.mrplant.com. (800)974-0488.
Franchise: Yes.
Description: Franchisees sell, rent, or lease foliage for interior landscaping. Ongoing maintenance is also provided to customers.
Requirements: The franchise fee is $14,950 and there is financing available for that. Startup costs amount to another $4,000.
Provisions: In addition to the training program at company headquarters, franchisees receive a home study course. Marketing support includes yellow pages advertising, co-op advertising opportunities, and ad slicks. Cooperative purchasing is available, but not required.

PACIFIC MEDICAL, 16516 Bernardo Center Dr., #300, San Diego, CA 92128; www.pacificmedical.com. (800)815-6334.

Franchise: Yes.
Description: Medical billing service.
Requirements: This is a low-cost franchise that starts at only $8,995 and there is financing available through the franchisor. There is no ongoing royalty fee either.
Provisions: Training is provided on-site or at corporate headquarters in a classroom setting. The training covers all aspects of the medical billing business, plus provides books, manuals, software and client leads.

PADGETT BUSINESS SERVICES, 160 Hawthorne Pk., Athens, GA 30606; www.smallbizpros.com. (800)723-4388.
Franchise: Yes.
Description: Provides payroll services, financial consulting, and tax services to small businesses.
Requirements: The franchise fee is $25,000 and arrangements can be made for third party financing. Startup costs require an additional $25,000. Experience in finance is definitely necessary.
Provisions: Training starts with 10 days at company headquarters and continues at the franchisee's location for at least 6 days. There are also annual conventions and seminars to keep franchisees up-to-date, particularly in regards to changes in tax codes.
Comments: Padgett has been in business for over 35 years and has over 400 franchisees.

PDP, INC., 750 East Highway 24, Building I, Woodland Park, CO 80863; www.pdpnet.com. (719)687-6074.
Franchise: No.
Description: Business consulting service matching jobs to people and people to jobs using an array of software programs to aid in the analysis.
Requirements: Total start-up costs estimated to be $50,900.
Provisions: The fee covers five days of formal training at corporate headquarters, a coordinator/technical manual, software user's guide, the software operating system, and ongoing support services.
Profit Potential: Not available.
Comments: PDP is a 13-year-old company with 30 licensees as far-flung as Brazil.

PROMENTUM LLC, 22 E. Lahon St., Park Ridge, IL 60068; www.promentum.com. (888)552-7761.
Franchise: No.
Description: Offer training programs and consulting services to companies. This involves working closely with clients to determine performance improvement issues within their organizations, and then implementing the appropriate consulting services and programs that resolve those issues.
Requirements: The total startup investment ranges from $34,000.
Provisions: The company offers a wide platform of training including business and management practices, market planning and development, sales strategies, project pricing and planning, performance consulting methods, client relationship management. Promentum also provides a lot of marketing and advertising support including marketing strategies, print advertisements, and brochures designed to generate leads.

PRIORITY MANAGEMENT SYSTEMS, 180, 13200 Delf Place, Richmond, B.C., Canada V6V 2A2; (800)672-6768. www.prioritymanagement.com.
Franchise: No.
Description: Priority Management has designed a program to help corporate employees

develop personal effectiveness skills. Specifically, employees are taught to manage time and projects, cope with stress, run meetings, delegate tasks, and communicate effectively. The purpose is to teach busy professionals to be able to control personal business lives while simultaneously reducing stress.

Requirements: Business operators are required to be educated, experienced, and highly motivated. The total investment required for this opportunity is under $100.

Provisions: Training starts with an intensive two-week session at company headquarters. Follow-up support is offered in several different ways.

Comments: This business is for experienced professionals who need to polish their skills. This is a lucrative market, but only heavy hitters survive.

PROFORMA, INC., 8800 E. Pleasant Valley Rd., Cleveland, OH 44131; www.proforma.com. (800) 825-1525/(216)741-0400.

Franchise: Yes.

Description: Sales of business products including forms, commercial printing, and computer and office supplies.

Requirements: The franchise fee is $14,900. You will need $5,000 for living expenses while you get started. The royalty is 8% and the advertising royalty is 1%. Marketing or executive management experience is required.

Provisions: The fee buys marketing systems, license agreement, ongoing support, trademarks, vendor relations, and lines of credit.

Profit Potential: Not available, but this is a huge industry.

Comments: This is a highly rated company with about 385 franchise operators.

RECRUITERS PROFESSIONAL NETWORK, 8 Grenada Circle, Nashua, NH 03062; www.RecProNet.com. (888)598-6633.

Franchise: No.

Description: RPN trains individuals to become physician and healthcare professional recruiters and consultants.

Requirements: The cost ranges from $315 to $515.

Provisions: The one-time fee buys the manual and unlimited training via telephone.

RENAISSANCE EXECUTIVE FORUMS, INC., 7855 Ivanhoe Ave., #300, La Jolla, CA 92037; www.executiveforums.com. (858)551-6600.

Franchise: Yes.

Description: Business consulting service.

Requirements: The ideal candidate for this franchise is a retired executive who has plenty of knowledge and experience to offer to clients. There is an orientation process which weeds out unqualified contenders. For those who make the cut, the investment starts at $45,000 with a hefty ongoing royalty fee of 20%.

Provisions: Franchisees are considered "partners." Extensive training is provided in all the key areas needed for success: marketing, presentation techniques, facilitation skills and coaching. The initial training is followed by an advanced certification program. The complete business startup package also includes an operations manual, all necessary stationery and office supplies, mail and phone sales support, press release kit, customized business plan, protected market, and field support. In addition, the corporate office will do all the invoicing and billing.

RESPOND INDUSTRIES, 5290 Vivian, Arvada CO 80002; (303) 403-9937.

Franchise: Yes.

Description: Respond Industries is a van-based route business. It provides quality

first aid and emergency medical supplies service and training to employers. Respond targets the majority of employers, which are the small businesses that do not have the resources for in-house medical clinics staffed with doctors and nurses.
Requirements: The total initial investment is $35,000. There are no royalties.
Provisions: Complete training is provided in technical, legal, personnel, and financial areas. Follow-up training and support are available at any time.

SANDLER SYSTEMS, 10411 Stevenson Rd., Stevenson, MD 21153; www.sandler.com. (410) 653-1993.
Franchise: Yes.
Description: Franchisees offer corporate training programs designed to help client companies boost productivity and generate more profits.
Requirements: The franchise fee is $30,000 with limited financing available.
Provisions: Complete training and follow-up support is provided.

SUPER COUPS COOPERATIVE DIRECT MAIL, The Mail House, 180 Bodwell St., Avon, MA 02322; www.supercoups.com. (800)626-2620.
Franchise: Yes.
Description: Franchisees sell ad space in their mailings to local and national businesses. They also design and write copy for the ads, but with extensive help from Super Coups.
Requirements: The franchise fee is $31,000.
Provisions: Complete training as well as exceptional follow-up support is provided.

SURVEILLANCE VIDEO SYSTEMS, 258 "A" Street #12, Ashland, OR 97520; (541) 482-4500.
Franchise: No.
Description: Selling security cameras, both live and simulated, to business owners with shoplifting, holdup and bad check problems.
Requirements: Under $100 puts one in business with sample products, sales aids, and point of sale material.
Provisions: You get 23 years of proven, profitable and needed products.

TIME PLUS, INC., 500 Colonial Center Pkwy., #650, Roswell, GA 30076; www.timeplus.com. (888)720-7587.
Franchise: No.
Description: Services for human resources departments including payroll, timekeeping, and other record-keeping systems.
Requirements: Minimum $15,000 for startup. There is financing available.
Provisions: Training in operations and marketing is provided in classroom session at corporate headquarters and on-site. An operations manual, training video, and online training is provided s well. Ongoing support is extensive, covering every possible scenario that might come up. Sales leads are also provided.

USA FOR HEALTHCLAIMS, INC., 39 E. Kings Hwy., Audubon, NJ 08106; www.usaforhealthclaims.com. (866)793-5583.
Franchise: No.
Description: Licensing program enables individuals to process medical claims electronically through a central clearinghouse. The company currently has over 1,500 licensees.
Requirements: $4,990 plus a PC.
Provisions: Fee buys software, manuals, marketing manuals, brochures, training class,

ongoing technical support and all updates.
Profit Potential: Unlimited.

WORLDWIDE EXPRESS, 2501 Cedar Springs Rd., #450, Dallas, TX 75201; www.wwex.com. (800)758-SHIP.
Franchise: Yes.
Description: Be an authorized Airborne Express reseller.
Requirements: The average total investment starts at about $40,000. You will also need a computer, fax and phone lines, fax machine, voicemail, and email.
Provisions: Your revenue stream will come from the difference between what you charge your customer and what you pay Airborne. Obviously, this is a repeat business in which the bulk of your efforts will be in obtaining clients. Once they sign up, you will continue to get a percentage of what they spend on Airborne services. Franchise territories are protected so other franchisees cannot sell in your zip codes. Complete training, software, weekly updates, marketing advice, and on-going support is provided.

HOME AND COMMERCIAL PROPERTY IMPROVEMENTS

Home improvement may be the single biggest industry represented in this book. Product sales alone top $160 billion each year and there doesn't appear to be a slowdown in sight. Put those products together with services and you have a whopping number of opportunities. The main reason for the size of this industry is that the number of homeowners is at an all time high. And most homeowners love nothing more than to make the biggest investment of their lives grow in beauty and in value.

To most of us, property improvement means remodeling. And there are indeed remodeling opportunities in this chapter. But there is much more to the property improvement industry than paint and carpentry. Included in this chapter's assortment of businesses are services that you may have thought of, such as carpet dyeing and repair, decorating services, floor coverings, handyman services, drapery cleaning, and lawn care.

There are also a few that you may not have considered. Water and gas leak detection provides a unique and valuable service. Porcelain refinishing is a popular alternative to bathroom fixture replacement for hotels, schools, interior decorators, and landlords. And businesses such as Foliage Design Systems offer unique services such as installing and maintaining interior landscaping.

Generally, the businesses in this chapter are very straightforward with no fancy image or special skills required. Down-to-earth working people who want the advantages of owning a business, such as greater income potential and freedom, will find some good possibilities here. Most of these businesses can also be run part-time, which is helpful if you are looking for something with flexibility.

ANCHOR CUSTOM PRODUCTS, P.O. Box 3477, Evansville, IN 47733;www.anchorinc.com. (812)867-2421.

Franchise: No.
Description: Design, sell, and install custom-made fabric awnings, canopies, and retractable patio awnings.
Requirements: $100 for dealer information.
Provisions: The $100 gets you the necessary sales tools; training is available by request.
Comments: This is a good add-on business for carpenters or remodelers.

ARCHADECK, 2112 W. Laburnum Ave., #100, Richmond, VA 23727; www.archadeck.com. (800)789-3325.
Franchise: Yes.
Description: Franchisees work with homeowners and builders to design and construct decks and gazebos. This is a very fast-growing company with over 80 franchise units added since 1985.
Requirements: The franchise fee is $28,000. Financing for half the franchise fee is available.
Provisions: Training and support.

BATHCREST, 2425 S. Progress Dr., Salt Lake City, UT 84119; www.bathcrest.com. (800) 826-6790/(801)972-1110.
Franchise: No.
Description: Bathcrest is in the porcelain refinishing business.
Requirements: The startup cost is around $25,000 for training, the costs of attending training sessions, a complete equipment package, printed materials and enough products to return $20,000 in gross sales.
Comments: This is a family business that has been around since 1974. They have substantial experience to offer.

BUDGET BLINDS, INC., 1927 N. Glassell St., Orange, CA 92865; www.budgetblinds.com. (800) 420-5374.
Franchise: Yes.
Description: Budget Blinds is the nation's largest window coverings franchise.
Requirements: The total investment is $64,950 including the franchise fee of $25,000. You will also need a fax machine, computer, and a cargo or minivan. The van can be owned or leased.
Provisions: The investment includes an operations manual, start-up supplies, personal web site, two weeks of corporate training including the cost of the hotel, and an exclusive territory.

COLOR-CROWN CORPORATION, 928 Sligh Avenue, Seffner, FL 33584; www.stardek.com. (800)282-1599.
Franchise: No.
Description: Color-Crown manufactures STARDEK products and has been in the concrete coating business since 1972. The products are used in the decorative concrete coating business.
Requirements: The only requirement is that you attend a free two-day training program. There is no franchise fee or minimum purchase required.
Provisions: "Unlike many companies that ask you to invest in them first only for you to find out it is not what they really told you or you just don't like it, we actually invest in you when you attend our free training class."

CONCRETE TECHNOLOGY, INC., 8770 133rd Ave. N., Largo, FL 33773; www.flycti.com. (800)447-6573.
Franchise: No.
Description: Company manufactures state-of-the-art concrete resurfacing product sold to a network of dealers and distributors worldwide.
Requirements: Exclusive territories are available through an initial inventory purchase of at least $10,000.
Provisions: 100% product inventory along with marketing materials, etc. to offer a turnkey operation.
Profit Potential: Average crew dealer has the opportunity to make $100,000 annually.

CREATIVE COLORS INTERNATIONAL, INC., 5550 W. 175th St., Tinley Park, IL 60477; www.creativecolorsintl.com. (800)933-2656.
Franchise: Yes.
Description: The CCI franchise system specializes in providing services for the repair, coloring, cleaning and restoration of leather, vinyl, cloth, velour, plastics and other upholstery surfaces and related services on a mobile basis primarily to commercial customers.
Requirements: The franchise fee is $19,500 and you will need $8,000 for supplies. The total investment, including minivan, is around $50,000. Financing is available for supplies up to $8,000.
Provisions: Two weeks of training at headquarters, one week in franchisee's territory, and ongoing support through newsletters, seminars, and an advisory council.
Profit Potential: This business can be expanded into all markets that have a need for repairing and re-dyeing of leather, vinyl, velour, plastics, etc.

CRITTER CONTROL, 9435 E. Cherry Bend Rd., Traverse City, MI 49684; www.crittercontrol.com. (231)947-2400.
Franchise: Yes.
Description: This is an interesting company that started out as a chimney cleaning service. So often animals were part of the debris stuck in the chimneys, that animal removal was offered as a service - not only from chimneys but attacks, decks, and other areas. Customers include both businesses and homeowners and also cities that do not have their own animal control agencies. Services have been expanded to include damage repair, pest management (such as screening vents or closing entry holes).
Requirements: This is a low-cost opportunity. Total startup can be under $10,000 including the $3,000 franchise fee. Experience is the main requirement. General business, marketing, and animal or wildlife control are all necessary.
Provisions:
Comments: The company has been around since 1983 and now has 90 franchisees.

DECOR & YOU, INC., 900 Main St. South, Bldg. #2, Southbury, CT 06488; www.decorandyou.com. (203)264-3500.
Franchise: Yes.
Description: Interior decorating.
Requirements: The total investment starts at approximately $28,000.
Provisions: The investment buys training at company headquarters, which covers all aspects of the decorating business from design to accounting. You also get on-going support.

DECORATING DEN, 19100 Montgomery Ave., Montgomery Village, MD 20866; www.decoratingden.com. (800) 686-6393/(301)272-1500.
Franchise: Yes.
Description: Decorating Den is a shop-at-home decorating service. The franchisee goes by appointment to a customer's home in a "ColorVan" containing over 5,000 samples of fabrics, wall coverings, carpets, draperies, furniture, and accessories. There is no charge for the decorating service because the profit comes from the difference between the wholesale and retail prices on the products sold to the customer. There are over 1,100 franchises operating throughout the U.S., Canada, United Kingdom, Japan, Europe and Australia.
Requirements: The franchise fee is $24,900. An additional $5,000 to $15,000 working capital is needed. Some business and decorating experience is preferred.
Provisions: The franchise fee covers complete training which takes about six months, national advertising, promotional materials, business and record keeping systems, access to quality products at wholesale discounted prices, a selection of product samples, and all the necessary paperwork down to printed checks and business cards.
Profit Potential: Not available.

DR. VINYL & ASSOCIATES, LTD., 821 NW Commerce St., Lee's Summit, MO 64086; www.drvinyl.com. (800) 531-6600.
Franchise: Yes.
Description: Dr. Vinyl franchisees repair vinyl, cloth, leather, strip molding, windshields, and plastic for car dealerships, restaurants, and doctors' offices.
Requirements: The franchise fee starts at $32,500 and you will need a van, new or used.
Provisions: The fee includes $5,000 worth of inventory, training, and ongoing support.

DURA-OAK CABINET REFACING PRODUCTS, 863 Texas Ave., Shreveport, LA 71101; (800)228-7702. www.dura-oak.com.
Franchise: No.
Description: Refacing existing cabinets, saving the homeowner about half the cost of a complete kitchen remodel.
Requirements: $10,000 investment with no royalty fee, no inventory, and no show room necessary. Financing is available.
Provisions: Exclusive territory, never ending sales training that includes videos and personal training, marketing tools, technical support, TV and radio ads, and manuals.

FLOOR COVERINGS INTERNATIONAL, 5182 Old Dixie Hwy., Forest Park, GA 30050; www.floorcoveringsintl.com. (800)955-4324.
Franchise: Yes.
Description: Mobile floor covering retailer offering convenient shop-at-home service to today's time-starved consumers.
Requirements: The franchise fee is $16,000 with total start-up costs ranging from $30,000 to $40,000; royalties are 5%; and the ad fund is 2%.
Provisions: Comprehensive training program, regional workshops, monthly newsletter, national accounts, national advertising, toll-free help line, marketing manual and materials, operations manual, annual convention, and buying group discounts.

FLOORTASTIC, 1638 S. Research Loop Rd., Suite 160, Tucson, AZ 85710; www.floortastic.com. (800)332-7397.
Franchise: Yes.

Description: This program offers state-of-the-art assortment of decorative, resinous floor coating systems, which transform ugly concrete or linoleum tiles into beautiful, ultra-tough, surfaces. These coatings are extremely durable and very low maintenance. They are designed to beautify and protect driveways, patios, garage floors, basements, walkways, pool decks, and interior flooring. For example, you can turn a common concrete garage floor into a simulated quartz texture or make a linoleum entryway look like elegant flagstone.
Requirements: The minimum startup cost is $39,500.
Provisions: Extensive training, ongoing support, and all the equipment, inventory and promotional materials you need.

FOLIAGE DESIGN SYSTEMS, 4496 35th St., Orlando, FL 32811; www.foliagedesign.com. (800)933-7351/(407)245-7776.
Franchise: Yes.
Description: Interior foliage design, sales, and or maintenance.
Requirements: The franchise fee depends on a market analysis performed by the company, but it ranges from $25,000 to $100,000 with additional costs amounting to about $15,000. The royalty is 4% of gross.
Provisions: Each franchise receives a protected territory, two weeks of training in Florida, operating manuals, operation systems, a computerized management information system to minimize administrative chores, leads from national advertising, and toll-free support. Plant materials can be obtained from over 200,000 sq. ft. of company owned greenhouses. Training covers tested and proven methods of record keeping, order writing, marketing, filing, collections, and accounting, as well as the care, design, and use of foliage in commercial and residential spaces.
Profit Potential: Not available.
Comments: This company has been in business since 1971 and has won numerous nationally recognized awards.

JET-BLACK SEALCOATING & REPAIR, 25 W. Cliff Rd., #103, Burnsville, MN 55337; www.Jet-Black.com. (888)538-2525/(952)890-8343.
Franchise: Yes.
Description: Asphalt/blacktop seal coating, hot rubber crack filling, oil spot treatment, patchwork, grass edging and striping.
Requirements: $39,500 includes the franchise fee.
Provisions: You get a complete business package including a trailer, equipment, uniforms, office supplies, a week of corporate training, and grand opening advertising.

KITCHEN SOLVERS, 401 Jay St., La Crosse, WI 54601; www.kitchensolvers.com. (800)845-6779.
Franchise: Yes.
Description: Kitchen Solvers has been in business since 1984 and now has 138 franchises throughout the US and Canada. The company specializes in custom cabinet refacing for the kitchen. Other services offered include pre-built & custom cabinetry, laminate, solid surface, & stone countertops, kitchen planning & design, kitchen accessories, bathtub & surround wall shower liners, glueless laminate flooring, and storage organizing systems.
Requirements: The franchise fee for an owner operator franchise is $25,000, plus the standard supplies package which is $7,995.
Provisions: Comprehensive supplies package, exclusive territory, two weeks of extensive training in the areas of installation, marketing, administration, software & design, product/

supplier knowledge, pricing, and ongoing corporate support.

KITCHEN TUNE-UP, INC., 813 Circle Dr., Aberdeen, SD 57401; www.kitchentuneup.com. (800)333-6385/(605)225-4049.
Franchise: Yes.
Description: Kitchen Tune-Up offers consumers a new way to renew, repair and remodel their kitchens. They offer "Kitchen Solutions for any Budget" with wood restorations, cabinet recoating, cabinet refacing and a brand line of custom cabinetry.
Requirements: The franchise fee is $25,000 and additional start-up expenses amount to about $9,000.
Provisions: The fee buys a protected territory, national supplier discounts, ongoing support, monthly newsletters, and regional and national conventions.

KOTT KOATINGS, 27161 Burbank St., Foothill Ranch, CA 92610; www.thebathtubpeople.com. (949)770-5055.
Franchise: No.
Description: Porcelain and fiberglass refinishing.
Requirements: The franchise fee is $17,500. There is financing available from the company for the franchise fee, equipment, and inventory.
Provisions: A dealer package includes 5 days of training at company headquarters, a complete custom "factory on wheels" trailer unit with generator, a complete equipment package of all necessary tools and supplies, a protected territory, and manuals.
Profit Potential: Not available.

LANGENWALTER INDUSTRIES, INC., 1111 S. Richfield Rd., Placentia, CA 92670; www.langdye.com. (800)422-4370.
Franchise: Yes.
Description: Franchisees do carpet color correction work for apartment, hotels, and commercial properties, saving the owners up to 85% on carpet replacement costs.
Requirements: Must have management experience and $30,000 liquid capital. This company is on the SBA approved list for financing.
Provisions: Fee includes five days of intensive training, operations manual, marketing package, complete equipment package, technical assistance, and ongoing support.

MAINTENANCE MADE SIMPLE, 9820 E. Dreyfus Ave., Scottsdale, AZ 85260; www.m2simple.com. (866)778-6283.
Franchise: Yes.
Description: Handyman and home maintenance services.
Requirements: Total costs including franchise fee runs around $35,000. There is financing available from third party sources. No experience is necessary.
Provisions: Training is provided at company headquarters and continues at franchisee's location. There is very strong marketing support including national and regional media, co-op advertising, an inbound and outbound call center, national accounts program, and catalog of marketing collateral.

MIRACLE METHOD, 4239 N. Nevada Ave., #115, Colorado Springs, CO 80907; www.miraclemethod.com. (800)444-8827/(719)594-9196.
Franchise: Yes.
Description: Since 1979 Miracle Method has provided expert refinishing of bathroom and kitchen tubs, tile, counters, sinks, and cabinets. Their process saves customers up to 70% versus the cost of replacement.

Requirements: The franchise fee is $18,500 with estimated start-up costs of $6,000 for equipment. Negotiable financing is available.
Provisions: Franchisees get proprietary bonding agent, access to hi-tech coatings, specific territory, initial and on-going training, customized advertising program, toll-free support, and free start-up package.

MR. ELECTRIC, 1020 N. University Parks Dr., Waco, TX 76707; www.mrelectric.com. (800)805-0575.
Franchise: Yes.
Description: Provides residential and light commercial electrical service and repair.
Requirements: Total startup costs start at $65,000. Only the franchise fee of $19,500 can be financed. Experience in the field of electrical repair is needed.
Provisions: Training is provided both at company headquarters and on-site. Ongoing support is provided via the Internet, toll-free phone line, meetings, and newsletters.
Comments: This company is owned by Dwyer, Inc., which owns other home maintenance franchise companies including Mr. Rooter, Mr. Appliance, Glass Doctor, and Rainbow Int'l.

NATIONAL CARPET EQUIPMENT, INC., 6801 Winnetka Ave., North, Minneapolis, MN 55311; www.nationalequipment.com. (800)245-0267/(612)535-8206.
Franchise: No.
Description: Rug making and tufting and carpet sculpting.
Requirements: $1,100 to $2,900.
Provisions: Investment buys complete training including hotel costs, continuing support from instructors after training, discounts on supplies, training on new applications and techniques as they come up, and referral system.

NATIONWIDE CARPET BROKERS, P.O. Box 1472, Dalton, GA 30720. (800)322-7299.
Franchise: No.
Description: This is a national floor covering and decorating business that offers agents major mill purchasing. You could elect to set up your car or van with the Nationwide logo and be ready to call on your in-home or in-office shoppers. Presently about 20% of Nationwide agencies are full-time businesses with the rest on a part-time basis.
Requirements: Minimum investment is $4,900 in areas where there are no other agents.
Provisions: For the minimum investment you would receive a complete collection of samples, training in your area, technical support, an 800 number for free quotes and inventory availability, video tape training, cards, invoices, letterheads, and basic forms to start your business.
Profit Potential: $30,000 and up depending on the person.

PARKER INTERIOR PLANTSCAPE, INC., 1325 Terrill Rd., Scotch Plains, NJ 07076; www.parkerplants.com. (908) 322-5552.
Franchise: Yes.
Description: Part I is the installation of plants, trees, flowers, silks, Christmas decorations, containers, etc. to offices, malls, atriums, etc. Part II is the continual care and maintenance of these plants and products on location.
Requirements: $35,000.
Provisions: Training from the largest, most successful, privately owned interior plantscaping company in the U.S. You will be taught all the secrets, operations, sources, etc. "We will start them in a successful enterprise."

Profit Potential: First year - after costs and salaries $20,000, second year $40,000, third year $60,000, etc. "It is almost like a pyramid. Each time you get an account, you should keep the monthly billing coming in. Each new account just adds to the last."

PUROSYSTEMS, INC., 6001 Hiatus Rd., Taramac, FL 33321; www.puroclean.com. (800)247-9047.
Franchise: Yes.
Description: Provides property restoration and reconstruction due to water, fire, and smoke damage.
Requirements: The total investment is around $50,000 with half of that going to the franchise fee.
Provisions: A total of 3 weeks of training is provided divided between company headquarters and the franchisee's site.

SCREEN MACHINE, 4173 First St., Livermore, CA 94557; www.screen-machine.com. (877)505-1985.
Franchise: Yes.
Description: A mobile service business specializing in the custom fabrication, replacement, and repair of window and door screens as well as other related services.
Requirements: The franchise fee is $25,000. An equipment and supplies package costs at least $11,350 and general business expenses are $5,500 minimum. The total initial investment ranges from $45,000 to $70,000.
Provisions: Your investment buys training in marketing strategies, advertising techniques, business management, basic accounting methods, operational procedures, and "hands-on" technical instruction on how to custom fabricate screens and perform screen repair and related work. Also provided are advertising materials, audiovisual training, ongoing support, and all of the materials, supplies, and equipment necessary for the basic operation of the business. A custom built mobile workshop with a generator and power miter box saw are all part of the equipment package.
Profit Potential: Not available.

SPRING-GREEN LAWN CARE, 11909 Spaulding School Dr., Plainfield, IL 60544; www.spring-green.com. (800)435-4051.
Franchise: Yes.
Description: Franchisees offer to residential and commercial customers regular lawn fertilization, weed control, lawn aeration, and pruning and feeding of trees and shrubs.
Requirements: The franchise fee is $21,900 and the total investment ranges from $80,000 to $90,000.
Provisions: You get an exclusive territory and complete training, computer hardware and software, equipment and vehicle.

STAINED GLASS OVERLAY, INC., 1827 N. Case St., Orange, CA 92665; www.stainedglassoverlay.com. (800)944-4746/(714)974-6124.
Franchise: Yes.
Description: The Stained Glass Overlay business is a patented process used to manufacture solid, seamless, one-piece stained glass in any design or pattern. It turns everyday glass into designer glass.
Requirements: The minimum investment is about $88,000. The franchise fee is $45,000, the franchise package that provides training, support materials, a business start-up package, and show quality display materials is $8,000, and other materials cost

an additional $3,000. Royalties run 5% of gross sales plus another 2% for the advertising fee.

Provisions: Training starts with 40 hours of classroom and hands-on instruction and includes manuals.

Profit Potential: Not available.

Comments: This franchise is available in the U.S., Australia, the United Kingdom, Israel, Japan, Norway, Thailand, and has locations in 13 other foreign countries.

STARSCAPES INTERNATIONAL, 427 W. Chilton St., Chandler, AZ 85224; www.starscapes.com. (602)926-1982.

Franchise: No.

Description: Licensees produce glow-in-the-dark ceiling murals of astronomically correct skyscapes. Clients include individuals, hotels, motels, resorts, etc.

Requirements: The complete start-up package is under $300.

Profit Potential: Up to $1,500 per day.

SURFACE DOCTOR, 4239 North Nevada Ave, #115, Colorado Springs, CO 80907; www.surfacedoctor.com. (800)735-5055.

Franchise: Yes.

Description: Surface restoration and refinishing service for tile, counter tops, bathtubs, sinks, metal appliances and more. Surface Doctor's technology allows bathrooms and kitchens to be transformed without the chaos and expense of conventional remodeling methods.

Requirements: Franchise fee is $15,000; start-up costs range from $7,800 to $11,780; royalties are $175 per month; and the ad fund is $25 per month.

Provisions: Comprehensive training program, marketing manuals and materials, operations manual, toll-free Help Line, annual convention, newsletter, ongoing training, and research and development.

TRIPLE A DYE & CHEMICAL, 1872 Del Amo Blvd., #C, Torrance, CA 90501; (800)228-3240.

Franchise: No.

Description: On-location carpet and upholstery dyeing.

Requirements: Training is at company headquarters in Los Angeles and is $300 for the first person for the first day; it is $250 a day thereafter.

Provisions: The company offers marketing assistance and technical training.

Profit Potential: Not available.

USE-WHAT-YOU-HAVE INTERIORS, 109 East 73rd St., New York, NY 10021 (212)288-8888. www.redecorate.com.

Franchise: No.

Description: Pioneer of one-day redecorating consultations.

Requirements: Talent and passion for interior design. Investment of $3,000 for training materials, certification dinner and other expenses.

Provisions: Weeklong decorator training program for novices and professionals and membership in the Interior Refiners Network. Trainees learn everything they need to know to have a home-based decorating consultation business plus certification in network.

LON WALTENBERGER TRAINING SERVICES, 5410 Mt. Tahoma Dr. S.E., Olympia, WA 98503; www.lonwaltenberger.com. (360) 456-1949.

Franchise: No.

Description: Repair/refinish porcelain, gel coat and acrylic bathtubs; sinks; counters (Formica-type and cultured marble); ceramic tiles; spas; ranges and hoods; refrigerators; and dishwashers. Use only primer that requires no acid etching or sanding for savings in labor and durability.
Requirements: The training fee is $295 and you will need about $2,000 for equipment and supplies. "You will repay your total investment with your first 10 jobs."
Provisions: The $295 buys a 14-hour video program plus two manuals with advertising examples, forms, prices, inventory of equipment, and all the information you will need to successfully manage your business. The company president insists that you should shop your hometown sources and manufacturers for all supplies. Technical support is available.
Profit Potential: Profit margin for this industry is high.

WEED MAN, 11 Grand Marshall Dr., Scarborough, ON M1B 5N6 Canada; www.weedman.com. (416)269-5754.
Franchise: Yes.
Description: Franchisees provide lawn management services to home owners.
Requirements: The total startup investment is around $50,000 including the franchise fee. The company provides help with third party financing for startup costs, the franchise fee, and equipment. General business experience is also required.
Provisions: Training is provided at company headquarters, at the franchisee's site, and other locations. Particular attention is paid to safety and security precautions.
Comments: Franchisees operate throughout Canada and the U.S.

RESIDENTIAL & COMMERCIAL CLEANING & MAINTENANCE

Residential and commercial cleaning businesses are the essence of service businesses. No products are exchanged, and no special skills are required. The basic purpose is to save customers time.

Home cleaning services is a $200 million a year industry, and it is growing all the time. "In John Naisbitt's best seller, Megatrends, maid services was listed among the six growth industries," says Frank Flack, chief executive officer of Molly Maid, the fastest growing international maid service. "Most American households are now two-income families. There are seventy million women in the work force - more than half of them have some form of domestic help. Juggling a career and family can take some doing. A working woman is likely to exchange money for time - something she has precious little of. She can save five or six hours a week to do things that are more gratifying than cleaning windows or dusting under the bed."

There are dozens of maid services, and more are entering the field every day. Most can be operated from home. Although they are not the least expensive home-based opportunities to get into, the potential return on investment is excellent. A well-run maid service, utilizing the team cleaning method, can expect to gross over $100,000 by the second year.

Also targeting the residential customer are carpet cleaning, chimney sweeps, and window washing services.

Other businesses in this chapter cater to commercial customers. Office cleaning, janitorial services, mobile power washing, and restaurant cleaning are among these opportunities. Commercial cleaning businesses tend to require bigger investments and more commitment of time and effort. On the plus side, commercial customers are often repeat customers and long-term contracts offer extra security.

One of the fastest growing services in this category is cleaning windows and window coverings such as shutters and blinds. According to the National Home Builders Association, there are 110 million single family homes in the U.S. More and more of these are being built with open floor plans with an average of 25-35 windows per home. That's almost 4 billion windows and coverings someone has to clean. You don't need a calculator to figure out that there is a lot of profit to be made.

AIR CARE, 3868 E. Post Rd., Las Vegas, NV 89120. (702)424-5515.
Franchise: No.
Description: Indoor air quality specialists clean and decontaminate air conditioning and heating systems in residential and commercial buildings.
Requirements: $5,000 to $15,000.
Provisions: Complete equipment package plus one week training in all aspects of the business. This also includes a toll-free help line.
Profit Potential: $50,000 to $200,000 annually.

AMERICAN LEAK DETECTION, 888 Research Drive, Suite 100, Palm Springs, CA 92262; www.americanleakdetection.com. (800)755-6697.
Franchise: Yes.
Description: Franchisees use electronic instruments and tools to find and repair water, gas, and sewer leaks in both commercial and residential buildings.
Requirements: The franchise fee is $57,500 and up. You also need a work vehicle and tools.
Provisions: Complete training, both business and technical, is provided.

BLIND DOCTOR'S TRAINING ACADEMY, LLC, 269 Market Place Blvd. Suite 342, Cartersville, GA 30121; www.blindsshadesandshutters.com. e-mail info@clean-money.com. (770) 975-9009.
Franchise: No.
Description: Cleaning, repairing, selling and installing blinds, shades and shutters to residential and commercial customers. The cleaning equipment employs a specialized mobile pressure washing system and is safe for all types - vinyl, metal, fabric, or wood. It's easy to transport and anyone can use it easily - even petite women.
Requirements: There are two programs to choose from when starting the blind cleaning and repair business. The cost for the "Starter Plan" is $2,990 and the most popular program is "Plan A" for $9,990. There are also two additional programs for cleaning, repairing, selling and installing blinds, shades and shutters that cost $14,990 and $17,990 respectively. "We recommend starting with "Plan A" and then moving on to selling and installing when the business is able to pay for the expansion." There are no geographic restrictions.
Provisions: This is a turnkey business opportunity that has all the benefits of a franchise

without ongoing fees, territorial restrictions and contracts. The fees include everything: the equipment, a how-to operational manual including all the forms needed to run the business, a hiring and training manual, how-to video training tapes on cleaning and repairing blinds, shades and shutters, marketing and advertising materials on CD ROM and hard copy for easy cost effective printing, a complete bookkeeping package, and a source for purchasing blinds and repair parts at wholesale cost. Also offered is unlimited consulting time and ongoing company support for one full year.

Comments: "Service two accounts each morning - working from 7am to 11am - and gross between $400 and $650 each morning Monday through Friday. The average blind takes 90 seconds to clean with our equipment."

CLOSEUP: Blinds Shades & Shutters

If you're like Kristie Sullivan, you've searched long and hard for a way to earn good money without having to work long hours. All you want is something you can build and count on, but you may wonder if you'll ever find it. After years of hunting and scouring magazines, Kristie finally found just such a business in an ad for Blinds Shades & Shutters. "I could tell just by looking at the picture in the ad that this was it," she says. "Everyone has blinds, but who has the time to clean them?"

Obviously there is a market, but what really caught Kristie's attention was the mobile system that is designed so that even a 4'11" woman such as herself could use it alone with ease.

With millions of blinds, shades and shutters being sold and installed in homes and businesses, the demand for someone to clean and repair them is unlimited. While the market potential is large, to date, it is virtually untapped. There is very little competition and the ones that are around are usually ultrasonic cleaners, which may void manufacturers' warranties.

Kristie learned everything she needed to know to start her new business in 3 days. When she came home from her training, she promptly placed an ad in the free local paper. She was astonished by the response. "It scared me," she laughs. "That ad booked me for 5 weeks solid. It was that fast!"

Both homeowners and businesses clamored for Kristie's service. She has long-term contracts with Dairy Queen and Burger King. "Business owners love this because I don't take the blinds away to work on them, instead I take them right outside. Busy establishments appreciate that because it doesn't disrupt business. And homeowners don't have to worry about when or if they'll get their blinds back."

So the training is thorough, the competition is almost nonexistent, and the market is vast. The downside? "The hardest part is going up ladders if you are afraid of heights," laughs Kristie. "There was a time when I couldn't go up past the third step on a ladder, but now I don't even think about it."

And the best part? "The money is the best part. I don't work that long and it's just not hard. I didn't have to invest that much either. I didn't even need a truck; I pull the trailer behind my little car."

Business just keeps getting better for Kristie. She hasn't advertised for over a year now because word of mouth keeps her busy. "I actually have to be careful not to build up more than I can handle," she says. "Besides, I have to leave some time to spend the money and enjoy it."

BEARCOM BUILDING SERVICES, 7022 South 400 West, Midvale, UT 84047; www.bearcomservices.com. (888)569-9533.
Franchise: Yes.
Description: The Laser Chem advanced carpet dry cleaning system thoroughly cleans carpet, dries quickly, and does not resoil. "This new system has revolutionized the carpet cleaning industry."
Requirements: The franchise fee is $9,900 and you'll need another $3,000 for startup.
Provisions: Month to month support via newsletter, toll-free technical assistance, and benefits of in-house research and development.

CEILTECH, 825 Gate Park Drive, #3, Daytona Beach, FL 32114; www.ceiltechinc.com. (800)662-9299.
Franchise: No.
Description: Ceiling cleaning service.
Requirements: Startup costs are about $13,000 and there are leasing plans available.
Provisions: The system includes all necessary equipment, supplies, and accessories to generate over $4,000 in gross income. Also included are marketing materials and a training manual.
Profit Potential: You can net in excess of $150 per hour.

CHEM-DRY CARPET, DRAPERY AND UPHOLSTERY CLEANING, 1530 North 1000 West, Logan, UT 84321; www.chemdry.com. (877)307-8233.
Franchise: Yes.
Description: Chem-Dry franchises clean carpet, drapery, upholstery and most fabrics with a patented, heated carbonating system. Chem-Dry specializes in the hard-to-remove stains and has four patents with several more pending.
Requirements: The franchise fee is $11,950. There is a financing plan available with $5,950 down payment with a full purchase price of $18,950 (including equipment, supplies, etc.). The remaining $15,000 is financed over 56 months at 0% interest.
Provisions: Your fee will get you all of the equipment, solutions, paperwork and training needed to start the business. Plus you can expect the constant support of the parent company, a technical department to help with any questions, newsletters, etc. The investment covers everything necessary to start a full-time business.

CLEAN & HAPPY WINDOWS, 10019 Des Moines Memorial Dr., Seattle, WA 98168; www.cleanhappy.com. (866)762-7617.
Franchise: Yes.
Description: Franchises clean windows, gutters, roofs, screens and awnings. Customers include home owners and businesses with buildings no taller than four stories.
Requirements: This is a very inexpensive franchise opportunity. There is no franchise fee and it can be started for $100. Business and marketing experience is the basic requirement. Must be comfortable working several stories up.
Provisions: Training is available and an online scheduling service is provided.
Comments: About half the franchisees are absentee owners.

CLEANNET USA, 9861 Broken Land Pkwy., #208, Columbia, MD 21046; www.cleannetusa.com. (800)735-8838.
Franchise: Yes.
Description: Provides a variety of professional cleaning services for commercial, retail and industrial facilities.
Requirements: This is an excellent opportunity that can be started for under $4,000. Financing is available.
Provisions: The amount of training is impressive considering the low cost. One to four weeks is provided at company headquarters and/or the franchisee's location.
Comments: This company has experienced tremendous growth over the past five years. There are now over 2,600 franchisees.

CLENTECH ACOUSTIC CLEAN, 900 Colorado Ave. S., Minneapolis, MN 55416; www.acoustic-clean.com.
 (800)328-4650.
Franchise: No.
Description: Acoustical wall and ceiling cleaning using atomized cleaning mist system.
Requirements: Price starts at $7,500.
Provisions: Equipment, training, protected territory, and enough supplies to triple your investment.

COVERALL CLEANING CONCEPT, 500 West Cypress Creek Rd., Suite 580, Ft. Lauderdale, FL 33309; www.coverall.com. (800)537-3371.
Franchise: Yes.
Description: Commercial cleaning services. These services include hard floor   care, carpet cleaning, restroom sanitation, lawn maintenance and painting. Coverall also offers pest control by Orkin.
Requirements: The franchise fee ranges from $6,000 to $32,200.
Provisions: Coverall offers a turnkey program that goes from startup through expansion. It includes complete training in the latest technology, innovative cleaning techniques, business management, and safety procedures. The fee includes an equipment package, an initial customer base, and participation in volume buying. There are financing options available as well as national membership opportunities.

THE DALE GROUP, dba Blind Butler, 23052 Alicia Pkwy., #H-202, Mission Viejo, CA 92692; www.myblindbiz.com. (888)922-5463.
Franchise: No.
Description: Mobile mini-blind wash and wax; on-site sales of blinds, drapes or shutters; and high tech window tinting.
Requirements: The cost is $3,000 and there is financing available.
Provisions: The investment covers all needed tools and equipment, working samples, proven marketing plan, tightwad advertising plan, and free ongoing support.

DELCO CLEANING SYSTEMS, 2513 Warfield, FT Worth, TX 76106; www.dcs1.com. (800)433-2113.
Franchise: No.
Description: Environmental mobile power wash service, i.e.: truck washing, building washing for store fronts and shopping malls, restaurant kitchen washing, and numerous other situations.
Requirements: Equipment, supplies, and training are all sold separately. Minimum required: $2,000. Financing is available.

Provisions: See above.
Profit Potential: $10,000 to $100,000.

DR. GLASS, 3573 Nyland Way, Lafayette, CO 80206; (888)282-3535.
www.docglass.com.
Franchise: No.
Description: Window washing service. This particular company has started more than 200 business operators across the country. It's a great part-time business with a proven system and very low start-up cost.
Requirements: The total cost is $2,660 with a down payment of $500 and the balance financed in-house.
Provisions: Turnkey system includes equipment to start a small scale residential window cleaning business. The system includes manuals, videos, template, marketing and advertising materials, e-mail bulletin board access, and all business materials.

FABRI-ZONE, 3135 Universal Dr., # 6, Mississauga, ON L4X 2E2 Canada; www.fabrizone.com. (888) 781-1123.
Franchise: Yes.
Description: Dry-cleaning and purification process for carpets and upholstery, ceiling cleaning, and insurance damage restoration.
Requirements: Total investment requires $15,000 minimum with a cash outlay of $6,000. There is financing available from the company.
Provisions: Training and ongoing technical and promotional support.
Profit Potential: Not available.
Comments: Franchise opportunities exist in both the U.S. and Canada.

HEAVEN'S BEST CARPET & UPHOLSTERY CLEANING, P.O. Box 607, Rexburg, ID 83440; www.heavensbest.com. (800)359-2095/(208)359-1106.
Franchise: Yes.
Description: An alternative to the traditional wet saturation carpet cleaning offering the advantages of modern, low moisture cleaning. "Our operators receive professional training. These factors with a low flat rate royalty fee insure success."
Requirements: The franchise fee is very low at only $2,900 and the royalty is $80 a month. Additional startup expenses amount to be $13,000.
Provisions: Complete equipment and training package, exclusive territory, and enough initial supplies to re-coop $10,000.

JANI-KING INTERNATIONAL, INC., 16885 Dallas Pkwy., Addison, TX 75001; www.janiking.com. (800)552-5264/(214)991-0900.
Franchise: Yes.
Description: Jani-King is the world's largest janitorial franchise. Operators perform light office cleaning and janitorial services for commercial and industrial buildings on a long-term contract basis.
Requirements: The franchise fee starts at $8,500, but can go as high as $32,000. Financing is available.
Provisions: All franchisees receive training, business forms, and ongoing support.

JANITIZE AMERICA, INC., 15449 Middlebelt, Livonia, MI 48154; www.jantize.com. (800)968-9182.
Franchise: Yes.
Description: Commercial cleaning service.

Requirements: The franchise fee range starts at $3,500 and the initial start-up package (computer system, equipment, supplies, etc.) is another $6,000. You can lower that cost by using the company's computer service instead which reduces the cost by $2,500. Monthly royalties are 8% of gross sales and the advertising fee is 1% of gross.

Provisions: In addition to the provisions stated above, Janitize provides all business forms, a supply of uniforms, and ongoing support.

Profit Potential: Not available.

JAN-PRO, 383 Strand Industrial Dr., Little River, SC 29566; www.jan-pro.com. (800)668-1001.

Franchise: Yes.

Description: This is a commercial cleaning franchise with over 2,800 franchisees throughout the United States and Canada.

Requirements: It is possible to start this business for under $1,000. The company even provides financing, but the royalty is a hefty 8%. Management skills are also needed.

Provisions: Training is provided for up to four weeks, first at company headquarters then at the franchisee's location. Ongoing support is provided.

MAID BRIGADE, 4 Concourse Pkwy., #200, Atlanta, GA 30328; www.maidbrigade.com. (800)722-6243.

Franchise: Yes.

Description: Supervised team-cleaning services for single-family homes.

Requirements: The franchise fee is $19,500. Operating expenses will require an additional $15,000+. The royalty is 3.5% to 6.9%. A business background is preferred.

Provisions: The fee buys the right to use the name, a one-week training class, operations manual, and a start-up kit that includes janitorial supplies, printed materials, training videos, and marketing materials.

Profit Potential: Not available.

THE MAIDS INTERNATIONAL, 4820 Dodge St., Omaha, NE 68132; www.maids.com/ (800) 843-6243.

Franchise: Yes.

Description: Completely computerized residential cleaning service.

Requirements: The franchise fee is $16,900. Another $25,000 will be needed for operating capital including leases for cars and computers, labor and advertising. The royalty ranges from 5% to 7% and the advertising royalty is 2%.

Provisions: The fee buys the use of the company name, the exclusive system, pre-training, corporate training, post-training, and a complete equipment and advertising package. Financing is available only for expanding territories.

Profit Potential: Not available.

CLOSEUP: Maid Services of America

Aspiring entrepreneurs who are successful in their careers often assume that they can expect even greater success as business owners. But the truth is, running a business requires special knowledge and skills sometimes totally unrelated to a chosen occupation. Even one who has already ventured out into the world of business ownership may not have a clue how to get from a small one-man band to a thriving business capable of succeeding in a competitive marketplace.

Naomi Parsons cleaned houses full-time for three years while her husband, Tom, worked as a firefighter. She liked her little business, but it was becoming increasingly difficult to handle it physically.

"People kept telling us that we should expand, but we didn't know how to do that," says Tom. "There is nothing you couldn't figure out with enough time, but we didn't have the time." The couple investigated the options which included everything from overpriced books to franchises. Ultimately, they decided to get their training from Maid Services of America (MSA).

"We chose MSA because it was not a franchise. We saw no reason why we should have to pay royalties out of our business when we had already been operating for three years with an established customer base. There were also no restrictions and we didn't have to give up our autonomy."

While working on her own, Naomi had been earning an average of $500 per week, doing everything from scrubbing floors to acting as confidant to her 30 regular customers. The first step to success was for Naomi to stop being a maid and start being a manager. She recalls, "I've heard my trainer say over and over, 'you can't push the business until you stop pushing the broom'. We had to start acting like a big business even though we are in our living room."

Within two years of training with MSA, the Parsons' business, Tidy Home Cleaning, has expanded to 126 customers, has 10 employees, and grosses nearly $200,000 per year. Their goal is to double that.

"From our own experience, we knew how to clean and how to charge for the services. That might seem like enough. It isn't. For instance, there were legal issues that we didn't even think of. Now we can expand our workforce without fear of crossing the law. We also didn't have the paperwork to impress new customers. MSA provided us with a printing package that included over two dozen professionally designed forms, everything from brochures to job contracts. Investing in a turnkey system like this was definitely the way to go," says Tom. "All we had to do was follow instructions. Don't get me wrong, running this business is hard work, but at least we know exactly what we have to do."

"From our own experience, we knew how to clean and how to charge for the services. That might seem like enough. It isn't. For instance, there were legal issues that we didn't even think of. Now we can expand our workforce without fear of crossing the law. We also didn't have the paperwork to impress new customers. MSA provided us with a printing package that included over 75 professionally designed forms, everything from brochures to job contracts. Investing in a turnkey system like this was definitely the way to go," says Tom. "All we had to do was follow instructions. Don't get me wrong, running this business is hard work, but at least we know exactly what we have to do."

MAID SERVICES OF AMERICA, 475 East Main St., Suite 151, Cartersville, GA 30121; www.maidservicesofamerica.com, email maidmoney@aol.com. Office (770) 387-2455 or voice mail (800)289-8642.
Franchise: No.
Description: Maid service and property maintenance.
Requirements: Fee is $4,995 (financing is provided with 50% down - no payments for 3 months)
Provisions: The comprehensive business plan includes unlimited consulting and support; instructional training manuals covering residential cleaning, move-in/move-outs, property maintenance, window washing, floor care and new construction cleaning; scheduling software; personalized business forms covering all aspects of the business; flyers, door hangers, direct mail coupons; accounting system; training videos; recruitment, hiring and training procedures for new maids; motivational programs and award incentives for recognizing the accomplishments and performance of the maids.
Profit Potential: The company claims anyone following their system should be able to gross $100,000 in sales by the end of the first year. There is also a new system, sold separately, for a mobile mini-blind washing system.
Comments: The company has an exceptional record. Of its 600+ independently owned and operated offices, none have failed to obtain the clientele needed to successfully operate their businesses.

MOLLY MAID, INC., 3948 Ranchero Dr., Ann Arbor, MI 48108; www.mollymaid.com. (800)665-5962.
Franchise: Yes.
Description: Regularly scheduled cleaning services with weekday business hours. This is an affordable investment in an exploding industry. Repeat cash business. "Award winning technology."
Requirements: No experience is necessary, but a business background is considered a plus. The franchise fee of $9,900 is included in the total investment of $35,000 to $70,000. The additional working capital is needed for leased cars, insurance, and bonding of the employees. The royalty decreases from 6% to 3% as sales increase. The advertising royalty is 2%.
Provisions: The fee buys exclusive rights to the territory, equipment and supplies, training, and start-up business documents.
Profit Potential: Not available, however, franchisees said that they were earning well into the six figures and grew so fast it was hard to keep the business at home.
Comments: This is the largest maid service franchise with over 400 operators and 16 years of experience. The company believes in projecting a quality image and it works.

NATIONAL PROCLEAN CORPORATION, 4320 Sable Ridge, Colorado Springs, CO 80918; www.nationalproclean.com. (800)796-4680.
Franchise: No.
Description: Complete program to establish cleaning contractors in janitorial, maid service, carpet cleaning, construction cleanup or restroom sanitation services.
Requirements: The program costs $300; optional equipment costs range from $500 to $3,000, and optional telemarketing service costs an additional $200 to $400.
Provisions: The program includes four training manuals, seven hours of instructional audiotapes, all necessary forms, advertising and bid materials, certification test and diploma, and free follow-up consulting.

OMEGASONICS, 330 E. Easy Street, Suite A, Simi Valley, CA 93065;

www.omegasonics.com. (800)669-8227.
Franchise: No.
Description: Omegasonics gives entrepreneurs and existing cleaning businesses the opportunity to expand into the ultrasonic blind cleaning service and sales market.
Requirements: Total costs range from $9,500 to $18,950. There is financing available.
Provisions: The company provides equipment, initial set of cleaning supplies, training manual, training video, two days of hands-on training at the factory, toll-free support line, annual convention and conference.

PRIME SHINE AMERICA, INC., 2525 Hospital Road, Saginaw, MI 48603; www.primeshinecleaning.com. (800)456-8588.
Franchise: No.
Description: Residential maid service.
Requirements: The complete start-up package costs $599. (There is also the option of getting training tape and manual for only $199.)
Provisions: Included in the complete package are supplies and equipment for your first maid team, a maid training video, an operations manual, and two days of training at company headquarters. Any of the above may be purchased separately.
Profit Potential: The company claims that following their procedures, you should be able to gross over $80,000 a year within two years.

PROFESSIONAL CARPET SYSTEMS, 4211-C Atlantic Ave., Raleigh, NC 27604; www.procarpetsys.com. (800)925-5055.
Franchise: Yes.
Description: Professional Carpet Systems is a leader in on-site carpet redyeing and a total carpet maintenance service. PCS services include carpet cleaning and repair, water/flood damage restoration, smoke removal, guaranteed odor control and more.
Requirements: Franchise fee is $14,950; start-up costs range from $18,000 to $50,000; and the royalties are 4-6% with rebates. Financial assistance is provided.
Provisions: Comprehensive training program, annual convention, newsletter, toll-free Help Line, and ongoing research and development. Training consists of two weeks in Raleigh, NC, (five days extended available), two days on site, and 11 two-day training sessions held every year for additional training, most with industry certification available. In addition to this, there are periodic workshops and an annual convention.
Comments: "Professional Carpet Systems is the leader in on site carpet redyeing, servicing thousands of apartment complexes, hotels, and motels worldwide. Complete carpet service is a niche that is not being filled in the market place by anyone else. Because service and replacement is offered, this business is very recession resistance. This is a business that is for someone who wants to build a company, not for the absentee owner, direct involvement is vital. "

SERVICEMASTER, 3839 Forest Hill Irene Rd., Memphis, TN 38125; www.ownafranchise.com. (800)255-9687.
Franchise: Yes.
Description: Professional residential and commercial cleaning and lawn-care services with more than two million customers worldwide.
Requirements: The franchise fee ranges from $16,900 to $43,000 depending on the type of franchise. You will need up to $10,000 for training, equipment, and supplies. The royalty is 10% and the advertising is 1%.
Provisions: The fee buys one week of training at headquarters and ongoing support. Financing is offered for up to 65% of total investment.

Profit Potential: Not available.
Comments: This is a franchise that everyone knows. It has been around since 1947 and now has over 4,200 franchise operators.

SERVPRO, 575 Airport Blvd., Gallatin, TX 37066; www.servpro.com. (800)826-9586.
Franchise: Yes.
Description: Full-service residential and commercial cleaning business that also specializes in fire restoration.
Requirements: The franchise fee is $26,000 with an equal amount needed for startup.
Provisions: Complete training and technical support are provided. Financing is available.
Comments: This is one of the oldest services businesses in the industry with over 1,000 franchisees.

SWISHER HYGIENE, 6849 Fairview Rd., Charlotte, NC 28210; www.swisheronline.com. (800)444-4138.
Franchise: Yes.
Description: Commercial restroom cleaning and sanitation. Products and services provided to 35,000 customers every week. "We are one of tne top 50 franchise in North America."
Requirements: Franchise fees start at $35,000 plus another $26,000 is required for startup expenses.
Provisions: Full initial and ongoing training, and access to an extremely successful business.

WINDOW GANG, 1509 Ann St., Beaufort, NC 28516; www.windowgang.com. (252)726-4314.
Franchise: Yes.
Description: Window, gutter, blind and pressure cleaning service.
Requirements: The franchise fee starts at $5,000 plus a minimum $9,000 for equipment. You will also need a truck.
Provisions: A complete business package and ongoing training in cleaning procedures, equipment operation, maintenance procedures, sales and marketing techniques, and cleaning solutions and application tips. Also provides telemarketing leads, group business and health insurance, national advertising, and initial credit line for supplies.

UNICLEAN SYSTEMS, INC., 1010 W. Queens Rd., #200, North Vancouver, British Columbia, Canada V7R 4S9; http://www.unicleansystems.com. (604)986-4750.
Franchise: Yes.
Description: Commercial cleaning service.
Requirements: The franchise fee is $1,500 and another $4,000 is required for startup expenses. Royalties start at $50 per $10,000 gross revenue.
Provisions: The franchise package includes training, office materials, equipment and supplies, an initial customer base, and ongoing support.
Profit Potential: Not available.

COMPUTER AND TECHNICAL SERVICES

After 20 or so years of computers making their way into the workplace, it is rare to find a business without one. This chapter is comprised mostly of businesses that either offer services for computer equipment or are based specifically on the services a computer can provide.

There are several opportunities in the computer training industry. In some cases, training services alone provides the income but usually these businesses also sell hardware and software. That can make a big difference in the bottom line, but obviously it also involves sales (which can be done by employees).

There are a lot of opportunities related to the Internet. You will find businesses here that offer Web design, Web hosting, domain names, e-commerce solutions, and other services to help people make the most of their Web experience.

Anyone who has tried to set up a new computer or figure out what to do when one crashed can appreciate a little onsite help. Companies like Geeks On Call come to the rescue with house calls, an idea whose time has definitely come. There are several newcomers to this field, which is growing hotter by the day. The best part is, you don't have to know a thing about computers yourself. Most of these businesses hire skilled college students to handle the actual service calls.

Computertots has an excellent curriculum for teaching computer skills to small children.

AIS MEDIA, INC., 115 Perimeter Center Terrace, #540, Atlanta, GA 30346; www.aisprivatelabel.com. (800)784-0919.
Franchise: No.
Description: Services include Web site design, Web hosting, domain registration, e-mail services, custom database development, programming, search engine registration, credit card merchant accounts and other e-commerce services.
Requirements: Start-up costs total $10,000.
Provisions: Training is provided via the Internet and over the phone. Advertising and marketing support is provided including sales leads.
Profit potential: Six figure income possible.
Comments: Can be run part-time.

CM IT SOLUTIONS, 537 Woodward Dr., #D, Austin, TX 78704; www.cmit.biz. (800)710-2648.
Franchise: Yes.
Description: Computer services and training for businesses.
Requirements: Startup costs range from $55,000 to $100,000 and there is no financing available. Business and marketing skills are also needed.
Provisions: There is a two-week training session at company headquarters followed by ongoing support via Internet and toll-free phone line.

COMPUCHILD USA, 602 Main Street, Suite 2, Rochester, IN 46975; www.compuchild.com. (800)619-5437.
Franchise: No.
Description: Educational and entertaining classes in computer education designed to give preschoolers a head start in the computerized world. This is the largest preschool computer education system in the world. It has grown tremendously since its inception

in 1994.

Requirements: The investment is $12,500 with no financing available.

Provisions: Intensive training is provided in all aspects of the business at the licensee's location. There is also plenty of follow-up support.

COMPUTER MEDICS OF AMERICA, 10322 Chain of Rock St., Eagle River, AK 99577; www.computermedicsofamerica.com. (907)694-0371.
Franchise: Yes.
Description: Mobile repair service for all kinds of PC's, laptops, and networks. Customers include both individuals at home and businesses.
Requirements: The startup total is $16,000 including $15,000 for the franchise fee. Financing is available.
Provisions: Training is conducted at company headquarters and ongoing support is provided primarily over the Internet.
Comments: Absentee ownership is allowed.

COMPUTER TROUBLESHOOTERS, 3904 N. Druid Hills Rd., #323, Decatur, GA 30033; www.comptroub.com. (770)454-6382.
Franchise: Yes.
Description: Provide computer services and support to business owners and home office owners.
Requirements: The total investment ranges from $10,000 to $18,000 with an ongoing royalty fee of $220 per month. In addition, you should have computer skills in hardware, Internet, networking, software or training.
Provisions: Proven business plan and marketing campaigns, training, worldwide network of support, and regularly updated utility CDs.

COMPUTERTOTS, 12715 Telge Rd., Cypress, TX 77429; www.computertots.com. (888)638-8722.
Franchise: Yes.
Description: Computertots is a computer enrichment program offered through day-care centers and private preschools to children ages three to six years. In addition to a complete computer system and an extensive software library of the latest educational software, Computertots uses alternate keyboards, light pens, graphic tablets, and computer-controlled robots to introduce computers to children in a fun and nonthreatening way.
Requirements: The franchise fee starts at $15,000 with an additional need for at least $13,000 to get started.
Provisions: The fee includes an exclusive territory, a collection of computer software programs, eight monthly curriculum packages, some hardware, master copies of printed materials, and complete training in every aspect of the business.

CONCERTO NETWORKS, 501 W. Broadway, #800, San Diego, CA 92101; www.concertonetworks.com. (866)482-6623.
Franchise: Yes.
Description: Franchisees provide mobile, on-site small office and residential computer and network solutions.
Requirements: The most important requirement is experience with computer repairs. The total cost of startup is about $35,000. The ongoing royalty is very high at 14%.
Provisions: The company provides strong training and support. Part of the royalty pays

for regional and national advertising designed to drum up business for franchisees.

CYGNUS SYSTEMS, INC., 1601 Stoneview Dr. Kokomo, IN 46902; www.cygnussystems.com. (765)854-0645.
Franchise: No.
Description: Graphics imaging system.
Requirements: $5,900 for the black/white video system and $24,000 for the color photography system complete with a 386 computer with digitizing hardware.
Provisions: A complete computer portrait system to do computer pictures.

ELECTRONIC VOICE SERVICES, INC., 16475 Dallas Pkwy., #350, Addison, TX 75001; www.evs7.com. (800)713-8353.
Franchise: No.
Description: Business offering completely automated computerized touchtone services ("Community Infoline"), which includes entertainment hotlines, talking time and temperature, etc.
Requirements: The cost is $695 plus you will need a Pentium computer and phone lines.
Provisions: Telecommunications boards, software, manuals, and technical support.

EXPETEC TECHNOLOGY SERVICES, 12 2nd Ave. SW, Aberdeen, SD 57401; (605) 225-0054.
Franchise: Yes.
Description: Provides mobile on-site, high-level technology services to commercial, small business, and consumer customers. Services include computer maintenance, consulting, computer upgrades, repairs, networking, Web hosting, Web design, and other business technology services.
Requirements: Although the investment is hefty at $62,000 to $83,200, the company has a program for those with qualifying credit so it is possible to start with as little as $5,000.
Provisions: The cost covers three weeks of training in a state-of-the-art training center, testing and diagnostic equipment, a business system, and a service vehicle called the TAV (Technical Assault Vehicle) which is equipped with a built-in custom networked repair center.

FRIENDLY COMPUTERS, 3145 N. Rainbow Blvd., Las Vegas, NV 89108; www.friendlycomputers.com/franchise. (800)656-3115.
Franchise: Yes.
Description: Computer sales, repair, and support for businesses and consumers. Services cover the entire range from helping beginners set up their first computer to installing networks and providing e-commerce solutions to large corporations.
Requirements: This is one of the better deals among franchises of this type. A franchise operation can be started for under $15,000. Business experience is required.
Provisions: Training start with one week at the company's site, followed by one week at the franchisee's site. Ongoing support is provided in a number of ways including the Internet, toll-free phone line, newsletters, and cooperative purchasing and advertising programs.

GATEPOST COMPUTER SERVICES, 13902 N. Dale Mabry Hwy., #300, Tampa, FL 33618; www.gatepostcomputers.com. (877)963-3129.
Franchise: Yes.

Description: Computer service including maintenance and repair.
Requirements: A minimum investment of $35,000. The $23,500 franchise fee is included and can be financed through the company.
Provisions: An all-inclusive package to help you establish and operate a computer services business that includes extensive initial training as well as ongoing support with proven sales, marketing and administrative programs.

GEEKS ON CALL AMERICA, 814 Kempsville Rd, #106, Norfolk, VA 23502; www.geeksoncalls.com. (888)667-4577.
Franchise: Yes.
Description: Providing computer support on-site including repairs, networking, and training.
Requirements: $20,000 franchise fee plus at least another $28,000 for startup. The royalty fee varies.
Provisions: Extensive training is provided with special emphasis on helping you build a business from the ground up. The company provides a comprehensive marketing plan, which is customized for your territory. State-of-the-art support system includes marketing research databases, prospect databases, telephone and central dispatching systems.

JUST THE FAX Restaurant Lunch Specials Fax Service, 711 Medford Center, #153, Medford, OR 97504; www.justthefax-bizop.com. (541)734-9260.
Description: A unique service that helps restaurants acquire customers and business people with their "where to go to lunch today" decision, by faxing Lunch Specials from local restaurants to businesses daily.
Requirements: $1,200 license fee and a computer with a modem and a phone line. There are three payment plans available.
Provisions: The license fee includes a 130-page business and marketing manual plus a new Website marketing report, rights to use the Just The Fax trademarked name and all copyrighted materials (provided on disk), free consulting, resale rights referral agreement, and a guarantee of satisfaction.
Comments: The owners of Just The Fax have been licensing their business in the US and Canada since 1996.

CLOSEUP: Just The Fax

"I must be an entrepreneur at heart because I'm always on the lookout for an additional source of income," says Dawn Harrington, of upstate New York. "Just The Fax really fit the bill. It must be the best sideline business there is."

Dawn is one of millions of people who work as full-time employees and run sideline businesses out of their homes. As an administrative assistant for a university, she thought at first that she wanted to leave her job, then realized all she really wanted was to supplement the family income.

Dawn's first attempt to go into business failed before it got started because she paid for an unscrupulous business opportunity that never delivered what it promised. She was more careful, downright leery, when she decided to try again.

"I figured I was already out $6,000 and I had a $3,000 computer just sitting there in my house. I was determined to find something that would work." Dawn found Just The Fax right here in *The Work-at-Home Sourcebook*. This time she was more careful about checking out the company.

"After seeing the preliminary package, it just didn't seem like it could lose," Dawn says. "Actually, it seemed like fun."

The Just The Fax business concept is simple. You fax daily lunch specials from local area restaurants to businesses where workers will likely go out to lunch on weekdays. It works because it's an inexpensive way for the restaurants to advertise and because it targets the customers they're after - the people who want to go out to eat.

Best of all, it takes only an hour a day to operate the business. Even in a small population area, the earnings are $1,200 a month with virtually no overhead. Larger areas can bring in up to $7,200 a month with very little extra time needed.

Dawn says if it can work where she lives, it can work anywhere. "This is a small area with a sluggish economy. But it was so easy to get started, it was surprising. I followed instructions and started sending letters copied verbatim from the manual. That was in December. By February 3rd I was up and running with enough restaurants to earn $1,000 a month."

Could you ask for a better part-time business? "I don't think so," says Dawn. "I can work full-time, and I don't have to take any extra time away from my kids. I do it after they're in bed. And the fringe benefits aren't bad either. I love to eat, and I've picked up a lot of recipes and cooking tips, too."

REMOTE BACKUP SYSTEMS, 319 Poplar View Lane West Suite 1, Collierville, TN 38017; www.remote-backup.com. (901)850-9920.
Franchise: Yes.
Description: This is an interesting concept that makes you wonder why someone didn't think of it sooner. Operators provide remote computer backup services for businesses and anyone else who uses a computer a lot.
Requirements: Packages available from $798, but can go higher if you don't already have the necessary computer setup. Free evaluation is offered.
Provisions: Advertising and marketing plans, phone support, technical support, and sales leads.

RESCUECOM, 2560 Burnet Ave., Syracuse, NY 13206; www.rescuecom.com. (800)737-2837.
Franchise: Yes.
Description: Computer consulting and repair service.
Requirements: Must qualify by being a top-notch computer professional such as a tech pro, computer executive or computer company owner. The investment is low. The franchise fee starts at just $2,500 with financing available.
Provisions: Complete business training and support.

SHOW ME PCS, 12010 Bammel N. Houston, #M, Houston, TX 77088; www.showmepcs.com. (866)600-7672.
Franchise: Yes.
Description: Franchisees provide a number of computer training services, both online and offline. Working one-on-one with customers in their homes and offices, they teach how to use various software programs, how to use e-mail, shop online, conduct Internet research, track and trade stocks, play games, develop Web pages, create and publish documents, make cards and banners, and scan and print photos.
Requirements: The franchise fee is just under $10,000 and an equal amount is needed for startup costs. General computer knowledge is expected; some sales experience is

needed.
Provisions: Training and ongoing support is provided along with regional advertising.

SOFT-TEMPS WORLDWIDE, 1280 NE Business Park Place, Jensen Beach, FL 34957; www.stfranchise.com. (800)221-2880.
Franchise: Yes.
Description: Provide on-site computer services to local small to midsize businesses using a database of skilled consultants.
Requirements: This is an excellent value at only $1,900 for startup including franchise fee. The 4% royalty includes 1% for advertising.
Provisions: Web site, full-time technical and corporate support, and a huge amount of marketing materials (brochures, videos, CDROM master, etc.). Minimum market area granted is 25,000 population per franchisee.

SUPPORT ON-SITE COMPUTER SERVICES, INC., 18 Technology, #160, Irvine, CA 92618; www.support-onsite.com. (888)497-4319.
Franchise: Yes.
Description: On-site service providing computer support, installation, maintenance, and servicing. The service is provided primarily to home computer owners whether for business or personal use. The service is designed to be consumer friendly and what could be friendlier than making house calls?
Requirements: The franchise fee is $15,000 and there is financing available for that. About another $23,000 minimum is needed for startup. The ongoing royalty fee is 6%.
Provisions: Complete training is provided which includes technical certification.

THRIFTY IMPRESSIONS, 1046 E. Walker St., Blackfoot, ID 83221; www.thriftyimpressions.com. (208) 782-0349.
Franchise: No.
Description: Computerized signs and banners for businesses and consumers.
Requirements: Total startup is about $2,000.
Provisions: Training is provided in classroom sessions at company headquarters, plus ongoing training is available in a manual, video, and online. There is ongoing support for advertising and marketing strategies, plus technical support online or on the phone. Sales leads are provided.

WSI INTERNET, 5915 Airport Rd., #300, Toronto, ON L4V 1T1 Canada; www.wsicorporate.com. (905)678-7588.
Franchise: Yes.
Description: This company formerly known as Worldsites provides Internet services to small- and medium-sized businesses.
Requirements: The bulk of the investment required is the $40,000 franchise fee.
Provisions: Training is available at company headquarters. There is ongoing support.
Comments: This company has grown quickly over the past five years. There are now over 500 franchisees throughout Canada and the U.S.

XSTREAM STUDIO, 2275 Huntington Dr., #514, San Marino, CA 91108; www.uxtm.com. (626)280-1793.
Franchise: No.
Description: Streaming media product sales.
Requirements: Startup costs total $5,000.
Provisions: There is plenty of training and support provided at company headquarters

and through a manual, video, by phone, and over the Internet. Marketing support is also strong and there are sales leads provided.

REAL ESTATE AND FINANCIAL SERVICES

Real estate is a business commonly based in a home office. Although there are no real estate businesses per se listed in this chapter, there are a variety of businesses closely associated with the industry. Home inspection services, for instance, are employed by real estate brokers and homebuyers to carefully check out buildings for hidden problems. Lindal Cedar Homes franchisees do more than sell homes, they offer personalized design services and sometimes act as contractors too. Income property owners need to check out new tenants before renting, and the National Tenant Network offers computerized tenant screening services.

Closely related to the real estate industry are financial services. U.S. Mortgage Reduction has been in the business of providing refinancing on mortgages for many years. There are several companies that focus on different ways to reduce costs and get refunds for customers that have been overbilled.

All of these businesses require a higher level of expertise and business acumen. If you consider buying one of these businesses, you should have a strong interest in the business and be able to deal effectively with people and project yourself professionally.

ALLSTATE HOME AND ENVIRONMENTAL INSPECTION, 2097 N. Randolph Rd., Randolph Ctr., VT 05061; www.allstatehomeinspection.com. (800)245-9932.
Franchise: Yes.
Description: Franchisees trained and licensed to perform home inspections, plus a number of environmental testing services like mold, radon, lead, water and more.
Requirements: Startup costs total about $24,000. Must have industry experience and complete four hours of marketing skills training, five supervised inspections, five independent inspections, and 40+ hours home inspection training.
Provisions: Training is provided at headquarters for 10 days plus as many as 15 days throughout the year for refresher and continuing education.

AMERICAN ELITE HOMES, INC., P.O. Box 1160, Kannapolis, NC 28082; http://www.constructionresources.net/americanelitehomescard.htm (800)792-3443 ext. 567.
Franchise: No.
Description: Market a full line of panelized homes and commercial buildings.
Requirements: There is no charge to become a representative, however, you are required to purchase or sell a house to get started. The initial down payment is $5,000.
Provisions: Model home to sell, live in, or use as office. Also books, manual, literature, blueprints, and complete construction information.
Profit Potential: $5,000 to $50,000 per sale.

AMERISPEC HOME INSPECTION SERVICE, 889 Ridge Lake Blvd., Memphis, TN 38120; www.amerispecfranchise.com. (800)426-2270.
Franchise: Yes.

Description: Amerispec is the number one home inspection company in North America. Business owners conduct a 400+ item home inspection and provide a computer-generated report for homebuyers and sellers.
Requirements: The franchise fee ranges from $19,900 to $29,900 with additional start-up costs estimated at $5,000.
Provisions: Amerispec has a network of customer services, marketing and trainers. You receive extensive marketing and technical training plus on-going training and support.

CASH IN, INC., 5386 Pleasant View Road, Memphis, TN 38134; www.phonerefund.com. (888)726-8044.
Franchise: No.
Description: Cash In is a telephone auditing practice serving the small and moderate sized business markets. You will negotiate refunds, credits, and lower costs on behalf of your clients. You do not do the audits; the corporate office does that.
Requirements: $495 training fee plus $50 for working capital.
Provisions: You receive 25% of Cash In's fees from your clients.

COST CONTAINMENT SOLUTIONS, INC., 9921 Fringe Tree Ct., Louisville, KY 40241; www.costcontain.com. (800)872-3709.
Franchise: No.
Description: Business to business contingency-based expense reduction service.
Requirements: The initial licensing investment is $29,900. You will also need a notebook computer.
Provisions: This is a turnkey expense reduction system that includes operations manuals, software templates, supplier networks, initial and on-going training and support.

CREATIVE ASSET MANAGEMENT, 1090 Broadway, Long Branch, NJ 07764; www.mymoneyadvantage.com. (732) 229-3262.
Franchise: Yes.
Description: Franchisees act as financial consultants to individual clients. This is a fee-based investment advisory franchise using MMA's, CD's, no-load mutual funds, fixed and variable annuities primarily. Franchise is building a practice with a client base they will service year after year, helping clients put together a diversified investment portfolio.
Requirements: The franchise fee starts at $17,500. Additional start-up is approximately $3,000. The monthly maintenance fee is $150/$300.
Provisions: Franchisees get a proven marketing system (13 marketing techniques), implementation system (set up investment portfolio with client), and a business system. There is also continual ongoing support.

DISABILITY ASSOCIATES, 4028 S. Sable Cir., Aurora, CO 80014; www.ssaconsultants.com. (303)766-1111.
Franchise: No.
Description:
Requirements: Startup costs total $2,500.
Provisions: Training is provided at the licensee's location and also via manual, video, Internet, and phone. There is ample marketing support including sales leads.
Comments: The company has 1,500 licensees.

ELLIOTT & COMPANY APPRAISERS, 3316-A Battleground Ave., Greensboro,

NC 27410; www.elliottco.com. (800)854-5889.
Franchise: Yes.
Description: As a franchisee, your office would be offering residential appraisals, commercial appraisals, land appraisals, relocation appraisals, appraisal reviews, and appraisal consultation. Employees would perform these services and you would act as manager.
Requirements: The franchise fee ranges from $900 to $9,900 and you will need another $5,000 for startup.
Provisions: The franchise offering is comprehensive. You will receive management training, all the software necessary to run an efficient business, ongoing training and support, leads from the company's national advertising efforts, exclusive territory, image materials, and much more.

HEALTHCARE DATA MANAGEMENT, INC., 303 West Lancaster Avenue, Wayne, PA 19087; www.healthserve.com. (800)859-5119.
Franchise: No.
Description: Help companies reduce health care expenses by reviewing and auditing hospital and medical bills and recovering overages.
Requirements: The full package costs $7,500, but there is a package available for only $2,495.
Provisions: The full package includes proprietary software, manuals, and two days corporate training. Without the two days training, the cost is $6,500. Since you will be paid on a contingency basis, typically $50 of recovered money, it is not difficult to obtain clients. Clients will be businesses, not individual consumers. You will provide highly qualified, specialized services and generate reports that are easy to understand.

THE HOMETEAM INSPECTION SERVICE, INC., 575 Chamber Dr., Milford, OH 45150; www.hmteam.com. (800)598-5297.
Franchise: Yes.
Description: Home inspections using the "team" concept, using multiple people on inspections which cuts the inspection time in half and gives a better inspection.
Requirements: The franchise cost ranges from $11,900 to $29,900 depending on population size of territory. Additional start-up costs are approximately $8,000.
Provisions: Designated franchise area; an extensive 14 days of training which includes: marketing, technical knowledge and business procedures; and continuous ongoing support.
Profit Potential: Average $100,000 annually.

HOUSEMASTER OF AMERICA, INC., 421 W. Union Ave., Bound Brook, NJ 08805; www.housemaster.com. (800)526-3939.
Franchise: Yes.
Description: HouseMaster has developed a complete system for doing business in the home inspection industry. It is not necessary to know anything about housing, engineering, real estate, or law to take advantage of this opportunity.
Requirements: The franchise fee ranges from $12,000 to $29,000. Other first year costs range between $10,000 and $18,000.
Provisions: The fee buys training, customized data base software, and ongoing support.

THE INTERFACE GROUP LTD., 2182 Dupont Drive, # 221, Irvine, CA 92612; www.interfacefinancial.com. (800) 387-0860.
Franchise: Yes.

Description: Franchisees provide short-term working capital for small businesses through an innovative invoice-discounting program.
Requirements: The initial franchise fee is $30,000; working capital required is $100,000+. Home based-franchisees need phone, fax, computer and a car.
Provisions: The fee covers all documentation, operations manuals, newsletters, full training program and extensive on-going support.
Comments: "We provide 30+ years of experience, extensive training and hand holding. Franchisees have the opportunity to be part of a 130-unit team and part of a trillion dollar world wide market place. This is a lifestyle business."

INTERNATIONAL HOMES OF CEDAR, INC., P.O. Box 886, Woodinville, WA 98072; www.ihoc.com. (800)767-7674.
Franchise: No.
Description: IHC produces custom pre-cut homes and commercial building packages featuring solidly engineered timber walls to provide superior energy efficiency, structural strength, reduced maintenance, and ease of construction.
Requirements: Purchase of model home.
Provisions: IHC provides training and technical support.

INTERNATIONAL MERGERS AND ACQUISITIONS, 4300 N. Miller Rd., #230, Scottsdale, AZ 85251; www.ima-world.com. (480)990-3899.
Franchise: Yes.
Description: Providing consulting and financing assistance to public and private companies with mergers, acquisitions and funding.
Requirements: This is a high level business that requires a solid background in management. Ideal candidates are former high-level executives from major national and international corporations, but other experts with hands-on experience would be considered if proven to be capable of working in the international business environment. The total investment required is $25,000 with no ongoing royalty fee.
Provisions: Upon completion of training, you will become part of a worldwide network of consultants with all the support that implies.

LINDAL CEDAR HOMES, INC., P.O. Box 24426, Seattle, WA 98124; www.lindal.com. (800)221-6063.
Franchise: No.
Description: Lindal Cedar Homes is the world's largest manufacturer of cedar homes.
Requirements: The cost of a dealership is $5,000.
Provisions: Comprehensive training and a comprehensive cooperative advertising program.

NATIONAL PROPERTY INSPECTIONS, 11620 Arbor St., Suite 100, Omaha, NE 68144; www.npiweb.com. (800)333-9807.
Franchise: Yes.
Description: Residential and commercial property inspections.
Requirements: The total investment, including franchise fee, is $21,800 with partial financing available.
Provisions: The fee includes two weeks of comprehensive training in Omaha, in-field training, on-going and responsive technical and marketing support, computer system that produces on-site reports, warranty program and award-winning National Relocation Referral Program.

NATIONAL TENANT NETWORK, INC., P.O. Box 1664, Lake Grove, OR 97035; www.ntnnet.com.(503)635-1118.
Franchise: Yes.
Description: This is a unique computerized tenant tracking and screening system for residential and commercial tenants.
Requirements: The franchise fee is $45,000. An additional investment of $20,000 is required for a marketing and feasibility study and for equipment.
Provisions: The franchise investment covers the cost of two fully programmed access terminals, modems, and telecommunications software as well as training and marketing assistance.

PAID INC., 4800 W. Waco Dr., #100, Waco, TX 76710; www.paidinc.com. (254)772-8131.
Franchise: Yes.
Description: Provides e-commerce financial services including electronic payment systems to business customers.
Requirements: The franchise fee of $24,500 is the entire investment required. Business and marketing experience is also necessary.
Provisions: Training at headquarters is short, lasting only 3 days. However, there is plenty of ongoing support and even onsite sales help if requested.
Comments: Absentee ownership is allowed.

PROVENTURE BUSINESS GROUP, INC., P.O. Box 338, Needham Heights, MA 02194. (781)444-8278.
Franchise: Yes.
Description: In this business, the franchisee would perform two functions: business brokering and franchise consulting.
Requirements: A solid background in top-level management and/or business ownership is required. The total investment for startup is about $35,000 of which $10,000 is the franchise fee. The monthly royalty is 6%.
Provisions: Training, software, leads, and marketing support.

U.S. MORTGAGE REDUCTION, 1282 N.E. Business Park Pl., Jensen Beach, FL 34957; www.usnetlink.com. (800)743-0001.
Franchise: No
Description: Through a national network of sales agents, U.S. Mortgage Reduction offers its Equity Acceleration Program to homeowners. As an agent for the firm, you will be demonstrating to homeowners why paying for their home with a long-term mortgage is a waste of many thousands of dollars in mortgage interest.
Requirements: Total startup costs including the licensing fee ranges from $250 to $699.
Provisions: The fee covers a presentation binder/flip kit, training manual, computer software, brochures, contracts, cassette training tapes, and client presentation video.
Profit Potential: Not available.
Comments: There are also opportunities in regional management.

ZAIO.COM, Suite 200, 1013 - 17th Avenue SW, Calgary, AB, Canada T2T 0A7; www.zaio.com. (877) 318-0537.
Franchise: Yes.
Description: ZAIO.COM is in the process of photographing each and every property

in cities across the country. The company has named this process "GeoPic." The database will be continuously maintained and updated as properties change. Franchisees earn fees in their exclusive geographic areas in a variety of ways. The digital images are accessed exclusively over the Internet by real estate, mortgage and insurance industries, police, fire and ambulance dispatching, and portals and media outlets.

Requirements: Must live in an available territory of at least 5,000 population. The total investment of $17,000 minimum includes the franchise fee. There is an ongoing royalty of 6%. Financing is available.

Provisions: Proprietary software, access to the database, and training in business and marketing techniques.

PERSONAL SERVICES

These days, busy working people are demanding all kinds of services. Some services are designed to make more quality time available while others help enhance the quality of life.

Through these businesses, customers can have their meals delivered to their door at dinnertime, have their pets and plants tended to while on vacation, find sitters for their children temporarily or nannies permanently, and find all kinds of help through personal referral services. They can also find potential mates, have someone else shop for them while they work, have their clothing custom-made, or have custom-made gift baskets sent to their kids in college. There's something here for everyone, customers and entrepreneurs alike.

One of the fastest growing services is elder care. Not only are we living longer, we are living healthier, more independent lives. Elder care services generally do not include medical treatments or supervision of any kind. Rather, it focuses on the routine chores of daily living. By offering these services, seniors can continue to live in their own homes without having to work too hard at maintaining their independent lifestyles.

A CARD-IN-THE-YARD TM, N9564 Onyx Ct., Appleton, WI 54915; www.acardintheyard.com. (920)830-8373.

Franchise: No.

Description: This is a unique and fun business that will literally turn heads and stop traffic. Just as the name implies, it involves producing a variety of yard sign designs, which can be personalized for virtually any occasion. The signs are generally whimsical in nature and are removable and re-usable after each use. Each set-up includes 6-foot high fun signs, a yard-full of props and decorations which customers rent from you to announce special occasions.

Requirements: $399 one-time licensing fee.

Provisions: The complete business system includes a business manual, 5 to-scale patterns, 50 sample ads, sample coupons and flyers, wholesale sources, record keeping forms and tips, and all the necessary instructions to make the business work. Ongoing support is available by phone.

CLOSEUP: A Card-in-the-Yard TM

One of the many advantages of having a home-based business versus a storefront is the ability to pick up and go. This kind of flexibility is important in a mobile society such as ours. We Americans now move every three years on average.

Dawn Coolahan is married to a man who serves in active duty in the Air Force. As anyone in a military family knows, a lot of moving around comes with the territory. For a while Dawn tried various jobs, but eventually that became too difficult with three children at home. She started looking for a good home-based business, something that would be portable, fun, and would flourish near a military base. It wasn't long before she found what she was looking for.

"I actually started working with the idea of putting big, colorful cards in people's yards on my own," recalls Dawn. "Things like baby announcements, congratulations, and birthday greetings - especially the over-the-hill kind -seemed like a great idea. But as I was trying to get started, I heard about A Card-in-the-Yard. They had already developed a business opportunity package along the same lines."

Dawn was quickly discovering that there was a lot to learn about the business. "I was just getting the card patterns together and trying to figure out what hardware to use. Then I was going to make the signs, figure out how to erect them on a lawn, come up with a way to market the service, and so on. On my own, that was a lot to figure out. A Card-in-the-Yard had all of that already laid out along with the whole business concept. It's like any business, it looks simple once it's up and running, but starting from scratch is not so easy."

Dawn invested in the system and was happy that now she had all the answers without having to find them the hard way. After ten years, she is still in touch with the company. "I called with a million questions in the beginning and after all this time we still chat on the phone. They just have so much information to share."

The original idea of putting fun signs in yards has been expanded. Now there are displays available for every occasion and theme you can imagine, like Halloween and corporate functions. And it's much more than just a big sign, too. Each display includes a yard full of colorful props. It's a real traffic stopper.

Although Dawn has moved her business several times, she's found it's easy to start up again in a new location. "Once people start seeing the different displays, it really catches on fast," she says.

"The feedback is fabulous and I've never had a displeased customer. I do this because it's so much fun," she says. "I know I'm going to bring a smile to someone's face."

AUSSIE PET MOBILE, 34189 Pacific Coast Hwy., #203, Dana Point, CA 92629; www.aussiepetmobile.com. (949)234-0680.
Franchise: Yes.
Description: This is a cute idea that makes a lot of sense. In this franchise, you would

offer a convenient, affordable, reliable and efficient service to pet owners by operating a mobile pet grooming service. You will use environmentally friendly products and bring a highly organized professional approach to mobile grooming.

Requirements: Must love animals, work well with people, and have at least $60,000 to invest.

Provisions: The investment covers the cost of training, the mobile grooming unit, which includes a heated hydrobath, regional and national advertising support, a national toll-free number with dispatch service, and full support.

BARK BUSTERS, 5901 S. Vine St., Greenwood Village, CO 80121; www.barkbusters.com. (877)280-7100.

Franchise: Yes.

Description: This is a non-aggressive dog training service performed in the dog owner's home.

Requirements: Must love animals, be willing to learn new techniques, and also work well with pet owners. The total investment is around $47,000.

Provisions: Training and support.

CALCULATED COUPLES, 4839 E. Greenway Rd., #183, Scottsdale, AZ 85254; www.cupidhelp.com. (800)446-2824.

Franchise: Yes.

Description: Provide matchmaking service through singles parties, plus get access to love advice and singles products.

Requirements: The total investment, including franchise fee, is $5,000.

Provisions: Training and ongoing support.

CANDY BOUQUET, 423 East 3rd St., Little Rock, AR 72201; www.candybouquet.com. (877)CANDY-01.

Franchise: Yes.

Description: Candy bouquets are floral-like creations crafted from gourmet chocolates and candies. They are customized into one-of-a-kind gifts that won't wilt, fade or die.

Requirements: Approximate initial startup costs ranges from $7,500 to $45,000.

Provisions: Exclusive territory, operations manual, trademarked name and logo, business training, marketing training, Candy Bouquet design training, discounts from suppliers, new design updates, online catalog, newsletters, and continuing support. There are no royalties.

CARE TRAK, INC., 1031 Autumn Ridge Rd., Carbondale, IL 62901; www.caretrak.com. (800) 842-4537.

Franchise: No.

Description: Care Trak manufactures electronic equipment that monitors and locates people who wander. This condition may be a result of Alzheimer's disease, Autism, Down syndrome, Prader-Willi Syndrome, or brain injury. The mobile locater can find a lost person up to a mile day or night, inside or out.

Requirements: The distributorship costs $6,000 for demo equipment, plus start-up costs are about $3,500.

Provisions: The fee covers demo equipment, videos, brochures, training, and support. Care Trak is currently the only company licensed by the FCC for this purpose.

COLOR 1 ASSOCIATES, 2211 Washington Cir. N.W., Washington, DC 20037; www.dressingsmart.com. (202)293-9175.

Franchise: No.
Description: Image consulting services combined with skin-care products.
Requirements: A minimum $300 investment.
Provisions: Training either at the company or at your location. Sales leads and ongoing support are provided.

COMFORT KEEPERS, 6640 Poe Ave., #200, Dayton, OH 45414; www.comfortkeepers.com. (800)387-2415.
Franchise: Yes.
Description: Care for seniors in their own homes. This service includes only assistance in the daily tasks of living and does not include any medical care. The franchisee is a manager, not a caregiver.
Requirements: The franchise fee is just under $20,000 with an equal amount needed for startup. There is an ongoing royalty ranging from 3-5%.
Provisions: Complete training and ongoing support.

COMPANION CONNECTION SENIOR CARE, 304 Park Ave. S., 11th Fl., New York, NY 10010; www.companionconnectionseniorcare.com. (800)270-6949.
Franchise: No.
Description: Provides live-in or live-out non-medical home care to seniors and infirm or disabled individuals.
Requirements: Startup costs total $10,000 and there is financing available.
Provisions: Provides a business manual and video plus training at headquarters. Marketing support includes sales leads and Web site.

CHRISTMAS CONCEPTS, 3960 S. Higuera St., San Luis Obispo, CA 93401. (805)782-0128; www.christmasconcepts.com.
Franchise: No.
Description: Rent Christmas decorations commercially to banks, hotels, restaurants, retirement homes, car dealerships, and malls.
Requirements: The startup cost ranges from $350 to $1800 including licensing fee and there is financing available from the company.
Provisions: Complete training is provided at company headquarters and on-site. The licensee also receives a training manual, portfolio, and video. There is plenty of ongoing support as well as advertising and marketing materials and the company will even help get accounts.

CHRISTMAS DÉCOR, P.O. Box 5946, Lubbock, TX 79408-5946; www.christmasdecor.net. (800)687-9551.
Franchise: Yes.
Description: Provide decorating services for holidays and other special events. Customers are both residential and commercial.
Requirements: The total investment is under $20,000. Half of that can be financed.
Provisions: Training is provided and there is plenty of ongoing support. Profits can be raised by participating in the company's cooperative purchasing program but it is not a requirement.

DISCOUNT BRIDAL SERVICE, INC., 4147 . Andrea Dr., Cave Creek, AZ 85331; www.discountbridalservice.com. (800)708-3363.
Franchise: No.
Description: Personal buying service for soon-to-be brides.

Requirements: The initial investment is under $500.
Provisions: You will be given an operations manual and advertising materials. From time to time there are mandatory training seminars you will need to attend, scheduled throughout the year at different locations. Ongoing support is available via phone and online and you can expect sales leads.

DRAMA KIDS INT'L, INC., 3225-B Corporate Ct., Ellicott City, MD 21042; www.dramakids.com. (410)480-2015.
Franchise: Yes.
Description: After-school children's drama program.
Requirements: The franchise fee is $25,000 and an additional $5,000 minimum will be necessary for startup. There is an ongoing royalty fee of 10%. No acting or teaching experience is required.
Provisions: Extensive training, marketing assistance, ongoing support, regular seminars, newsletters, and Internet connections are provided.

DRY CLEANING TO-YOUR-DOOR, 1121 N.W. Bayshore Dr., Waldport, OR 97394; www.dctyd.com. (800)318-1800.
Franchise: Yes.
Description: Franchisees pick up dry cleaning from customers' homes and drop it off the next day, for free. A cleaning bill is presented to the customer at the end of every month.
Requirements: Total investment of $40,000. You will also need a van.
Provisions: Training and support, racks, logos and paint for the van, uniforms, heavy-duty laundry bags, hangers, computer calling board and routing database, web site, new customer kits, and more.

ENTREES ON TRAYS, INC., 3 Lombardy Terrace, Fort Worth, TX 76132; (817)735-8558.
Franchise: No.
Description: A dinner delivery service operated without labor or inventory. You would work with 20-50 local restaurants within a six-mile radius, acting as a home delivery service, not a caterer. The business is run from home from 5:00 to 9:00 p.m.
Requirements: The one-time license agreement fee is $8,750.
Provisions: You will receive two days of training, working hands-on in Fort Worth. Also included with your fee is all equipment and materials necessary to initiate business (except radios negotiated on a local basis).
Profit Potential: See below.
Comments: This is a great business idea that has been perfected by this company. Entrees on Trays has delivered 100,000 dinners amounting to over $1 million annually in the Fort Worth metroplex while 11 out of 11 competing companies have gone out of business.

GIFT BASKET CONNECTION, 3 Juniper Ct., Schenectady, NY 12309; www.agiftbasketconnection.com. (800)437-3237.
Franchise: No.
Description: International gift basket wire service similar to FTD.
Requirements: $200 per year for already existing retailers. The manual is $56.

GRISWOLD SPECIAL CARE, 717 Bethlehem Pike, #300, Erdenheim, PA 19073; www.griswoldspecialcare.com. (215)402-0200.

Franchise: Yes.
Description: Home care for seniors who need help with daily tasks. This does not include medical care. People being cared for may be disabled, bed- or wheelchair-bound, recovering from illness or surgery, or just needing to give a respite to family members.
Requirements: Franchisees in this business need to be caring people in addition to having management skills. The cost is low, starting at $6,000 and there is no franchise fee. There is partial financing available.
Provisions: Training and proprietary software.

GYM ROMPERS, 193 W. Oakridge Park, Metairie, LA 70005; www.gymrompers.com. (504)833-2155.
Franchise: No.
Description: This is a parent-child interactive music and movement program for young children, 3 months - 4 years. The purpose is to develop learning skills through fun play activities and to help develop sensory-motor skills. Over 40 pieces of specially chosen play equipment are used to enhance a child's developing gross motor skills, basic coordination and sensory-motor learning.
Requirements: It's possible to start with only $500, but the investment can go higher depending on the goals of the licensed operator.
Provisions: Training is provided at company headquarters in Louisiana with follow-up support available over the phone and the Internet.

HAWKEYE'S HOME SITTERS, 14920-95 A St., Edmonton, AB, Canada T5E 4A6; www.homesitter.com. (888)247-2787.
Franchise: Yes.
Description: An expanded home sitting service that includes everything from security checks to lawn maintenance.
Requirements: You must be adaptable, willing to be of service, and be extremely reliable. The cost is based upon population and starts at $4,000.
Provisions: You receive a comprehensive startup package, a proven business system, continuous support, and the benefits of national and regional advertising campaigns.

HIGH TOUCH-HIGH TECH, 12352 Wiles Rd., Coral Springs, FL 33076; www.hightouch-hightech.com. (800)444-4968.
Franchise: Yes.
Description: Franchisees provide 90-minute, hands-on science programs at schools from pre-school to high school. The programs cover the physical, natural, environmental and mathematical sciences and meet the National Board of Education Student Science Performance Standards. Additional income comes from "Sizzlin Science" birthday parties. Franchisees run the business, but usually don't provide the actual programs at the schools. They hire educators who are required to have a four-year teaching degree from an accredited college or university, as well as a certificate in teaching science or eligibility for one.
Requirements: Investment of about $20,000 plus business and marketing experience.
Provisions: Provides training and ongoing support.

HOME HELPERS, 10700 Montgomery Rd., #300, Cincinnati, OH 45242; www.homehelpers.cc/franchise.html. (800)216-4196.
Franchise: Yes.
Description: Franchisees hire caregivers who in turn provide companionship, transportation, a "perk-up" in the morning and a "tuck-in" at bedtime. Services include

shopping, running errands, preparing meals, and checking in on clients over the phone. Care is provided mostly to seniors, but also new mothers.
Requirements: This is non-medical, in-home care so no medical experience is required. It costs about $20,000 to get started and most of that can be financed.
Provisions: Training and ongoing support. Marketing materials including electronic ads and presentation formats.
Comments: The company is affiliated with Direct Link, an in-home emergency monitoring system.

HOME TUTORING, P.O. Box 536, Meadow Vista, CA 95722; www.hometutoring.com. (888)368-8867.
Franchise: No.
Description: A home tutoring service.
Requirements: An interest in furthering the education of children is the most important prerequisite. The investment is small, only $495.
Provisions: Training is provided both at the company's location and the licensee's. You will receive a complete business package including an operations manual, software, and ongoing support via phone and on the Internet.

HOMEWATCH INTERNATIONAL, INC., 2865 South Colorado Blvd., Denver, CO 80222; www.homewatch-intl.com. (800)777-9770.
Franchise: Yes.
Description: Full service house-sitting by trained, bonded, and insured adults for people who are away from home on business or vacation; companion sitting (non-medical); and handyman services.
Requirements: The fee ranges from $15,500 to $19,500 for a franchise, plus additional costs of approximately $7,500. You must be capable of affording the franchise, be a compassionate people-oriented person, and have the desire to succeed in business.
Provisions: The fee buys a geographic area with a population of 200,000, five days of training including software training, logo, manual, bond/insurance for one year, exclusive area, ongoing support, and advertising materials. You will also get a grand opening at your location. Financing is available, but only when buying multiple territories.
Comments: This is a good part-time business for retired or semi-retired people.

INNERACTIVE INC., 11949 Jefferson Blvd, #105, Culver City, CA 90230; www.aura.net. (800)578-5810.
Franchise: No.
Description: Aura Video Systems and Aura Shop. This business is for health and wellness oriented entrepreneurs. The system is used to check your clients' emotional and energetic state and also provide energy balancing products.
Requirements: The investment starts at $8,995.
Provisions: The complete video system plus Aura Shop Products, training, and support.

INTERQUEST DETECTION CANINES, 21900 Tomball Parkway, Houston, TX 77070; www.interquestfranchise.com. (281)320-1231.
Franchise: Yes.
Description: With this franchise, you would use highly trained dogs to detect drugs and other contraband (such as weapons) in public schools, private schools, and businesses. Other services to offer include providing trained dogs to police departments and offering security consulting and drug testing programs.
Requirements: The investment required is about $50,000.

Provisions: This is a comprehensive offering with everything you need to start and run a successful business.

JUNE WEDDING, INC., 19375 Pine Glade, Guerneville, CA 95446; www.junewedding.com. (415)279-7423.
Franchise: No.
Description: Be a wedding, event, and/or party consultant.
Requirements: Startup costs amount to about $5,000.
Provisions: The investment includes a three-month home study course, manual, forms, certification, and on-going technical support. To find out more, check out the web site. Mail inquiries require $15 and letter of request.

LITTLE PRINCESS TEA PARTIES, P.O. Box 41, Gainesville, VA 20156; www.princesstea.com. (800)489-0832.
Franchise: Yes.
Description: Providing mother/daughter and special events tea parties, as well as etiquette courses.
Requirements: The franchise fee is $7,500 and additional startup costs run around $1,500.
Provisions: You will receive an Operations Manual, protected territory, 5 full days of training, protected territory, use of the trademarked name, a Web page, initial start-up supplies, and access to wholesale suppliers.

NANNIES PLUS INC., 615 W. Mt. Pleasant Ave., Livingston, NJ 07039; www.nanniesplus.com/. (800)752-0078.
Franchise: No.
Description: Nanny placement service.
Requirements: One-time licensing fee is $22,500 with operating capital of an additional $5,000. Financing is available.
Provisions: Licensees receive a complete package: five days of training in New Jersey, three days training on-site, promotional materials, ongoing support, a hotline, and office forms.

PARAGRAPHICS CORP., 517 S. Commerce Rd., Orem, UT 84058; www.paragraphics.net. (800)624-7415.
Franchise: No.
Description: Ultra high-speed custom engraving to personalize valuables for decoration and anti-theft purposes.
Requirements: The complete "Parapak" system costs $2,399.
Provisions: The fee covers dealership privileges, an ongoing support program, all equipment necessary to perform the service, training videos, and illustrated manuals.
Profit Potential: Not available.

PETS ARE INN, 5100 Edina Industrial Blvd., #206, Minneapolis, MN 55439; www.petsareinn.com. (866)343-0086/(952)944-8298.
Franchise: Yes.
Description: Performing pet lodging service in private homes - not the owner's, but a network of hosts that you, the franchisee, develop. You provide the pick-up and delivery of the animals. It's a unique alternative to the usual boarding and kennels.
Requirements: The minimum startup cost is $20,000.
Provisions: This is a turnkey opportunity that includes all marketing, promoting, and

operating systems for this specialized service. Included is proprietary software that makes the service dependable, efficient, and easy to manage. The company's master insurance plan makes it possible for all franchisees to obtain liability insurance. Follow-up support is provided through e-mail and a toll-free phone number.

PET-TENDERS, P.O. Box 23622, San Diego, CA 92193; www.pet-tenders.com. (619)283-3033.
Franchise: Yes.
Description: In-home pet/housesitting service that cares for pets in the comfort of their own home.
Requirements: The total investment is between $10,500 and $13,900. The royalty fee is 5% of gross sales per month and the advertising fee is 2%.
Provisions: The costs include the franchise fee (for which you are given an exclusive territory), training, and a complete operation and training manual for your business. The training package includes up to five days of lectures, hands-on training, telephone techniques, voice training, and on-the-job training with a working pet-sitter.
Profit Potential: Not available.

PRE-FIT FRANCHISES, INC., 10926 S. Western Ave., Chicago, IL 60643; www.pre-fit.com. (773)233-7771.
Franchise: Yes.
Description: A home-based mobile preschool fitness program of sports, exercise, and health classes designed for two to six year olds.
Requirements: The franchise fee is $8,500; additional start-up costs are $1,250 to $3,500.
Provisions: Your fee buys uniforms, initial and continuous training program, lesson plans, workout routines, marketing tools, bookkeeping materials, class equipment, exclusive territory, and toll-free support.

PRESSED4TIME, 8 Clock Tower Pl., #110, Maynard, MA 01754; www.pressed4time.com. (800)423-8711.
Franchise: Yes.
Description: Franchisees provide pick-up and drop-off services to local businesses, delivering items to local dry cleaners. They also collects clothing, shoes, handbags and luggage for repairs.
Requirements: This franchise costs about $20,000 to start. Marketing skills are also needed.
Provisions: Training is provided at headquarters and at the franchisee's location. Marketing support includes ad slicks and other marketing materials plus a public relations program designed to bring in new customers.

SAFETY MATTERS, 478 Barberry Road, Highland Park, IL 60035; www.safetymatters.com. (800)9SAFE06.
Franchise: Yes.
Description: This is a baby-proofing service.
Requirements: About $35,000 including franchise fee. The royalty is 5%.
Provisions: Training and inventory, plus continuous support.

SITTERS UNLIMITED, 2351 Sunset Blvd., Suite 170, PMB 120, Rocklin, Ca 95765; www.sittersunlimited.com. (800) 328-1191.
Franchise: Yes.

Description: A coast-to-coast sitting service for children, the elderly, homes, and pets, on both a temporary and permanent basis. In addition to quality in-home care, traveling families can rely on hotel and convention care services.
Requirements: The franchise fee for an exclusive territory is $13,000.
Provisions: The fee includes five days of corporate training, ongoing training and support, and one month's free supply of required materials. Literature, business cards, and all required forms are designed for you. No purchasing of products except an answering machine and forms is necessary.
Profit Potential: Not available.
Comments: The company has been in business since 1979.

SPACE WALK/INFLATABLE ZOO, 450 31st St., Kenner, LA 70065; www.herecomesfun.com. (504)464-5851.
Franchise: No.
Description: Provide inflatable rides for private party rentals and corporate events. Space Walk was the original inflatable amusement ride and it's been around for 25 years now.
Requirements: $3,000-$5,000 start-up costs.
Provisions: Training is provided at company headquarters in all aspects of operating this business. Advertising and marketing strategies are provided along with sales leads. Ongoing support is available by phone, Internet, meetings, and newsletters.

STRETCH-N-GROW, P.O. Box 7955, Seminole, FL 33775; www.stretch-n-grow.com. (727)596-7614.
Franchise: Yes.
Description: Fitness classes for children are taught at child-care and recreation centers, elementary schools, YMCA and YWCA centers, Mothers' Day Out programs and Head Start facilities. Franchisees offer other programs, too, including after-school programs, birthday parties and sports camps. All are designed to help children stay fit and healthy.
Requirements: The investment totals around $20,000. The royalty is a flat $150 per month. A strong desire to work with children is a prerequisite.
Provisions: Training is provided in Florida and followed up on the Internet and on the phone. Marketing support includes ads in day-care center publications.

TOP SECRET SCIENCE CORP., 10 Tower Office Park, #310, Woburn, MA 01801; www.topsecretscience.com. (781)935-9925.
Franchise: No.
Description: If you've ever lamented the state of American education, this business is for you. It's a fantastic hands-on approach to teaching science and math to children. You'll be offering programs that are exciting, magical and fun and designed to get kids to discover & explore the world around them. Kids get to interact with lots of weird experiments and state-of-the-art high-tech equipment.
Requirements: In addition to having an interest in education, you should enjoy children and be a highly motivated businessperson. The startup costs are low at only $2,500 and there is financing available from the company to make it even easier to get started.
Provisions: Training is provided in person and online, plus you'll have a manual and video to refer to. Follow-up support continues via phone and the Internet. Sales leads are also provided.

VISITING ANGELS, 28 W. Eagle Rd., #201, Havertown, PA 19083; www.livingassistance.com. (800)365-4189.

Franchise: Yes.
Description: Franchisees provide living assistance services to homebound customers. Services include hygiene assistance, meal preparation, light housekeeping, errands, shopping, and companionship. No medical services are provided.
Requirements: The total cost including franchise fee is around $22,000. The royalty fee is low, from 2.9% down to 2%.
Provisions: The initial training at headquarters is followed by five regional training meetings each year. Marketing support includes ads in national media, Internet marketing, and a public relations program.

PHOTO AND VIDEO SERVICES

Of the opportunities described in this chapter, few actually involve traditional, still-shot photography. The Visual Image is perfect for anyone who loves children and animals. It caters to the proud parents of preschoolers and devoted pet owners by providing keepsake portraits.

Some other businesses here are in the booming video market. Each services a different and unique function. MDM International trains business operators to use videotape to record weddings and other special events in a modernized version of standard photography services. And for Spielberg wannabe's, Home Video Studio will have you producing videos in your own home video studio.

As technology changes, opportunities automatically open up. There are still plenty of 8mm home movies that need to be transferred to videotape and now people want their videotapes transferred to DVDs.

These opportunities offer some interesting possibilities for people interested in photography or video. It is a market that is sure to continue growing and changing.

AMERICAN ENTERTAINMENT DISTRIBUTORS, 2514 Hollywood Blvd., #200, Hollywood, FL 33020; www.aed1.us. (954)929-6860.
Franchise: No.
Description: DVD rentals through automated machines located is located in all kinds of retail establishments, apartment buildings, and office buildings.
Requirements: Cost of startup runs around $40,000.
Provisions: This is a turnkey business with all the training, support, and supplies provided. The company provides basic installation and maintenance. Ongoing technical support is provided over the phone toll-free and via the Internet.

CREATIVE PHOTO CONCEPTS, 18027 Hwy. 99, #D, Lynnwood, WA 98037; (800)833-5655.
Franchise: No.
Description: Photo glazing system.
Requirements: Total startup is $5,000.
Provisions: Extensive training in the classroom and at your location plus through manual, video, and online. There is also plenty of help along the way with technical support, advertising advice, sales leads, etc.

DIGITOGRAF STUDIO, CRA Productions, 23532 El Toro #9, Lake Forest, CA 92630; www.cra-pro.com. (949)261-7066.
Franchise: No.
Description: Your customers will send any films or original documents to the company studio to have the images scanned, manipulated and a digital art file created and then printed on oil base canvas media thus creating a "painting".
Requirements: Total investment of $25,000.
Provisions: The cost includes hardware and software, the licensing fee, and training.

DVDESIGNGROUP, INC., 3747 Levy Ln., Huntingdon Valley, PA 19006; www.digitalvideodesign.com. (800)872-7896.
Franchise: No.
Description: DVD transfer and duplication services. Customers are both corporate and consumer.
Requirements: You can start this business for under $500, depending on how much equipment you already have.
Provisions: There is plenty of training available, both at the company's location and yours. Backup materials include a manual, video, plus ongoing newsletter. Technical support is available over the phone.

FACES N CUPS, INC., 6130 W. Flamingo Road, #455, Las Vegas, NV 89103; www.facesncups.com. (702)365-6847.
Franchise: No.
Description: This is a photo imaging system used to transfer photos to mugs, shirts, mouse pads, plates, puzzles, and a variety of small products.
Requirements: $9,950.
Provisions: Fee buys complete video imaging system, training and installation at your site, on-going technical support (365 days a year), monthly newsletter, and marketing assistance.

HOME VIDEO STUDIO, INC., 8148 Raven Rock Dr., Indianapolis, IN 46236; www.homevideostudio.com. (800)464-8220.
Franchise: No.
Description: Producing videos from your own home video studio. Products and services include: photo videos, duplication, editing, tape repair, international conversion, audio tape duplication, format conversion, home movie transfer, video prints, and full service video tape production.
Requirements: The full cost of startup is about $89,900. The company does offer financing.
Provisions: Training is extensive and offered both at the company's location and your own. There is plenty of handholding available after startup.

IDENT-A-KID SERVICES OF AMERICA, INC., 2810 Scherer Dr., Ste 100, St. Petersburg, FL 33716; www.ident-a-kid.com. (800)890-1000.
Franchise: Yes.
Description: There are nearly one million children reported lost, missing, or separated from their parents each year. It was this realization and the personal experience of a close friend that inspired the company founder, Robert King, to start this company in 1986. The business involves producing identification cards for children that are sold en masse through schools.

Requirements: The cost of the franchise is $29,500 including exclusive territory, equipment, inventory, and comprehensive training.

Provisions: Equipment package includes a notebook PC, desktop PC, Digital card printer, wide format forms printer, digital photography equipment (camera, fingerprint scanner, lighting, backdrop, etc.), and miscellaneous office equipment. Four custom software packages are also included enabling quick and easy processing of ID cards and forms. Inventory includes 10,000 marketing pieces, components to produce 8,400 ID cards, and various marketing supplies. This inventory is designed to provide you with enough initial income to pay for the entire cost of the franchise. Training includes a comprehensive operations manual, an audio CD, two video CDs, two weeks of phone pre-training, and three days of on-site field training. The on-site training is preformed in your territory, both performing the program at a local school and marketing to other schools in your community.

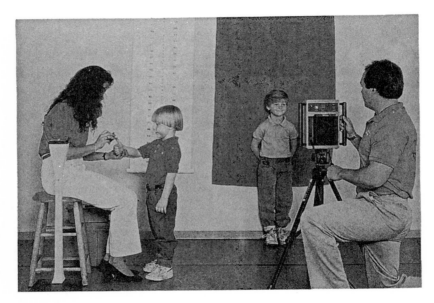

CLOSEUP: IDENT-A-KID

IDENT-A-KID, a franchise based in Florida, provides credit-card-sized ID cards for parents to carry; the card contains the photograph, fingerprint, weight, measurements, and other identifying information about their child. The cards sell for six dollar to ten dollars depending on quantity. Since the service is primarily offered through schools, those quantities can run into the thousands.

Not only does IDENT-A-KID provide a much-needed service, but it offers the kind of flexibility necessary to have a fulfilling family life as well. Before starting her franchise 14 years ago, Joyce Johnston, of Greensboro, North Carolina, worked as a supervisor for a mortgage corporation. At that time, as a single parent, getting home after six each night made her very unhappy. Now her schedule is hers to make as she sees fit.

"I work when I want to," she says. "I don't work on Monday, I reserve Fridays for computer work, and when the kids come home from school I'm done. With children you can't beat that." Joyce takes the photos and gathers all the necessary data at the schools, then returns home to produce the cards, a process that takes about four days. To further reduce her time away from home, she recently hired somebody to go out and do the photo shoot.

As a parent, Joyce felt comfortable in the school and daycare environment. Her first order of business was to line up appointments to make her presentations. She has yet to be turned down and her business grew so fast she was working to capacity right away. She now services over 100 schools. "I do the schools during the school year and save the daycares for summer."

You might think that cutting down on hours means cutting down on income. But Joyce says, "You can't even compare incomes. My business went over $100,000 this year. I could never go back to working for someone else."

LIL' ANGELS, 4041 Hatcher Cir., Memphis, TN 38118; www.lilangelsphoto.com. (800)358-9101.
Franchise: Yes.
Description: Provides professional "dress up" photography services in day-care centers and preschools.
Requirements: The total investment, including franchise fee and professional studio equipment, comes to $30,000. Sales experience is also needed.
Provisions: Training is provided at headquarters and on-site. Marketing support includes special opportunities and meetings so that franchisees can network and build on multi-location accounts.

LUKSA INDUSTRIES, INC., 3150 Innisdale Rd., Mississauga, Ontario, Canada L5N7T3; www.luksa.com. (905)785-9018.
Franchise: No.
Description: Aerial photography from a tripod extending up to 60 feet. The operator can view and select each photo on the ground console. The system has over 100 applications.
Requirements: Minimum startup is $5,450.
Provisions: Equipment package consisting of a custom telescoping tripod and remote control robotics plus business training at the company's location.

MCGRUFF SAFE KIDS, 15500 Wayzata Blvd., #812, Wayzata, MN 55391; www.mcgruff-safe-kids.com. (888)209-4218.
Franchise: Yes.
Description: Computerized children's identification system.
Requirements: The franchise fee is $30,000 and there is financing available. Business experience is also required.
Provisions: Training and ongoing support.

MDM INTERNATIONAL MULTI MEDIA, 7949 Woodley Ave., #215A, Van Nuys, CA 91406; www.webmdm.com. (888)663-6932.
Franchise: No.

Description: Digital video and photography production and services.
Requirements: $8,900.
Provisions: This is a turnkey business designed to launch your own wedding and event photography, videography and DJ services. It includes a comprehensive training and marketing package for quick startup without a huge learning curve. There is free phone support for the first year with additional years of phone support available for $350 per year. The initial (and intensive) training session lasts from four to six days and covers all aspects of photography, videography and editing, and mobile disc jockey services.

VIDEOMASTERS, 2200 Dunbarton Drive, Suite D, Chesapeake, VA 23325; www.vdsvideo.com. (800)836-9461.
Franchise: No.
Description: Videotaping service.
Requirements: $25,900 for a turnkey system.
Provisions: The price includes a complete equipment package based on the Amiga computer, training, marketing materials, and ongoing support.
Profit Potential: Over $100,000 annually.

VIDEO LEARNING LIBRARY, 15838 N. 62nd St., Scottsdale, AZ 95254; www.videolearning.com. (480)596-9970.
Franchise: No.
Description: Renting how-to and special interest videos. While your local video rental store may carry a few dozen such videos, there are over 15,000 available through this company.
Requirements: You can start for under $100.
Provisions: You will receive a manual describing how the business works, plus phone support.

THE VISUAL IMAGE, INC.100 E. Bockman Way, Sparta, TN 38583; www.thevisualimageinc.com. (931)826-2800.
Franchise: Yes.
Description: If you always wanted to be a photographer, you'll probably enjoy this franchise, which will get you the warm-and-fuzzy business of photographing kids and pets. You'll take portraits of young children by working through preschools and portraits of pets will be taken in their owners' homes.
Requirements: Obviously, you should love working with children and animals. You don't need to have any experience as a photographer. The startup cost is $35,000 including the franchise fee. Financing is available. No experience is required.
Provisions: Training in starting and operating this business as well as photographic skills and techniques. The investment covers the price of all necessary equipment and supplies for a portable studio.

PUBLISHING

There has been an opportunity explosion in the publishing industry that has not been seen since Guttenberg invented the printing press. Technology has made it possible for anyone, anywhere, interested in any subject, to become a publisher with a minimal amount of money and experience. This is an industry where home-based business operators can buy into a low-cost business opportunity and realistically expect to make it big. There are actual cases of business owners who started at home and built publishing empires worth millions of dollars. Without a doubt, the opportunities in this chapter offer the greatest potential of any of this book. Fees start as low as $149 and top out at only $20,000. Some require experience, but most do not.

The actual involvement in the business of publishing ranges from simply signing up advertisers, to snapping some pictures and writing editorials, to performing every task necessary to publish a complete book.

Probably the best way to choose a publishing business is to decide what subject you are most interested in. If you like children's books, then you might want to take a closer look at Hefty Publishing. If you love bingo, Bingo Bugle would be a better choice for you. Other opportunities presented in this chapter cover real estate, television, fashion, entertainment, shopping, travel, and wedding information. Plus there are unique opportunities to publish specialty items such as maps, church directories, and coupon books.

BINGO BUGLE NEWSPAPER, K & O Publishing, Inc., P.O. Box 527, Vashon, WA 98070; www.bingobugle.com. (800)327-6437.
Franchise: Yes.
Description: Monthly publication for bingo players. Franchisee is responsible for sales, publishing, and distribution.
Requirements: $1,500 to $5,000 plus cost of telephone, camera, automobile, typewriter and/or computer if franchisee doesn't own one.
Provisions: A 2-day training session is provided to franchisees, along with manuals and start-up materials. A monthly package is provided each month that includes camera-ready copy, clip art, industry news, etc. Other support is given as needed.

COFFEE NEWS USA, P.O. Box 8444, Bangor, ME 04402-8444; www.coffeenewsusa.com. (207)941-0860.
Franchise: Yes.
Description: Weekly restaurant newspaper.
Requirements: This is one of the lowest investment franchises you can get. The total startup cost is under $5,000. Experience is required in business, marketing, sales, and particularly ad space sales since that is where the profit comes from.
Provisions: Training is provided and there is an ongoing mentoring program. Marketing materials are also supplied.
Comments: This is such a great franchise that 94% of franchisees own more than one unit.

THE COUPON TABLOID, 5775 Jean Rd., #101, Lake Oswego, OR 97035; www.coupontabloid.com. (800)888-8575.
Franchise: Yes.
Description: The Coupon Tabloid is a direct mail advertising business. All graphics are done through the company's production department.
Requirements: The one-time investment is $3,500. Sales experience is necessary.
Provisions: The fee covers an exclusive territory, one week of intensive training in your area, marketing materials, start-up materials, printed business supplies and other support materials, and ongoing support by a team of professionals.
Profit Potential: "Excellent."

CREATE-A-BOOK, INC., 1232 Paula Cir., Gulf Breeze, FL 32561; www.hefty.com. (800)732-3009.
Franchise: No.
Description: Producing personalized children's books. This company originated the concept 20 years ago.
Requirements: Only $99.
Provisions: You'll receive a manual plus additional instructions and support online. There is phone support, technical support, and some sales leads are provided.

DISCIPLE'S DIRECTORY, INC., P.O. Box 100, Wilmington, MA 01887; www.disciplesdirectory.com. (800)696-2344
Franchise: No.
Description: Publish award-winning local Christian business and ministry guides (Christian Yellow Pages).
Requirements: $6,000 plus sales experience.
Provisions: Investment covers complete training, all materials needed to start a business, three days of on-site training, sample directories from other areas, and marketing materials.

FIESTA CARTOON MAPS, 942 N. Orlando, Mesa, AZ 85205; www.fiesta-cartoon-maps.com. (800)541-4963.
Franchise: No.
Description: Dealers sell cartoon maps of area, usually as a fund raising project for local organizations. Licensees can grow as large as desired. Maps are updated each year resulting in an annual money making venture.
Requirements: The one-time fee for a territory large enough for a 100 ad map is $6,495. Additional territories are $1,500 each. No experience is necessary.
Provisions: The fee covers hotel and round trip airfare to Phoenix for three days of training, operations manual, sales manual, 100 maps for samples, invoices, business cards, reference letters, in-house production, ongoing support, and promotional materials.
Profit Potential: Net profit for a 100 ad map is $30,000.
Comments: This can be run part-time or as an absentee ownership. Part of the training course is devoted to hiring, training, and managing sales teams.

GRAFFITTI GRAPHICS, 3 Micasa Pl., Victoria, BC, Canada V9B 1S3; www.puzzlemachine.com. (350)384-5555.
Franchise: No.
Description: Producing custom jigsaw puzzles. There are three main markets: personal gift giving, commercial advertising (more fun than a pen), and fund raising. This is a high profit margin business which reportedly does especially well during slow economic times.
Requirements: Total startup costs run around $9,000.
Provisions: You'll learn to use the machine with a manual and a video. Other support, such as marketing, is provided over the Internet and by phone. Some sales leads are provided.

HOMES & LAND PUBLISHING CORP., 1600 Capital Cir. S.W., Tallahassee, FL 32310; www.homesandland.com. (850)574-2111.
Franchise: Yes.
Description: Homes & Land is the largest publisher of community real estate magazines in the United States with over 275 communities now being serviced by franchisees.

The pictorial magazines are published either in black and white or in color, and each contains property listings of real estate companies. Franchisees sell advertising space to real estate brokers and distribute the magazines throughout the community.
Requirements: The franchise offering is $25,000. Royalties vary. Aside from the franchise fee, about $25,000 will be needed to cover initial printing costs and operating expenses. It is common for franchisees to own more than one franchise, and the company expects that all franchisees will operate on a full-time basis. No experience is required.
Provisions: The fee pays for training, field assistance for obtaining initial sales, sixty distribution racks, business cards, invoices, copy folders, stationery, and rate sheets. Training is a one-week orientation at company headquarters covering production, sales, and financial management. An operations manual and sales aids are provided at this time. Franchisees can start as soon as training is completed.

THE HOMESTEADER, Knox Trail Office Bldg., 2352 Main St., Concord, MA 01742; www.thehomesteader.com. (978) 461-0028.
Franchise: No.
Description: Publish a local newspaper for new homeowners. This is a good opportunity for anyone with a sales, publishing, or business background.
Requirements: Franchise fee is $5,000; other costs vary from $3,000 to $17,000.
Provisions: Fee covers exclusive territory, training, support, and monthly editorial packages to use in local publication.

INDUSTRY MAGAZINE, 317 S. North Lake Blvd., #1020, Altamonte Springs, FL 32701; ww.industrymagazine.com. (866)256-9550.
Franchise: Yes.
Description: Fashion and beauty magazine.
Requirements: The franchise fee is $25,000 and another $10,000 is needed for startup expenses. Business and marketing experience is also required.
Provisions: Training is provided. Marketing support includes national advertising.

THE NEWSLETTER PLACE, 14461 Redhill Ave. #D, Tustin, CA 92780; www.thenewsletterplace.com. (888)550-7460.
Franchise: No.
Description: Operators offer a full, turnkey newsletter service to companies and organizations. This includes writing, design, list management and deployment. Both electronic and print versions are available.
Requirements: Must be self-motivated and be responsible for your own sales office. No investment is required.
Provisions: Ongoing monthly residual commissions of $40-150 per customer.

SPECTRUM UNLIMITED, 2261 Market St., Ste 276, San Francisco, CA 94114; www.clientbrithday.com. (415)647-1070.
Franchise: No.
Description: Computer software for IBM compatible systems that creates beautiful birthday or anniversary greetings. The cards highlight the events that occurred on any date back to the year 1880.
Requirements: $149 for the software plus you will need a PC.
Provisions: The fee includes News of the Past software and 200 greeting forms. You also get on-going support via fax, Internet, and telephone.
Profit Potential: The individual greetings sell for $1 to $3 each; the greeting forms cost only 20 cents each.

TRAVEL

Computers have made it possible for the first time for travel agencies to be run from home. You will find several companies here that can get you set up in your own agency or work as an associate.

Discount travel has also become big recently. Through TIX you can offer major discounts to traveling consumers, plus tickets to concerts and sporting events as well.

Being a travel agent is one of those occupations that straddles the line between business ownership and employment. There are several opportunities for travel agents listed in the Job Bank. They are there because no investment is required in those instances.

Specialty travel is gaining in popularity. Wheelchair Getaways and Outdoor Connection are two good examples of prepackaged travel and tours that cater to travelers with specific interests and needs.

CONDOMINIUM TRAVEL ASSOCIATES, INC., 2001 W. Main St., Suite 140, Stamford, CT 06902; www.condotravel.com. (866)864-5966.
Franchise: No.
Description: Vacation rental service. The vacation rental market is four times greater than the cruise sector and there is very little competition.
Requirements: The start-up fee is $495 and there is an annual renewal fee of $250.
Provisions: You get training, all materials necessary to run the business, a marketing plan and advertising collateral, consumer lead referrals, familiarization trips, and an annual conference.

CRUISE PLANNERS, 3300 University Dr., #602, Coral Springs, FL 33065; www.cruiseagents.com. (888)582-2150.
Franchise: Yes.
Description: This is an exclusively homebased travel agency franchise specializing in cruise packages.
Requirements: The franchise fee is under $10,000. Other startup expenses could add up to another $8,000.
Provisions: Training is provided in Florida and followup support is available online or with a toll-free phone line. Marketing support includes national and regional advertising campaigns.

CRUISEONE, 1415 N.W. 62nd St., #205, Ft. Lauderdale, FL 33309; www.cruiseone.com/franchise. (800)892-3928.
Franchise: Yes.
Description: Travel agency specializing in cruises.
Requirements: The franchise fee is $9,800 and additional startup expenses could be as much as $15,000.
Provisions: Training is conducted at headquarters for eight days. Ongoing support includes Internet, toll-free phone line, newsletters, and regular meetings.

CRUISES INC., 1415 N.W. 62nd St., #205, Ft. Lauderdale, FL 33309; www.cruisesinc.com. (877)714-4072.

Franchise: No.
Description: A travel service dealing exclusively with cruise packages.
Requirements: The startup cost is under $500.
Provisions: Complete training is provided at company headquarters. Ongoing support is available in a variety of ways. Sales leads are provided.

FRANKEL TRAVEL WORLDWIDE, 80 Eric Ct., Oldsmar, FL 34677; www.frankeltravel.com. (800) 277-7657.
Franchise: No.
Description: Full service travel company with focus on vacation packages and cruises.
Requirements: $275 is required for ITC package.
Provisions: Comprehensive program provides all the resources and tools needed to book travel. All members receive a major portion of the travel agent commission. Free marketing and promotional materials plus excellent customer support is provided as well.

OUTDOOR CONNECTION, 424 Neosho, Burlington, KS 66839; www.outdoor-connection.com. (620) 364-5500.
Franchise: Yes.
Description: Market fishing and hunting trips to corporations and individuals in their area.
Requirements: The franchise fee is $9,500 and there is financing available for half. The total additional start-up costs range from $900 to $5,900.
Provisions: You get master catalogs with complete information on the 100+ lodges you will represent, corporate banners for trade shows, training at the corporate office, daily corporate support and guidance.

TIX TRAVEL & TICKET AGENCY, INC., 201 Main St., Nyack, NY 10960; www.tixtravel.com. (800)269-6849.
Franchise: No.
Description: Travel agency with ticket brokerage offering sold-out concerts, sports and theater tickets.
Requirements: $3,495 dealership fee. Software is not included in price.
Provisions: Classroom training takes place at company headquarters and backed up with a manual, video, and online instruction. Sales leads are provided along with ongoing support in all areas of the business. Includes access to premium ticket inventory, Web site, reservation system, and back-up service.

TRAVELER'S CHOICE, INC., 12751 County Rd. 5, #100, Burnsville, MN 55337; www.travelerschoice.org. (952)894-7777.
Franchise: No.
Description: Home-based travel agency offering a full range of services.
Requirements: No licensing or experience is required. The total startup cost is under $3,000 and there is in-house financing available.
Provisions: Training is provided at your location and is followed by online instruction. Online support is provided in a variety of ways and you'll get sales leads, too.

TRAVELINK2000, 7 W. Main St., Bay Shore, NY 11706; www.travelink2000.com. (800)519-1852.
Franchise: No.
Description: Travel agency.

Requirements: $495.
Provisions: This is a dealership with few frills. Training is provided exclusively over the Internet although there is phone support.

WHEELCHAIR GETAWAYS, INC., P.O. Box 605, Versailles, KY 40383; www.wheelchair-getaways.com. (800)536-5518.
Franchise: Yes.
Description: Wheelchair Getaways, Inc. provides wheelchair accessible van rentals for people with disabilities. One can rent a full-size and minivans on a daily, weekly, or monthly basis.
Requirements: There is a one-time franchise fee of $17,500. There is a cost of $550 per van for national advertising and a royalty fee of $550 per van per year.
Provisions: You get national advertising, on-going support, name recognition, training, national insurance plan, and leasing program for vans.

MISCELLANEOUS

Many changes in consumers' needs have taken place in recent years, and home-based businesses have proven flexible enough to meet those needs. New businesses are started all the time to fill market niches that never even existed before. In this chapter you will find an assortment of business opportunities, most of which defy classification. If you are looking for something just a little different, this chapter is for you.

AIR WAVES,INC., 7787 Graphics Way, Lewis Center, OH 43035; www.airwavesinc.com. (800)468-7335.
Franchise: No.
Description: Creating heat transfers for T-shirts, mouse pads, tote bags, coasters, and puzzles. The main customers are schools, churches, and real estate agencies.
Requirements: The cost is $300.
Provisions: Initial inventory.

ALOETTE COSMETICS, 4900 Highlands Pkwy., Smyrna, GA 30082; http://usa.aloette.com. (800)ALOETTE.
Franchise: Yes.
Description: Aloette is the only cosmetics franchise opportunity that does not require a storefront.
Requirements: The franchise fee is $20,000. Financing is available.
Provisions: Training in sales and management skills is provided along with manuals and videos, an accounting manual and journals.
Comments: The profit potential is tremendous for those who follow through with the training.

AMERICAN MOBILE SOUND, 1213 State St., Suite J, Santa Barbara, CA 93101; www.amsdj4u.com. (805)899-4000.
Franchise: Yes.
Description: Mobile entertainment business providing DJs and MCs for weddings, school dances, reunions, or any event which needs great music.

Requirements: The franchise fee ranges from $6,000 to $15,000, marketing materials cost $2,400, and system with music is $6,000.
Provisions: Full training in Santa Barbara and marketing training on-site.

BALLOON WRAP, INC., 433 W. Renwick Rd., Glendora, CA 01840; www.balloonwrap.com. (800)229-WRAP.
Franchise: No.
Description: This business involves putting all kinds of things (not just gifts) in balloons. The possible markets include business shows, fairs and carnivals, weddings, and decorating hotels. Typical part-timers earn $200 to $3,000 per weekend while full-time wrappers make $30,000 to $100,000.
Requirements: Start-up costs range from $850 to $2,700.
Provisions: Fee covers free unlimited consulting, the Balloon Wrap machine, training in everything from sales to balloon decorating, and all supplies and inventory needed for a turn-key operation.

CAJUN COUNTRY CANDIES, P.O. Box 70, Scott, LA 70583; www.cajuncountrycandies.com. (337)232-8990.
Franchise: No.
Description: Distribute homemade candy via mail order.
Requirements: Cost of total business package is $80. There is a 30 day unconditional refund privilege. Must be able to follow directions.
Provisions: You will receive a business operations manual with marketing instructions, drop ship directions (so you don't have to stock candy), a box of candy samples, 100 promotional advertising mailers, sample ads, plus unlimited phone consultation. Also included in the price is $80 worth of inventory.
Profit Potential: Unlimited.

CANINE CAVIAR PET FOODS, INC., P.O. Box 6526, Anaheim, CA 92816; www.caninecaviar.com. (800)392-7898.
Franchise: No.
Description: Delivery service that involves a premium line of pet foods. This is naturally preserved allergen-free food with no chemical preservatives, animal by-products, corn, wheat, or soy. It does include human grade meats and grains, flaxseed and fish oils for the skin and coat, alfalfa and kelp for the stomach, and yucca for the hips and joints.
Requirements: Need a delivery van, warehousing capability, and dedication to building the business. The total investment amounts to about $35,000.
Provisions: Inventory, on-site training, ongoing support, and national advertising.

COMPLETE MUSIC, INC., 7877 L St., Omaha, NE 68127; www.cmusic.com. (800)843-3866.
Franchise: Yes.
Description: Music disc jockeys provide the entertainment for parties and celebrations of all kinds. About 70% of the time, they are used for wedding receptions. The disc jockeys bring everything, including stereo sound and light equipment as well as a music tape library. The tape collection is the largest music disc jockey collection in the country, with over 30,000 selections in all categories. The entire system packs easily into a compact car.
Requirements: The entire initial investment is $26,500 in most markets.
Provisions: Start-up package, 14 days of training, and ongoing support.

Profit Potential: 33% net.
Comments: This is the nation's largest DJ entertainment service with 129 franchisees now in operation.

THE DENTIST'S CHOICE, 774 Mays Blvd., #10-297, Incline Village, NV 89451; www.thedentistschoice.com. (800)757-1300.
Franchise: Yes.
Description: Franchisees primarily repair, rebuild and maintain all models of dental drills. Other services include rethreading and burring tools, replacing fiber optics, and selling new handpieces to dentists.
Requirements: The total investment for startup is around $30,000. Marketing skills are necessary.
Provisions: Training and ongoing support is provided. Marketing support is exceptional and includes an extensive marketing manual.

GLOBAL SECURITY PRODUCTS LTD., 1727 E. Springfield Ave., Spokane, WA 99202; www.macesecurityproducts.com. (800)735-1797.
Franchise: No.
Description: This is a manufacturer of pepper spray personal protection products offering distributorships.
Requirements: Startup costs are zero.
Provisions: Purchase products at wholesale; sell at retail.

GUMBALL GOURMET, 1460 Commerce Wy., Idaho Falls, ID 83403-3111; www.gumballgourmet.com. (866)486-2255.
Franchise: Yes.
Description: Gumball machine kiosks.
Requirements: Total investment including franchise fee is around $25,000. Some background in business is required.
Provisions: Training, support, toll-free phone line, kiosk signs, and Internet marketing.

GYMSTERS, INC., Phoenix, AZ 85003; (408) 315-0351.
Franchise: Yes.
Description: This is a fitness and sports skills program that is offered to kids from ages two to twelve at their daycare centers, private schools, preschools, family providers, etc.
Requirements: The franchise fee is $12,000. A physical education degree and some experience are preferred.
Provisions: The fee buys training and materials.

HANDPIECE EXPRESS, 1020 Railroad Ave., #A-1, Novato, CA 94945; www.handpieceexpress.com. (800)895-7111.
Franchise: No.
Description: Home-based business providing rapid repair service to dentists.
Requirements: $37,500, some technical ability, sales and marketing ability, and hard work. Financing is available.
Provisions: Investment covers training, manuals, videos, software package, toll-free support for one year, specialized tools, and $9,000 parts inventory.

HAYES HANDPIECE, 5375 Avenida Encinas, Carlsbad, CA 92008; www.hayeshandpiece.com. (760)602-0521.

Franchise: Yes.
Description: Franchisees offer dental handpiece repair with free pick-up and delivery service and 24-hour turnaround. They also occasionally sell new handpieces, but they specialize in selling rebuilt, used handpieces.
Requirements: Total startup expenses including the franchise fee run around $50,000. The franchisor also wants to see business and marketing experience and especially sales skills.
Provisions: Training is provided at headquarters and the franchisee's location. Marketing support includes co-op advertising, ad slicks, regional and national advertising, and a call center.
Profit Potential: Since dentists typically need to repair 5-15 handpieces a year, there is tremendous opportunity for repeat business.

I9 SPORTS, 1463 Oakfield Dr., #135, Brandon, FL 33511; www.i9sports.com. (813)662-6773.
Franchise: Yes.
Description: Franchisees operate local amateur sports leagues, tournaments, clinics and special events in two dozen sports, including baseball, soccer, golf and bowling. Additional profit comes from selling sponsorships, sporting goods, and customized uniforms.
Requirements: Startup costs start at about $25,000. A background in business is required along with marketing skills.
Provisions: Training is provided at headquarters and the franchisee's location plus refresher training is available at any time. This business is highly dependent on good marketing and therefore, the marketing support is excellent. It includes co-op advertising programs, ad slicks, national and regional advertising, and ongoing guidance with sales and PR. Also provided are administrative services, billing and commission payment support; and visits from field support.

KINDERDANCE INTERNATIONAL, INC., 268 North Babcock St., Melbourne Beach, FL 32951; www.kinderdance.net. (800)554-2334.
Franchise: Yes.
Description: Kinderdance is a program for preschool children that is designed to develop motor and cognitive skills through dance and movement. Ballet, tap, acrobatics, and modern dance are blended with numbers, colors, and shapes in the basic program. This is taught to boys and girls three to five years of age, and it is offered through nursery schools and day-care centers.
Requirements: You must have a desire to work with young children or to manage a team of instructors. Costs range from $9,350 to $20,600 including franchise fee. KD offers up to 50% financing of the franchise fee.
Provisions: The fee buys training, an operations manual, printed materials including promotional materials and forms, props, dance wear, cassette and videotapes, and file cabinet.
Comments: This company has an excellent reputation and the opportunity is ideal for someone who loves children, has an educational background, and enjoys dance.

KINDERMUSIK INTERNATIONAL, P.O. Box 26575, Greensboro, NC 27415; www.kindermusik.com. (336)273-3363.
Franchise: Yes.
Description: Kindermusik is a unique, highly creative, music and movement learning experience for children 18 months to 7 years of age. Professional curricula workshops

are designed to acquaint participants with the principles of the Kindermusik curricula and prepare them to teach the program.
Requirements: $125 to $200.

LE GOURMET GIFT BASKET, INC., 723 Anderson St., Castle Rock, CO 80104; www.legift.com. (800)934-4386.
Franchise: Yes.
Description: Providing elegant and affordable gourmet gift baskets for any occasion including birthdays, weddings, showers and for corporate clients. The baskets can be custom made for any occasion or theme and shipped worldwide.
Requirements: There are three programs ranging in price from $3,500 to $8,500. This is a one-time fee; there are no royalties or additional fees.
Provisions: Training in person or by videotape. Also provides equipment, inventory, negotiated vendor deals, and referrals.

LITTLE SCIENTISTS, 14 Selden St., Woodbridge, CT 06525; www.Little-Scientists.com. (800)FACT-FUN.
Franchise: Yes.
Description: Children's science educational "hands on" franchise.
Requirements: The fee is $20,000. No science education background is needed.
Provisions: Training, protected territory, and enough supplies for 40 children.

MAGIC RICE, INC., P.O. Box 592457, Orlando, FL 32859; www.magicrice.com. (407)438-6650.
Franchise: No.
Description: Personalized rice jewelry for necklaces, bracelets, key chains, and earrings.
Requirements: The cost ranges between $300 and $1,000.
Provisions: Supplies and instructions. The markup is very high - nearly 800%.

MARTY WOLF GAME COMPANY, 2120 Highland Ave., Las Vegas, NV 89101; www.gamblersjunkyard.com. (702)385-2963.
Franchise: No.
Description: Own and operate a charity gambling casino for fundraising activities. It can be started in your garage part-time.
Requirements: The total investment for the complete party business package ranges from $220 to $5,000. There is financing available. You will also need a garage or storage area to store equipment.
Provisions: The investment covers all the tables, equipment and supplies required to stage a Las Vegas Style Gambling Party. A complete gambling casino accommodates 100 charity party gamblers. It also includes a five-day, casino dealer workshop in Las Vegas where you will learn and qualify to deal Blackjack, Craps, and Roulette; learn and qualify to train your own party dealers. There is ongoing support and training in how and where to find clients.

MINI-GOLF, INC., 202 Bridge St., Jessup, PA 18434; www.minigolfinc.com. (570)-489-8623.
Franchise: No.
Description: Portable, prefabricated miniature golf courses that can be used indoors or outdoor. Courses are easy to set up, move and store. The courses can be rented for a wide variety of events from parties to fund raisers.
Requirements: $5,900.

Provisions: You get a portable, prefabricated miniature golf course with all the necessary accessories, and operators manual with ideas and promotions, and continuous support.

P & 1 INFLATABLES, INC., P.O. Box 1200, New Lenox, IL 60451; www.jumbousa.com. (888) 586-7464.
Franchise: No.
Description: Inflatable amusement devices used in party rental business.
Requirements: Start-up costs are about $3,000 depending upon size and design of unit purchase.
Provisions: Cost includes products, manuals, and toll-free support.

PALM BEACH SPECIALTY COFFEE, 3965 Investment Ln., #A-8, West Palm Beach, FL 33404; www.palmbeachcoffee.com. (561)881-0803.
Franchise: No.
Description: Espresso machine sales.
Requirements: Start-up costs total $12,000.
Provisions: Training is provided at headquarters and the franchisee's location. There is also a complete manual. Marketing support includes sales leads.

PATTY-CAKES INTERNATIONAL, INC., 1726 W. Third St., Montgomery, AL 36106; www.patty-cakes.com. (334)272-2826.
Franchise: Yes.
Description: Make the actual impression of a child's hand and foot and cast them in bronze. The bronzed impressions are then mounted on a variety of wall plaques to make a lasting keepsake.
Requirements: $7,900 for franchise and equipment fee.

PEE WEE WORKOUT, 34976 Aspenwood Ln., Willoughby, OH 44094; www.peeweeworkout.com. (800)356-6261.
Franchise: Yes.
Description: Aerobic fitness program for children.
Requirements: The franchise fee is $2,500 and start-up costs are another $300.
Provisions: Programs, training, and start-up materials.

PERSONAL TOUCH PRODUCTS, INC., 2187 Vista Court, La Verne, CA 91750; www.PersonalTouchProducts.com. (877)593-1249/(909)596-1166.
Franchise: No.
Description: Utilizing your computer and the unique supplies offered by this company, you can create a wide variety of unique personalized gift items including framed keepsakes, jewelry boxes, mouse pads, ceramic plates, address books, key chains, clocks, calendars, etc. Among the special features offered by this company is the "Gifts on Art Business Software", which includes a database containing over 100,000 first names origins, plus an extensive collection of personalize-able poetry. The software is easy to use to personalize and then print first names and poetry on any one of their 100+ specialty art backgrounds. The entire process takes about two minutes to create a gift. Both English and Spanish versions are available.
Requirements: The start-up investment is low at only $850. You will need a computer, but no technical experience is required.
Provisions: The system includes personalization software, a first names database, a poetry database, master books, specialty art backgrounds, instructions, order forms,

brochures, training, and support. Enough starting inventory is supplied to recoup your initial investment several times over.

PROFITABLE HOBBIES, 517 S. Commerce Rd., Orem, UT 84058; www.profitablehobbies.com. (800)624-7415.
Franchise: No.
Description: Custom engraving system using micro-sandblasting and airbrush.
Requirements: Startup costs range from $1,000 to $14,000.
Provisions: Provides training, marketing, and equipment.

PROTOCOL, LLC, 1370 Mendota Heights Rd., Mendota Heights, MN 55120; www.protocolvending.com. (800)227-5336.
Franchise: Yes.
Description: Personal product vending franchise involving wall-mounted units that vend specialty products ranging from OTC medications to feminine hygiene and breath fresheners.
Requirements: $500 franchise fee and an investment in equipment and inventory of around $8,000.
Provisions: Marketing manual with step-by-step startup instructions and regional manager support to establish your business. There is also a national account program whereby the company lands major accounts such as malls, theaters and restaurants and passes them on to the franchisees.

SPORTSLIFE ENTERPRISES, INC., 1455 Old Bridge Rd., Suite 204, Woodbridge, VA 22192; www.sportslifeinc.com. (800)909-5433.
Franchise: No.
Description: Dealers market sporting goods to schools, leagues, and businesses.
Requirements: Initial investment is $495 and there is a $30 ongoing fee each month.
Provisions: Price includes manual, directories, catalogs, monthly newsletters, and free business consulting.

STORK NEWS OF AMERICA, INC., 1305 Hope Mills Rd., Suite A, Fayetteville, NC 28304; www.storknews.com. (910)426-1357.
Franchise: Yes.
Description: Stork News is a newborn announcement service primarily providing outdoor display signs. Other products include announcement cards, newborn clothing for christening, and party supplies.
Requirements: The franchise fee starts at $5,000. Additional tools, advertising expenses, operating capital, equipment, and inventory can cost as much as $5,000.
Provisions: The fee buys a complete start-up package including introductory advertising materials, administrative supplies, and enough equipment and supplies to get started. Protected territory. This franchisor has an exclusive partnership with Babies R Us.

TEAM DOUBLE CLICK, W10530 Airport Road, Lodi, WI 53555; www.TeamDoubleClick.com. (608)592-3050.
Franchise: No.
Description: Team Double Click is a virtual staffing agency with over 1,300 homebased workers in their database. The company now has an affiliate program that is custom made for staffing firms looking to expand into the cutting-edge world of virtual staffing.
Requirements: The affiliate fee is a one-time $1,500.
Provisions: The system is turnkey and includes two weeks training via phone and instant

messenger plus ongoing support. Under the agreement, Team Double Click receives 25% of the affiliate's net profit. Provides 100% funding of client receivables and payroll for all virtual staffing contractors.

UNCO INDUSTRIES, INC., 7802 Old Spring Street, Racine, WI 53406; www.vermiculture.com. (800)728-2415.
Franchise: No.
Description: The business concerns producing night crawlers and organic fertilizer. The company has been in business for 17 years.
Requirements: You will need a small spare room, a portion of your garage, or a corner of your basement. You will need to spend 2 hours every 2 weeks per kit. Startup costs $3,900 and includes complete training. Financing is available.
Provisions: Everything is supplied including step-by-step training.

VENDX, 3808 E. 109th N., Idaho Falls, ID 83401; www.vendx.com. (800)527-8363.
Franchise: No.
Description: Bulk candy/nut vending of nationally advertised products such as M&Ms, Skittles, etc.
Requirements: Startup costs amount to about $7,000.
Provisions: You will be advised of which candies sell best, and where to purchase your products. You will be provided with proven management tools. You will receive a sample route record keeping system, bi-monthly newsletter, product and vending information, operations manual, support materials, and ongoing support. Financial assistance is available.
Profit Potential: On most products, you will receive 64-84% gross profit.

MARKETS FOR HANDCRAFTS

This chapter is for serious artisans and handcrafters who want to spend more time producing their products than selling them. The traditional route for many crafters is to rent booth space at craft fairs, feeling more like a retail clerk than an artist. When going the craft fair route, it is often necessary to travel around in order to find enough events to keep busy. Plus, craft fairs tend to be very seasonal, leaving little opportunity for sales in the winter months. If you would rather be in your home studio doing the work that you love, this is the chapter for you.

The listings in this chapter include shops, galleries, and mail order catalogs that will consider buying your handcrafts. While these buyers are willing to give new artisans a chance, they have no patience for hobbyists. You must deal with them on a professional level, making them believe you mean business.

There are also quite a few manufacturers' representatives and wholesalers listed. These are agents who deal regularly with numerous buyers, from small shops to huge chain stores. They work on a percentage commission, so you have to build that percentage into your pricing. You should only consider a rep if you can produce your crafts in quantity. They are not in the business of dealing with one-of-a-kind items.

To approach any buyer, follow the instructions exactly. Start with a letter of introduction, preferably typed on letterhead. Always supply a self-addressed envelope. Keep the information brief and concise. Describe what you have to offer, stressing the quality of the work and materials used.

Include a price list. Keep in mind that a shop that buys outright will generally split 50/50, while you can expect another 10% if it is a consignment sale. Don't price yourself out of the market, but make sure you can make a healthy profit. Otherwise, you won't be in the handcrafts business for long. It is an acceptable practice to set minimum orders, but keep them small, say a half dozen for example.

Send the best quality photos or slides of your work that you possibly can. You don't have to hire a professional photographer. Set up one or two items on a plain contrasting background such as a sheet or drapes. Keep the focus close enough to show the detail of your work. Remember, this is the first, and possibly only, impression that a potential buyer will have. Never send samples unless asked. Label the back of every photo with your name and address.

Contact more than one shop at a time. By doing business with several, you can be assured of making it through seasonal fluctuations and other lean times. Give plenty of time for shops to respond. Rather than contacting the same shops repeatedly, go on to some others if you need more business. But do be patient. It is not unusual for several months to pass before you get a response from a buyer. Do not call them in the meantime. If they are interested, you will hear from them when they are ready.

Finally, make sure that you are capable of handling the volume of business each shop requires. It's very disappointing for everyone when an item is selling well, but the crafter can't -or won't -produce enough.

ACCESSORY RESOURCES, 7 W. 36th St., New York, NY 10018.
Items Wanted: Fine jewelry including custom pieces, other fashion accessories.
Payment: Pays commission every 30 days.
Instructions: Send photos or slides along with wholesale and retail price lists.

ALLYN AND COMPANY, 8 East 36th St., New York, NY 10016.
Items Wanted: Quality, unique jewelry and accessories. Particularly interested in silver items. Accepted items are marketed worldwide.
Payment: Sells items wholesale and takes a standard commission.
Instructions: Send slides, artist resume, brochures, and wholesale prices.

AMERICRAFT CRAFT BROKERS, Stillwaters, 210 Lockes Village Rd., Wendell, MA 01379.
Items Wanted: This wholesale rep handles handcrafts of all kinds, home accessories, pottery, and personalized items.
Payment: Sells items wholesale and takes a standard commission.
Instructions: Submit your bio and contact information, product description, catalog sheet or brochure or photo, wholesale price list, and sample.

AMISH ACRES, 1600 West Market Street, Nappanee, IN 46550; www.amishacres.com.
Items Wanted: This is a nonprofit organization that represents over 200 crafters. Visit the Web site and browse the wholesale catalog to get a good view of the types of products handled here.
Payment: Takes items on consignment paying 60% to the crafter. Provides a detailed report of sales activity with payment on the 15th of each month.
Instructions: Submit product description with brochure or photo and price.

ANNE MENAKER GORDON & CO., 2300 N. Stemmons Fwy, Dallas, TX 75258.
Items Wanted: Giftwares, fine jewelry (prefers silver), and fashion accessories.
Payment: Sells items wholesale to stores in the Midwest and takes a commission.
Instructions: Send slides, documentation, and wholesale price list. Be sure to include information on quantity available of any given item as this is a manufacturer's rep.

THE APPLE TREE, 54 East Street Road, West Chester, PA 19382.
Contact: Jill Butler.
Items Wanted: Giftwares of all kinds, home and bath accessories, garden products, gifts for babies and children, pet products, books and stationary, and general collectibles. Looking for new and deferent items of good quality in the country or traditional style.
Payment: Buys outright.
Instructions: Submit product description, catalog or brochure or photo, wholesale price, and sample. Also indicate if there are any stores in this local area carrying your products.

ARTIQUE, INC., 259 Godwin Avenue, Midland Park, NJ 07432.
Items Wanted: Good quality items based on Early American designs. Also, items that can be customized. Only interested in items that can be reordered. No precious metal items. No extremely fragile items or paper items.
Payment: Purchase with terms; credit references can be furnished.
Instructions: Send photos and price list. Later, samples may be requested. If necessary, would like craftsperson to drop ship via UPS.

ARTISANS GALLERY, PO Box 256, Mentone, AL 35984; www.folkartisans.com.

Items Wanted: Folk art, weather vanes, quilts, paintings, carvings, etc. Visit the online catalog to see the type of products carried.
Payment: Purchases outright for sale in both the print catalog and online store.
Instructions: Send product description, photo, and price sheet to either Matt Lippa or Elizabeth Schaaf.

ARTISTS' PARLOR, 126 Laurens Street, NW, Aiken, SC 29801.
Items Wanted: Pottery, wood, jewelry, whimsical but not country. Animal images are good.
Payment: Purchase outright.
Instructions: Any information is helpful; all will be returned.

ARTS & ARTISANS, LTD., 108 S. Michigan Ave., Chicago, IL 60603.
Items Wanted: Blown glass in all forms, jewelry, wood, ceramic, frames, clocks, dolls, boxes - all media.
Payment: Purchase; net 30.
Instructions: Send photos, slides and prices (wholesale). Your background would also be helpful. This is a group of 4 galleries in downtown Chicago.

ARTWORKS PARK CITY, 461 Main St., Park City, UT 84060.
Items Wanted: Sophisticated, whimsical, contemporary crafts with an emphasis on hot glass, clay, and jewelry. There are over 200 artists represented here.
Payment: Mainly consignment 60/40; or purchase 50%.
Instructions: Send photos, prices, and information about the artist.

AVITA, INC., 136 Cedar St., Corning, NY 14830.
Items Wanted: All types of decorative glass items for nationwide distribution.
Payment: Pays wholesale minus commission 30 days after sale.
Instructions: Send photos or slides along with wholesale price list and description of artist's work.

BARBARA SCHWARTZ ACCESSORIES, 392 Fifth Ave. Lobby, New York, NY 10018.
Items Wanted: High end gift items and silver jewelry.
Payment: This wholesale rep takes a standard commission on items sold.
Instructions: Send slides, brochures, resume, and price list.

BOATEAK, Bluff Island, 102 Holly Circle, Fayetteville, NY 13066.
Items Wanted: Varies. Good quality and unusual.
Payment: 50% wholesale; 1/3 commission on consignment with 2/3 to craftsperson.
Instructions: Contact Cookie Tomaiuoli. "The Boateak is a seasonal store open from Memorial Day through the second week in September. My customers are those islanders who move up to the river from all over the country. They in turn bring their company, many of which are from all over the world. The store will be in existence 12 years next summer. Today, we represent over 300 craftsmen from all over the U.S. and Alaska. January and February are the months in which I plan for the season. I would be happy to hear from any craftsmen."

BOB TURNER, INC., 50 Lenape Lane, Doylestown, PA 18901.
Items Wanted: Any interesting gift items including interesting novelties for nationwide distribution.

Payment: Pays wholesale less commission upon sale.
Instructions: Send slides or photos along with brochures and price list. Send only information on items that can be produced in quantity.

BONNIE BUTLER SHOWROOM, North Stemmons Freeway, Dallas, TX 75258.
Items Wanted: This is a jewelry wholesaler that is also interested in quality accessories and gift items.
Payment: Pays wholesale less commission.
Instructions: Send slides, photos, and samples if appropriate. Include price list and any helpful documentation.

BRASS SMITH HOUSE, 59 Middlesex Turnpike, Room 168, Bedford, MA 01730.
Items Wanted: Interesting and unique crafts that would be appropriate for gift giving. Items are sold wholesale to department stores and smaller shops nationwide.
Payment: Pays wholesale minus standard commission.
Instructions: Send slides or photos, brochures, and price list. Indicate quantities available and delivery schedule.

BROOKLYN WOMEN'S EXCHANGE, INC., 55 Pierrepont St., Brooklyn, NY 11201.
Items Wanted: Hand-knitted sweaters, handmade toys, dolls, clothing for children.
Payment: Consignment 70/30 (this is a non-profit group).
Instructions: Send photos and prices to be reviewed by consignor committee. This is a non-profit organization staffed by volunteers continuing operation since 1854.

BUYLINK CORPORATION, 222 3rd Ave. SE. Suite 8, Cedar Rapids, IA 52401; www.buylink.com.
Items Wanted: This company was one of the pioneers of wholesaling online. Here you can put your catalog online for the 20,000+ store owners and other wholesale buyers to see.
Payment: Arrangements are made between the buyers and vendors (you).
Instructions: Visit the Web site and click on "Vendor" for instructions and/or contact Dave Stoddard. The cost of participating is $49.95 a month.

CAMBRIDGE SALES, 451 East 58th, Suite 2145, Denver, CO 80216.
Items Wanted: Country style crafts of the highest quality. Items are sold wholesale throughout the Western region of the U.S.
Payment: Pays cash less standard commission.
Instructions: Send photos or slides, price list, brochures, and samples if possible.

CARNEGIE ART CENTER, 109 South Palouse, Walla Walla, WA 99362.
Items Wanted: Handcrafted art items including pottery, jewelry, weavings, glass paperweights, vases, wooden toys, fabric toys, etc.
Payment: Consignment preferred; 60% of retail price goes to the artist.
Instructions: Send photos or slides, artist's catalog, resume, and personal statement if available. "The Center is a non-profit art gallery with a gift shop. Art classes for children and adults are offered."

CATS 'N CRITTERS GIFT SHOP, 715 Merchant Street, Ambridge, PA 15003.
Contact: Karen Miller.
Items Wanted: This is a gift shop for animal lovers. Looking for any handcrafted items

with animals on them. This includes general gift items, home accessories, garden products, gifts for babies and children, pet products such as treats and toys, books and stationary, and jewelry. No stuffed animals.

Payment: Buys outright at standard wholesale discount or accepts items on consignment.

Instructions: Submit product description, catalog or brochure, photo, and/or sample. Items should be unique (inexpensive to upper moderate price range).

COLDWATER CREEK HOME, 5 Coldwater Creek Drive, Sandpoint, ID 83864; www.coldwater-creek.com.

Items Wanted: This high-end mail order catalog offers a variety of products, but is only looking for handcrafted home décor items and furniture. Will not consider any item that uses animal by-products (feathers, bones, etc.).

Payment: Buys outright at wholesale prices.

Instructions: Visit the Web site and look in the Home & Gifts section to get a good understanding of the kind of items carried. Then submit a letter of introduction to the merchandizing department that includes your experience with other catalogs, how long in business, production capabilities, color photos or catalog, and whole price list. Do not send samples unless requested.

COLLAGE GALLERY, Attn: Delisa, 1345 18th St., San Francisco, CA 94107.

Items Wanted: Contemporary crafts, bowls, clocks, jewelry, mirrors, picture frames, candleholders, and furniture.

Payment: Consignment; 50/50.

Instructions: Send photos with price list. "Functional crafts sell really well."

CONGREGATION BETH ELOHIM SISTERHOOD GIFT SHOP, 86 Hasell St., Charleston, SC 29401.

Items Wanted: All Judaica only! Candleholders, sabbath, sever, matzo plates, dreidles, menorahs, and jewelry.

Payment: Outright purchase and consignment.

Instructions: Send photos, slides, and/or brochures. "We are open to the public - tourists are welcome."

CORVALLIS ARTS CENTER, LINN-BENTON COUNCIL FOR THE ARTS, 700 SW Madison, Corvallis, OR 97333.

Items Wanted: Jewelry, fine crafts, mostly functional.

Payment: On consignment: 60% to artists by the 20th of the month.

Instructions: Send photos or samples. Items are "juried" by a panel of several people so it often takes at least a full week to make a decision. Contact Alice Hall or Hester Coucke.

CRAFTER'S ATTIC, 1910 Cochran Rd., Pittsburgh, PA 15220.

Contact: Kim, Tim, or Renee.

Items Wanted: All mediums are represented and styles of handcrafts are represented here. Items are accepted only after going through the jury process.

Payment: Pays a generous 75% to the consigning crafter. If retail customer uses a credit card, the crafter is charged 3% fee.

Instructions: Submit product description, good photos, and bio.

DAFA SALES, 2100 N. Stemmons Freeway, #1733, Dallas, TX 75207.

Items Wanted: Gift items of any material, particularly that could be sold as souvenirs

through mass distribution. Think college bookstores and you get the idea. Distributes mainly in the South.
Payment: Pays wholesale prices less standard commission.
Instructions: Send photos, slides, and/or samples. Make sure you only offer items that can be produced in quantity within reasonable time period. Include brochures, wholesale prices, etc.

DAVLINS, 2652 Southdale Center, Edina, MN 55435.
Items Wanted: Quality, unique wood gifts (some furniture), no country.
Payment: Consignment - monthly; net 30.
Instructions: Send photos, slides, or brochures. Contact Dave Loonet.

DENNIS PAUL ASSOCIATES, 389 Fifth Ave., Room 712, New York, NY 10016.
Items Wanted: This is a quality wholesale jeweler that distributes its line all over the world through mass merchandising, wholesaling, and mail order.
Payment: Works on standard commission.
Instructions: Submit slides and/or photos, documentation, brochures, resume, and wholesale prices.

ESPECIAL DAY, 9A Trolley Square, Wilmington, DE 19806.
Items Wanted: Creative, useful gifts, jewelry cards made in the USA- "in this economy the more practical items are best".
Payment: Net 30 days.
Instructions: Send all information to the attention of Elizabeth Clayton.

ETOYS, 12200 Olympic Blvd., Los Angeles, CA 90064; www.etoys.com.
Items Wanted: Toys and gifts for children of all ages. This is probably the most successful online toy store.
Payment: Buys outright with purchase order; pays within 30 days.
Instructions: Visit the Web site first and get familiar with the extensive product line. Send your product description, photo, sample, and wholesale price to the merchandising department, attention "Product Submissions." If samples are too large for UPS shipment, send all other information and indicate the size.

ETCO, INC., 6100 4th S., Seattle, WA 98108.
Items Wanted: This is a manufacturer's rep that handles handcrafts, pottery, sculpture, and hand blown glass.
Payment: Works on standard commission agreement.
Instructions: Submit product description, photo, and/or catalog or brochure along with wholesale price list.

EZIBA, 120 Mass Moca Way, North Adams, MA 01247; www.eziba.com.
Items Wanted: This is a mail order catalog that buys handcrafted items of all kinds, especially unique, hard to find products. "We buy handcrafted objects from around the world."
Payment: Pays within 30 days.
Instructions: Submit product information in the form of printed color catalogs, photographs, and price sheets. Do not send samples unless requested. Send information to the attention of the merchandising committee.

FIREBURST, 83 Royalston Rd., Orange, MA 01364.

Items Wanted: This is a national jewelry wholesaler who markets to high end retailers, museum shops, and catalogs. Will consider unique fashion jewelry and accessories.
Payment: Pays cash with various contract options depending on particular distribution involved.
Instructions: Submit as much information as possible: color photos, slides, videos, brochures, catalogs, resumes, price lists, etc.

FRANZEN ENTERPRISES, 222 Merchandise Mart Plaza, Chicago, IL 60654.
Items Wanted: This is a manufacturer's rep for country crafts, folk art, and Victorian items.
Payment: Works on standard commission agreement.
Instructions: Submit photos and/or samples along with wholesale price list.

FUSION FINE CRAFTS, 118 E Orange St., Tarpon Springs, FL 34689.
Items Wanted: Fine, handcrafted goods - no country crafts.
Payment: Purchase at wholesale and keystone.
Instructions: Send brochure or photos and wholesale price list to above address.

GALERIA ELDORADO, 1054 Ashford Ave., Condado, PR 00907.
Items Wanted: High end sculptures in glass, wood, metal or ceramic.
Payment: Consignment with end of month inventory/payment.
Instructions: Prefer color pictures returnable upon selection. "We are an art and decor gallery, specializing in fine pieces of art, sculpture and porcelain. We are located on Main Avenue with both tourist and local trade."

GALLERY OF THE SANDIAS, Box 311, Sandia Park, NM 87047.
Items Wanted: Most crafts (interested in proven crafts), also discontinued items and slight irregulars.
Payment: COD or check within 7 days of receipt.
Instructions: Send photos or slides.

GALLERY/SHOP AT WESLEYAN POTTERS, 350 S. Main St., Middletown, CT 06457. Contact: Maureen LoPresti.
Items Wanted: Fine, contemporary American handcrafts in all media except clay. Items are juried first. No country.
Payment: All work, after jurying, is on consignment at 37%; payment made every 60 days.
Instructions: Invitation to submit work for jurying is made after viewing photos and price list. Send SASE for return of photos. "We are primarily a craft education center, non-profit, run as a cooperative. Most of our members are potters so we have more than enough clay work from them to sell."

GRASSROOTS HANDCRAFTS, 93 East Main Street, Newark, DE 19711; www.grassrootshandcrafts.com.
Contact: Marilyn Dickey.
Items Wanted: This is a very successful chain of four retail stores that has been in business for over 26 years and won numerous awards. They specialize in quality handcrafted contemporary gift items including American handthrown pottery, sterling silver jewelry, candles, ironware, fine wood items, etc. Visit Web site for complete picture of their product line.
Payment: Buys outright.

Instructions: Submit photos and/or samples along with wholesale price list.

H.O.M.E., INC., Route 1, Orland, ME 04472.
Items Wanted: H.O.M.E. stands for Homeworkers Organized for More Employment. It is a non-profit co-operative founded in 1970 for the purpose of marketing handcrafted products from this economically depressed area. H.O.M.E. operates a country store, many types of craft and trade workshops, a child-care center, the Learning Center for adult education, a sawmill, a shingle mill, a woodlot and two hospitality houses. It also publishes a quarterly newspaper ("This Time") and a crafts catalog, and builds homes for otherwise homeless neighbors. Currently has 3,500 members. Anyone living in the area is encouraged to participate.

HONEYSUCKLE CRAFTS, 317 Nelson Rt 3 Box 150, , Cambridge, NE 69022.
Items Wanted: Country wood dolls, signs, bunnies, bears, doll furniture; all items must retail for under $20.
Payment: Cash monthly for what has sold on consignment the previous month.
Instructions: Send photos.

HUSTED GALLERY & ART FRAMES, 9776 Holman Road, NW, #111, Seattle, WA 98117.
Items Wanted: Fine American made crafts: wood, glass, jewelry, pottery, Christmas.
Payment: Consignment 50/50 paid monthly or sooner if large sales accumulate.
Instructions: Send sample or photo with SASE for return. "We attract upper middle class repeat customers in this well established N. Seattle business. We are in our 16th year doing custom picture framing and showing original artwork as well as gifts, cards and crafts."

J. MARCO GALLERIES, 758 Medina Road, Medina, OH 44256; www.jmarco.com.
Items Wanted: This is a mail order catalog that also has an online showroom. Interested in jewelry, gifts, apparel, and home décor items.
Payment: Buys outright.
Instructions: Submit catalog or photo with wholesale price list and contact information. Send to the attention of Christa Ondrey.

JULIE HALL, 5915 Park Lane, Dallas, TX 75201.
Items Wanted: Jewelry, accessories, novelties, and especially textiles for distribution throughout the South.
Payment: Works on commission.
Instructions: Send photos and/or samples (samples preferred), brochures, wholesale price list, and contact information.

KAH-NEE-TAH GALLERY, 4210 W. Highway 61, Lutsen, MN 55612.
Items Wanted: This gallery carries only quality original work from Minnesota and regional artists and craftspersons. Items include pottery, jewelry, baskets, carvings, metal work, weaving, and local photography.
Payment: Consignment and outright purchase.
Instructions: Prefers to see work in person, but if not, send slides with resume and price range.

KENNEDY BROTHERS MARKETPLACE, 11 Main St., Vergennes, VT 05491.
Items Wanted: Leather, stoneware, glass, wood and other crafts.

Payment: Pays for consignments on the 10th of each month.
Instructions: Send photos and/or samples to Edwin Grant.

LOOSE ENDS, 2065 Madrona Ave., SE, Salem, OR 97302; www.4loosends.com.
Items Wanted: This mail order catalog carries "organic" products for home and garden. Is looking for country and rustic gifts, garden and outdoor items, floral, baskets, ceramics and pots, handmade paper and stationary, etc.
Payment: Buys outright; pays within 30 days.
Instructions: Send sample, product description, and wholesale price to Product Development.

LOVE OF COUNTRY, 137 Ault Rd., Urbana, OH 43078.
Items Wanted: Collector bears and dolls only.
Payment: Buys outright usually on net 30 days.
Instructions: Send photos. "I no longer buy and sell crafts - only dolls and sometimes bears."

MANSFIELD ART CENTER, 700 Marion Ave., Mansfield, OH 44903.
Items Wanted: The Gallery Shop carries work of original design in all of the art mediums ie, jewelry, glass, fiber, ceramics, wood, paintings, metal, etc. "We do not carry work made from kits!"
Payment: Both wholesale and consignment. Net 30 on wholesale; 60/40 on consignment.
Instructions: Photos and slides accepted as well as wholesale catalogs and price sheets. The gallery shop within the art center is open all year. Contact co-buyers Judy Cole and Judy Bemiller.

MARKET MASTERS, 6800 West 115th, Suite 258, Overland Park, KS 66211.
Items Wanted: This is a giftwares wholesaler working in the Midwest. Always on the lookout for quality crafts that could become collectible, but also wants to see items that are whimsical as well as functional.
Payment: Works on standard commission.
Instructions: Send catalog if you have one along with photos, quantities available, prices, etc.

MARTY WASSERBERG & ASSOCIATES, PO Box 367, New Vernon, NJ 07976.
Items Wanted: This wholesale rep deals in many different type of items including home décor items, nature and wood crafts, florals, and pottery.
Payment: Pays cash on sale minus commission.
Instructions: Send samples, brochure or catalog, wholesale price list, and any other supporting information.

METAL, THE TRANSFORMATION OF MYTH INTO MATTER, 125 Paseo del Pueblo Norte, Taos, NM 87571.
Items Wanted: This is a gallery of one-of-a-kind and limited edition jewelry and art objects made of metal. Especially interested in figurative as well as abstract pieces that bridge the gap between art and function. Items carried are in the $50-$2,500 range.
Payment: Offers consignment contracts.
Instructions: Send for more information and ask for an artist contract.

MIKE FEINBERG CO., 1736 Penn Ave., Pittsburg, PA 15222.
Items Wanted: This rep deals in many different type of items, but is particularly

interested in party supplies. Will also look at toys, novelties, and get-well items.
Payment: Pays cash on sale minus commission.
Instructions: Send samples, brochure or catalog, wholesale price list, and any other supporting information.

MILES KIMBALL, 41 W. 8th Avenue, Oshkosh, WI 54906; www.mileskimball.com.
Items Wanted: This well established mail order catalog carries a wide variety of gifts, home accessories, seasonal items, and garden products.
Payment: Buys with purchase order and pays within 30 days.
Instructions: Submit printed product information, wholesale prices, and photo. Send to the merchandising division. Do not send samples unless requested.

MOONSTONE GALLERY, 4070 Burton Dr., Cambria, CA 93428.
Items Wanted: This gallery carries truly unique items such as kinetic art, kaleidoscopes, moonstone jewelry, holographic glass sculptures, waterfalls, and wood jewelry boxes. Over 200 artists are represented here and the competition is stiff, but if you have something you think will make the grade, they are willing to take a look.
Payment: Both outright purchase and consignment.
Instructions: Send photos, brochures, resume, etc.

MOSSY CREEK POTTERY, Attn: Jeanne Davis, P.O. Box 368, Gleneden Beach, OR 97388.
Items Wanted: Handmade (thrown, slab or?) pottery. No commercial molds, please! All styles, glazes and price ranges considered.
Payment: Cash upon delivery (50% of retail price) of approved items or 60% of retail paid 1st of every month for consignment items.
Instructions: Send photos or slides; bring samples in person. Phone contact best initially; (503)996-2415. Oregon, Washington potters only. "We require exclusive sales rights within 20 mile radius. Willing to work with young or new potters or potters establishing market for new or different items."

NAPERVILLE FINE ART CENTER & GALLERY, 508 N. Center St., Naperville, IL 60563.
Items Wanted: This is a wonderful nonprofit gallery open to all kinds of arts and crafts. Items can be any style or material as long as the design is unique, original, and made with quality.
Payment: Consignment 60/40.
Instructions: Send photos, prices, and lead time needed.

NORTHFIELD ARTS GUILD, Attn: Ellie Lundblad, Executive Director, 304 Division St., Northfield, MN 55057.
Items Wanted: High quality original handcrafted items - more fine arts - less "crafts".
Payment: Consignment: 60 artist/40 shop. Wholesale: 30 days.
Instructions: Send photos, slides and/or samples. "Our shop is part of a center for the arts that includes a gallery, recital room, dance school and classrooms. We'd appreciate having information about the artists represented in the shop since many of our customers like this 'personal' touch."

NORTHWEST IMAGES, 6100 4th Ave. South, Room 363, Seattle, WA 98108.
Items Wanted: Any gift items with a country theme. Only takes on items that can be produced in sufficient quantity for distribution through drug stores, department stores,

and other mass merchandising outlets in the Northwest.
Payment: Pays wholesale prices less commission.
Instructions: Send samples, catalog, letter of introduction, and wholesale and retail price lists.

NOVICA WHOLESALE, 11835 W. Olympic Blvd. Suite 750E, East Tower, Los Angeles, CA 90064; www.novica.com/wholesale.
Items Wanted: NOVICA is one of the world's leading wholesalers of handcrafted products with offices around the world and online. They handle hundreds of unique jewelry, accessories, and home decor collections. Over 100,000 buyers come to the Web site to buy wholesale for their stores.
Payment: Web site order management system tracks all incoming order. Orders and payments are all processed through NOVICA.
Instructions: Visit the Web site and take the "Seller Tour" for instructions.

OCTAGON CENTER FOR THE ARTS, 427 Douglas, Ames, IA 50010.
Items Wanted: Pottery, jewelry, stationery, fiber, children's items, books, wood, metal, sculpture, art.
Payment: Consignment 50/50 paid 15th of the month when items have sold.
Instructions: Contact Alissa Hansen to set up an appointment. Otherwise send letter with photos, slides, etc. "We also buy things outright, but we prefer consignment. We specialize in Iowa handcrafted art and art that coincides with our exhibit in the gallery."

THE ONLINE GIFT SHOW, www.giftswholesale.com.
Items Wanted: This online wholesale business is where 5,000 gift shops, gift basket makers, florists, and other retail businesses come to order their inventory wholesale online. For $19.95 per month, you can present your products and make them available for buyers and reps to view and order without having to have your own Web site.
Payment: Arrangements are made between you and the individual buyers.
Instructions: Visit the Web site for more information.

POOPSIE'S, 107 S. Main St., Galena, IL 61036.
Contact: Susan Landes.
Items Wanted: Eccentric, unusual, and fun crafts of all kinds ranging in price from $5 to $2,000. Always looking for the original, innovative, and delightful. Carries only contemporary quality products.
Payment: Some outright purchase; some consignment.
Instructions: Send photos or slides along with descriptions, prices, and any helpful information about the artist such as how and where products are currently being marketed.

THE POTTER, ETC., Box 305, 331 Main St., Jerome, AZ 86331.
Items Wanted: The shop inventory includes pottery, baskets, jewelry, clothing, candles, books, cards, handwovens, dried floral arrangements, and wall sprays. "We carry only handcrafted items."
Payment: Prefers wholesale purchase, but consignment considered on very high-end items.
Instructions: Send brochures. "We are interested in high quality crafts. I have no crocheted or knitted items nor am I interested in what I call the work of "loving hands at home!"

PRAIRIE HOUSE, 3013 Lindberg Blvd., Springfield, IL 62704.

Items Wanted: Fine contemporary crafts, no country crafts or perishable items. The gallery has been in business for over 30 years and now represents the work of over 300 American artists.

Payment: Prefers purchase, but will consider consignment as long as quality is there.

Instructions: Prefers slides, but photos are acceptable. Include as much documentation as possible such as brochures and show history.

PRINTS & PATCHES, 38 Main St., Stowe, VT 05672.

Items Wanted: Fabric related handmade items that are one of a kind or repeated design of products welcome.

Payment: Consignment: 2/3 goes to artisan.

Instructions: Send samples. "I have an agreement they must sign."

PUTTIN' ON THE DOG, 5140 Shadow Path Lane, Lilburn, GA 30047.

Items Wanted: Canine motif gifts, accessories, and collectibles. This includes art, gifts, apparel, jewelry, etc. Items should be available for at least 15 different breeds and must be breed specific.

Payment: Pays outright.

Instructions: Send information package including product description, dog breeds available, your bio and contact information, wholesale price, availability and delivery time, and photos. Samples are accepted, but will not be returned.

THE QUILT RACQUE, 37 Terrace St., Dallas, PA 18612.

Items Wanted: Quilted wallhangings, runners for the table, placemats, coasters, pillows, and baby quilts.

Payment: Prefers consignment with 2/3 to maker, 1/3 to shop. Will consider purchase if on approval basis for minimum two months.

Instructions: Photos would be best. "I prefer handquilted items but good machine quilted articles are acceptable, if price can be kept moderate. People want handcrafted look but the price will always get compared to the 'imports'. It's a constant education to the public, i.e. quality, handmade one of a kind, etc. My shop is not a fabric shop with supplies, etc. It is a one of a kind finished product, antique and new quilts, linens and lace and - no imported linens or quilts!"

QUILTS LTD., 625 Canyon Road, Sante Fe, NM 87501.

Items Wanted: High quality quilts, pillows, and wearables.

Payment: Consignment; 50/50.

Instructions: Send photos, prices, and SASE to the attention of Trisha.

REFLECTIONS, Attn: Richard, 199 West River St., Leland, MI 49654.

Items Wanted: Prints, posters, greeting cards, crafts, pottery, photography, wood, ship and sailboat models.

Payment: Buys outright or 45% consignment.

Instructions: Send photos or slides, brochures, catalog, or samples. "We've been in business since 1970."

ROAD TO WEALTH, INC., dba DISCOUNT MARKETPLACE,
4631 N.W. 31st Ave., Suite 136, Fort Lauderdale, FL 33309; www.discountmarketplace.com.

Items Wanted: This is a cyber catalog showroom that sells handcrafted items of all kinds wholesale. This is a volume market where over $500,000,000 in orders are processed annually. This is a rare case where the public is invited to buy wholesale as well as store buyers. Looking for products that are unique and acceptable to the world market.

Payment: Orders are drop-shipped by you and payments are processed through the company.

Instructions: Go to the Web site and print out the "Suppliers Form". The form should be mailed or faxed to the Buying Committee.

SAMCO, 5105 Tollview Dr., #180, Rolling Meadows, IL 60008.

Items Wanted: Quality giftwares for distribution in the Midwest.

Payment: Wholesale less 15%.

Instructions: Send samples, catalog, price list, etc.

THE SASSY CAT, 88 N. Main St., Chagrin Falls, OH 44022.

Items Wanted: One-of-a-kind works in wood, fabric, or other materials. Handmade toys and home decorations are especially popular.

Payment: Consignment.

Instructions: Bring in samples.

SASSY SOUTH, Atlanta Apparel Mart, Atlanta, GA 30303.

Items Wanted: Unique hand crafted jewelry for wholesale distribution.

Payment: Works on standard commission.

Instructions: Send photos or slides, brochures, resume, wholesale price list.

SCREAMING FROM LA, 127 East 9th St., Los Angeles, CA 90079.

Items Wanted: This wholesaler deals mostly in the West and the Midwest and is primarily interested in hand crafted jewelry and textiles for the gift market.

Payment: Takes 15% commission from wholesale.

Instructions: Send photos, brochures, complete description of artist's work, price list, etc.

SEVENTEENTH COLONY HOUSE, 3991 Main St., Hilliard, OH 43026.

Items Wanted: Hand carved Santas, Noah's Arks, Uncle Sams, decoys, etc. Woven throws, placemats, jewelry, country stoneware.

Payment: COD or AmEx.

Instructions: Send photos and sizes. "We look for any items that are collectible or can be used in the home."

SHOW OF HANDS, 210 Clayton St, Denver, CO 80206.

Items Wanted: Fine American contemporary craft. No country. No wearables except accessories.

Payment: Purchase/ consignment.

Instructions: Send slides and SASE with description, dimensions, and prices. Slides are viewed the second Tuesday of each month except December.

STATEMENTS UNLIMITED, 17526 Aurora N., Seattle, WA 98133.

Items Wanted: Traditional crafts to be sold in gift and interior design shops throughout the Northwest. Specializes in the Victorian theme.

Payment: Works on standard commission.

Instructions: Send samples and plenty of documentation to prove you can produce the quality and quantity required by a wholesaler.

SUSI'S GALLERY FOR CHILDREN, 348 Huron Ave., Cambridge, MA 02138.
Items Wanted: Whimsical, colorful, jewelry, furniture, clothing, mobiles, and picture frames.
Payment: Consignment 50/50.
Instructions: Send photos or slides. Contact Susi Cooper. "I'm looking for something that appeals to the child in all of us."

TERRY'S COUNTRY SHOPPE, 1049 Queen St., Southington, CT 06489.
Items Wanted: Country items for the home; seasonal, wood, ceramic, etc. No jewelry or contemporary art.
Payment: No consignment, COD, Net 15-30 (preferred).
Instructions: Send written description or photos (no slides) and price list. Include care or safety instructions where required. "We have a 5,000 square foot retail store open year round. We feature many one-of-a-kind items and carry many lines of collectables. We have been in business since 1983."

TOTAL ACCESSORIES, 250 Spring St., NW, Atlanta, GA 30303.
Items Wanted: This wholesaler deals mostly with textiles, but will also consider unique jewelry.
Payment: Pays wholesale prices less commission.
Instructions: Send photos first, then samples if requested. Include price list and thorough description.

THE UNIQUE, 1708 W Colorado Ave., Colorado Springs, CO 80904.
Items Wanted: Handcrafted items in all media; wood, jewelry, glass, etc. Must be of excellent quality and design. Typical "bazaar items" not wanted.
Payment: Pays on the 10th of the month following month of sale.
Instructions: Send photos, slides, or samples. "This is our 30th year in business in the same downtown location."

VILLAGE OF THE SMOKY HILLS, Osage, MN 56570.
Items Wanted: Crafts of all kinds made by local home-based craftspeople are sold at the Village. Currently has over 350 participants.

CLOSEUP: Village of the Smoky Hills

Village of the Smoky Hills is an award-winning cottage industry center in Osage, Minnesota. Fifteen buildings nestled amid 67 acres of pine forest, showcase every imaginable type of handcraft.

Founder Lorelei Kraft came up with the idea in 1984 as a way to employ her neighbors without forfeiting the clear air and natural beauty of the area. At that time, unemployment was over 20%; the area was the poorest in the state. Kraft says she was inspired by Rockefeller's Appalachian quilting project, but rather than send the handcrafted products away to be sold, she gave the plan a whole new twist. She envisioned a village so unique it would not only attract customers, but would charge admissions to cover the cost of personal appearances by the craftspeople.

It took two months to develop the original business plan, during which time Kraft and 11 other social activists formed The Founding Mothers, Inc. From that point, it took only five months to locate the land, apply for a loan, get a zoning variance, build the entire complex, interview and train employees to run it, and open to the public.

Over 350 local artisans bring their products from home to be displayed and sold. The Village takes care of inventory, staffing clerks, advertising, etc. Everything is of high quality, nothing "plastic" is accepted. Each building houses something different; Woodworking, Stenciling, Pottery, Indian Arts, Mrs. Santa's House, Bake Shoppe, Candle-Dipping, Quilting, Stained Glass, "Country", Old-Tyme Photo, and Ice Cream Parlor.

If this sounds like just another cutesy shopping center, it's far from it. In addition to displaying the crafts, the group demonstrates how they are made. The Pavilion in the center of The Commons features special demonstrations throughout the summer. There's soap-making, birchbark weaving, making tea from common plants, spinning and weaving, chain-saw sculptures, tole painting, basket-making, silver-smithing, and more.

Visitors are invited to get involved, too. Want a souvenir T-shirt? Stencil your own! Or dip your own candles, or grind your own flour at the Bake Shoppe. The biggest project so far has been the erection of an authentic log cabin.

The key to the Village's success is participation. 20,000 visitors were expected the first year, but 100,000 came from all over to get involved in all the fun activities. For that, the Village won the State Travel Marketing of the Year Award, swept the top awards at the 1984 Minnesota Tourism Conference, and the Regional Development Award for outstanding tourism development. The latter was won an unprecedented two years in a row.

What's in the future? Kraft sees a lot of growth. Plans are in the works to build another 30 to 50 buildings (on the 500 acres bought recently) which will expand the number of crafts tremendously. A spin-off will be a direct mail catalog.

Kraft describes her group as the "Superstars of Cottage Industry in Minnesota." Not only has her innovation paid off for 350 home workers, but she breathed economic life into an otherwise impoverished area. She says, "We've proved here that cottage industry is a viable (economic) alternative!"

VILLAGE WEAVERS, 418 Villita, San Antonio, TX 78205.
Items Wanted: Handwoven items.
Payment: Consignment: "after item sells we pay 1st day of following month."
Instructions: Contact Romayne Mertens to discuss. "Village Weavers is located in a tourist area along the San Antonio river. Our customers are from - everywhere."

THE WEED LADY, 122 4th Avenue South, Edmonds, WA 98020.
Items Wanted: Quality handcrafts that are unique; rustic bird houses, jewelry, containers, candles, etc.
Payment: Store keeps 35% of consignment; pays quarterly.
Instructions: "We prefer to view items personally. Our shop is somewhere between country and Victorian. We specialize in dried flower products, and do our own floral design work. We carry antiques and do-it-yourself materials such as ribbon, cards, books, etc."

WENDY GORDON GLASS STUDIO, INC., & CRAFT GALLERY, P.O. Box 878, Stevensville, MD 21666.
Items Wanted: Some whimsical and nautical themes in glass, wood, ceramics, fiber, jewelry. (Not limited to described themes though). No country. Priced at $2 to $2,000.
Payment: Consignment, 70% to artist; purchase 50/50.

Instructions: Send photos and prices. Would like to know delivery time as well. The Craft Gallery is on Kent Island in Chesapeake Bay. It also has a working stained glass studio established in 1980.

WHOLESALE CRAFTS, INC., 2783 Martin Rd #125, Dublin, OH 43017; www.wholesalecrafts.com.
Items Wanted: This online wholesaling company is looking for serious handcrafters only. You must have a proven and successful track record supplying at least two retail locations before being considered. No work from kits, patterns, molds, etc. Only quality handcrafts will be considered.
Instructions: Visit the Web site for more information.

WOODSTOCK GALLERY, INC., 904 Green Bay Rd., Winnetka, IL 60093.
Items Wanted: Contemporary fine crafts that are also functional. Materials include glass, ceramics, wood, jewelry, metal and fabric.
Payment: Some purchases and some consignment.
Instructions: Send slides, artist documentation, and wholesale price list.

YVETTE FRY, 54 W 39th St. # 5, New York, NY 10016.
Items Wanted: This nationwide rep is always on the lookout for new handcrafted items such as silver jewelry and accessories.
Payment: Works on 15% commission.
Instructions: Send photos, description, letter from artist, and prices.

TELECOMMUTING AND OTHER EMPLOYEE OPTIONS

If you are like most people, you think that if you want a job working at home, you will have to give up your present job and start from scratch, and look for a new job that could be done at home. The fact is, however, that for 19 million Americans, taking their work home at least one day a week is routine. These home workers are commonly referred to as "telecommuters."

Telecommuting is an often-misused term. It means transporting work to the worker rather than the worker to the workplace. This can be accomplished in a number of ways, but most often it involves the use of electronic communications — telephones, fax machines, the Internet and email.

In this book, telecommuting will be defined as an option open to employees who are currently working for a company and have an express need to take their work home. A temporary need might be illness, temporary disability, pregnancy, or the need to take care of family members. Some workers desire to move home in order to work more productively on long projects, cut down on commuting, or spend more time with family.

Some telecommuting is done temporarily, some is part-time, and some is permanent. It is becoming a very common option in the corporate world with as many as 500 corporations reporting some kind of work-at-home option available to employees on an informal basis. A few of those have formal programs with the rules for working at home laid out in very specific detail.

If you are already working and you want to work at home, look in your own back yard first. Many employees have the opportunity to work at home and just don't know it. Before looking elsewhere for a new job that can be done at home, why not start by discussing with your manager the possibility of moving your present job home? You might be surprised by the answer.

The listings in this section should be considered as examples of successful telecommuting programs only. None of them are open to inquiries from anyone who is not currently an employee.

Moving Your Work Home

Moving your present job from its current location to your home is an option that you should explore before looking for a new employer.

Large corporations are most likely to accept the telecommuting arrangement. Of the several hundred major corporations in the U.S. that have home workers on the payroll, few hire home workers directly from the outside. As a rule, they want to develop confidence in their employees before allowing them to take their work home. Therefore, the very first thing to do is make sure you are known for being a valuable and trustworthy employee.

Next, develop a plan of action. Define the job tasks, which are feasible for homework. Don't ignore problems that could arise later and undermine your position. Consider all of the possible problems and devise a "worst case" scenario and alternative solutions for dealing with each of them. That way, you will be prepared and can confidently assure your company there will be no unpleasant surprises.

You will need to sell your homework idea to your employer, focusing on the ways moving your work home will benefit the company. Remember, your employer is in business to make a profit, and while he/she probably prefers happy employees, the bottom line is ultimately the highest priority. You can take comfort in the fact that the benefits employers gain from work-at-home arrangements are well documented. If you want to refer to some success stories, see the company profiles scattered throughout this book. In addition, the following information is likely to grab your employer's attention.

The number one benefit to employers is increased productivity. The best-documented cases are from Blue Cross/Blue Shield of South Carolina, which reported productivity gains of 50%, and from Control Data Corp., which showed gains of 35%. Employees at home tend to work at their individual peak hours, don't get paid for long lunch hours and time spent at the water cooler, and often continue to work while feeling slightly under the weather rather than take time off.

The second greatest benefit to employers is the cost savings from not spending money on additional office space, utilities, parking space, etc. This is especially helpful for growing companies and also for home-based businesses that need to expand, but want to limit the costs of doing so. Some companies have even sent employees home and rented out the unoccupied space to compatible firms. As a direct result of its homework program, Pacific Bell closed three offices in one year, saving $40,000 in rent alone.

Another advantage to employers is a far lower turnover rate among employees allowed to work at home. In some industries, rapid turnover is a serious problem. The insurance industry, for instance, has a turnover rate between 30% and 45%. As you would expect, recruiting and training costs are very high in such industries.

Even governments have come to view telecommuting as a viable solution to some of society's most pressing problems-air pollution, traffic congestion, and energy consumption. It has been estimated that a 20% reduction in commuting nationwide could save 110,000 barrels of gasoline a day! For these reasons, several states-including California, Washington, and North Dakota-have formally endorsed telecommuting. California even offers tax incentives to companies that will send some of its employees home to work.

All of this should give you ample ammunition to convince your manager(s) to let you try working at home. It's usually best not to try for an immediate move to full-time homework, though. Start slowly, asking to take your work home a couple of times in the afternoon, and then proposing a two-day project. While you're testing the waters, make sure you check in by phone to see if anything has come up at the office that you need to take care of. After a few months of occasional home work, you'll be ready to go to your manager and point out that you get more accomplished when you're not distracted by office routines and don't have to waste valuable time commuting. Remember, you're not asking for favors. You are simply offering what every employer wants-a motivated, efficient worker interested in increasing productivity.

COMPANIES WITH TELECOMMUTING PROGRAMS

ADC TELECOMMUNICATIONS, INC., Minnesota.

ADC makes telecommuting an option for employees as the need arises. An employee need only get the okay from their supervisor.

AETNA LIFE & CASUALTY, Connecticut.

Aetna has a formal program that includes over 2,000 employees. Among the telecommuters are claims representatives, sales consultants, claims processors, and account consultants.

AIR PRODUCTS & CHEMICALS, INC., Pennsylvania.

This is a very large company with over 10,000 employees. Of those, only 50 are telecommuters, which is actually a small percentage. There is no formal arrangement and telecommuting is allowed on an individual basis as needed.

ALLERGAN, INC., California.

Allergan is a well-known manufacturer of eye care products. For the last decade, company programmers have been working at home due to lack of space at company headquarters. The policy has saved the company considerable money (from not having to expand) and given employees freedom and flexibility.

ALLSTATE INSURANCE COMPANY, Illinois.

Allstate's telecommuting program originally started as an option for disabled employees, all of whom were programmers. The first was a systems programmer who was injured in a car accident. Then came some entries placed by Lift, Inc. Now, Allstate is open to the telecommuting option for any current employee with a job suitable to be taken home on an alternating schedule.

AMERICAN EXPRESS TRAVEL RELATED SERVICES COMPANY, INC., New York.

Over 50 travel counselors are offered telecommuting as an incentive program to top performers only.

AMERICAN INSTITUTES FOR RESEARCH, California.
Ten researchers and analysts telecommute; each has made individual arrangements to do so.

AMERITECH CORPORATION, Illinois.
Most of Ameritech's 250 telecommuters are in sales or customer service.

AMF BOWLING PRODUCTS GROUP, INC., New York.
Office-based employees are provided with computer terminals and telecommunications equipment for after-hours telecommuting. Most telecommuting is done by company programmers.

AMTRAK, Washington, DC.
Amtrak's Customer Relations Group has increased its productivity and employee morale by implementing telecommuting on a small scale. Nine writers in the group work at home on a rotating schedule, with one writer working one day at home, then the next taking one day, and so on.

ANASAZI, INC., Arizona.
Programmers, engineers, and other high level technical personnel work at home. Company is very careful who is selected for telecommuting. Only persons who have proven that they are self-managing, have some experience working at home, and have proper technical equipment can participate. Employee status remains intact.

ANDREWS GLASS COMPANY, INC., New Jersey.
Glass lamp work and tool work on laboratory glass products is dispensed as an option for extra income for after-hours work for established employees only.

APOLLO GROUP, INC., Arizona.
Apollo Group is the corporation that owns University of Phoenix. About 100 employees in various positions ranging from enrollment representatives to financial aid coordinators work from home.

APPLE COMPUTER, INC., California.
Telecommuting at Apple is a natural. All employees receive an Apple computer for their home use and are part of the company's electronic network automatically. Couple that with the company's liberal attitude toward its employees in general and you have a lot of people working at home whenever it seems appropriate.

ARIZONA, DEPARTMENT OF ADMINISTRATION, Arizona.
The state of Arizona began telecommuting in 1990. Now over 800 employees work at home.

ARTHUR ANDERSEN & COMPANY, Illinois.
Only about 80 of this company's 64,000 employees work at home. They are mostly in management positions, although the arrangement is open to all employees. The company's telecommuting program launched in 1998 formally and is considered to be just one of several flexible work options.

AT&T, California.
AT&T, like most of the "Baby Bells," is not only a participant in the telecommuting

trend, but a leader as well. The company took a giant step forward when it launched "Telecommuting Day" back in 1994.

Telecommuting is so commonplace within the company that it is hard to estimate how many employees take advantage of the option at any given time. However, it is estimated that as many as 29% of the total workforce are indeed telecommuters. That's tens of thousands! The policy is so liberal even newly hired employees can arrange to telecommute right from the start if that is the custom of the group they will be working with.

In addition, AT&T helps set up telecommuting programs for other companies in the Southern California area.

BALTIMORE EVENING SUN, Maryland.

The work-at-home option, used by writers of all kinds, is available to any employee with the necessary equipment.

BANKERS TRUST COMPANY, New York.

Bankers Trust conducted its initial telecommuting pilot program with the help of Electronic Services Unlimited. Twenty employees worked at home for six months on a part-time basis only. The usual time spent at home working was two days a week unless the particular project allowed for longer periods of time. Employees were supplied with IBM PCs tied into the mainframe in Manhattan. The work was done in the local mode using and transferring floppies. The pilot was successful so the program has been expanded to include more people.

BATTERYMARCH FINANCIAL MANAGEMENT COMPANY, Massachusetts.

Batterymarch is an international investment-counseling firm with $12 billion worth of funds, mostly corporate pensions, to manage. Operation requires a 24-hour vigilance in order to keep up with world markets. Most employees, 30 out of 35, have terminals at home connected to the company's mainframe. 20 professional brokers are also "on-line" with their own PCs. If a broker has a problem with the system, he/she can call one of the others at home for help. Throughout the night, the company's "Phantom Program" monitors the system automatically and transmits wake-up calls if something goes wrong.

"We've been using this system for over 10 years. Since starting the work-at-home routine, our productivity has increased tremendously. The owner had a vision that at some time everyone would work at home unless they absolutely could not."

BELL ATLANTIC, Pennsylvania.

Bell Atlantic has over 1,500 full-time telecommuters and many other employees who telecommute from time to time. Most are claims representatives and consultants.

BELL COMMUNICATIONS, New Jersey.

Experienced employees in the Research Department can make arrangements with their managers to take their work home on a project-by-project basis. There have been some full-time telecommuters, but the situation is not the rule.

BELL SOUTH, Arizona.

Bell South conducted an experimental two-year telecommuting program before making it a company-wide policy. Telecommuters are all regular employees of Bell South and include both high-tech and low-tech personnel, mostly middle managers and marketers.

BENEFICIAL CORPORATION, New Jersey.
Data processors and the top brass share the telecommuting option at Beneficial.

BEST WESTERN HOTELS INTERNATIONAL, Arizona.
This is an interesting project where the home workers telecommute from their home in prison. About 10 women prisoners in the Arizona State Prison handle telephone reservations for the hotel chain. They are provided with computer terminals, telecommunications hookups, extra phone lines, and complete training.

BLUE CROSS/BLUE SHIELD OF MARYLAND, Maryland.
This particular branch of Blue Cross/Blue Shield allows experienced employees to work at home as cottage keyers. They are part-time employees with part-time benefits.

BLUE CROSS/BLUE SHIELD OF THE NATIONAL CAPITOL AREA, Washington, DC.
This program was fashioned after the similar program at Blue Cross/Blue Shield of South Carolina's data entry program. Basically, cottage keyers enter data from insurance claims directly into the company's mainframe. The main difference is that here, all cottage keyers are former employees. Each worker has a quota of at least 400 claims per day. PC terminals with modems are leased to the home workers. The company pays so much per claim on a biweekly basis.

BOOKMINDERS, INC., Pennsylvania.
This is a unique company that provides bookkeeping services to over 200 small companies. It operates with a virtual staff meaning everyone works from home. Each time an employee is hired, a technician is dispatched to the worker's home office to do the necessary installations including software and phone lines.

BORG-WARNER CHEMICAL COMPANY, West Virginia.
Sales personnel are equipped with PCs at home, which are hooked up to the company's mainframe. Telecommunications capabilities include E-mail. Sales people can now do analysis and forecasting without going into the office. Other professionals on staff are similarly equipped and can work at home as the need arises.

BRISTOL-MYERS SQUIBB COMPANY, New York.
Working Mother Magazine named this corporation one of the best companies in America for working mothers three years running. Among the many flexible work options for women in this company is telecommuting. The option is available to the 44,000 employees company-wide.

BRONNER MANUFACTURING AND TOOL COMPANY, New Jersey.
Work to take home is assigned only to regular in-house employees that wish to earn extra money at home. Work involves milling, turning, deburring, drilling, and lathe work. Pays piece rates.

BROWN WILLIAMSON TOBACCO COMPANY, Kentucky.
Systems programmers work on a contract basis and divide their time between home and office. Only programmers that were previously employed in-house are chosen.

CALIFORNIA STATE DEPARTMENT OF GENERAL SERVICES, California.
After two years of planning, The California State Telecommuting Project was finally

conducted. State workers from 14 different state agencies volunteered to participate. That included anyone who thought his/her job could be done at home can volunteer. About 200 participated in the pilot program with job titles ranging from clerk typists to managers. Locations included the greater Los Angeles area, San Francisco, and (primarily) Sacramento.

Telecommuters were outfitted with PCs and ergonomically correct furniture. An electronic bulletin board replaced the "water cooler" as the center of internal communications. All workers were required to return to the office of origin at least once a week.

Jack Nilles, sometimes known as the "father of telecommuting" wrote the 150-page "Plan For Success" and was been selected to direct the project. David Fleming, who initiated the idea, hoped the experiment would serve as an example of successful telecommuting and thereby open up telecommuting opportunities elsewhere in government and private industry. To that end, many aspects will be monitored and evaluated to conclude how much fuel was saved, effects on traffic flow, possible effects on air quality, etc.

Fleming was gratified by the success of the program and the State has implemented and hugely expanded the program.

CHATAS GLASS COMPANY, New Jersey.

Glassblowing and grinding of laboratory glassware can be done as a secondary income opportunity by established employees. Only part-time work is allowed at home. Pick up and delivery of supplies and finished work is provided. This is handwork, so no machinery is needed. Pays piece rates.

CHILTON CREDIT REPORTING, Massachusetts.

In-house employees must be thoroughly experienced before moving work home. About 14 workers have taken advantage of the option. They proof computer sheets and analyze the "decisions" made by the computers. Pays piece rates equaling approximately the same as in-house workers doing similar work.

CIGNA CORPORATION, Pennsylvania.

Several hundred employees telecommute including underwriters, claims representatives, and accountants.

CITIBANK, New York.

Citibank offers telecommuting as an option to regular employees on an informal basis as the need arises. Employees most often work at home during temporarily disability or pregnancy.

COLORADO DEPARTMENT OF PERSONNEL, Colorado.

About 60 employees in a wide variety of positions telecommute in a formal program.

COLORADO NATIONAL BANK, Colorado.

This major Colorado bank started telecommuting by conducting a pilot telecommuting program within the MIS department only. The purpose of the project was to determine whether telecommuting could help cut costs as it has in so many other organizations. The telecommuters wrote systems documentation four days a week. The workers provided their own PCs. Colorado National subsequently expanded the program to include other employees at the end of the pilot phase.

THE COMPUCARE COMPANY, Virginia.
Several high level employees have found working at home necessary for various personal reasons.

CURTIS 1000, Connecticut.
Company offers homework arrangement as option to in-house employees with proven need. For example, one disabled worker does hand inserting and other mail processing work at home.

DATA GENERAL CORPORATION, Massachusetts.
Data General manufactures, designs, and sells business systems. One product is the "Comprehensive Electronic Office" system, which includes e-mail, spreadsheet analysis and more. Working at home is an option to in-house employees on a departmental level. Those taking advantage of the option are most often programmers, engineers, and word processors involved in software development.
Employee's department is responsible for providing necessary equipment, generally a PC and modem which will be logged onto the company mainframe. This is usually older equipment that has already been costed out. "Working at home has proven to be a convenient and useful tool. The key benefits are convenience and being close to family."

DECORATED PRODUCTS COMPANY, Massachusetts.
About 8 employees here make extra money by taking extra work home. They inspect nameplates manufactured at the plant. They are required to pick up and deliver the work themselves. Pays piece rates.

DENVER, CITY AND COUNTY, Colorado.
In an effort to combat air pollution in the Denver area, the city and county offers telecommuting wherever it was feasible. There are now about 150 employees including data entry operators, engineers, and supervisors working at home on a regular basis.

DETROIT FREE PRESS, Michigan.
Reporters, columnists, and editors telecommute. PCs are supplied. Work is transmitted to mainframe via telecommunications network. Examples of telecommuters include one-person bureaus in Los Angeles and Toronto, and a columnist who lives 40 minutes away from the office and has no reason to commute anyway for that type of work. Telecommuting was implemented as a company policy in 1984. Detroit Free Press also has several home-based freelance photographers who work on an assignment basis. Currently has about 20 home workers. All telecommuters are staff members and are paid the same salary and benefits they would receive if they were in-house. Freelancers are paid by the job.

DIGITAL EQUIPMENT CORPORATION, Massachusetts.
Digital, like Apple, has a very progressive attitude about its employees. Most of the technical workers have computers in their home offices and are allowed to work at home at their own discretion. Informally, the number of telecommuters (who work at home only part of the time) may run into the thousands.

EASTMAN KODAK COMPANY, New York.
About 25 sales representatives work from home with full benefits.

116

EQUITABLE LIFE ASSURANCE, New Jersey.

Telecommuting started here with several programmers and managers participating in the company's telecommuting program. Work involved database development, technical support, troubleshooting, budgeting, project monitoring and progress reporting. All equipment was supplied. Home terminals were connected to the large mainframe IMS. There was also a generous allowance for furniture. Employees were salaried with employee status intact. After final review of pilot, Equitable decided to expand telecommuting option to other departments.

CLOSE UP: Equitable Life Assurance

Success is a word that is rapidly becoming synonymous with telecommuting pilot programs. Equitable Life Assurance is no exception.

In 1992, Equitable relocated some of its departments from corporate headquarters in midtown Manhattan to Secaucus, New Jersey. For most employees involved, this was merely a matter of traveling in a different direction; some even lived in New Jersey and it meant less traveling. But, for those who lived on Long Island, travel time would double and it was feared that would be too much for some.

It was clear that something had to be done to avoid the costs of replacing valuable personnel. Telecommuting was offered to key people as an incentive to stay with Equitable. Six people, programmers, analysts, and one administrative assistant, were encouraged to stay home two or three days a week. They were each given all necessary equipment, a $400 furniture allowance, and retained their salary levels and employment status.

Telecommuting project coordinator, Jack Tyniec, credits Electronic Services Unlimited with providing the necessary training and guidance. ESU worked closely with Equitable's legal department, personnel manager, and prospective telecommuting managers to avoid problems in advance.

"We had no idea how many things could just creep out of the woodwork. ESU helped us spell out the issues and deal with them in advance - things like local zoning restrictions, labor laws, insurance liability both for company provided medical coverage and Workmen's Compensation, and even seemingly innocent wordings in our company personnel policy."

Words like "...work to be performed in company office...," found in standard employment contracts, may not have been intended to restrict working at home, but that is the legal effect, Tyniec points out. To rectify that situation, a supplementary contract was drawn up to specifically allow work at home.

The first formal review of the Equitable telecommuting program indicated that all was going well. The telecommuters loved it, Tyniec says, and their managers were equally enthusiastic. "Not only have we kept good people, but productivity has increased as well. We've measured productivity in terms of quality, not quantity, from a managerial point of view. The managers were unanimously in favor of continuing the program. The consensus is that these people (telecommuters) were good anyway, but now they're even better."

Telecommuting has since been formally integrated into Equitable's overall personnel policy. "It will spread now of its own accord," says Tyniec. "Our personnel manager gave a presentation to other company PMs at their urging. It seems that somebody has to slay the dragons first, but once that's been done and it's been clearly demonstrated that it works, others will follow. At least for corporations, someone has to champion the effort to get telecommuting started."

FEDERAL RESERVE BANK, Georgia.

Federal Reserve Bank offers a work-at-home option to its regular professional staff. First started as an experiment in the early 80's with more than 65 employees in the research department participating, working at home is now an option incorporated into departmental policy for anyone who performs tasks such as writing or editing either full-time or part-time. Computers, when used, are usually PCs owned by the employees. "Reports of our home work program have been greatly exaggerated by the media. When they (employees) can work better at home, they do. It's a simple as that."

FIRST NATIONAL BANK OF CHICAGO, Illinois.

This company has a formal home work program intended especially for data processing and other non-technical personnel. Program guidelines are designed to insure success. "It basically uses a foundation of trust and it's up to the managers to make it work. There is support from top management in the company." There are no number goals or monitoring of employees. Working at home is considered a career option, which managers can use as a possible solution to employees' problems as they arise. "We've had some good experiences. In the case of some clerical, there has been a 30% increase in productivity." Any necessary equipment is paid for by the business unit budget. This is a program for experienced current employees only.

FT. COLLINS, Colorado

Working at home is a citywide option open to all city employees. If work can be done at home, it will be permitted. Several hundred city employees are currently working at home in Ft. Collins. Any necessary equipment, furniture, or supplies will be provided. Employees retain full status, pay and benefits.

GANNETT, Virginia.

Newspaper reporters and editors who are currently employed by Gannett can work at home with manager approval.

GE PLASTICS, West Virginia.

Although the bulk of GE Plastics 100 telecommuters are sales and sales support staff, anyone here may telecommute as long as there is manager approval. Most employees have their own computers at home, but the company will sometimes supply the necessary equipment for telecommuting.

GENERAL TELEPHONE, California.

GTE first experimented with telecommuting during the '84 Summer Olympics as part of a citywide call for people to reduce commuting as much as possible. The pilot program involved technical and programming personnel and systems analysts. All were provided with PCs, modems, printers, and pagers and all were kept on straight salary. The experiment was considered a complete success and now GTE is broadening the scope of telecommuting across departmental lines. Planners of the program feel management skills should improve after telecommuting employees are trained in self-management skills and managers learn to gauge productivity rather than count heads. GTE is also participating in telecommuting as part of the Southern California Association of Governments' plan to reduce traffic congestion and pollution. "We think telecommuting over a period of time will have a substantial impact on traffic in Southern California. There is a lot of potential here."

GEORGIA POWER, Georgia.

Like many government entities endorsing telecommuting, Georgia Power has done so in response to environmental problems, in this case smog in the Atlanta area. Workers across the board are encouraged to work at home, particularly on official smog alert days. Those telecommuting on a regular basis - and there are over 250 of them - have a budget of up to $9,000 to cover the expenses of a computer and other home office necessities.

GTE, California.

Over 400 employees including administrative staff and marketing representatives telecommute in GTE's formal telecommuting program.

HARRIS TRUST AND SAVINGS BANK, Illinois.

Harris Trust has an informal agreement that allows certain experienced employees to work at home on computer terminals to complete paperwork.

HARTFORD INSURANCE GROUP, Connecticut.

Hartford first conducted a telecommuting pilot project in 1995 with guidelines developed by a special committee. Employees, all volunteers, were required to have a good performance record with the company, be highly productive, not be working on "sensitive projects", and have a manager's approval. Each worked four days a week at home and one day a week at the office. Hartford supplied computer equipment hooked up to the company's mainframe plus extra phone lines. Employee status and salary remained unchanged.

Although some problems were reported early on, telecommuting has since been integrated into Hartford's overall personnel policy. There are currently about 4,000 employees working at home. Each has been supplied with equipment, furniture, and office supplies.

HEWLETT PACKARD LABORATORIES, California.

Working at home as an option is offered department-wide. Home workers (over 3,000) are usually programmers, hardware and software engineers, applications engineers, research scientists, speechwriters, and managers. Most work at home part of the time during the week; some do so in addition to in-house work. Equipment is provided as necessary. Individuals are responsible for their own phone bills, but can avoid toll charges by calling the company mainframe and requesting a callback - made at company expense.

HOLT, RINEHART, & WINSTON, New York.

In-house copy editors and proofreaders can get permission to work at home if they have a need for any personal reason. Employees must have editor's approval.

HOMEQUITY, INC., Connecticut.

Telecommuters do programming, evaluating, systems analysis, and software development. Homequity is a leading relocation service company. Its primary business consists of finding new housing for transferred corporate employees. Phase One of the telecommuting pilot project lasted about four months and gave the company a chance to evaluate cost savings and productivity. The initial findings were excellent and Phase Two, "continuation and expansion," is now in progress. Since most of the participants in Phase One were computer personnel, they were supplied with PCs and modems. "Telecommuting only makes sense because the future of this business is in computers."

HONEYWELL, INC., Minnesota.

Working at home is an informal option for Honeywell employees on a departmental level. One example of its use involves handicapped phone operators. The operators have dedicated phone lines in their homes which route long distance calls on weekend and nights. Calls are relayed from Honeywell employees on the road who don't have access to touch-tone phones. Home-based operators patch through the calls, using a network. Pays salary plus benefits.

HOUSEHOLD INTERNATIONAL, Illinois.

This financial services company has several dozen telecommuters, mostly working in customer service.

THE H.W. WILSON COMPANY, New York.

Like Information Access Company (see below), this company is in the abstracting and indexing field. Although the number is smaller than its competitor, H.W. Wilson's indexers also work at home utilizing the company's electronic network and Federal Express.

IBM, New York.

Home-based work is a company option for IBM employees only. IBM has provided over 8,000 PCs for its employees to use at home, either part-time during regular business hours or after hours. Working at home is allowed during regular hours on a project basis as a convenience to employees. The company recently participated in a formal two-year telecommuting experiment conducted by The Center for Futures Research at U.S.C.

INDUSTRIAL INDEMNITY INSURANCE, California.

Approximately 125 insurance auditors in the company have been outfitted with Visual Commuter Portable Computers, Hayes modems, HP printers, and Super Audit software at the expense of the company. The purpose was to reduce commuting time to and from the office and to increase overall productivity. Both goals have been achieved.

INFORMATION ACCESS COMPANY, California.

This company collects information from magazines and trade journals to maintain databases, including Magazine Index, Management Contents, and Trade and Industry Index; all of which are found in most libraries. At one time, Information Access had a fairly large homework operation with over 150 home-based indexers. Upon moving the operation to California, however, the homework program was scaled back severely. Now home-based indexers work only on weekly or monthly publications so deadlines can be met comfortably.

Workers come in once or twice a week to get supplies, materials, and any special instructions and to meet with their supervisor.

Company provides Apple PCs and special software. (Indexes are written on disks,

CLOSE UP:
Fort Collins, Colorado

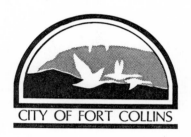

Ft. Collins, Colorado, a city of 85,000 located 60 miles north of Denver, is the first municipality to institute routine telecommuting. The foundation for the project is a large electronic mail network set up by Peter Dallow, Information and Communications Systems Director. The system was originally designed as a good means of communications between city employees and city council members. Each user had to be supplied with a computer, of course, and once several hundred of them were linked together by the system, telecommuting was simply the next logical step.

Asked about surveys or other scientific bases for the project, Dallow shrugs off any such notion. "It was no big deal once the equipment was in place."

As a matter of fact, the program's policies and procedures are found on a one-page sheet outlining blanket acquisition procedures for necessary hardware and software. Any other issues that may arise will be handled on a case-by-case basis. Thus far, no problems have been reported.

"Normally, you don't tell an employee to be sure and take home some supplies—that would be called pilfering. But, now we encourage them to take home the whole office," says Dallow.

It would take a lot of software, disk drives and other equipment and supplies to equal the cost of building more office space. The personal computers had to be purchased regardless of where they would be used, and telecommuting has proven to be an excellent way to deal with Ft. Collins' office space crunch.

Several hundred city workers on many different levels are now participating in the project, which includes council members, accountants, data processors, rate analysts for the utility department and secretaries. Most work at home part of the time with a small percentage doing so full-time. Prime candidates for telecommuting, says Dallow, are top level professionals such as programmers and systems engineers. Just about everybody is eligible for part-time participation except the police and fire fighters.

Dallow cites benefits for both the workers and the city. For the workers, there is flexibility, job enrichment, a way to retain employee status during maternity leave, and new opportunities for Ft. Collins' handicapped citizens. For the city, there is increased productivity, a partial solution to the office space problem, lower costs, greater employee retention and the ability to attract employees in otherwise hard-to-fill jobs.

which are returned to the office.) Workers are full-time employees with benefits and promotional opportunities equal to those of their in-house counterparts. Home indexers are used because they are more productive and have fewer errors.

JET PROPULSION LABORATORY, California.
Telecommuting is an employee option to be used only for health reasons.

LAFAYETTE VENETIAN BLIND, Indiana.
About 40 sales representatives work at home on a full-time basis.

LANIER BUSINESS PRODUCTS, INC, Georgia.
Lanier makes "Telestaf," a product used in telecommuting, which was used in American Express' initial homebound training program. It includes features such as voice mail and is transcription-facilitated. Within Lanier, homework is allowed as a necessary option. Usually home workers are word processors and secretaries working at home part-time as the need arises.

LENCO ELECTRONIC, INC., Illinois.
Lenco is an electronic manufacturing company. Experienced employees perform a small part of the job at home, connecting and soldering wires onto transformers.

ARTHUR D. LITTLE, INC., Massachusetts.
Telecommuting is an informal option offered to staff members. Most telecommuting is done by information systems consultants. Equipment is provided as necessary.

LOS ANGELES COUNTY, California.
In 1989, Los Angeles County joined a small, but growing, number of government entities that have decided to combat the problems associated with heavy work-related traffic with a telecommuting program. About 150 county employees started working at home as part of the initial pilot program. As many as 2,000 of the county's 17,000 employees could be telecommuting within the next 5 years. All departments have been instructed to identify and select potential telecommuters within their employee pools.

MARINE MIDLAND BANK, New York.
Regular employees of Marine Midland have the option of working at home as the need arises. The option is most often taken by professionals on staff in cases of temporary disability or pregnancy. The company is planning to develop more definitive guidelines for telecommuting in the future after current reorganization is completed.

MCDONALD DOUGLAS, California.
At one time (before the company went through reorganization) there were 200 full-time telecommuters, plus another 2,000 employees that worked at home part of the time. These were mostly consultants, project managers, sales and marketing personnel, programmers, and engineers. Homework is not quite as prevalent now, but it is still an available option on an informal basis. Any experienced worker whose job can be done at home can request permission from the manager in charge of their department.

MEGAHERTZ CORPORATION, Utah.
It only makes sense that a company that designs and manufactures communications products for mobile computer operators would have telecommuters. About three dozen

sales representatives and their managers work from home.

MELLON BANK, Pennsylvania.
Mellon Bank has made personal computers available to its programmers and other personnel for several years. Mostly the PCs are used at home for after-hours work, but some employees, programmers in particular, can work at home full-time on a project-by-project basis. Working at home is also used as a perk to boost the morale of management level employees.

MERRILL LYNCH, New York.
This leading financial services provider has been endorsing telecommuting for seven years now. Currently there are about 2,500 employees working at home.
The company does not offer telecommuting frivolously. Investing in home office equipment is just the beginning of the process. Home offices are inspected for safety and ergonomics at the outset and employees are thoroughly trained in all aspects of working at home including technical as well as psychological ones.
In addition, each is expected to attend the "Telework Simulation Lab" for six full days before beginning any work at home. Think of this as a sensory deprivation experience. The participant has access to a computer, phone/fax, and that's it!

METROPOLITAN LIFE INSURANCE COMPANY, New York.
Metropolitan has several handicapped computer programmers trained by Lift, Inc. (see listing). Agents are also home-based. Necessary equipment and phone lines are provided. All home workers are paid full benefits.

METROPOLITAN WATER DISTRICT OF SOUTHERN CALIFORNIA, California.
This is one of several southern California government agencies that entered into a formal telecommuting program as a way to ease traffic congestion and air pollution. Most of the 50 telecommuters are computer programmers.

MONSANTO AGRICULTURAL GROUP, Missouri.
About 25 employees, mostly involved in computer programming, telecommute under informal arrangements.

MONTGOMERY WARD & COMPANY. INC., Illinois.
Montgomery Ward uses home-based workers to handle mail opening and other jobs involved in the direct mail operation for insurance companies and other financial service clients. Only current employees or people referred by employees are considered. All are local residents.

MULTILINK INCORPORATED, Massachusetts.
MultiLink is in the teleconferencing business, so telecommuting comes naturally. About a dozen employees involved in setting up teleconferences do so from home.

NEW YORK LIFE INSURANCE COMPANY, New York.
About two dozen home workers are insurance claims processors and contract programmers. Equipment is provided as necessary. Employees retain in-house status and benefits.

NORTEL NETWORKS, North Carolina.

This company is another natural candidate for telecommuting since it produces telecommunications equipment. The HomeBase program has been successfully operating since 1994.

Telecommuting is huge and growing at a steady clip here with 250 more employees heading home each month and a total of over 5,000 already there.

The company not only pays to outfit home offices for its full-time telecommuters, it even has several office modules available on display to choose from. And that includes furniture.

NORTH CAROLINA NATIONAL BANK, North Carolina.

Telecommuting is being offered on a limited basis, along with other work options, as part of this company's personnel policy. The purpose of offering options is to answer some of the family issues raised in an employee survey. Currently, three women are taking advantage of the telecommuting option by dividing their work equally between home and office.

NORTHWESTERN BELL INFORMATION TECHNOLOGIES, Nebraska.

Northwestern Bell conducted a two-year telecommuting experiment involving middle managers, marketing personnel, and data processing personnel. The guidelines for the program were developed by the Center for Futures Research at USC. After conclusion of the experiment, telecommuting was evaluated and integrated into the company's permanent overall policy.

ORTHO PHARMACEUTICAL CORPORATION, New Jersey.

Although telecommuting started small here with just a handful of computer programmers and data processors, it is an option that is being offered to any employee who deems it appropriate. Supervisors have reported increased productivity; therefore many more employees will likely be working at home in the future with management's blessing.

ACIFIC BELL, California.

Engineers, marketing planners, project managers, forecasters, analysts, programmers and some technicians and service reps work for Pacific Bell at home. Currently has over 200 telecommuters in both Northern California and Southern California. Though not all positions require computers, PCs are supplied as necessary. Pagers and extra phone lines are also provided as necessary.

PEAT, MARWICK, MITCHELL & COMPANY, New York.

Throughout its 100 offices nationwide, this major accounting firm has provided its field auditors with MacIntosh computers in order to increase productivity. The auditors are now able to work for several days without actually returning to the office.

Like most major accounting firms, this one also has a "stable" of on-call accountants that handle assignments on a freelance basis during peak periods. These independent accountants are mostly former employees or are highly recommended by current employees.

J.C. PENNEY COMPANY, INC., New York.

Telemarketers take catalog orders in Milwaukee, Columbus, Sacramento, Richmond, Buffalo Grove (Illinois) and Atlanta, where the company catalog distribution centers are located. This program has increased from about 18 home workers in 1981 to over 200 today, making it one of the largest and most technologically advanced

Rick Higgins, Pacific Bell Marketing Manager

CLOSEUP: Pacific Bell

Pacific Bell has a work-at-home program that, after only five months, was hailed as a complete success. While most telecommuting programs to date have been designed specifically for data processing personnel only, from the start Pac Bell wanted to prove that any job could be done at home. And they have done just that.

75 employees went home in the program's first year, and 100 more are expected to make the move shortly. All are volunteers and no restrictions have been placed on job titles. The range of job classifications is broad-everything from marketing personnel to engineers.

Computers are used only by those who needed them before moving their work home. Second phone lines and pagers are the most added equipment. Geographically, the home workers are spread out all over the state of California.

Being closer to clients was the first noticeable benefit. "This made us much more effective in servicing our clients," says Leslie Crawford, Marketing Manager for the Pacific Bell Telecommuting Department. "We soon realized how much 'windshield time' (time wasted behind the wheel commuting) was actually being spent on driving to the office first, then to the client."

The company was naturally pleased to improve service to clients, but there have been other benefits as well. For one thing, moving the work home has resulted in closing three offices with savings on space leases totaling $40,000 annually. There were no deliberate plans to close the first office; all the employees went home and there simply was no one left to mind the store. Two other offices then closed down and several more are expected to close soon.

But the biggest advantage to the program, according to Crawford, is flexibility for everyone concerned-for the company, for the employees, and for the clients. Increased flexibility has meant many jobs have been redefined with a new look at what they are, what they should accomplish, and how.

The program is working so well that Pac Bell's account executives have been looking at telecommuting as a possible solution to clients' problems. Pointing to themselves as a prime example is often the best way to sell the idea. "To some, however, the very word 'telecommuting' sounds foreign. To them, we point out that their own salespeople have been doing it for years. Telecommuting is just a new word to describe it. When they realize that, it doesn't seem like such a weird idea after all."

This may all sound unrealistically positive, but when asked about disadvantages, Crawford said she couldn't think of any. "Maybe it's because everyone in the program volunteered," she said. "They knew their jobs, their managers knew them, and they knew from the advance planning what to expect. No one has voiced a problem and no one has left the program.

If there is a problem, she added, it would be not enough people. "More bodies in more homes around the state would be good for us," she laughs, "We are very, very pleased with the success of our telecommuting program and the enthusiasm with which it has been received. It has already been established that telecommuting works for data processing professionals. Now we have proved it is possible for all fields."

---

telecommuting programs in the country. Computer terminals (hooked up to the company mainframe) are supplied, along with two phone lines - one for data and one for voice contact with the customer. Supervisors visit home workers to make sure the homework space is adequate. They expect a minimum of 35 square feet of workspace that is isolated from family activities (noise).

Home workers are paid the same as in-house workers. In order to qualify to participate in the telecommuting program, a worker must have worked in a Penneys phone center for at least a year. The program is expected to grow even more, since it will save the company a lot of money by not having to build new facilities.

PRIME COMPUTER, INC., Massachusetts.

At any given time, about 100 of Prime's 12,000 employees are working at home on company provided computers. Most are in the customer service area, but others are in management and marketing. To take advantage of the telecommuting alternative, employees must first demonstrate the need.

PUBLIC SERVICE COMPANY OF NEW MEXICO, New Mexico .

Working at home is an option offered to permanent employees who need to. PCs are provided as necessary.

QWEST, Colorado.

Nearly 6,000 engineers, writers, computer programmers, and their supervisors work at home. Telecommuting has become a fully-accepted way of working at Qwest because it has proven to be very economical for the company. Equipment is supplied as necessary. Home workers are represented on the project planning team by The Communications Workers of America. Employee status remains unchanged.

REDMOND, Washington.

Redmond's telecommuting program began as an effort to ease traffic congestion. So far there are only a few dozen telecommuters, but any city employee can apply for the option.

SNET, Connecticut.

SNET (Southern New England Telecommunications, Inc.) has over 100 telecommuters in several job categories.

SOUTHERN CALIFORNIA ASSOCIATION OF GOVERNMENTS, California.

SCAG started its telecommuting program in 1992 with 20 staff members, including accountants, legal staff members, planners and writers. The purpose of the program is to find a way to reduce work-related driving in Southern California by 12% by the year 2000. This project was one of several being conducted under the umbrella of the Central City Association. During the initial project, the home workers kept a log of transportation charges, telecommunications usage and utilities usage. Each was periodically interviewed to determine the best methods for expanding the program. Workers have their choice of part-time or full-time telecommuting. There is no change in salary, benefits, or employee status for anyone who chooses to work at home.

SOUTHERN NEW ENGLAND TELEPHONE, Connecticut.

Working at home is an option open to all Southern New England Telephone employees. If the option is needed for any reason, working at home will be okayed as long as the job can be done at home.

STATE OF SOUTH DAKOTA, South Dakota.

Working at home is facilitated on a statewide level by several electronic networks and PCs that are provided to all professional personnel in all state agencies. Working at home is considered informal, but is clearly acceptable; especially since it is donated time.

SUN MICROSYSTEMS COMPUTER CORPORATION, California.

About 200 employees telecommute on a regular basis, but up to 4,000 are registered to do so at their discretion.

TANDEM COMPUTERS INCORPORATED, California.

Most of Tandem's 200 telecommuters are software developers and technical writers.

3COM CORPORATION, California.

3Com started experimenting with telecommuting in 1993. Today, there are about 85 employees in a wide variety of jobs who regularly work at home.

TRAVELER'S LIFE INSURANCE, Connecticut.

Resident claims operations adjusters are provided with laptop computers so they don't have to return to the office from the field to finish work. Data processors are also provided with home terminals, e-Mail, formal training in telecommuting procedures, and a telecommuting handbook. Telecommuting is a formal program for established DP employees only.

TRAVELING SOFTWARE, Washington.

Traveling Software started a telecommuting program as part of an effort to reduce long commuting times and enhance productivity. There are about 60 programmers, sales staff, and public relations staff involved.

UNION MUTUAL LIFE INSURANCE COMPANY, Maine.

Union Mutual's "Flex-Program" is an option offered to employees as needed. Examples of need include, but are not limited to pregnancy or temporary disability. "Currently, the program is driven solely by managers/employees' interests. After expressing a desire to work at home, employees must demonstrate a legitimate need for an alternative work arrangement to their managers."

UNITED PRESS INTERNATIONAL, Washington, DC.

Most of UPI's news bureaus are small operations scattered around the country and abroad. It only makes sense to allow the news correspondents and sales reps to work from home if they choose. Since home-based correspondents and reps are regular salaried employees of UPI, normal hiring procedures and requirements apply.

UNITED SERVICES AUTOMOBILE ASSOCIATION, Texas.

Programmers for this insurance company are provided with PCs, both for after-hours work and also on a project-by-project basis.

UNIVERSITY OF WISCONSIN HOSPITAL AND CLINIC, Wisconsin .

Medical transcribers handle physicians' notes for 50 clinics. To qualify for working at home, employees must first gain experience by spending six months in the office doing the same work that will be done at home. Work is to be completed on 24 to 48 hour turn-around schedule; same as for in-house workers.

Dictaphones and word processors are provided. Home workers are regular employees with salaries and benefits identical to that of in-house workers. Performance is measured by characters typed (home workers are found to be 40-50% more productive than in-house workers). Home workers are represented by Local 2412 of the Wisconsin State Employees' Union. "There is an interest here in expanding the program. We can add one home worker for every one-and-a-half in-house workers."

U.S. GENERAL SERVICES ADMINISTRATION, Washington, DC.

The federal government's telecommuting program is called Flexiplace and is sponsored by the President's Council on Management Improvement. Almost 3,000 employees now participate regularly.

WENDY'S INTERNATIONAL, INC., Ohio.

A couple dozen employees in a wide variety of administrative positions work at home as needed. Wendy's has supported telecommuting for a number of years and now provides laptop computers to those who need them at home.

WEYERHAUSER COMPANY, Washington.

Marketing personnel can work out of their homes full-time. In-house employees

Linda Anapol, Director of Teleservices Applications for Pacific Bell, at work in her home office. (Photo curtesy of Pacific Bell.)

in Washington have the option to work at home part-time on an informal basis. The option is usually used on a project-by-project basis. Weyerhauser has a very flexible time policy in general. The work-at-home option is most common among systems developers, technical professionals and sales personnel in the Research & Development and Data Processing departments.

LEARNING AT HOME
TO WORK AT HOME

Although there are plenty of opportunities listed in this book for people with limited skills, you have probably noticed many that do require education or skills you don't possess. Of course, additional skills generally bring additional pay, so the incentive to learn new things is strong.

The same reasons you have for wanting to stay home to work probably affect your ability to leave home to go to classes. How do you attend classes 35 miles away after working all day? And even if you were able to find childcare during the day, can you also find it in the evening? For these reasons, home study courses have become more popular than ever before.

Home study, also known as distance learning, involves enrolling in an educational institution that offers lessons specially prepared for self-directed study. The lessons are delivered, completed, and returned by mail one at a time or over the Internet. Each lesson is corrected, graded, and returned to the student by a qualified instructor who provides a personalized student-teacher relationship.

Generally, home study courses include only what you need to know and can be completed in a much shorter time period than traditional classroom instruction. With home study, you don't have to stick to somebody else's schedule. You don't have to give up your job, your time, leave home, or lose income. As in a home-based job, you work at your own pace with the school coming to you instead of you going to the school.

In the past, home study involved books and binders, audio tapes and videos. Those materials are still used, but today the majority of home study courses are available over the Internet. In some cases, that is the only way you can get the course. The Internet has proven to be an excellent way to get education and training. Although it started only 15 years ago, now all colleges and universities in the United States offer courses, either with or without credit, online. In fact, you can get anything from a high school diploma to a PhD online from any educational institution you can name. And the degrees are every bit as valid as those earned by students who attended "real" classes on campus.

Listed in this section are dozens of home study schools. All of them are fully accredited by the National Home Study Council. Although there are hundreds more such institutions, the ones presented here have been selected because they offer instruction that could help you take advantage of opportunities listed in this book.

ACCOUNTING

Educational Correspondence Training School, LLC, 3520 West 26th Street, Erie, PA 16506; www.ectschool.com.

ERI Distance Learning Center ; www.eridlc.com.

Hemphill Schools, 2500 Wilshire Blvd. #704, Los Angeles, CA 90057.

Education Direct, P.O. Box 1900, Scranton, PA 18501; www.educationdirect.com.

University of Phoenix; www.phoenix.edu.

ADVERTISING

Columbia School of Broadcasting, Metro Washington DC Communications Center, 3947 University Drive, 2nd Floor, Fairfax, VA 22030; http://columbiaschoolbroadcas.com.

Education Direct, P.O. Box 1900, Scranton, PA 18501; www.educationdirect.com.

ADVERTISING ART

Art Instruction Schools, 3309 Broadway Street NE, Minneapolis, MN 55413.

ARTS, FINE AND COMMERCIAL

Art Instruction Schools, 3309 Broadway Street NE, Minneapolis,MN 55413.

Artist Career Training, 2013 Kiva Road, Santa Fe, NM 87505; www.artistcareertraining.com.

BOOKKEEPING

Education Direct, P.O. Box 1900, Scranton, PA 18501; www.educationdirect.com.

Hemphill Schools, 2500 Wilshire Blvd. #704, Los Angeles, CA 90057-2998.

Home Study International, 12501 Old Columbia Pike, Silver Spring, MD 20914; http://www.hsi.edu.

COURT REPORTING

Stenotype Institute of Jacksonville, Inc., 500 9th Avenue North, Jacksonville Beach, FL 32250.

DRAWING

Hemphill Schools, 2500 Wilshire Blvd. #704, Los Angeles, CA 90057-2998.

Education Direct, P.O. Box 1900, Scranton, PA 18501; www.educationdirect.com.

DATA ENTRY

Thomas Edison State College, 101 W. State St., Trenton, NJ 08608; www.tesc.edu.

DRESSMAKING

Hemphill Schools, 2500 Wilshire Blvd. #704, Los Angeles, CA 90057-2998.

Education Direct, P.O. Box 1900, Scranton, PA 18501; www.educationdirect.com.

Lifetime Career Schools, 101 Harrison St., Archbald, PA 18403.

ELECTRONICS

Cleveland Institute of Electronics, 1776 E. 17th, Cleveland, OH 44114; www.cie-wc.edu.

Grantham College of Engineering, 34641 Grantham College Road, Slidell, LA 70469; http://www.grantham.edu.

Heathkit/Zenith Educational Systems, 455 Riverview Dr., Benton Harbor, MI 49022.

Hemphill Schools, 2500 Wilshire Blvd. #704, Los Angeles, CA 90057-2998.

Education Direct, P.O. Box 1900, Scranton, PA 18501; www.educationdirect.com.

GRAPHIC DESIGN

Sessions, www.sessions.edu/wwl.

INCOME TAX

National Tax Training School, 67 Ramapo Valley Rd. Suite 102, Mahwah, NJ 07430; www.nattax.com.

Professional Career Development Institute, 430 Technology Parkway, Norcross, Georgia 30092; www.pcdi-homestudy.com.

INFORMATION TECHNOLOGY (IT)

Advantage Career Training, 110 W. Ocean Blvd, Suite 531, Long Beach, CA 90802.

DeVry University, One Tower Lane, Oakbrook Terrace, IL 60181; www.devry.edu.

Educational Correspondence Training School, LLC, 3520 West 26th Street, Erie, PA 16506; www.ectschool.com.

Grantham College of Engineering, 34641 Grantham College Road, Slidell, LA 70469; http://www.grantham.edu.

Heathkit/Zenith Educational Systems, 455 Riverview Dr., Benton Harbor, MI 49022.

Hemphill Schools, 2500 Wilshire Blvd. #704, Los Angeles, CA 90057-2998.

Education Direct, P.O. Box 1900, Scranton, PA 18501; www.educationdirect.com.

PC Age IT Institute, 1259 Route 46 East, Building 4C, Parsippany, NJ 07054; www.pcage.com.

JOURNALISM

Education Direct, P.O. Box 1900, Scranton, PA 18501; www.educationdirect.com.

LANGUAGES, FOREIGN

Berlitz International, 40 West 51st St., New York, NY 10020, www.berlitz.com.

Home Study International, 12501 Old Columbia Pike, Silver Spring, MD 20914; http://www.hsi.edu.

Laural School, 2538 North 8th St., Phoenix, AZ 85006.

LEGAL TRANSCRIPTION

Laural School, 2538 North 8th St., Phoenix, AZ 85006.

Virtual Learning Center, 1925 Pine Ave. Suite 9035, Niagara Falls, NY 14301; www.thevlc.com.

MARKETING

Education Direct, P.O. Box 1900, Scranton, PA 18501; www.educationdirect.com.

MEDICAL BILLING

Meditec.Com, 190 S Fort Lane Ste. 5 Layton, UT 84041; www.meditec.com.

National Electronic Billers, 2226-A Westborough Blvd., #504, South San Francisco, CA 94080; www.nebazone.com.

MEDICAL TRANSCRIPTION

American Health Information Management Association, 233 North Michigan Avenue, Suite 2150, Chicago, IL 60601.

At-Home Professions, 2001 Lowe St., Fort Collins, CO 80525; www.At-HomeProfessions.com.

CAI Transcription, 116 Stillwater Road, Barnegat, NJ 08005.

Laural School, 2538 North 8th Street, Phoenix, AZ 85010.

Meditec.Com, 190 S Fort Lane Ste. 5 Layton, UT 84041; www.meditec.com.

MTEC, Inc., 3634 West Market Street, Suite 103, Fairlawn, OH 44333; www.mtecinc.com.

NOTEREADING

At-Home Professions, 2001 Lowe St., Fort Collins, CO 80525; www.At-HomeProfessions.com.

Stenotype Institute of Jacksonville, Inc., 434 9th Ave. N., Jacksonville Beach, FL 32250.

PHOTOGRAPHY

Hemphill Schools, 2500 Wilshire Blvd. #704, Los Angeles, CA 90057.

Education Direct, P.O. Box 1900, Scranton, PA 18501; www.educationdirect.com.

REAL ESTATE

Premier Schools, Inc., 11600 W. Olympic Blvd. Los Angeles, CA 90064; www.premierschools.com.

RETC, 22215 Northern Blvd., Bayside, NY 11361.

SALESMANSHIP

Education Direct, P.O. Box 1900, Scranton, PA 18501;
www.educationdirect.com.

SECRETARIAL / ADMINISTRATIVE ASSISTANT

Allied Schools, 22952 Alcalde Drive, Laguna Hills, CA 92653,
www.alliedschools.com.

Laural School, 2538 N. 8th St., Phoenix, AZ 85006.

SEWING

Hemphill Schools, 2500 Wilshire Blvd. #704, Los Angeles, CA
90057.

Education Direct, P.O. Box 1900, Scranton, PA 18501;
www.educationdirect.com.

Lifetime Career Schools, 101 Harrison Ave., Los Angeles, CA
90064.

TECHNICAL WRITING

Barnes & Noble University, www.barnesandnobleuniversity.com.

University of Washington, 4311 11th Avenue Northeast, Seattle,
Washington 98105; www.outreach.washington.edu.

TYPING

Home Study International, 12501 Old Columbia Pike, Silver Spring,
MD 20914; www.hsi.edu.

WRITING

Art Instruction Schools, 500 South Fourth St., Minneapolis, MN
55415.

Columbia School of Broadcasting, Metro Washington DC
Communications Center, 3947 University Drive, 2nd Floor, Fairfax,
VA 22030; http://columbiaschoolbroadcas.com.

Hollywood Scriptwriting Institute, 1605 N. Cahuenga Blvd., Suite 211, Hollywood, CA 90028; www.moviewriting.com.

THE WORK-AT-HOME JOB BANK

Getting a Home-Based Job, Step-by-Step

The first step in getting the home-based job of your choice is to define exactly what it is you want. You should ask yourself what kind of a commitment you are willing to make. Are you looking for a long-term career or just a short-term job? Do you need to support yourself or do you just need some extra income? Do you want to work in the same industry where you've always worked or try something new?

A wide range of occupations is covered in this book. Do you see something you like? If not, back up and give some thought to the type of jobs that can be done at home. While opportunities for homework span a wide spectrum of employment possibilities, not all work can effectively be moved home.

First of all, homework is work, which can be easily measured. Why? Because you and your employer need to know what to expect, such as when the work will begin and when it will be completed. If you are paid a piece rate, which is very common, this factor is crucial. Besides that, your employer wants to know that he's getting his money's worth. Along these same lines, the work should require minimal supervision after initial training.

It is also important to know whether there are physical barriers to doing a particular type of work at home. Work that requires minimal space and no large and/or expensive equipment is ideal. In some cases, the type of equipment and the amount of space used for homework is restricted by local zoning ordinances.

Where The Work Is

In general, homework tends to be available at very large corporations and at very small companies. Mid-sized firms often lack the management expertise available at large companies and may be less willing to take risks than small companies. There are many exceptions to this, however, especially among companies that originally started using home workers.

Information-intensive industries such as the banking industry, the

139

insurance industry and the computer software industry are prime candidates for homework because so much of their work is done via computer and telephone.

All types of sales organizations have traditionally been open to working at home. Real estate, publishing, insurance, pharmaceuticals, apparel, cosmetics, and printing are just a few of the businesses that typically use home-based representatives.

Home businesses are often forced by zoning ordinances to use other home workers or else move out of their original home base. Such businesses may need secretaries, sales reps, bookkeepers, assemblers, shipping clerks, artists, copywriters, public relations consultants, programmers, lawyers, and accountants.

Any rapidly growing company may also be a good bet. Whenever a company suddenly outgrows its available space, the option of having additional workers provide their own space can be very appealing. Besides, if the growth were temporary, the money spent on additional facilities would be wasted. It is normally far cheaper for a company to pay for extra phone lines, computer terminals, or other equipment for employee's homes than to build new office space.

Moving Your Work Home

Now that you have zeroed in on the job you would like to have at home, you have two options. You can either start from scratch and find a new job starting at home, or you can move your present (or future) job from its current location to your home.

Large corporations are most likely to accept the latter option. There are presently several hundred major corporations in the U.S. that have home workers on the payroll. As a rule, however, they don't allow new hires to work at home right from the start. As a rule, they want to develop confidence in their employees before allowing them to take their work home. Therefore, the very first thing to do is make sure you are known for being a valuable and trustworthy employee.

Next, develop a plan of action. Define the job tasks, which are feasible for homework. Don't ignore problems that could arise later and undermine your position. Consider all of the possible problems and devise a "worst case" scenario and alternative solutions for dealing with each of them. That way, you will be prepared and can confidently assure your company there will be no unpleasant surprises.

You will need to sell your homework idea to your employer, focusing on the ways moving your work home will benefit the company. Remember, your employer is in business to make a profit, and while he/she probably prefers happy employees, the bottom line is ultimately the highest priority. You can take comfort in the fact that the benefits employers gain from work-at-home arrangements are well documented. If you want to refer to some success stories, see the company profiles scattered throughout this book. In addition, the following information is likely to grab your employer's attention.

The number one benefit to employers is increased productivity. The best-documented cases are from Blue Cross/Blue Shield of South Carolina, which reported productivity gains of 50%, and from Control Data Corp., which showed gains of 35%. Employees at home tend to work at their individual peak hours, don't get paid for long lunch hours and time spent at the water cooler, and often continue to work while feeling slightly under the weather rather than take time off.

The second greatest benefit to employers is the cost savings from not spending money on additional office space, utilities, parking space, etc. This is especially helpful for growing companies and also for home-based businesses that need to expand, but want to limit the costs of doing so. Some companies have even sent employees home and rented out the unoccupied space to compatible firms. As a direct result of its homework program, Pacific Bell closed three offices in one year, saving $40,000 in rent alone.

Another advantage to employers is a far lower turnover rate among employees allowed to work at home. In some industries, rapid turnover is a serious problem. The insurance industry, for instance, has a turnover rate between 30% and 45%. As you would expect, recruiting and training costs are very high in such industries.

All of this should give you ample ammunition to convince your manager(s) to let you try working at home. It's usually best not to try for an immediate move to full-time homework, though. Start slowly, asking to take your work home a couple of times in the afternoon, and then proposing a two-day project. While you're testing the waters, make sure you check in by phone to see if anything has come up at the office that you need to take care of. After a few months of occasional home work, you'll be ready to go to your manager and point out that you get more accomplished when you're not distracted by office routines and don't have to waste valuable time commuting.

Remember, you're not asking for favors. You are simply offering what every employer wants-a motivated, efficient worker interested in increasing productivity.

Starting From Scratch

If you're presently not working and need to find a job you can do at home right from the start, there is a good chance the type of work you're looking for is secondary to your need to be at home. (This has proven to be true about 75% of the time.)

The first thing you should do is examine your skills and match them up with possible job types. If you don't see anything here that you're already trained in, consider what you would like to learn. Many jobs offer training at a central location or right in your home.

Preparing a Resume

It's time to prepare a resume that stresses skills needed to work at home. In other words, you should emphasize anything that demonstrates your ability to work well without supervision. Because your employer won't see you very often (or ever, in some cases), your reliability is extremely important. For every job you apply for, you should write a cover letter openly stressing your desire and ability to work efficiently and effectively at home.

There are basically two kinds of resumes-chronological and functional. Both include identifying information, work history, and educational background. Neither is necessarily better than the other, but generally speaking, employers prefer the chronological style because its format is quick and easy to read.

The chronological resume simply lists your work history according to dates, starting with the most recent and working backwards. Educational background is handled in the same way.

The functional resume presents essentially the same information, but in a different order. The purpose of this type of resume is to emphasize your skills. Instead of starting with dates, you head each descriptive paragraph with a job title.

Regardless of the style of resume you choose, the following rules apply:

• Include only information that is directly relevant to the job for which you are applying. While it is great to have many skills and accomplishments, employers are only interested in what you can offer them in particular.

• Limit your resume to two pages. A ten page resume may look impressive, but what employer has time to read it? It will be easier to keep your resume brief if you carefully follow the rule above.

• Present a professional image. Your resume should be typed or typeset in a neat and orderly fashion. Leave sufficient margins and double space between paragraphs. Proofread carefully. Grammatical errors and typos could cost you a highly desirable job.

The Cover Letter

A cover letter is a personalized letter stating your interest in a job in clear, concise terms. You should indicate which job you are applying for and point out a few good reasons why you should be considered. There is no need to repeat any of the information included in the resume.

Letter of Interest

In some cases an employer is more interested in your aptitude and enthusiasm than in your background. This is often the situation when a training course will be provided, or for "people jobs" such as sales, customer service, and market research positions. The basic requirement here is an ability to relate to people and communicate effectively. How do you prove that ability with a resume? You can't, really, so you use a letter of interest.

A letter of interest is similar to a cover letter except that you (briefly) describe any background or personality traits that are applicable to the position and then request an application or an interview, or both.

Phone Interviews

Prospective home workers are often interviewed over the phone; many are hired without ever meeting their new employers.

After sending in an application, you can normally expect to be called within a week or two if you are going to be considered for an opening in the near future. Of course, you won't know exactly when to expect the call, but you should be prepared right from the start.

• Find out as much as you can about the company ahead of time. Then, make a list of questions you want to ask about the job. Keep the list and a copy of your application near the phone. Don't forget to keep a pen or pencil and paper handy, too.

• Try to use a phone in a quiet part of the house where you will not be interrupted.

• Listen carefully, take your time and answer all questions in a clear, steady voice. Don't mumble. Speak with confidence and honesty.

• Be polite and friendly, but not "chummy."

• Be enthusiastic even if you're not sure you want the job. You can always change your mind later.

• Be prepared to give references if asked.

Most important, you want to present yourself as the right candidate for the job. Ask yourself one question: "Why should this company hire me?" This is, after all, what they are calling to find out.

Don't Expect Too Much

Looking for a job that you can do from home is essentially no different, and definitely no easier, than looking for a job in a "traditional" work place. You cannot assume that because an employer uses home workers, that somehow means the employer is desperate for help and getting the job is going to be easy. On the contrary, employers often offer the work-at-home option as an incentive in order to have a larger pool of applicants to choose from. A single small ad in a local newspaper mentioning a job that can be done at home typically elicits hundreds of responses. That means competition, and lots of it, for you. It's up to you, and you alone, to convince any prospective employer that you're a cut above the rest and that you will handle the job professionally with a minimal amount of supervision.

Most home worker employers never advertise at all (like most of the ones in this book). They don't need to because the jobs are so sought after, word-of-mouth alone often creates a waiting list of eager applicants. If you should apply to any of these firms and don't receive a reply, understand that they don't have the manpower or the time to do so and your name has been placed on file for possible future openings. Rather than sit around waiting for a response that may not come for quite a while, your time would be better spent seeking out new opportunities in your field that nobody else knows about yet.

IN ANSWER TO YOUR QUESTIONS....

1. How are the listings in the book obtained?

Compiling a list of opportunities as diverse as those in this book requires constant searching. The listings actually come from many different sources including government agencies, industry associations, trade directories, advertisements, and telephone surveys of certain types of businesses. Of course, some companies write in asking to be listed, but most of the time it's not that easy.

2. How do I know these listings are legitimate opportunities?

There are thousands more real work-at-home opportunities than are listed in this book, and yet The Work-at-Home Sourcebook is still the most extensive listing of real work-at-home jobs and business opportunities available. To the best of our knowledge, there have been no reports of deceptive practices among the employers listed-and this is after 18 years of publication. Each listing has been verified, and those firms, which write in asking to be listed, are screened with special care. If there is any question as to the legitimacy of the offer, an interview with at least one worker is required before listing the company.

3. What if I don't find what I'm looking for in my area?

The majority of the listings in the job bank that can be done either in a large region or anywhere in the country. And, most of the business opportunities can likewise be operated from wherever you are. But if you still want to pursue a particular job type in a town where there is none listed in this book, you need only follow the instructions found at the beginning of The Work-at-Home Job Bank. Do not contact an employer that can only hire local residents if you don't live in the same area. You will only be wasting your time and theirs.

4. Is it okay to call a prospective employer?

Unless there is a telephone number published with the listing, the answer is definitely no. Most employers simply don't have the manpower available to talk to anyone who might have questions or be somewhat interested in their company. If you call before you are invited to, you will only alienate a potential employer.

5. Is it better to send a letter of interest or a resume?

That depends. If an employer has a preference, it will be stated in the listing. Most of the time, a letter of interest is welcomer. A resume is best in the case of professions requiring a high level of education and experience.

6. What should I do when I don't get a reply to my letter of interest or resume?

If you don't get a response within a few weeks, you have to assume that there is no interest or no openings. In either case, you shouldn't sit around waiting for that to change. Look for opportunities elsewhere. Finding the work-at-home job you want takes time and diligence.

7. Will I have to pay money to work for any of these companies?

Just as a general rule, you should always be wary of any employer that requires money to work for them. (This does not pertain to business opportunities, which almost always involve an investment.) There are exceptions, however. Positions in sales often require a deposit for a sales kit to get started. All of the listings in this book that require money upfront will refund your money if you change your mind and return the kit in reusable condition. Never pay money to a company if you don't know exactly what the job is and what you are getting for your money.

8. How do you handle complaints about listings?

Fortunately, this is a rare problem. Readers' complaints are usually about a company that has moved, changed its policy towards working-at-home, or simply hasn't responded. Sometimes, an employer will become swamped with applications and ask to be removed from the listings. These requests are always complied with at the first available opportunity.

9. Can I work for more than one company?

Since most work-at-home job opportunities are for independent contractors, it is your right (and obligation according to the I.R.S.) to seek out multiple sources of income. Most employers know that you will need to do this and understand if there is an occasional conflict. If the position or business will require full time participation, the company will tell you before you begin.

10. Are there any shortcuts to find the listings I want in the book?

Much thought has gone into the organization of this book. It is not always easy to categorize an opportunity. The lines between job opportunities and business opportunities, for instance, are not always clear. Likewise, it is not always easy to decide in what grouping a particular type of opportunity should be placed. For these reasons, and so that you will not miss out on anything, you should take the time to browse through the entire book. You would do yourself a disservice to go to the location index and, seeing that there are not many listings in your particular area, give up before you even get started. If you know exactly what you're looking for, though, you can save a lot of time by looking first at the Table of Contents. There you will see the layout of the book and find the general categories broken down into major sections. There are also several indexes in the back of the book to help you zero in on specific companies and their locations.

OPPORTUNITIES IN ARTS

Artists of all kinds have been working at home since the beginning of time. An artist is a special breed of worker, with a need for freedom that may be stronger than the need for security. To be able to work when the flash of inspiration strikes is important to the artist; not being forced to work when there is no inspiration is equally important.

Included in the following pages are freelance opportunities for graphic artists, illustrators, designers, calligraphers, photographers, writers, and editors. To get work in any artistic field, the primary requirement is proof of talent, skill, and dependability. Some prospective employers may require evidence of previous publication; others are on the lookout for new talent and will take a look at samples.

Graphic art is a growing field that has traditionally accepted the work-at-home option. Currently, about 80% of all graphic artists work in their own studios as independent contractors. They design, by hand or computer, the visuals for commercials, brochures, corporate reports, books, record covers, posters, logos, packaging, Web sites and more. Their major clients are ad agencies, publishers, broadcast companies, textile manufacturers, Web hosts, and printers.

Illustrators and calligraphers may find that work is more sporadic. Illustrators often work for publishers, but both illustrators and calligraphers will find the most opportunities among ad agencies and greeting card publishers. Both of these are huge industries. Photographers, writers, and poets will also find this to be fertile ground for homework.

The biggest field for photographers is still advertising. Agencies large and small are in constant need of professional photographers who can deliver high quality work according to the concept developed by the agency. Rarely will an agency use an inexperienced photographer; the business is too fast-paced to risk losing time on a photographer who may not work out. A freelance photographer looking for any kind of work should be prepared with a professional portfolio of his/her best work, tear sheets of previously published photos if possible, a resume, business cards, and samples that can be left on file.

ADELE'S II, INC., 17300 Ventura Blvd., Encino, CA 91316; www.adeles2.com.
Positions: This producer of high quality personalized giftware uses freelance artists for product design.
Requirements: Submit resume along with photographs of work samples.

AMCAL, 2500 Bisso Lane #500, Concord, CA 94520.
Positions: Artists and writers for greeting cards and fine art calendars. Themes include country, nostalgia, Christmas, and many others that fall within the fine art categories.
Requirements: Artists send samples in 5" x 7" size along with SASE. Writers send samples of verses. No humor or long poetry. Most commonly purchased are friendship and birthday messages. It's best to check out company's style first before submitting.
Provisions: Pays royalties.

AMERICAN GREETING CORPORATION, 1 American Rd., Cleveland, OH 44102.
Positions: Artists, writers, and photographers. Company makes cards, wrapping paper, posters, calendars, stationary, and post cards. Work is on a freelance basis; some is assigned, some is bought.
Requirements: Must send for submission forms first, then send samples of work with letter of interest. If appropriate, ask to arrange for a personal interview to show portfolio.

AMERICAN INSTITUTE OF PHYSICS, 2 Huntington Quad #1NO1, Melville, NY 11747.
Positions: Scientific publisher seeks copy editors and proofreaders.
Requirements: Bachelor's degree required. Good knowledge of English a must. Experience a plus. Send resume and salary history.
Provisions: Provides training.

AQUENT; www.aquent.com/careers.
Positions: This is a placement agency that specializes in placing creative workers including copywriters, technical writers, photographers, and artists. It is a little different than most agencies in that here the workers are the ones who are represented and "sold."
Requirements: Technically, you can live anywhere in the U.S. but you will need to come into an office for an interview and to show your portfolio. Start by going online and filling out the online application.
Provisions: Pays top rates.

ARGONAUT PRESS, 1706 Vilas Ave., Madison, WI 53711.
Positions: Photographers. Company produces postcards with contemporary themes.
Requirements: Submit transparencies along with resume. A guideline sheet is available upon request.
Provisions: Pays for photos outright or in royalties.

BCC, INC., 25 Van Zant St., Suite No. 13, Norwalk, CT 06855; www.BCCResearch.com.
Positions: Freelance writers for market research assignments. This is a US-based international publisher who hires seasoned writers/market researchers who are capable of preparing technical/economic market research reports discussing components of any one of these industries: biotechnology, healthcare, chemicals, technical ceramics, glasses, polymers and advanced materials, electronics, electronic materials, energy, flame retardancy, membranes/separations, packaging, waste, water, and air treatment, food/

beverage, banking, telecommunications and many other allied industries.
Requirements: In addition to having a broad knowledge of your chosen industry and good economic/market research skills, you must be able to meet deadlines and adhere to format requirements which are supplied by the publisher. You will find an author guide, report template and sample full-length report all downloadable at http://buscom.com/guide. A Bachelor's degree is the minimum requirement. Applicants should e-mail a copy of their resume and indicate the industries/technical areas of greatest interest. If there is a potential match, a detailed application procedure guide will be e-mailed.
Provisions: Compensation includes an advance against royalties and expense reimbursement.

BEAUTYWAY, 555 S Blackbird Roost St., Flagstaff, AZ 86001.
Positions: Photographers. Company produces postcards, calendars, and posters. Interested mostly in scenics and animals.
Requirements: Submit any size transparencies. Guidelines are available; include SASE with request. Prefers to work with previously published photographers.
Provisions: Pays one-time fee for each photo used.

BENTLEY HOUSE, 1410 Lesnick Lane #J, Art Sources Department, Walnut Creek, CA 94596.
Positions: Bentley House has been a major national publisher of art for over eight years. They sell to major accounts, print shops, and distributors at the rate of 100,000 per month. For the first time, new artists are being sought. Preferred subject matter includes anything of interest to "Middle America;" nostalgia, country, scapes, local folk arts, people, animals, etc. Can be any medium: oils, watercolor, acrylics... Original art will be reproduced for mass sale.
Requirements: No prior publishing is required. Bentley House is most interested in long term working relationships. To be considered, send slides (only) of your work plus a cover letter to introduce yourself. Be sure to number your slides and keep a file of them at home for later reference. Bentley House requires no investment of any kind and suggests strongly that any artist who is approached by a buyer of any kind asking for money up front Beware.
Provisions: Reproduced prints sell in the $15 to $60 range. Different arrangements are worked out with different artists; buys outright, on commission, and other. A new line is introduced every four to five months.

BIRDS & BLOOMS, 5400 South 60th Street, Greendale, WI 53129; www.reimanpub.com.
Positions: Freelance photography throughout the U.S. The company uses photos of backyard flowers, gardens, senior citizens, landscapes/scenics, rural, travel, agriculture and birds, for a bimonthly magazine.
Requirements: Query with resume of credits and stock photo list. Send unsolicited photos by mail for consideration and the company will keep samples on file. Be sure to include SASE.

BOOK EDITING ASSOCIATES; www.book-editing.com.
Positions: Freelance fiction editors (mainstream and genre, esp. sci-fi) perform both developmental editing and copyediting.
Requirements: Applicants will receive several short editing tests (developmental editing

and copyediting). Failed tests will not be marked and returned. Must have 5+ years of fiction editing experience with a history of edited books that have been subsequently published by subsidy/royalty publishing houses (not self-published). Must have time available to accept regular job offers. Submit resume as Word or RTF attachment. Your resume or e-mail must contain a list of books edited for published authors (excluding self-published).

BRADFORD EXCHANGE, 9333 N. Milwaukee, Chicago, IL 60714.
Positions: Bradford is a manufacturer of collectible plates. Freelance professional artists are used to design landscapes and portraits that will be reproduced on the plates.
Requirements: Submit resume, samples that can be kept on file, and references or tear sheets.

BREAKTHROUGH DIGEST; http://breakthroughdigest.com.
Positions: Consumer medical writers.
Requirements: Must be able to intelligently conduct interviews with research scientists, review research programs and translate medical/tech speak into interesting briefs (300-600 words). Please send resume, published writing samples (or links), and your per-word rate.

BUCKBOARD ANTIQUES, 5025 Brettshire Way, Oklahoma City, OK 73107.
Positions: Folk art and other traditional country crafts like rag dolls and quilted items will be considered.
Requirements: Send photos and prices you want along with an SASE.

BUSINESS COMMUNICATIONS COMPANY, INC., 25 Van Zant Street, Norwalk, Ct 06855.
Positions: Newsletter editors. This is an international publishing firm that produces technical and economic evaluations of advanced technologies, market forecasts and industry newsletters in all major markets.
Requirements: Must be able to produce market research reports and newsletters for any of the markets BCC caters to (which covers just about any industry you can imagine).
Provisions: Assignments are contracts lasting about 12 weeks. Pays per contract on a very competitive basis. You can work from anywhere in the world if qualified.

THE CALIFORNIA INSTITUTE OF INTEGRAL STUDIES, 1453 Mission Street, San Francisco CA 94103; http://ciis.edu.
Positions: Dissertation editors work from home throughout the U.S. This is on a part-time, ad-hoc, basis with a quick turnaround when the work is assigned. The editors review dissertations for correct format, style, and citation methods according to CIIS dissertation guidelines.
Requirements: Demonstrated extensive editing experience for academic publications for at least 3 years. Need expertise with at least one of the following formats: APA, MLA, Chicago, and/or American Anthropological Association. Must provide the names of 2 professional references and authors of the recent dissertations that you edited. Send those references along with a brief resume listing relevant experience, cover letter, and a list of PhD and/or PsyD dissertations edited.
Provisions: Contracts pay fixed rate of $25 hour.

CAMARES COMMUNICATIONS, INC., 3 Wing Drive, Suite 200, Cedar Knolls, NJ 07927; www.camares.com.

Positions: Freelance high tech marketing copy writers work from their home offices in Canada. This is a full-service advertising agency serving the high tech business-to-business marketplace with services that include research, planning, marketing, advertising and pubic relations.

Requirements: Requires superior writing skills, 4-5 years experience writing for companies in the high tech B-to-B market, and knowledge of the hardware, software, telecom and/or instrumentation market space. Must be able to write excellent white papers, Web content and case studies. Must have fully equipped home office including high-speed Internet access and mobile phone accessibility. Forward resume, work samples and hourly rates.

CARLTON CARDS, 1 American Rd., Cleveland, OH 44144.
Positions: Artists, writers, and photographers design cards and calendars.
Requirements: Artists should submit sketches; photographers submit color transparencies. Send sample portfolio with return postage included. Writers should submit ideas on 3x5 index cards. Be sure name and address is on the back of each card submitted.
Provisions: Payment depends on individual situation. Sometimes ideas are purchased outright, sometimes work is assigned and paid for by the project. New talent is actively solicited.

CHESAPEAKE BAY MAGAZINE, 1819 Bay Ridge Ave., Suite 200, Annapolis, MD 21403.
Positions: Freelance writers and photographers.
Requirements: Any material about the Chesapeake region will be considered. Photographers submit color photos only. Writers can submit either proposal or complete manuscript.
Provisions: Pays on acceptance.

CMP PUBLICATIONS, 3 Park Ave. # 30, New York, NY 10016.
Positions: Editors, associate editors, reporters, and writers are all outfitted with computers and modems in order to transmit material from the field. Freelance stringers are hired to cover business news from all over the country.
Requirements: Hard news reporting experience a must. Must feel comfortable going to top industrial companies looking for stories and information. Apply with resume and previously published clips.
Provisions: Payment varies. Some reporters are salaried, some are paid by individual contract. Phone charges are reimbursed.

COMMUNICATIONS DYNAMICS CORPORATION, 800 Roosevelt Rd., Glen Ellyn, IL 60137.
Positions: Freelance copywriters and technical writers.
Requirements: Must be reliable and experienced. Send resume and work sample. Must be local resident.
Provisions: Pays by the job.

COMSTOCK CARDS, INC., 600 S. Rock Blvd., Suite 15, Reno, NV 89502.
Positions: Photographers, artists, and writers are used to design outrageously funny stationery and novelty items.
Requirements: Submit color transparencies, cartoon drawings, or brief verses with strong, but short lead.

Provisions: Pays $50 for each assignment. Will consider royalty arrangement.

COURAGE CARDS, 3915 Golden Valley Road, Golden Valley, MN 55422.
Positions: This is a non-profit rehabilitation and independent living center for children and adults with various disabilities. They produce mostly Christmas and other holiday cards using fine art theme only.
Requirements: Unsolicited samples are not accepted. Send letter of interest.

CRAIG COMMUNICATIONS, 444 Silver Lane, Oceanside, NY 11572.
Positions: Graphic art.
Requirements: Experience required in marketing graphics, advertising and printing. Also, strong desktop publishing skills required. Local residents only-send resume.

CUP OF COMFORT, P.O. Box 863, Eugene, OR 97440.
Positions: Freelance writer of creative nonfiction.
Requirements: Experience is a plus, but it is not required. For guidelines, send SASE or go to www.cupofcomfort.com.

CUSTOM STUDIOS, 4353 N Lincoln Ave., Chicago, IL 60660.
Positions: Freelance photographers on assignment basis only for Christmas card department. Offer over 100 assignments annually.
Requirements: To be considered, send letter of interest with SASE requesting "Photo Guidelines." Include business card.
Provisions: Pays by the job, $50 minimum.

DEADY ADVERTISING, 17 E. Cary St., Richmond, VA 23236.
Positions: Freelance illustrators.
Requirements: Must be very experienced in the advertising field. Local artists only. Submit resume and work samples.
Provisions: Pay methods vary from project to project.

DISPLAY CONNECTION, INC., 131 W Commercial Ave., Moonachie, NJ 07074.
Positions: Freelance artists. Company manufacturers advertising display fixtures.
Requirements: Must have experience working in the advertising field and, in particular, with display fixtures. Submit work samples or photos of work and resumes. Prefers local artists.
Provisions: Pays by the project.

EDITFAST, Kanagawa, Japan; www.editfast.com.
Positions: Editors, writers, copy editors, and proofreaders telecommute from all over the world for this company. Projects include novel manuscripts, Web pages, scientific journal articles, technical documents, magazine articles, and computer documentation.
Requirements: Must be reliable with professional experience and qualifications. To be considered as a potential EditFast freelancer you must first register online.
Provisions: Projects are paid by the word on a project to project basis.

ELANCE; www.elance.com/testquestions.
Positions: Elance Online has partnered with a national publisher of standardized achievement tests and is seeking teachers (active, retired, or unemployed) to write Science and Social Studies test questions for student assessments (Grades K - 12).

Requirements: Must have teaching experience or formal education in K-12 Science and Social Studies including biology, chemistry, life sciences, physical sciences, history and civics. Apply online.
Provisions: Accepted writers will be able to work remotely, on a part-time basis, from home. Training is provided for accepted applicants. Pays competitive rates for work completed per specifications.

ENESCO IMPORTS CORPORATION, Attn: Ms. Karen George, Art Department, 1 Enesco Plaza, Elk Grove Village, IL 60007.
Positions: Enesco provides freelance opportunities in their art department for artists, designers, and sample makers for their giftware line.
Requirements: Artists and designers must have exceptional creativity and the work samples to prove it. Sample makers must have all necessary tools to produce samples from artists' renderings. Must be local resident. To inquire, write to the address above. Absolutely no phone calls will be accepted!
Provisions: Artwork is often bought outright. Others are paid by the project or by the hour.

EDUCATION DIRECT; www.EducationDirect.com.
Positions: Subject matter experts and authors work at home throughout the U.S. and Canada developing associate degree programs to be delivered via distance education. Education Direct was formerly known as ICS Learning Systems and Harcourt Learning Direct. Visit Web site for information on current subject needs.
Requirements: Minimum qualifications include a bachelor's degree in an appropriate discipline and experience in the respective fields. A directed writing sample will be required. Interested individuals should send resumes to the attention of James Shemanski, Project Manager. E-mail: jim.shemanski@thomsonlearning.com.

EDUCATIONAL TESTING SERVICE K-12 WORKS, INC., 666 Rosedale Road, Princeton, NJ 08541.
Positions: Education assessment specialists. This job entails writing, editing and revising test questions and related educational products. You will also be asked to analyze curriculum and government standards, create outlines for new educational products, and plan/monitor test development.
Requirements: Prefers Bachelor's degree in education or related field. Prefers teachers with 3 years experience. Apply with 2 copies of resume and cover letter.
Provisions: Will offer professional training to qualified freelance writers and teachers. Pays salary and benefits.

EVERETT STUDIOS, INC., 5 N Greenwich Rd., Armonk, NY 10504.
Positions: Graphic artists and freelance photographers and videographers.
Requirements: Need experienced people who have worked in production, lab, or studio end of the business. Local residents only. Send resume.

FABJOB.COM; www.fabjob.com.
Positions: Writing career guides on a contract basis. Prefers full-time, but will consider part-time.
Requirements: Experience required. For full requirements and application instructions, visit Web site.
Provisions: Pay is $1,500 per career guide.

FREEDOM GREETING CARD COMPANY, 774 American Dr., Bensalem, PA 19020.
Positions: Writers and artists. Writers sell verses outright. Artists work on assignment only.
Requirements: Samples of work, letter of interest, and SASE required for either type of work.

GERBIG, SNELL, & WEISHEIMER, 500 Olde Worthington Rd., Westerville, OH 43082.
Positions: Freelance illustrators and photographers used for the production of advertising materials.
Requirements: Works only with local experienced people. Submit resume, tear sheets, and business card.

HANSEN PRINTING, 557 Fischer Blvd., Asbury Park, NJ 08753.
Positions: Graphic designers for work on full color brochures, advertising, wedding and tourism books.
Requirements: Knowledge of PC or Mac necessary. Local residents send resume.

HARCOURT BRACE & CO., 525 B St., #1900, San Diego, CA 92101.
Positions: Freelance writing assignments are available from this major business publisher. Artists also work on assignment.
Requirements: Only very experienced writers will be considered. Apply with resume and writing samples along with letter of interest. Artists should send samples of work along with letter of interest and bio describing in detail background experience.

HERFF JONES, 226 Public St., Providence, RI 02905.
Positions: Freelance illustrators and designers. Company makes medals, trophies, and class rings.
Requirements: Several years of experience is required. Submit resume and samples.
Provisions: Pays by the project.

IKON OFFICE SOLUTIONS, 70 Valley Stream Parkway, Malvern, PA 19355.
Positions: Content writers to produce business training kits. Topics covered are career advancement, sales achievement, time and productivity enhancement, entrepreneurial development, and small business opportunities.
Requirements: Send contact information and area of interest.
Provisions: Pays flat fee per project.

IMPACTDEVELOPMENTS; www.impactdevelopments.com.
Positions: Fundraisers, strategists, planners, writers, researchers, and business plan analysts. Company serves non-profit and for-profit clients based on need, budget and mission.
Requirements: Especially looking for specialists in health, education, arts and culture, environment, youth, women's issues, faith, media programming, and civil rights. Experience required in grant writing, letters of inquiry, business plans, Web page content, collateral materials, and reports to funders. Apply online.

INTERCONTINENTAL GREETINGS, LTD., 176 Madison Ave., New York, NY 10016.
Positions: Freelance artists for greeting cards, gift-wrap, calendars, posters, and

stationery. Prefers very graphic designs with some cartoon style illustrations.
Requirements: Works only with professionals. Send resume, work samples, and include SASE.
Provisions: Generally pays royalties.

KERSTEN BROTHERS, P.O. Box 1765, Scottsdale, AZ 85252.
Positions: Writers and artists for greeting cards. All cards are humorous and seasonal; Christmas, Thanksgiving, Halloween, Mother's Day, Father's Day, Graduation, Easter, Valentine's Day, and St. Patrick's Day.
Requirements: Writers submit batches of short verses for consideration. Artists send sketches or photocopies of finished originals.

LILLIAN VERNON CORPORATION, 543 Main Street, New Rochelle, NY 10801.
Positions: Freelance artists. Lillian Vernon is one of those rare "kitchen table" success stories. The company is one of the most successful of all direct mail catalog marketers. Products include all kinds of paper products, textiles, house wares, Christmas decor, etc. Freelance artists design and illustrate on assignment only.
Requirements: Only New York metropolitan area artists are used. Only uses artists with previous experience. Send letter of interest with tear sheets or samples that can be kept on file.
Provisions: Pays flat fee.

LOMA, 2300 Windy Ridge Parkway SE #600, Atlanta, GA 30339.
Positions: Writers for curriculum and text development and achievement tests. This entails writing and editing at the university level on topics such as insurance, finance, and business.
Requirements: Excellent research skills, the ability to write technical material. Education in insurance, finance, business, or law preferred. Professional experience or degree preferred but not required. Limited travel is required. Samples are required along with a series of rigorous interviews.
Provisions: Pays salary and benefits. Offers flexible hours and the opportunity to telecommute after training period.

MAGIC MOMENTS GREETING CARD PUBLISHING COMPANY, 10 Connor Lane, Deer Park, NY 11729; www.magicmoment.com.
Positions: Freelance artist.
Requirements: Go online and become familiar with the published content before inquiring. Submit portfolio, artwork, or samples and make sure you include postage if you want them returned.

MERION PUBLICATIONS, INC., 2900 Horizon Dr., King of Prussia, PA 19406.
Positions: Freelance staff writers for newspaper read by health professionals.
Requirements: Must live in the area. Need experience and resume with samples.
Provisions: Story leads are provided for features.

METRO CREATIVE GRAPHICS, 519 8th Ave., New York, NY 10005.
Positions: Freelance illustrators. Metro is a clip art dealer that works with dozens of artists.
Requirements: Must apply with resume and request personal interview to show portfolio of professional work samples. Prefers New York artists, but will consider anyone with real talent.

Provisions: Pay worked out on an individual basis.

NEWSBYTES NEWS NETWORK, 406 Olive St. W., Stillwater, MN 55082.
Positions: Newsbytes is similar to AP and UPI in that it is a news service. The difference is that it specializes in news about the computer industry. The entire staff is comprised of a dozen writers scattered throughout the world, each running his or her own bureau from home. Each is a permanent, though part-time, employee of the company.
Requirements: Resumes are accepted from experienced computer industry reporters.

NEWSTANDARD; http://newstandardnews.net.
Positions: Company is building a substantial network of freelance reporters, stringers, photographers and cartoonists in numerous fields, to generate content for the NewStandard Web site.
Requirements: It is essential that you visit the Web site and study the type of news published there. Make sure you read all instructions for applicants and familiarize yourself with the content on the site before you apply.

NOBLEWORKS, 115 Grand St., Hoboken, NJ 07030.
Positions: This company has been called the "Marx Brothers" of the greeting card industry. They purchase photos and some illustration. It is important that you study this company's line first before submitting anything.
Requirements: Send letter of interest first.
Provisions: Pays royalties.

NU-ART, INC., 6247 W. 74th St., Chicago, IL 60638.
Positions: Writers and artists for greeting cards, wedding invitations and accessories, and boxed stationery. Cards are for Christmas only.
Requirements: Writers submit verse along with design ideas for total concept. Artists submit color roughs or finished art.

OATMEAL STUDIOS, Box 138, Rochester, VT 05767.
Positions: Writers and illustrators for greeting card design.
Requirements: The first step for both positions is to send for Oatmeal's guidelines and current market list. Include SASE with your request. Then send several samples with a letter of interest.
Provisions: Writers are paid for each idea that is accepted. Pay for artists depends on the situation. 90% of Oatmeal's work is done by freelancers.

PARAMOUNT CARDS INC., 400 Pine Street, Pawtucket, RI 02869.
Positions: Writers, artists, and photographers for greeting card production and promotional work. Cards are seasonal and everyday with a humorous theme (studio style).
Requirements: First send for instruction sheet, including SASE with request. Then send samples with letter of interest. Be sure to include SASE with any samples.
Provisions: Specific art assignments and purchase agreements are given to freelance artists/designers. Pay methods vary.

PHILLIPS PUBLISHING, INC., 7811 Montrose Road, Potomac, MD 20854.
Positions: This newsletter publisher uses up to ten freelance writers.
Requirements: Must have the necessary expertise to write on high technology topics. Prefers local residents.

Dana Cassell, President
Writer Data Bank

"To make it as a writer, you've got to be competitive. Start by making your manuscript look better. The look of it has a lot to do with whether you get the assignment. It's just like you look and talk, it's the image that sticks.

"If you have no specific field, try a little bit of everything until you find your niche. Look for the field where you are getting the highest ratio of return from query letters, then sales, and so on..."

Provisions: Equipment such as personal computers and fax machines are provided as needed.

PLATINUM MEDIA WORLDWIDE, 81 Osborne Terrace, Newark 07108.
Positions: Graphic artists to work on magazines.
Requirements: Professional work experience producing commercial magazine ads is preferred. This is a contract position so you must own your equipment, tools, supplies, etc. Send resume and work samples to the attention of Contract Personnel Dept.
Provisions: Pays per ad plus bonuses for productivity.

PORTAL PUBLICATIONS, 201 Alameda Del Prado #200, Novato, CA 94949,
Positions: Freelance writers. Company produces greeting cards especially for young adult working women.
Requirements: Study the line first and send for market guidelines. Then submit verses on index cards in small batches with SASE.

RED FARM STUDIO, 1135 Roosevelt Ave., Pawtucket, RI 02861.
Positions: Writers and artists. Company produces greeting cards, gift wrap, and note papers. Artwork used is mostly watercolor.
Requirements: Send for a current market list; include a business size SASE. Then send letter of interest with work samples.
Provisions: Writers are paid by the line. Artists' pay varies depending on the situation.

REED STARLINE CARD COMPANY, P.O. Box 2368, Lake Arrowhead, CA 92352.
Positions: Artists and writers for work involved in the production and promotion of greeting cards. 100% of all work is done by freelancers on assignment basis only.
Requirements: To be considered for any of the hundreds of project assignments each year, start by sending for company guidelines and market list; include SASE with request. Then send samples of your style with SASE. Include business card, which will be kept on file for future assignments.

RENAISSANCE GREETING CARDS, 505 Main St., Sanford, ME 04073.

Positions: Writers and artists for all occasion and Christmas cards.
Requirements: Writers send verse ideas; especially likes humorous verse. Include ideas for design. Artists send samples of full color work in batches of a dozen; include resume. Prefers bright cartoons. Guidelines are available. Be sure to include SASE with your request.

SAMS PUBLISHING; www.samspublishing.com.
Positions: Technical editors / reviewers with technical expertise in an existing or emerging development tool, application or programming environment.
Requirements: Review the guidelines on the Web site for more information and instructions.
Provisions: Can live anywhere in the U.S.

SAN FRANCISCO BAY GUARDIAN, 2700 19th St., San Francisco, CA 94110.
Positions: Freelance writers produce over half of the contents of this alternative news weekly.
Requirements: Only previously published Bay Area writers will be considered. Especially interested in investigative reporters. Send query with clips of previously published work.

SANGAMON INC., Route 48 West, Taylorville, IL 62558.
Positions: Writers and artists for greeting card and gift wrap design.
Requirements: Writers should submit verses with SASE included. Artists submit finished art or color sketches.

SHULSINGER SALES, INC., 799 Hinsdale Street, Brooklyn, NY 11207.
Positions: Freelance artists design greeting cards and gift-wrap with Jewish themes.
Requirements: Submit work samples and resume.

SMALL BIZ COMMUNITY; www.smallbizcommunity.com.
Positions: Freelance writers are assigned press releases, media submissions, and placement follow-ups on a national level.
Requirements: Need not have extensive previous publicity experience, but must have a strong work ethic, solid writing abilities and good speaking skills. No set hours are required, and we will work around family obligations. Work at home moms, emerging business owners and students are encouraged to apply. Visit Web site and e-mail resume.

SPORTS-SHOT; www.Sports-Shot.com.
Positions: Freelance sports photographers for this company that serves the online marketplace for high school/college sports photos.
Requirements: Must have own equipment and lens capability to capture action. Apply online. Company is expanding nationwide.

ST. MARTIN'S PRESS, 175 Fifth Ave., New York, NY 10010
Positions: Freelance copy editors.
Requirements: Must be computer literate, experienced, New York resident.
Provisions: Apply by sending resume to the managing editor, trade division.

SUITE 101.COM, Family Topics.
Positions: Part-time opportunities to write articles and surf the Net in a family topic area that you are knowledgeable about and have a passion for. Suite 101.com is a

community based best-of-web guide seeking contributing editors to cover a variety of topics ranging from computers to sports to politics. Different levels of participation are available.
Requirements: Good writing skills and web knowledge. No HTML required. All work is submitted via simple to use online forms. Further information can be found at: wwwsuite101.com.

SUNRISE PUBLICATIONS, INC., P.O. Box 4699, Bloomington, IN 47402.
Positions: Writers and artists for production of greeting cards.
Requirements: First, send for Sunrise's Creative Guidelines and current market list. Then send letter of interest with work samples. Include SASE.
Provisions: Payment varies.

SYNERGY 6, INC., 336 West 37th Street, 14th Fl, New York, NY 10018; www.synergy6.com.
Positions: Advertising copywriters work on a project basis doing direct mail, Web site content, and copywriting.
Requirements: Send examples of your work and resume.
Provisions: Can live anywhere in the world.

TAYLOR CORPORATION, 1725 Roe Crest Dr., North Mankato, MN 56003.
Positions: Freelance artists are used to design wedding invitations.
Requirements: Send samples of work to be kept on file.

3DTOUR; www.3DTour.com.
Positions: This is a virtual tour company providing national coverage and personalized service to clients. The company needs more digital photographers to join its network of over 200 photographers for various 360 degree virtual tour and other digital photography projects.
Requirements: Must have your own digital camera. Send your contact info, qualifications, and coverage area (within one hour drive)
Provisions: Training provided for those without virtual tour experience. A job list will be supplied each week and will allow you to set the photo shoots around your schedule.

TRINITY REAL ESTATE SOLUTIONS, 15303 Dallas Parkway, Suite 510, Addison, TX 75001; www.trinityinspection.com.
Positions: Part-time positions for photographers to take digital pictures of houses in your local area for the real estate industry.
Requirements: Must have a digital camera and Internet access. Must be able to take 3 digital photos of each property or properties as requested,(front and both sides of the home), and return them via e-mail same day.

TURNROTH SIGN COMPANY, 1207 E Rock Falls Rd, Rock Falls, IL 61071.
Positions: Freelance artists design billboards and other kinds of signs on assignment.
Requirements: Submit letter of interest with sketches or finished work samples. Include SASE with all correspondence.
Provisions: Pays flat rates for each project.

UC BERKELEY EXTENSION; http://learn.berkeley.edu/jobs.
Positions: Course developers and online instructors work from home via the Internet for UC Berkeley Extension Online.

Requirements: Applicants must possess at minimum a master's degree, and for some courses, a doctorate. Computer skills and a strong knowledge of the Internet are required. Experience with online education is preferred.
Provisions: There are numerous positions available. For complete information on openings, requirements, and compensation, visit online.

UNIVERSITY OF NEW HAVEN, 300 Orange Ave., Public Relations Department, West Haven, CT 06516.
Positions: Freelance photographers take shots of campus life, working on assignment basis only. Work is used in all sorts of PR presentations.
Requirements: Send letter of interest along with resume and at least one sample shot to be kept on file. Include SASE and business card. You will be contacted for an interview. Be ready with a portfolio. Local photographers only.
Provisions: Pays by the hour at a minimum of $20.

VECTOR ART, 117 Madison Circle, Horseheads NY 14845; www.vectorart.com.
Positions: Vector Art Inc publishes high quality original, monochromatic artwork for the sign, engraving, tattoo, CAD, and routing industry worldwide. The art department is always open to viewing the work of new artists for licensing and publication.
Requirements: To be considered, send electronic samples in ai,eps or jpeg format to Ms. Devon Cottrell, Art Director.

VIDEO HOME TOURS, 1350 East Touhy Avenue, Suite 110W
Des Plaines, IL 60018; www.vht.com.
Positions: VHT provides service to the real estate industry in 65 major U.S. metropolitan cities. They have a nationwide network of photographers and videographers and are always looking for more quality, professional people with photography knowledge and a passion for real estate.
Requirements: Excellent customer service and organizational skills are essential. E-mail resume to HR@VHT.com.

WARNER PRESS, INC., 1200 E. 5th St., Anderson, IN 46012.
Positions: Writers and artists for work on greeting cards, calendars, posters, postcards, and plaques. Artists work on assignment. Writers are freelance.
Requirements: Before applying, write for current market list and guidelines. Include SASE. Be sure to study company's style before sending samples. Talented new artists are especially sought.
Provisions: Pay varies.

WCITIES, 340 Brannan St., San Francisco, CA 94103.
Positions: Writers with photographic skills to remove restaurants and other social establishments for this online global publishing company. Assignments are currently available in Canada. Take a look at the Web site to get a good idea of what's needed and the style of presentation: www.wcities.com.
Requirements: Send resume and cover letter.

WEBMD, 669 River Drive, Center 2, Elmwood Park, NJ 07407; www.webmd.com.
Positions: Freelance healthcare copywriters work via the Internet for this major consumer health information Web site.
Requirements: Experience is required. Must be able to write creative, effective healthcare (preferably pharmaceutical) copy with little or no supervisory rewrite. Must

have experience in writing for the Web plus healthcare agency experience. Reply with letter and resume. Copy samples will be requested.
Provisions: Salary to $75 per hour.

WILLITTS DESIGNS, 1129 Industrial Ave., Box 178, Petaluma, CA 94953.
Positions: Designers and illustrators for porcelain and earthenware giftware. Some calligraphy. All designs are three-dimensional and range from the light and whimsical to the detailed and serious.
Requirements: Submit full color design samples with resume.
Provisions: Pay methods vary from outright purchase to royalties.

WORDS4NERDS, 1464 Edgeware Road, Victoria BC V8T 2J4; www.words4nerds.com.
Positions: Freelance technical writer. This is not a full-time or payroll position, but an as-needed contract arrangement only. For U.S. or Canadian writers.
Requirements: Must have minimum 2 years' professional experience in tech writing, exceptional spelling and grammar skills, ability to proof and edit your own work, 100% reliability in meeting deadlines, ability to code clean HTML and CSS by hand, and strong knowledge of Word (styles, macros, templates, indices, etc.), FrameMaker, and Acrobat. Qualified applicants should visit Web site, then e-mail a brief outline of your experience and skills, and a link to your online portfolio - do NOT send attachments.

OPPORTUNITIES IN CRAFTS

A craft is any occupation that requires manual dexterity or artistic skill. In this section, you'll find quite a few crafts represented - jewelry making, knitting, embroidery and merrowing, sewing, and silkscreen among others.

Knitting is one of the original seven industries that were banned from using home workers in 1938 under the Fair Labor Standards Act. The ban was lifted on knitting alone in December of 1985, after many years of struggling in the courts. Now there are dozens of companies that are certified by the U.S. Dept. of Labor to hire home workers. Most of these companies are based in New England, where home knitting has been a traditional occupation for generations.

Most knitting is still done by hand, but knitting machines are being used in increasing numbers. As you can imagine, using a knitting machine speeds up the process and allows the knitter to make more clothing and therefore more money.

Sewing is among the remaining six industries that are still banned from using home workers. Actually, only certain types of sewing are banned and most have to do with women and children's apparel. That doesn't mean there isn't any home sewing going on. There are tens of thousands of home sewers across the country, but most are working underground. The companies listed here are located in states with labor laws that allow home sewing under specific certification procedures. (State labor laws supercede federal laws.)

Sewing is a skill that most women learn to some extent, but that doesn't mean that every woman is qualified to be a professional home sewer. Most home sewing is specialized so that each sewer works on a particular type of garment or, in many cases, a particular piece of garment. Employers have indicated that it isn't easy finding workers who are capable of doing quality work. Sewing jobs are generally of two types: pattern making and production work. Pattern making is highly skilled work that requires one to work closely with the designer. Experience is always required for this position. The main requirement for production work is consistency. Be forewarned that if any piece that does meet quality or consistency standards will be rejected and you will not be paid for that piece.

One word of caution: do not pay for this kind of job. There are plenty of scams out there that require you to put up money for supplies and instructions. It sounds good on paper, but chances are you're going to be disappointed - and lose your money.

AMERICAN CRAFTS, 13010 Larchmere, Cleveland, OH 44120.
Positions: Contemporary fiber arts are accepted on consignment.
Requirements: Submit slides (only) and prices you want. Include SASE.
Provisions: Pays 50/50 split.

AMERICAN GLOVE CO. INC., 98 Alpine St., Lyerly, GA 30730.
Positions: Home manufacture of work gloves. There are currently 34 home workers.
Requirements: Must be local resident and be skilled.

BARRY MANUFACTURING COMPANY, INC., 15 Bubier St., Lynn, MA 01901.
Positions: Stitching and hand assembly of infant and children's shoe parts.
Requirements: Experience is required. Must be local resident.
Provisions: Some of the work requires machinery, which is supplied by the employer. Pays piece rates equal to minimum wage, which is the same in-house workers are paid for the same work.

BEADNIKS; www.junkyjewelry.com/beadniks.htm.
Positions: Beaders and jewelry makers.
Requirements: No experience is necessary, company will train. You do not need to buy any kits!
Provisions: Average pay is $12.00 per hour depending on design and materials. Only USA residents, over 18 years of age will be considered. Apply online.

BERLIN GLOVES CO., 150 W. Franklin, PO Box 230, Berlin, WI 54923-0230.
Positions: Home stitchers manufacture gloves. Currently there are 18 home workers.
Requirements: Must be local resident and be skilled.

BLUEBERRY WOOLENS, P.O. Box 318, Randall St., Anson, ME 04911.
Positions: Machine knitting of whole sweaters for wholesaler. This is an established and growing company with close to $1 million in annual sales. Currently has a pool of 60 knitters.
Requirements: Enrollment in company's training classes and submission of acceptable samples is required. Must own a knitting machine or purchase one from the company. Must be local in order to pick up and deliver supplies and finished sweaters.
Provisions: Pays per finished sweater. Hours can be full time or part time. Workers are independent contractors. Inquiries are welcome as company continues to grow.

CHICAGO KNITTING MILLS, 3344 West Montrose Ave., Chicago, IL 60618.
Positions: Home-based sewing of emblems onto outerwear. Currently there are no openings available.
Requirements: Must be local resident and be skilled. Must obtain a home workers certificate from Illinois Department of Labor.

CHIPITA ACCESSORIES, 110 E. 7th St., Walsenburg, CO 81089.
Positions: Between 75 and 250 home workers handcraft jewelry using beads, stones, semi-precious stones, silver, crystal, and gold. The number of home workers fluctuates with the time of year, number of orders, and number of available workers in this rural area in southern Colorado. Walsenburg is, like most rural areas, economically depressed, but has a history of handcrafts of all kinds created by local artisans. Chipita started by producing and selling one kind of beaded earrings and grew from there. Home workers here are completely independent, having total control over their hours, how often and

when they work, etc. The company will sell kits to workers, will show and attempt to sell from new sample designs for workers, or will buy outright as much jewelry as a worker can produce as long as it meets quality standards. A worker can work part-time or full-time, with the opportunity to earn a regular income.
Requirements: Must be a local resident. Contact the company with letter of interest.

COUNTRY CURTAINS, INC., 705 Pleasant St., Lee, MA 01238 .
Positions: Sewing trim on basic curtains. Currently has about 31 home workers.
Requirements: Need sewing machine. Must be local resident.
Provisions: Pick up and delivery provided. Pays piece rates equal to minimum wage.

DAINTY MAID MANUFACTURING COMPANY, 12 North St., Fitchburg, MA 10420.
Positions: Sewing waitress aprons.
Requirements: Must be local resident and own sewing machine. Experience is required.
Provisions: Material is supplied. Pays piece rates. Company only has 2 home-based employees; opportunities are extremely limited.

DELAWARE CENTER FOR THE CONTEMPORARY ARTS, 103 E. 16th Street, Wilmington, DE 19801.
Positions: Freelance artist for contemporary crafts in any media.
Requirements: Submit letter of inquiry, resume, and up to 20 slides with a corresponding slide sheet describing the work in detail. Be sure to include an SASE if you want your slides returned. This opportunity is open to Delaware residents only.

DRG, Product Development Department, 103 North Pearl Street, , Big Sandy, TX 75755.
Positions: Sewers, crochet and needlework specialists.
Requirements: Must be expert in cross-stitch, crochet, and plastic canvas needlecraft mediums. Must have proven stitching ability and be committed to completing assignments on deadline. This is not for hobbyists; only serious professionals need apply. Apply with contact information, letter of interest, description of abilities and stitching experience. Include good photos of work samples.

ERIC ANTHONY CREATIONS, Live Oaks Boulevard, Casselberry, FL 32707.
Positions: Making wooden frames.
Requirements: Area residents only.

FRENCH CREEK SHEEP & WOOL COMPANY, INC., 600 Pine Swamp Rd., Elverson, PA 19520.
Positions: Knitting sweaters on hand-operated machines. Currently has about 40 workers.
Requirements: Must be local resident in order to pick up and deliver supplies and finished sweaters.
Provisions: Some training, specific to the work here, is provided. Pays production rate, which is "well above minimum wage."

ESTELLE GRACER, INC., 950 West Hatcher Rd., Phoenix, AZ 85021.
Positions: Knitting and crocheting jackets and sweaters. Work has previously been done by hand only, but company is now going into machine knitting. Currently has over 50 home workers; that number fluctuates up to 200. "Inquiries are always welcome."
Requirements: Must be experienced. Phoenix residents only.

Provisions: Specific training is provided. Home workers are full-time employees. Pays for production.

FLANNERY AND ANGELI; http://flanneryandangeli.com.
Positions: Seamstresses make aprons for this designer apron company.
Requirements: Quality seamstresses only. Need to know how to make a self-bias trim and welt pockets. Company is based in Fresno, California, so you must live in the central valley.
Provisions: Pays per piece. Part-time contract work only.

INDIAN JEWELERS SUPPLY, 2105 San Mateo Blvd. NE, Albuquerque, NM 87110.
Positions: Jewelry making. There are currently 7 home workers.
Requirements: Must be local resident.

K-C PRODUCTS, 1600 East 6th Street, Los Angeles, CA 90023.
Positions: Sewing vinyl travel bags, garment bags, mattress covers, and appliance covers. Up to 16 home workers are employed.
Requirements: Need ordinary sewing machine. Must live nearby.
Provisions: Pays piece rates.

LEISURE ARTS, INC., 5701 Ranch Rd., Little Rock, AR 72212.
Positions: Knitting of outerwear. Currently there are 177 home workers.
Requirements: Must be local resident with experience.

LIVING EARTH CRAFTS, 600 E. Todd Rd., Santa Rosa, CA 95407.
Positions: Production of several types of crafts. Most work consists of sewing bags, vinyl pieces, sheets, blankets and pad covers.
Requirements: Must own sewing machine. Must live in Santa Rosa. Experience is required.
Provisions: Materials are supplied. Workers are considered regular employees with medical and dental insurance, paid holidays and sick leave. Pays piece rates. Applications are kept on file indefinitely.

MIA GYZANDER DESIGN, 5427 W. Pico Blvd., Suite 204, Los Angeles, CA 90019; www.miagyzander.com.
Positions: Pattern makers, sample makers, cutters, and seamstresses for costume construction and also for the fashion division. This is a fast moving and creative costume and fashion company.
Requirements: Must be experienced. Local residents only.
Provisions: Part-time and/or full-time on contract basis. Compensation is about $12-$15 an hour depending on how fast you work.

MORIARTIE'S HATS AND SWEATERS, P.O. Box 1117, 112 Main St., Stowe, VT 05676.
Positions: Mrs. Moriartie started this company in the late 1950's when she hand knitted a hat for her son and almost single-handedly launched the New England home knitting industry as it is today. Moriartie's has a reputation for being the best hat and sweater store in the world. Home knitters make hats, Christmas stockings, ornaments, and sweaters. Work is done on hand-operated machines. Company sells products wholesale as well as retail. Currently has 17 permanent home workers.
Requirements: Must be local resident in order to come in once a week to get supplies.

Must own machine.

Provisions: Knitters can select designs, patterns and yarns from stock and make as many or as few items as they like. Can accept custom orders, too. "Each knitter has something they like to do especially and they usually stick to it. Some prefer to knit hats that only take 25 minutes to complete. Others prefer sweaters that take much longer. It's up to them." Pays piece rates.

MOUNTAIN LADIES & EWE, INC., Box 391 Route 7, Manchester Village, VT 05254.
Positions: Knitters make ski hats and sweaters. Products are sold both retail and wholesale. Currently has 25 permanent home workers.
Requirements: Prefers workers that live within a 60-mile radius of Manchester Village. Must own knitting machine. Pick up and delivery of supplies and finished work is required of each knitter.
Provisions: Specific training is provided. All supplies are provided. Pays production rates, but workers are considered regular employees and receive basic benefits provided by law. Inquiries are welcome from qualified applicants.

RUTH HORNBEIN SWEATERS, 8804 19th Avenue Apt 2, ., Brooklyn, NY 11214.
Positions: Knitting of outerwear. Currently there are only 5 home workers.
Requirements: Must be local resident.

SOUTHERN GLOVE MFG. CO., INC., 749 Ac Little Dr., Newton, NC 28658.
Positions: Stitching of gloves.
Requirements: Must be local resident.

SWEET AND VICIOUS, 2046 Treasure Coast Plaza #357, Vero Beach, FL 32960; www.sweetandviciouslingerie.com.
Positions: Seamstress for samples and finished product line. The product is a line of lingerie.
Requirements: Positions available only in Atlanta. Requires attention to quality and detail. Must have skills in sewing narrow fabrics, lace, nylon, lycra, etc. Proof of skill is required (i.e.: portfolio, sample garments).
Provisions: Pays per piece, how much depends on the complexity of the individual design. It should amount to about $15 per hour. Part-time hours only.

TOMORROW TODAY CORPORATION, P.O. Box 6125, Westfield, MA 01085.
Positions: Handwork consists of tying bows and working with flowers to make decorations. Currently has 23 home workers.
Requirements: Must live in Westfield.
Provisions: Pays minimum wage.

UNIQUE 1, P.O. Box 744, 2 Bayview Street, Camden, ME 04843.
Positions: Knitting of sweaters using both wool and cotton yarn for retail shop. Currently has 9 home workers.
Requirements: Must be experienced and be a local resident.
Provisions: Training is provided. If home worker doesn't own a knitting machine, Unique 1 will lease one. Pays piece rates. "Camden is tourist town, so the summer is the best time for us, especially for custom orders."

VONE FASHION; www.vonefashion.com.

Positions: This is an up-and-coming fashion line designed by Vonett Trotman. There is an opportunity for a seamstress to work on a project basis.
Requirements: Must own sewing machine and be experienced. Must live in Brooklyn, New York. Visit Web site and apply via e-mail indicating background, rates, etc. Qualified applicants only.
Provisions: Pays reasonable rates. Work is part-time only at this time.

ZAUDER BROTHERS, INC., 10 Henry St., Freeport, NY 11520.
Positions: Handwork involved in the manufacture of wigs, toupes, and theatrical makeup. Up to eight home workers are employed here.
Requirements: Must have specific experience with this kind of work. Must be local resident.

COMPUTER-RELATED OPPORTUNITIES

This section includes any situation that specifically requires a computer to get the job done. This doesn't necessarily mean that you must own your own equipment, but it typically does. In some cases, companies provide PCs and the necessary software, but those are usually telecommuting situations. On the other hand, a contract programmer not only needs to own a computer, but often several different computers.

By its nature, technical jobs such as you will find here, are the highest paying positions for home workers. In order to compete for these opportunities, you do need to know your stuff. Fortunately, the learning curve has diminished with time and getting training and experience is not nearly as difficult as it was just a few short years ago. There are classes available at most community college, vocational schools, and on the Internet. If you want to do computer-based office work, but lack the necessary skills or need to brush up on the latest software, you can get paid while you learn by signing on with a temporary help agency. Kelly Services and Manpower, to name just two, have excellent training programs, including cross training on different systems, available to anyone who is on the roster and available for work.

The field for contract programmers has opened up considerably since the last edition of this book. There are all kinds of work available, but the bulk of it is in Web-based applications and e-commerce. In this global marketplace, there is also a lot of translation to be done. Programmers today cannot only work for companies all over the U.S., but all over the world. The key to getting work as a programmer is to continue learning about languages, compilers, and systems design. Employers like programmers who are enthusiastic about what the company is doing, pay attention to deadlines, document their work properly, and submit clean programs.

Graphic artists are in demand, too. Up until recently, graphic art was mostly about print media. Today, it is more common for a graphic artist to need a certain level of computer savvy including some programming skills. These jobs generally involve making software applications and Web sites appear visually appealing and are vital to making these things "user friendly."

While the jobs mentioned above require a considerable amount of formal education and references, there is still plenty of opportunity for the self-trained computer geek. Web mastering is now considered a tedious job, lacking in the creativity that most programmers crave. Just about anyone with a couple of Web sites to show and a working knowledge of HTML, Frames, and Dreamweaver can land a job as a Web master. There are even tutorials on the Internet that can teach you these skills in a weekend.

ABILITY GROUP, 1255 New Hampshire Ave. NW #112, Washington, DC 20036.
Positions: Word processing specializing in transcription of medical, legal and verbatim tapes. Occasional assignments are mostly overflow.
Requirements: Must be local resident. Word processing equipment is required. Any major word processing software is okay as long as it is PC so that it can be converted. Experienced professionals only.

ACT 1 TECHNICAL, 111 Pine Street Suite 915, San Francisco, CA 94111.
Positions: FileNet developers for high tech consulting company.
Requirements: Must have at least 2 years experience developing imaging Web-based applications. Working experience with Visual Basic, Visual C++, and Oracle a must.
Provisions: Pays very competitive salary.

ADD2NET, INC., Lunarpages Division, 14730 Beach Blvd, Suite 102, La Mirada, CA 90638 ; www.lunarpages.com.
Positions: System administration.
Requirements: Send resume outlining experience.
Provisions: Various shifts available. Can live anywhere. This is full-time work. Salary starts at $12.00/hour depending on experience.

ADVANCED AUTOMATION ASSOCIATES, 900 Middlesex Turnpike, Billerica, MA 01821.
Positions: About 9 home-based keyboarders input data for this data management service.

ALLTEL PUBLISHING, 50 Executive Parkway, Hudson, OH 44236.
Positions: Distributed systems/LAN professionals. ALLTEL provides information-based solutions to financial, telecommunications and mortgage clients in over 47 countries worldwide. These services include information technology outsourcing, call center solutions, and more.
Requirements: Requires college degree or equivalent experience as well as five years experience in the implementation, support and design of Local Area Networks (LANs) or microcomputer based systems or three years experience in a management position in a related technical field. Experience in both LAN and WAN environments strongly preferred. Submit resume with your salary requirements.

ALPHA PRESENTATIONS, 5405 Alton Parkway, Irvine, CA 92714.
Positions: Typesetting.
Requirements: Must have Mac computer with Quark Express and Pagemaker for advanced graphic layouts, design and typesetting. Prepare for quick turnover. Local residents mail resume.

AMERICAN EXPRESS BANK, LTD., American Express Plaza, New York, NY 10004.
Positions: Word processors.
Requirements: Must be local, physically handicapped and disabled. Job requires transcription skills.
Provisions: Complete training and equipment package are provided. Telephone lines link the homework station to company headquarters on Wall Street. A company supervisor can dictate into the system from anywhere; likewise a home worker is able to access the system any time 24 hours a day to transcribe the dictation. The finished product in hard copy form is then sent back to headquarters electronically. All activity is

identified and monitored through the Control Center. "Project Homebound" currently has 10 full-time regular employees of American Express.

ANALYSTS EXPRESS, INC., 12902 Glenyork Court, Cypress, TX 77429.
Positions: WebSpeed developer.
Requirements: Specific experience with WebSpeed design and development is required. Provide URLs with samples of your work along with your resume.
Provisions: This is a full-time contract position. Pays top rates.

APPALACHIAN COMPUTER SERVICES, Highway 25 South, P.O. Box 140, London, KY 40741.
Positions: Appalachian Computer Services is among a growing number of service bureaus that has solved the problem of stabilizing workflow with a homework program. The initial pool of cottage keyers was formed out of former in-house employees. Most of them had left their jobs because they needed to be at home with their families. The program accomplished what it was supposed to. The workflow went smoothly, the keyers were happy with the arrangement (no one dropped out), and the company overhead fell. Now that Appalachian Computer Services is sure the homework program is the solution they've been looking for, plans are underway to expand the program to an ultimate goal of 200 home keyers. These additional workers will be hired from outside the company.
Requirements: Since there are no telecommunications available, all recruiting will have to be done within the township of London. The only requirement will be a typing speed of 45 wpm. Experienced applicants will spend two days in-house learning to use the Multitech PC. Those with no experience in data entry will spend an additional 3 days in the company's standard training program. There is no pay for time spent in training. Each worker goes into the office to pick up the work and receive instructions. When the job is finished, he or she returns the work on disks (which are provided).
Provisions: The cottage keyers are all treated as part-time employees, not independent contractors. Each works a minimum of 20 hours a week. No one works over 30 hours a week at any time so the part-time status remains intact. There are no benefits due to this part-time status, however, the company is looking into ways of providing some benefits as the program progresses. In the meantime, there are production bonuses offered in addition to the guaranteed hourly wage. The necessary PCs are provided at no charge.

APPLIED ANALYTIC SYSTEMS, INC., 3418 Estate Dr., Carnegie, PA.
Positions: Online researcher for software development and consulting firm.
Requirements: Must understand how to identify content driven Web sites that would be appropriate and willing to provide links either as an exchange or unilaterally. Sites must be personally visited. While this is the basic thrust of the job, there are other miscellaneous research tasks, which will come up from time to time. E-mail resume to ir100901@aasdt.com or apply online http://www.aasdt.com.
Provisions: There is about 10 hours of work per week, paying $8.50 an hour plus bonuses.

ART & LOGIC, Box 56465, Sherman Oaks, CA 91413.
Positions: This is an office-free software services company that develops commercial-quality applications, middleware, drivers, and components. Programmers work entirely online from their own home offices.
Requirements: Experience with C++, Windows and Mac OS. Applicants will take a programming test online at www.artlogic.com/careers.

ARTIZEN, INC., 990 Industrial Rd., San Carlos, CA 94070; www.artizen.com.
Positions: Programmers for software consulting firm.
Requirements: Minimum three years experience with OO, Java, Small Talk, Forte or C++ required. Job starts in office. Send resume.

ARTSCI, INC., P.O. Box 1428, Burbank, CA 91507; www.artscipub.com.
Positions: Contract programmers to translate programs between PC and Mac. Programmer's guidelines are available only to those who send acceptable resumes.
Requirements: Resume and references required.
Provisions: Pays by the project.

ARTWORX SOFTWARE COMPANY, 6017 Pine Ridge Road #280, Naples, FL 34119.
Positions: Programmers are contracted to do conversions from other computers to major brand computers.
Requirements: Resume, work samples, and references required.
Provisions: Pays by the job.

ASSOCIATION OF FLIGHT ATTENDANTS AFL-CIO, Attn: Personnel, 1275 K Street, NW Suite 500, Washington, DC 20005.
Positions: Web master. Duties include daily maintenance of Web site plus organization of Internet-based campaigns.
Requirements: Minimum 2 years experience with electronic communications and Web mastering. Apply with resume.
Provisions: This is a salaried position.

AT-HOME PROFESSIONS, 2001 Lowe Street, Ft Collins, CO 80525; (800)347-7899.
Positions: At-Home Professions is a unique institution established in 1981. It develops and provides career education specifically for the types of jobs that are commonly performed at home. The courses utilize home study methods and can be done at the student's own pace. Some of the courses include: medical transcription, medical coding, medical claims and billing, massage, legal transcription, bookkeeping, paralegal, wedding and event planning, accounting services, veterinary assisting, day care, and introduction to computers.
Requirements: Admission standards vary somewhat for each course, but generally an applicant must be a high school graduate, hold a GED, or pass an admissions test. Tuition also varies and can be paid as-you-go with no interest.
Provisions: In addition to providing top quality training programs and course materials, this organization also includes great follow-up services. At-Home Professions provides placement services, promotion of graduates through advertising and events such as trade shows, continuing employment instruction and advice, and personal counseling in job-search techniques. At-Home Professions is accredited by the Accrediting Commission of the Distance Education and Training Council.

BANCTEC, 2120 Industrial Parkway, Silver Spring, MD 20904; www.banctec.com.
Positions: Software engineers.
Requirements: Three years experience with C programming language and UNIX system call interface plus one year programming with Network Management (MIB, SNMP, SMI), Workflow Technologies, or Mass Storage Devices (Optical or Tape). Informix or Oracle DBMS programming a plus. Travel required. Send resume.
Provisions: Flexible schedule with telecommuting option, salary, and full benefits.

BCF TECHNOLOGY, 1508 Grandview Road, Vista, CA 92984; www.bcftech.com.
Positions: Application specialists in Javascript, MS IEDOM, C#, and XML Transforms work with the largest insurance carriers and agency management systems in the industry. Primary responsibilities include developing, enhancing, testing, supporting, and debugging insurance-based software.
Requirements: Three years minimum experience. Strong data mapping and scripting skills required. Telecommuting, insurance-experience, and ACORD industry standards, a plus.
Provisions: Pays $50,000 annually. This is a telecommuting company.

BI-TECH ENTERPRISES, INC., 140 Raynor Avenue. Ronkonkoma, NY, 11779; http://www.bi-tech.net.
Positions: Contract programmers write communications and database software according to company specifications for PCs.
Requirements: Must be local resident. Extensive experience required. Submit resume and references.
Provisions: Pays by the project.

BLUE CROSS/BLUE SHIELD OF SOUTH CAROLINA, Columbia, SC 29219.
Positions: Local cottage keyers (data entry operators) for coding health claims. Full-time, 8-hour days. Openings are offered first to in-house employees, who are preferred for their company experience, but will also hire from outside applicants. Prefers to train in-house for 6 to 12 months if possible. Currently have over 100 workers.
Requirements: Must live in the area.
Provisions: Pays by the line on computer. Training and equipment (including computer and modem) is provided. Home workers are considered part-timers and receive virtually no benefits; employer/employee relations are excellent, however, and the program is considered by all parties concerned to be very successful. Inquires are welcome, but you should expect to be put on a waiting list.

BOYD PRINTING COMPANY, INC., 49 Sheridan Avenue, Albany, NY 12210; www.boydprinting.com.
Positions: Typesetting input operators.
Requirements: Must be local resident. Experienced operators with own equipment only.
Provisions: Pays by the word.

BUREAU OF OFFICE SERVICES, INC., 361 S. Frontage Road, Ste 125, Burr Ridge, IL 60521.
Positions: Home-based workers do transcription and word processing for both general and medical work.
Requirements: Must have PC and be experienced. Local residents only.
Provisions: Company furnishes all supplies, transcribers, and computer equipment may be rented. Telecommunications has replaced almost all need for pickups and deliveries, but when necessary it is done by company messengers. All home workers are employees (not independent contractors) who are paid by production but who also receive benefits.

BUSINESS COMMUNICATIONS COMPANY, INC., 25 Van Zant St., Suite 13, Norwalk, CT 06855; www.buscom.com.
Positions: A publisher of technical/economic evaluations of advanced technologies,

market forecasts, and industry newsletters, is seeking seasoned writers who are capable of preparing self-contained technical/economic market research reports discussing select components of any of these industries: biotechnology, chemicals, healthcare, banking, advanced materials, electronics, energy, flame retardancy, food/beverage, Internet, telecommunications, membranes/separations, plastics, packaging, waste, water, and air treatment, and allied industries.
Requirements: In addition to having a broad knowledge of their chosen industry, the successful applicant must be able to meet publication deadlines and adhere to finished copy format requirements, which are supplied by the publisher. Minimum requirements for these contract assignments are a Bachelor's degree in a relevant field. Applicants should send a resume, list of publications, and a brief cover letter identifying the industries/technical areas of greatest interest.

BUSINESS GRAPHICS, 3314 Vasser Dr. NE, Albuquerque, NM 87107.
Positions: Typesetting input operators.
Requirements: Must be local resident. Experience and computer required.

BUYSELLWEBSITE; www.buysellwebsite.com.
Positions: BuySellWebsite is actively hiring database designers with at least one year of experience.
Requirements: Applicants need to have database skills employing ASP in a FrontPage environment running on a Windows 2000 server. Contact with a resume and examples of your work.
Provisions: The position is telecommute and available to Canadian and U.S. residents only. Bi-weekly paychecks and flexible hours.

CAL-BAY SYSTEMS, INC., 3070 Kerner Boulevard, Suite B, San Rafael, CA 94901; www.calbay.com.
Positions: Software engineers for engineering firm specializing in PC-based process automation. Projects cross a broad range of industries and therefore, offer a lot of creative interest. Each project can last anywhere from 3 months to 3 years.
Requirements: Must prefer to work in a changing, dynamic environment and be flexible and eager to work in different areas. Technically, requires coding in Visual Basic and LabVIEW, instrumentation experience of GPIB and RS232, plus in-depth understanding of hard and systems integration. An engineering degree and at least four years experience working with automation software and/or hardware is required. Apply with resume.
Provisions: You will be provided with cutting edge PC and cell phone. Pays competitive salary and provides profit sharing and full benefits package.

CAPITAL DATA, P.O. Box 2244, Palm Harbor, FL 34682.
Positions: Openings for programmers to work from home using RPG 400 on the AS/400.
Requirements: Must live in Georgia, Florida, or the Carolinas. Minimum three years experience of RPG 400 on the AS/400. Company will supply the AS/400. Must have development and maintenance programming experience. Need the ability to work independently. Manufacturing or distribution background a major plus. Send resume.
Provisions: Excellent salary with full benefits package.

CARLISLE COMMUNICATIONS, 4242 Chavenelle, Dubuque, IA 52002.
Positions: Typesetting input operators. Currently have 17 home keyers.
Requirements: Must live in Dubuque in order to pick up and deliver manuscripts and

disks. Must be excellent typist with high rate of accuracy.
Provisions: Training and equipment provided. Pays by the character.

CENTRAL ILLINOIS LIGHT CO., 300 Liberty St., Peoria, IL 61602.
Positions: Computer programming.
Requirements: Must be local resident with experience and equipment. Apply with resume.

CIRCLE GRAPHICS, INC., 8835 Columbia 100 Parkway, Columbia, MD 21045.
Positions: Typesetting input operators. Company has 12 operators on call.
Requirements: Must be local resident in order to pick up and deliver work. Computer required; any brand okay.
Provisions: Pays by the character. Will train for company code.

CIRITH CONCEPTS, 8727 FM 1960 East, Suite B, Humble, TX 77346.
Positions: Internet programmers.
Requirements: Proven experience in hand-coding HTML, CSS, DHTML, ASP, Visual Basic, VBS, SQL, and Access. Graphics, basic design and layout experience also needed.
Provisions: These are contract positions available to telecommuters in the Texas area.

CLARITY CONSULTANTS, 1901 South Bascom Ave., Pruneyard Towers, Suite 1300, Campbell, CA 95008.
Positions: Technical writers for online and printed customer documentation for complex Internet telephony products.
Requirements: College degree or equivalent experience, minimum 3 years technical writing in commercial software development, experience in telecommunications or database technical writing, and skills using HTML, Adobe FrameMaker, and ForeHelp. Must be familiar with Windows and UNIX environments. Must live in or around the Silicon Valley. Apply online at www.clarityconsultants.com.

COGHILL COMPOSITION COMPANY, 7640 Whitepine Rd., Richmond, VA 23224.
Positions: Typesetting input operators. Company handles all types of commercial typesetting jobs.
Requirements: Must own PC and have high speed Internet capabilities. Local residents only.

Provisions: Pays by the character.

COMMLINK CONSTRUCTORS, 1525 Flowerfield Drive, Concord, NC 28025.
Positions: Drafters for communications firm.
Requirements: Experience with AutoCAD needed. Local pros send resume.
Provisiors: Full-time or part-time hours. Will train for CATV drafting.

COMPUTER SOLUTIONS, 814 Arion Parkway, Suite 101, San Antonio, TX 78216.
Positions: Software engineers for development including object-oriented systems, three-tier architectures, and Web technologies.
Requirements: BS in computer science, engineering or equivalent work experience.
Need minimum 1 year of Java development experience for productions systems plus 2 to 3 years total software engineering, programming experience.
Provisions: Salary, full benefits, and bonuses.

COMPUTEREASE, 3016 Harrison Ave., Cincinnati, OH 45211.
Positions: Programmers.
Requirements: Positions are in the Cincinnati area. Requires experience in C++, VBasic, and/or Access. Send resume.

CONCURRENT TECHNOLOGIES, 150 Allen Road, # 107, Basking Ridge, NJ 07938.
Positions: IT business development.
Requirements: At least five years selling IT solutions with proven record of success. Experience must be in the area of e-commerce strategies, sales force automation, sales order management, and customized design and development in major industries such as telecomm and insurance.
Provisions: Pays draw on commission. Offers full-time or part-time contracts. Provides paid training and technical support when needed.

CONNECT ONLINE SERVICES; www.topwebpromotion.com.
Positions: Search engineers.
Requirements: Must have knowledge and experience of search engine positioning work. A proven and verifiable track record of successful positioning and ranking projects is required. Applicants must possess good communication and writing skills, along with good skills in all of the following: HTML, CGI, Perl, and Java. Also accepting applications for part-time and full-time homebased positions. Send resume.
Provisions: Can live anywhere in the U.S.

CORNADO; Cornado.com
Positions: Programmers, Web engineers, graphic designers, and content providers (writers).
Requirements: For programmers, preference is given to those with proven experience with PHP and SQL databases such as MySQL and PostgreSQL. Experience with Unix based operating systems and Apache a major plus. Graphic designers must be inventive, visual people who can create icons and images for Web sites and Web-based user interfaces.
Provisions: Variable hours and pay depending on qualifications. Prefers telecommuters.

CORPIMAGES.NET, 131 11th. Street, SE, Suite "B", Washington, DC 20003; www.CorpImages.net.

Positions: Web site designers and freelance Web site programmers
Requirements: Visit Web site to submit resume.
Provisions: "We are constantly looking for self-motivated, creative individuals anywhere in the world."

CROMLAND, INC., 2200 N. Irving St., Allentown, PA 18103; www.cromland.com.
Positions: Part-time web developer.
Requirements: CGI experience required for wholesale book dealer doing business online. Local residents send resume.
Provisions: Flexible hours available.

CROSS-CURRICULAR CONNECTIONS; www.crosscurricular.com.
Positions: Software testers work part-time from home for this virtual educational services company.
Requirements: Must have minimum two years of QA software testing experience including Web-based applications. Prior experience designing software testing strategies and familiarity with Macromedia Flash are strongly preferred. Must be thorough, flexible, have great attention to detail, and be able to work unsupervised from home. Need to have hardware for testing, including both Mac and PC. Familiarity with ASP.net, editorial skills, and Quality Assurance are a plus. Apply online.

CSG, 2708 Commerce Way, Suite 203, Philadelphia, PA 19154.
Positions: Typesetting for design firm.
Requirements: Experience typesetting on Quark platform is required. Local residents apply with resume.
Provisions: Offers flexible scheduling.

CYBERCODERS, 95 Argonaut, Suite 220, Aliso Viejo, CA 92656.
Positions: ASIC developers.
Requirements: Minimum five years professional experience with ASIC development and manufacturing.
Provisions: Pays minimum $80,000 plus extremely generous benefits.

DAOU-SENTIENT, INC., 10410 N. Kensington Parkway, Kensington, MD 20895.
Positions: Numerous opportunities exist for technical professionals with experience in M technology. Design, code test and implement technical solutions for leading healthcare institutions.
Requirements: Two years of MUMPS or MIIIS programming experience is required. Previous healthcare industry experience and knowledge of IDX, SUNQUEST, Compucare, HIS, CHCS or RPMS is desired. Apply with resume.
Provisions: Telecommuting is available.

DATA PROCESSING CAREERS, INC., 2720 Stemmons Freeway, #1207, Dallas, TX 75207.
Positions: Programmers with Visual Basic and/or C++ experience. Apply with resume.

DENTAL BENEFIT PROVIDERS, INC., 800 King Farm Blvd. # 600, Rockville, MD 20850.
Positions: Level II and III software engineers needed to develop, design, and enhance custom web-based, 3 tier applications.
Requirements: Client server and/or web-based application experience and three years

working with Visual Basic. One year MS ActiveX or MS InterDev preferred. Send resume with salary requirements.
Provisions: Offers excellent, ongoing training opportunities, full benefits, sign-on bonus, and the option to work from home.

DIART STUDIO, www.diartstudio.com.
Positions: Web designers.
Requirements: Apply online at http://www.diartstudio.com/job/index.html.
Provisions: Can work from anywhere nationwide.

DIGNUS, 8354 Six Forks Road Suite 201, Raleigh, NC 27615; www.dignus.com.
Positions: Software developers.
Requirements: Experience with IBM mainframe, OS/390, and C and/or C++. BS in computer science is also required. Local programmers preferred. Send resume.
Provisions: Pays competitive salary.

DS SEWING, INC., P.O. Box 8983, New Haven, CT 06532; www.ds-sewing.com.
Positions: Internet Web designers, programmers, and graphic artists.
Requirements: Programmers must know HTML, XML, some PERL, some CGI, VB 6, some SQL 7, MS Access, and have network admin skills. Graphic artist must know Adobe Photoshop. Digital photography knowledge is a plus. Must know and use HTML without using an editor. Extensive site design and graphics experience is required. Telecommuters must live in the area.

DUARTE DESIGN, INC., 800 W. El Camino Real, Suite 250, Mountain View, CA 94040; www.duarte.com.
Positions: Duarte Design has a broad network of contractors who help build Web-based marketing programs for businesses. "We are always looking for creative people to join our studio."
Requirements: Must be highly skilled in PhotoShop, Illustrator, PowerPoint, Flash, Director, HTML, etc. and portfolio of your work to show. Submit resume with cover letter and samples, via e-mail to WeWantYou@duarte.com.

DYNAX RESOURCES, INC., 6800 Jericho Turnpike #240W, Syosset, NY 11791; www.dynax.com.
Positions: MVS Systems programmers.
Requirements: Must have own PC. CICS, DB2, VTAM experience a plus. Send resume.
Provisions: Work any hours. Pays $35 to $40 per hour.

ECHO MANAGEMENT GROUP, P.O. Box 2150, 15 Washington Street, Conway, NH 03818; www.echoman.com.
Positions: This national software company specializes in the medical and social service markets. They need programmers to help develop new Windows applications using Delphi # and SQL databases.
Requirements: Need experience with Delphi, PowerBuilder, or Visual Basic. Position is in the Conifer/Bailey area and telecommuting is an option. Apply online.
Provisions: Pays salary commensurate with experience plus benefits.

ECTONE, INC., 2475 Augustine Drive, Ste 202, Santa Clara, CA 95054.
Positions: Software engineers.
Requirements: Minimum five years experience with Java technologies. Must have

proven proficiency writing JDBC and servlets and developing server-side applications. Must understand WebLogic, e-commerce security, XML, EDI, and nTier applications. Apply with resume.

EDWARDS BROTHERS, INC., 2500 S. State Street, Ann Arbor, MI 48106; www.edwardsbrothers.com.
Positions: Typesetting input operators, proofreaders, and layout for book typography business.
Requirements: Local residents only. Must have necessary skills.
Provisions: Equipment and specific training provided. Home workers are considered company employees.

ELECTRONIC ARTS, 209 Redwood Shores Pkwy, Redwood City, CA 94065; www.ea.com.
Positions: Contract programmers for conversion work. Also regularly backs talented software developers on original programs. Company mainly produces entertainment software for the home market. Some technical writing is assigned for documentation.
Requirements: Must have experience on equipment owned. Must have fervent interest in company's products. "We look for someone specifically suited to the project."

ELITE SOFTWARE DEVELOPMENT, INC., 2700 Arrington Road College Station, TX 77845; www.elitesoft.com.
Positions: Contract programmers for program components such as algorithms.
Requirements: Must own and have experience with PC. Prefers programmers who properly test their work and are capable of writing their own documentation.
Provisions: Generally pays by the hour, total sum not to exceed predetermined amount.

FEDERATION OF THE HANDICAPPED, Automated Office Services, 52 Duane St. # 26, New York, NY 10011.
Positions: Automated Office Systems is the newest of the Federation's programs for homebound disabled workers. It is similar to the typing/transcription department, except that all workers use computers and telecommunications equipment to perform the work.
Requirements: All positions require evaluation through lengthy interviews and personal counseling. All workers must live in New York City.
Provisions: Automated Office Services provides training in word processing procedures. Computers, telecommunication equipment and a phone-in dictation system are provided. All positions pay piece rates. Disability insurance counseling is provided.

FINGERTWICE, INC., 85 Bluxome Street, Suite 302, San Francisco, CA 94107; www.FingerTwitch.com.
Positions: Videogame development company uses coders for porting projects.
Requirements: Must thrive on working with multiple, evolving and emerging mobile development environments. You need to be able to work under limited supervision, be able to port, code and debug mobile device software, and have a keen sense of the constraints of mobile devices and their affect on speed and gameplay. The ideal candidate would have the ability to program software on various mobile platforms: J2ME, BREW, SymbianOS, PalmOS, etc. Send resume via e-mail to devjobs@fingertwitch.com.

FIRST ANALYSIS, 1030 W. Wrightwood Ave., Chicago, IL 60606.
Positions: IT projects involving Web application and database development.
Requirements: Ability and experience with IIS, SQL Server 7.0, ASP, VB, JavaScript,

XML, NT, Linux, and Exchange.
Provisions: These are contract positions that are available for telecommuting.

Carolyn Hyde
Blue Cross/Blue Shield of SC

"The best thing about working at home is being able to work my own hours, not being confined to a 9 to 5 job. The pay is better, too. Since I get paid by the line, all I have to do is work more to get paid more. It's nice to get paid for what I do."

GATEWAY TECHNICAL SERVICES, 11403 Cronridge Dr., Suite 200, Owings Mills, MD 21117.
Positions: Software development.
Requirements: Need solid experience in software development for PC applications. Send resume describing language capabilities.

GEICO DIRECT, One GEICO Plaza, Washington, DC 20076.
Positions: GEICO is a leading direct auto insurer with huge databases. Systems Programmers are south at all levels with any of the following individual or combined skill sets: DC/DB, IMS, CICS, DB2 MQ Series, DBA, Storage Management, Capacity Planning, Performance Management, MVS, and Unix.
Requirements: Positions are available at the Chevy Chase, MD and Fredericksburg, VA offices. Qualified residents in those areas send resumes.
Provisions: Excellent salary, full benefits, profit sharing, and telecommuting option.

GENERATION Z, P.O. Box 820372, Fort Worth, TX 76182; www.generationz.com.
Positions: Internet developer. This would be an R&D software systems engineer with experience working with leading edge technologies as well as existing Web technologies.
Requirements: Advanced degree in computer science, engineering or information systems OR 3-4 years equivalent experience in advanced engineering. Advanced skills in UNIX, NT, ODS SQL, and relational databases. Apply by e-mailing your resume to development@generationz.com.

GLASSWORD USA, 20859 King Hezekiah Way, Bend OR 97702; www.glassword.com.
Positions: Software engineers.
Requirements: Experience with MOSeries and ability to write software using Java, C++, and Visual Basic. Send resume.

Provisions: This is a 100% telecommuting position. Be sure to include contract rates with your application.

GROOVY LOGIC, 1228 East 2ND St., Loveland, Colorado. 80537; http:// groovylogic.com.
Positions: Professional Web site design/development from home.
Requirements: Must have experience and ability to build both small and large-scale sites. Must have knowledge in Knowledge in Dreamweaver MX and/or other WYSIWYG platforms, HTML, DHTML, Photoshop, Fireworks and Flash. You should also possess knowledge in some or all of the following, but it is not required: ASP, CFM, JSP, XML, Perl, Java, JavaScript, and building backend design with SQL and Access.
Provisions: Pays $15 per hour. Can live anywhere. Visit Web site to apply and put "Web Designer Position" in the 'Position applying for:' text field.

HARD SYSTEMS, 200 Stonehenge Lane, Carle Place, NY 11514.
Positions: This data processing service specializes in keeping inventories for major department stores. More than 600 home-based data processing employees and their managers work throughout Nassau and Suffolk counties.
Requirements: Must live in one of the two counties mentioned. Must own a personal computer. There is a 24-hour turn-around requirement and workers must pick up and return their work to the company if they live in Nassau County or to a manager's home if they live in Suffolk County.
Provisions: Pays piece rates (by the line). Pay ranges up to $15 an hour depending on the speed of the individual worker. Managers receive a base salary plus a 10 percent override on workers. This can amount to $12,000 to $15,000 for a 94-day cycle. This work is very seasonal and is therefore not available all the time. The best times to apply are July and August and again in January and February.

IISTEK CORP., 2645 Executive Park Dr., Suite 509, Weston, FL., 33331; http:// iistek.com.
Positions: Search engine optimization specialists. The positions will require the ability to analyze keywords, manage reporting software, customer service, and research new techniques.
Requirements: Must have some Web development experience and extensive experience with the Internet. At least 2+ year's experience required, optimizing Web pages for Google, Yahoo, and MSN with success. A complete understanding of search engine trends and search engine algorithms is a must. The ideal candidate has experience with WordTracker online keyword analysis, WebPosition Gold rank reporting, GRSEO optimization software, and WebTrends traffic analyzer.
Provisions: Can live anywhere. Apply online.

IMAGE WORKS, P.O. Box 3184, Vernon, CT 06066; www.imagesites.com.
Positions: Graphic designer. ImageWorks, employs full time artists and designers, and needs freelance artists from time to time as well.
Requirements: Knowledge of Adobe or Macromedia product line a definite plus, but not entirely necessary. "Show us something persuasive."
Provisions: Can live anywhere in U.S.

IMPRESSIONS, INC., 2016 Winnebago St., Madison, WI 53704.
Positions: Typesetting input operators for book typography.

Requirements: Local residents only. Excellent keyboarding skills are required. Must own computer equipment.
Provisions: Hours are flexible. Pays by the character.

INTELLISTREAM TECHNOLOGIES, INC., 801 West Street, Wilmington, DE 19801; www.intellistream.com.
Positions: Network engineers, software developers, and database application developers.
Requirements: Visit online for complete information.
Provisions: Can live anywhere in the U.S. Moonlighters welcome.

INTRACORP, 1601 Chestnut St., Philadelphia, PA 19102; www.intracorp.com.
Positions: Intracorp develops software for the healthcare management industry. This is a large and well-established company with multiple opportunities for programmers.
Requirements: Minimum two years experience required in any of the following: Oracle Database, Oracle Financials, C++ and C, DEC/VAX VMS, Rdb, RMS, CDD, DEC C, SQL Module, DIBOL, COBOL, and BASIC. Know of UNIX Shell, relational databases, 4GL's, Powerbuilder, object-oriented design and development, Windows NT and Internet technologies a plus. Apply with resume.
Provisions: Telecommuting is available to local professionals. Offers professional development/technology training opportunities, competitive salary and full benefits.

ISC CONSULTANTS, INC., 14 East 4th St., Suite 602, New York, NY 10012; www.isc.com.
Positions: ISC, an award-winning Internet and call center consulting firm, seeks freelance graphic designers, producers, and HTML jockeys. The company develops web sites that people use to perform work. People use ISC systems to: select and buy products online, define and display reports, easily retrieve answers from databases, and transact with other online users.
Requirements: Applicants should have the ability to present complex information clearly, and to create "intuitive" easy-to-use visual interfaces. Expertise with HTM editors, Photoshop, Freehand, and Delabelizer is relevant.

JNANA, 10 Rockefeller Plaza, Suite 1110, New York, NY 10020; www.jnana.com.
Positions: Java programmers. This company makes advanced software platforms focusing on markets in the financial services, law and compliance, and CRM.
Requirements: Substantial experience working with Java.
Provisions: Good salary, full benefits package, and the opportunity to work from anywhere in the world.

JDA PROFESSIONAL SERVICES, 701 N. Post Oak Rd., Suite 610, Houston, TX 77024; www.jdapsi.com.
Positions: Applications programming.
Requirements: Experience with implementation in Lawson, Epic, or Cerner Millennium. Some clinical experience as a nurse or technician is desirable. HIPPA or HL7 would be major advantage. Houston residents preferred. Send resume.
Provisions: Full-time contract pays $65,000 to $125,000.

LABMENTORS; www.labmentors.
Positions: MSCE mentors. LabMentors provides guided on-line labs for Web-based training in real-time lab environment over the Internet. Participants can log on anywhere, anytime to gain hands-on experience and advice in the study of Linux, Windows2000,

NT, Cisco, or Novell training programs/certification tracks. Programming and database labs will be available soon.
Requirements: Requires very good communication skills (typing is essential), fast and reliable Internet connection, and commitment to work hours (essential).
Provisions: Can live anywhere in U.S.

LAYKIN, Los Angeles, CA; www.laykin.com.
Positions: HTML coders.
Requirements: Experience maintaining multiple mid-sized sites plus skills with Java and PERL. Must understand graphics interfaces and cross platform functions. Apply online at www.laykin.com/lc/lc.htm.
Provisions: Telecommute with full benefits.

LEISTEN ONLINE SERVICES; www.leisten.
Positions: Web designers work at home and complete all work via the Internet.
Requirements: Ideally, you should have experience in one of the following areas: HTML, JAVA, Visual Basic, Shockwave, Real Audio, and FrontPage 98, FrontPage 2000, Net Objects Fusion, or Dream Weaver. You may send a short e-mail message describing your relevant experience or complete the application form at www.leisten.com/Employment.htm.
Provisions: Pay depends on experience and current skill sets. Can live anywhere in the U.S.

LETTER PERFECT WORD PROCESSING CENTER, 4205 Menlo Drive, Baltimore, MD 21215.
Positions: Company operates a mailing center and publishes three newsletters for businesses in mail order. About a dozen home-based word processors and typists work mostly on mailing lists and the company's two monthly newsletters.
Requirements: Must be Baltimore resident. Must own PC and have experience using it. Word Perfect software is preferred. Typing speed of 100 to 110 wpm is average among workers here.
Provisions: Will train on Nutshell software. Pays piece rates, which run much higher than in-house rates.

LIFT, INC., PO Box 4264, Warren, NJ 07059.
Positions: Lift, Inc., is a nonprofit organization that trains and places physically disabled people as home-based computer programmers for corporate employers. In the past 14 years, program participants have been placed with over 70 major corporations.
Requirements: Applicants must have a severe but stable disability, such as MS or impaired limbs. Pilot programs for blind and deaf workers are underway, too. Standard aptitude tests are applied to find traits as motivation, drive, self-control, and an aptitude for computer programming. Occasionally the candidate already has some training, but prior training is not necessary for entry into the program. Each candidate is trained to specifically meet the needs of the corporate client using whatever language and equipment the employer chooses. Most candidates are trained in systems programming and business applications.
Provisions: Upon completion of training, the programmer will work under contract with Lift for one year. The salary is comparable to that of any other entry-level programmer, with medical and life insurance provided. After the year is up, the corporate employer then has the option of employing the programmer directly. The placement record has been exceptional. Lift operates in most states now and plans to include all

50. Qualified persons are encouraged to apply from any urban location. (All workers are required to go into the employer's office at least once a week and most corporations are located in densely populated areas.)

MACARTHUR ASSOCIATES, 500 Fifth Ave, Suite 305, New York, NY 10110.
Positions: Database administration for credit card company.
Requirements: Must have strong experience working with SQL. Must be able to go into the Trenton office at least once a week.
Provisions: Pays salary starting at $75,000 plus full benefits.

MARYLAND STATE GOVERNMENT, Office of Personnel Services & Benefits, 301 W. Preston St., Baltimore, MD 21201.
Positions: Information Technology positions working on finance, health, assessments and taxation, public safety insurance, the environment, retirement, agriculture, the treasury, and other applications. Applications are continuously accepted for: Computer Information Services Specialist I, II; Computer Network Specialist Trainee, I II; DP Programmer Analyst Trainee, I, II; Lead/Advanced.
Requirements: On resume, list any computer programming languages in which you have expertise.
Provisions: In certain cases sign-on bonuses or tuition reimbursements may be offered.

MAVERICK PUBLICATIONS, P.O. Box 5007, Bend, OR 97701; www.mavbooks.com.
Positions: Keyboarding and proofreading. This is a small book producing company, established in 1968, that uses cottage labor where economics make it advantageous. An optical character reader is used to transfer manuscripts to magnetic disks. Computerized photo typesetting allows corrections to be made on the computer.
Requirements: Must be local resident.

MICROPROSE SOFTWARE, INC., 180 Lake Front Dr., Hunt Valley, MD 21030.
Positions: Company uses contract programmers for conversion work and is always open to freelance submissions of original software, particularly productivity tools.
Requirements: Must be nearby resident. Freelancers should send letter describing finished program on disk along with documentation. Contract programmers, send resume. Both should be thoroughly experienced and work with their own Mac or PC.
Provisions: All programmers are paid on a royalty basis.

MINDBUILDER, Northbrook, IL; mindbuilder.com.
Positions: MindBuilder develops and produces multimedia presentations and training materials for Fortune 500 corporations.
Requirements: Talented computer professionals should be self-directed and Internet-ready. Currently needs hardcore Visual Basic 5 developers with minimum two years experience. Need absolute knowledge of Microsoft Access and Oracle. Also coding projects available for C++, HTML, CGI, Perl, or Java. Any web development experience is a big plus. Apply online to imageek@mindbuilder.com.
Provisions: Pays competitive salaries plus full benefits.

MINNESOTA DEPARTMENT OF HUMAN RESOURCES, 444 Lafayette Rd., St. Paul, MN 55155.
Positions: Programmers and systems analysts. The Department has two very large IBM mainframe applications written in Natural using ADABAS as the dbms.

Requirements: Minimum of two years programming experience required. Need experience with Natural and ADABAS, or with other 3rd or 4th GLs. Apply with resume.

MONARCH/AVALON HILL GAME COMPANY, 4517 Harford Road, Baltimore, MD 21214.
Positions: Monarch/Avalon has been making adult board games for 30 years. Company now produces adult computer strategy games. Contract programmers are used for conversions from one computer to another and also for original program writing to company specifications.
Requirements: Must own and have experience with PC or Mac. Some game experience is preferred, particularly with "our type of games." Send resume and include references. Programmers are encouraged to send for free "Programmer's Guidelines."
Provisions: Pays by the job or royalties or a combination of both. Can live anywhere. "We have programmers as far away as Hungary." Currently has up to 25 contract programmers working at a time.

MONOTYPE COMPOSITION COMPANY, 2050 Rockrose Avenue, Baltimore, MD 21211.
Positions: Typesetting input operators for book typography. This is a union shop, so in-house workers are guaranteed work first. Any overflow goes to independent contractors. There are about 6 full-time and another 12 on-call home keyed on the roster.
Requirements: Local residents only. Must own computer equipment and have experience.
Provisions: Pays by the character.

MOONWOLF ENTERPRISES, 5303 Quintana St., Riverdale, MD 20737; www.moonwolf.net.
Positions: Language support technician for Web design/hosting company.
Requirements: Fluency in English and one of the following: Danish, Dutch, Finnish, French, German, Greek, Italian, Norwegian, Portuguese, Russian, Spanish, or Swedish. Also need experience with HTML, PHP, CGI, Perl, Java, Flash, and/or UNIX. Job involves translation of inbound and outgoing e-mail technical support issues and translation of design contract Web sites to target language.
Provisions: Payment for translation of Web site design is a percentage of total quoted contract.

NATIONAL READING STYLES INSTITUTE, P.O. Box 737, Syosset, NY 11791; www.nrsi.com.
Positions: Desktop publishing and typesetting.
Requirements: Educational publisher has overflow work only for professionals experienced with Ventura. Local residents only send resume.

NET CONSULTANTS, INC., 8000 Towers Crescent Dr., Suite 1350, Vienna, VA 22182.
Positions: This company provides software consulting and placement services for leading firms in the area. Part-time work-from-home jobs are available for ASP, Cold Fusion and HTML development.
Requirements: Apply online at nc-inc.com.
Provisions: Subscribe free to e-zine of local Internet developer events and jobs.

NETWORK ENGINEERING, 3010 LBJ Freeway, Suite 1500, Dallas, TX 75234.

Phil Neal
Contract Programmer, Maine

"I live in such a remote area I do as much as possible over the phone. I start each job by traveling to the worksite to do a requirement analysis and determine what needs to be done. I then report on what the client will need, how long it will take, and when they can expect parts of the system to be tested. From there, all the work is done strictly from my house. Living in such a remote area, it would be difficult to envision working in any other way."

Positions: This company started offering engineering services in 1985. They are currently looking for RF engineers with knowledge of LMDS-Point to Multipoint radio systems, including network frequency planning, antenna selection and modulation. Send resume.

NORTHWESTERN UNIVERSITY, 720 University Place, Evanston, IL 60208.
Positions: Maintaining database.
Requirements: Must be local resident with experience and equipment. Must obtain home worker certificate from Illinois Department of Labor.

NPD, 900 West Shore Road, Port Washington, NY 11050; www.npd.com.
Positions: NPD is one of the largest market research firms in the country. They have begun to employ home-based data entry operators to process batches of source documents. The operators are divided into groups of 20 each, with a supervisor for each group. Supervisors are also home-based and are treated the same as in-house data entry supervisors with salaries, benefits, etc. They are provided with PCs for their homes, but do not do data entry work.
Requirements: Good typing skills are necessary. Must be local resident. Must attend quarterly meetings. Must pick up and deliver work about every three days.
Provisions: PCs and all necessary supplies are provided. Training is provided in NPD office for one to two weeks. Work is part-time, therefore, only sick leave and vacation benefits (prorated) are provided; no insurance benefits. Pays piece rates equal to that of in-house workers. Applications are accepted, but there is a waiting list.

ON WORLD, INC., San Diego, CA; www.onworld.com.
Positions: Engineers, market analysts and Web researchers.
Requirements: Visit www.onworld.com/html/theTeam.htm.
Provisions: Can live anywhere in the world.

ONLINE JOB TRAINING, 2610 Central Ave., Union City, CA 94587; www.ojt.com.
Positions: Technical writer to document new product assembly and testing procedures

of semiconductor test equipment.

Requirements: At least 5 years of solid experience relevant to this job. Excellent skills with software graphics and text editing programs. Must be local resident. Apply online at www.ojt.com/team/index.html.

Provisions: This can be a staff or a contract position with about a third of the time spent working at home.

OPSOL INTEGRATORS, INC., Opsol Business Park, 1566 La Pradera Dr., Campbell, CA 95008; www.opsol.com.

Positions: Web designers for visualizing and developing Web clients to interface with back-end servers.

Requirements: Minimum 1 year experience using HTML and Java. Work samples will be required. Telecommuting is allowed part-time only so only local applicants will be considered. Visit Web site for current openings and apply online.

Provisions: Pays hourly rated based on experience.

ORUS INFORMATION SERVICES, 3012 Huron St., Ste 300, Denver, CO 80202.

Positions: Programmers for long and short-term contracts.

Requirements: Generally requires at least 5 years of programming experience working on NT platform with Visual Basic, ASP, HTML, Oracle, and XML. Will consider college graduates with the right background.

Provisions: Pays competitive salary and benefits.

PACVIEW INC., Santa Clara, CA/ www.pacview.com.

Positions: Java developers.

Requirements: Must be skilled in Java, Servlets, JSP, Struts framework, Hibernate, Tag Libraries and have experience with Oracle or other relational databases. Need knowledge of NT, UNIX, Web Servers, Apache/Tomcat, WebLogic, and iPlanet/Netscape. U.S. applicants only.

Provisions: Pays excellent salary and comprehensive benefits.

PLATINUM MEDIA WORLDWIDE, 81 Osborne Terrace, Newark, NJ 07108.

Positions: Graphic artist for print publisher.

Requirements: Experience working on commercial magazine ads is preferred. Must have your own equipment and materials.

Provisions: Pays on a performance basis.

PORT CITY PRESS, INC., 1323 Greenwood Rd., Pikesville, MD 21208.

Positions: Typesetting input operators for book typography.

Requirements: Local residents only. Experience and equipment required.

Provisions: Pays by the character.

PRATT SYSTEMS, PO Box 12405, La Jolla, CA 92039; www. prattsystems.com.

Positions: Flash designers for company that provides Web design, Internet marketing, Web hosting, technology projects, and computer security to business clients.

Requirements: Experience using Flash, Photoshop, and Dreamweaver. Page layout skills needed. Send resume with work samples.

Provisions: Can live anywhere in the U.S. Pays $15 per hour.

PRAXICOM CONSULTING SERVICES; www.praxicom.com.

Positions: LINUX programmers and sys/admin support for remote servers.

Requirements: Experience with LINUX, Apache, PHP, MySQL, SSH, SendMail, and Tomcat.
Provisions: Can live anywhere in the world. Work is part-time.

PROSITES, INC., 32209 Camino Caliari, Temecula, CA 92592; www.prosites.com.
Positions: Part-time and full-time designers for Web sites, print advertisements and other graphic design works.
Requirements: Must be capable of compelling work. Expertise in Dreamweaver, Flash, Fireworks and Photoshop is a major plus. Visit www.prosites.com/careers.htm for more information on application process.

PUBLISHERS CLEARING HOUSE, 382 Channel Dr., Port Washington, NY 11050.
Positions: Data entry operators work on PCs at home entering names and addresses and other data for mailing lists.
Requirements: Local residents only. Experience, speed, and accuracy are required.
Provisions: Pays piece rates. There is currently a waiting list of 6-9 months because the turnover is so low among the home-based workers.

QUEUE, INC., 1450 Barnum Ave. # 207, Bridgeport, CT 06610.
Positions: Contract programmers for writing educational software for Macintosh and/ or PCs. Freelance programmers also do conversions and programming to company specifications.
Requirements: Local people are definitely preferred. Apply with resume and references or work samples. Quality of work is very important.
Provisions: Pays by the job or royalty. Inquiries are welcome.

REMINGTON INTERNATIONAL, 10900 Wilshire Blvd., Suite 550, Los Angeles, CA 90024.
Positions: Applications software developers for major online mortgage lender.
Requirements: Must possess strong skills in VB, SQL, COM, DCOM, and working on Windows 3-tier architect on NT platform. Prefers local residents.
Provisions: Pays competitive salary and offers excellent benefits package.

RIGHT ON PROGRAMS, 778 New York Ave., Huntington, NY 11743.
Positions: Contract programmers for computer-to-computer conversions. Company produces educational programs for PC and Mac. Also accepts freelance submissions.
Requirements: Must be highly qualified. Submit resume and references.

ROXBURY PUBLISHING COMPANY, P.O. Box 491044, Los Angeles, CA 90049; www.roxbury.net.
Positions: Freelance home-based typesetters are used by this textbook publisher.
Requirements: Must have typesetting equipment (not PC; this is not embedding, this is actual typesetting). Los Angeles residents only. Minimum of five years experience. Send resume and indicate equipment type.
Provisions: Pay method varies. Inquiries welcome from qualified people, but there is a waiting list.

SPHERION, 475 Sansome Street, Suite 800, San Francisco, CA 94111; www.spherion.com.
Positions: This is an agency that outsources Web masters, Web designers, technical writers, and quality assurance testers.

Requirements: Minimum five years experience is required in each job area. Apply with resume and references.
Provisions: Offers competitive salaries and great benefits including profit sharing and 401K.

SIGNAL CORPORATION, 6354 Walker Lane, Alexandria, VA 22310.
Positions: COBOL programmers and systems developers.
Requirements: Strong working knowledge of COBOL, MDSII, and ECL required. Experience with Unisys 1100/2200 a must. Need BS degree with five years experience in software development. Positions are based in Pax River, Maryland, but telecommuting is an option. Apply with resume and salary requirements.
Provisions: Pays competitive salary, benefits, and retirement plan.

SOFTWARE TECHNOLOGY GROUP, Santa Clara, CA; www.stgglobal.com.
Positions: Oracle forms programmer analysts and Oracle junior DBA testers.
Requirements: Programmers must be skilled with Oracle forms design, specifications, coding, testing, and PL SQL. Testers must be skilled in configuring Oracle databases and unit and subsystem testing.
Provisions: Pays $10 per hour. Can live in any U.S. or Canadian city.

SPSS, INC., 233 S Wacker Dr. Fl 11, Chicago, IL 60611.
Positions: Contract programmers and technical writers. Programmers do conversions of business graphics software. Technical writers are used for documentation and promotional materials.
Requirements: Programmers must have experience with mainframe or super-minis. Applicants for both positions must send resume and previous work samples.

STANDARD DATA-PREP, 6 Dubon Ct., Farmingdale, NY 11735.
Positions: Data entry operations.
Requirements: Good skills, experience required. Local residents only. Send resume.
Provisions: Home workers are full-time employees with 37 1/2 hour work week, benefits, vacations, holiday pay, and 401K.

SWORDSMITH, PO Box 242, Pomfret, CT 06258; www.swordsmith.com.
Positions: Freelance coders work from their own homes on their own computers, adding the edits and typesetting codes to authors' disks for everything from romances to college textbooks.
Requirements: Applicants must have a strong eye for detail, a love of books and reading, and strong word-processing skills. Typing skills are a plus.
Provisions: Coders may work full or part time, and are paid by the job, not by the hour (experienced coders average about $15 per hour, but this varies from job to job). Coders must live within easy driving distance of Swordsmith to pick up and drop off manuscripts, and must be able to train at Swordsmith for a week. "Many of our coders are mothers with small children at home."

TECHNICAL RESOURCE GROUP, 5 Concourse, Ste 2160, Atlanta, GA 30328; www.dreamjob.com.
Positions: Systems engineers. This company develops and sells automated testing solutions and targets the healthcare vertical (specifically Meditech and Cerner) hospitals.
Requirements: Experience in Cerner or Meditech. Since this company targets Meditech and Cerner Hospitals, it is important that the person they hire is familiar with at least

one of these software packages. While you may work remotely from anywhere in the country, they prefer those in the NorthEast. There is also travel involved.
Provisions: $70-$85K.

TECHNOCRACY CORPORATION, www.technocracyinc.com.
Positions: C++ Developers.
Positions: Must have Artifical Intelligence knowledge and be very skilled with C++. Coding will be brand new, starting from zero on up, so people with heavy UNIX or Windows backgrounds only need not apply.

3D TEK INFORMATION SYSTEMS, INC., Orlando, FL.
Positions: 3D Tek is an Information Technology staffing company specializing in Pick or Pick-like, UniVerse, Unidata, SB+, and Masterpack. They provide quality computer professionals to clients across the U.S., sometimes on contract, sometimes permanent. To apply, fill out application located at www.3dtek.com/apply.htm.

TIG FIRST SOURCE, 2211 Norfolk, Suite 510, Houston, TX 77098; www.tigfirstsource.com.
Positions: Software developers for GUI programming on NT platform..
Requirements: Minimum three years experience working with VC++ plus MFC and development on NT platform. Educational requirements will be waived only if proven experience is sufficient. Experience with Com, Dcom, and ActiveX is preferred, but will train in those areas if necessary. Only local residents need apply.
Provisions: Pays competitive salary plus benefits.

TOPWEBPROMOTION, 321 Main Ave. Suite #2, De Pere, WI 54115; www.TopWebPromotion.com.
Positions: Search engineers for Web site design and promotion services company.
Requirements: Must have skills in HTML, CGI, Perl, Java, ASP/Chilesoft, and Unix / Linux / Redhat / server environments. Must have knowledge and experience of search engine positioning work or related technologies including PPC based software is an advantage. A proven and verifiable track record of successful projects is required. Applicants must possess good communication and writing skills, as some customer interaction is necessary.
Provisions: Can live anywhere.

UNIBASE DATA ENTRY, 510 Park Land Dr., Sandy, UT 84070.
Positions: This is a data entry service bureau that employs several hundred home-based keyboarders.
Requirements: Must be a Salt Lake City resident, have basic knowledge of keyboarding skills, and perform at the level of 10,000 keystrokes per hour including both letters and numbers (that's about 55 wpm typing with no errors).
Provisions: Training is provided over a six-week period in the head office. Training continues with the "clients" until the worker reaches 99.9% accuracy, then the work can be taken home from that point on. Work is picked up and delivered daily and this is done on a rotational basis by members of a car-pooling group of home workers living within close proximity to each other. Home workers are included in company social functions. Home workers are paid per item keyed.

UNIMATRIX INTERNATIONAL, 2101 East Main St., Richmond, VA 23223; www.unimatrix.com.

Positions: This is a large computer and Internet company with a wide array of products and services including hardware, software, networking, consulting, repair, Web design and hosting, e-commerce, publishing, etc. There are many positions available for IT professionals including: HTML designers, graphic artists, Shockwave and Flash editors, programmers (CGI, Perl, Java), and e-commerce specialists.
Requirements: Specific experience is not required though the appropriate skills are. The company is mostly looking for qualified individuals who are highly motivated. Apply by sending cover letter and resume to careers@unimatrix.com.
Provisions: Pays excellent hourly rates. Can live anywhere.

UNIVERSAL HEALTH SERVICES, P.O. Box 61558, King of Prussia, PA 19406; www.uhsinc.com.
Positions: MIDAS analyst.
Requirements: Ability with GUI software environment, ASCII file structure and project management experience. Some travel will be required. Local qualified applicants can send a resume via e-mail to cjohns@uhsinc.com.
Provisions: This is a full-time position.

USPAGES.NET, INC; www.uspages.net.
Positions: Web page designer/builders for database.
Requirements: PHP, MySQL (i.e. server-based database setup and programming) experience required. UNIX experience required, as all USPages.net, Inc. Web sites are currently hosted on UNIX servers. Must be proficient in HTML. Send resume including URLs of completed Web site projects to employmentdb001@uspages.net.
Provisions: Compensation package consists solely of USPages.net, Inc. stock or stock options. Only part-time positions are available. Can live anywhere.

V-STAFFING, 9 Woodcreek Road, Brookfield, CT 06804; www.v-staffing.com.
Positions: Email optimization and search engine optimization.
Requirements: Must be experienced with meta tags, title tags, keywords, submission to all major search engines and search engine optimization. If you are qualified, send your resume, four references and times and days you would be available for a phone interview.
Provisions: Pays $10-13 per hour, every two weeks.

VISDA ENTERPRISES, INC., 7509 Madison Avenue, Suite 114, Citrus Heights, CA 95610.
Positions: Hardware engineers working with OEM solutions for high-speed networking, digital broadcasting and data storage.
Requirements: Minimum six years experience in directly related work. Must be specifically skilled with RAID Controller, BSCS/BSEE, and hardware architecture and implementation.
Provisions: Offers full-time positions starting at $100,000 plus impressive benefits.

VISIONARY WEB SERVICES, P.O. Box 9053, Midland, TX 79708; www.visionarywebservices.com.
Positions: Web design experts.
Requirements: Must have knowledge of ASP.NET, .NET, HTML, FLASH, ETC. Submit resume.
Provisions: Can live anywhere.

WAVERLY PRESS, INC., 351 West Camden Street, Baltimore, MD 21201.
Positions: Waverly Press has been using home keyers for over 10 years to embed code for typesetting medical and scientific publications. This is a high volume operation typesetting over 250,000 pages a year.
Requirements: Applicants must type fast and very accurately. "Some are surprised at the level of skill required for this work. This is not just a typing job." Must live in the area. Also has a pool of proofreaders; must be able to read at a certain rate (about 27,000 characters per hour while simultaneously checking for errors in the copy. A test is given upon application).
Provisions: Initial training is conducted in the plant for six weeks. Workers are then supplied with PC, furniture, miscellaneous office supplies, and "an endless supply of manuscripts." Pay is dependent upon accuracy with 3 different rates: low, medium, and high. "Two thirds of our keyers are in the high range." Pays by the keystroke with the complexity taken into consideration; the computer is programmed to measure the work. Piecework with no benefits except a pension plan is available to those with over 1,000 hours a year. Daily van service is available to those who need it.

J. WESTON WALCH, Box 658, Portland, ME 04104.
Positions: Company publishes educational courseware. Freelance programmers can submit finished program with documentation for consideration. Contract programmers are also used for conversions and modifications.
Requirements: Freelancers should send only proposal. Contract programmers should submit resume, work samples, and complete information describing particular expertise.

WENGER CORPORATION, 555 Park Drive, Owatonna, MN 55060.
Positions: Contract programmers for conversion, modifications, and original programming to company specifications. Company publishes educational programs on the subject of music only. All programs are written by freelancers.
Requirements: Submit resume, samples, and references.

JOHN WILEY & SONS, INC., 605 3rd Ave., New York, NY 10158.
Positions: Contract programmers and technical writers. Company produces technical applications software for the engineering and scientific fields. Various types of work are contracted out to programmers, including conversions, testing, debugging, and some original development. Technical writers do documentation work.
Requirements: Must own and have thorough knowledge of Mac and PC machines. Send resume, work samples, and references.
Provisions: Payment methods vary according to the situation.

WILSON, HEWITT & ASSOCIATES, INC., 1700 Market, Suite 2200, Philadelphia, PA 11903.
Positions: Software development.
Requirements: Candidate should have knowledge of many software packages. Send resume.

WORLD SINGLES NETWORKS, 12030 Gatewater Drive, Potomac, MD 20854; www.worldsingles.com.
Positions: IT developers, database engineers, and Web programmers.
Requirements: Send resume to jobs@worldsingles.com.

YORK GRAPHICS SERVICES, INC., 3600 West Market Street, York, PA 17404.

Positions: Typesetting input operators and proofreaders for book typography.
Requirements: Local residents only. Operators must have good typing skills. Proofreaders must be detail oriented and have excellent English skills.
Provisions: All home workers are independent contractors and should understand that there are no guarantees of work assignments. All available work is overflow.

OPPORTUNITIES IN
OFFICE SUPPORT POSITIONS

Desk jobs" are among the fastest-growing categories of homework opportunities. Just about any kind of job that is performed in an office setting can just as easily be done at home. The availability of inexpensive office equipment combined with various telephone service options makes it easier now than ever before.

Some companies hire home office workers directly. But many times, they are hired through service bureaus. For instance, insurance policies have been typed by home workers for many years. But the insurance companies have nothing to do with the hiring of home typists. Instead, the insurance companies contract with policy processing service bureaus. The service bureaus are responsible for all phases of the policy processing and do all the hiring and training.

Service bureaus are popping up everywhere in the medical transcribing field. Medical transcribing is the top of the line of word processing. Not only is it the most financially rewarding of all keyboarding jobs - it is also an industry that continues to grow at break neck speed and there are more openings for jobs than most employers can fill.

The job involves typing doctors' reports and correspondence from recordings, which are usually accessed via the Internet with a WAV player. Employers often require several years of experience and test applicants to ensure they have a thorough knowledge of medical terminology. To get the necessary background, there are courses available through community colleges, private vocational schools, and on the Internet. A complete course generally takes from three to six months. But even then, you will need some practice in order to keep up with the 24-hour turnaround time required by most companies. One good way to gain some experience is to sign up with one or more temporary employment agencies. Explain what you're trying to do and ask to be assigned to any medical office jobs that come up.

Foreign language translation is included in this section because so much of the work requires office skills such as word processing, proofreading, typesetting, and transcribing. Again, this is a field handled almost entirely by service bureaus. Most translators work at home and many work for service bureaus located in another state or even another country.

Translation is not a job for amateurs. It requires a high level of proficiency in a foreign language and some bureaus will only hire native language translators. It is also necessary to have special expertise in a given field in order to be able to work with the terminology peculiar to that field. For instance, if you are a translator specializing in the legal field, you would need an understanding of legal terminology not only in English, but in the foreign language as well.

There is a new kind of service bureau that is still in its infancy: the virtual staffing agency. Companies such as Team DoubleClick are able to provide office support services of all kinds, from office administration to business writing, to clients worldwide. They draw from a database of hundreds of workers that will never leave home and never meet the client they're working for. They even get paid online. More of this kind of service bureau will surely be included in the next edition of this book.

A STAT TRANSCRIPTION, 712 Pine Forest Trail E., Port Orange, Florida 32127.
Positions: Medical transcribers and editors work full-time from home nationwide.
Requirements: Requires five years experience as a transcriptionist. Must have computer system with Win98, Win2000 Professional, Win ME or Win NT, and Word for Window 95 version 7.0 or Word for Windows 98 version 8.0 or Word 2000. Must have high speed Internet access, either cable modem or DSL.
Provisions: Compensation is dependent upon experience. Send resume.

A WORD ABOVE, INC., 12012 Wickchester Lane, Houston, TX 77095.
Positions: Medical transcriber.
Requirements: Three years experience transcribing consultations, discharges, and physicals from digital equipment. Need compatible Dictaphone system. Local residents send resume.

ABELSON LEGAL SEARCH, 1700 Market Street. Philadelphia PA 19103; www.abelsonlegalsearch.com.
Positions: This is a placement agency serving the legal field. Occasionally has positions that allow for working from home.
Requirements: Must be qualified, experienced, and live in the Philadelphia area. Should have good computer system.
Provisions: Check Web site for opportunities and more information.

ABS MEDICAL TRANSCRIPTION SERVICES, suite 301 - 2275 Atkins Avenue, Port Coquitlam, B.C. V3C 1Y5; www.absmed.com.
Positions: Medical transcriptionists work at home throughout Canada.
Requirements: Must be qualified MT with typing speed of 60 wpm or better, at least 2 to 3 years of hospital/radiology experience, and experience in one of the following: General surgery, orthopedics, oncology, cardiology, neurology, or gynecology. Need to have high speed Internet, MS Word 2000, FTP software, WAV pedal and headphones, and medical dictionaries.

ACADEMIE LANGUAGE CENTER, 124 S. Lasky Dr., Beverly Hills, CA 90212.
Positions: Foreign language translations of documents.
Requirements: Certification required. Local residents only. Apply with resume.

ACCU-DOC, 32 Pin Oak Road, Skillman, NJ 08558; www.accu-doc.net
Positions: Medical transcriptionists work from home nationwide. Work is mostly for doctors' offices.
Requirements: Minimum ten years working experience as a transcriptionist. You will need MS Word and FTP software.
Provisions: Starting pay is .08 per 65 characters including spaces.

ACCURAPID TRANSLATION SERVICES, INC., 806 Main St., Poughkeepsie, NY 12603.
Positions: Technical translators in all languages. Company specializes in business, engineering and scientific documents.
Requirements: Thorough knowledge of foreign language and English is required. Must also have experience in one of the three specialties. For translators outside the area, a computer and modem is required. Submit resume, noting areas of technical expertise and type of computer and telecommunications equipment.
Provisions: Pays by the word on most contracts.

ACCUPRO SERVICES, 30181 W 231st St., Spring Hill, KS 66083.
Positions: Medical transcriptionists work full-time from home throughout U.S. and Canada.
Requirements: Minimum two years experience of hospital transcription in any specialty. Experience specifically doing hospital discharges and ops for all specialties. You will need a WAV pedal, Internet access, and FTP software.
Provisions: Company supplies transcription software (MPWord).

ACCUSTAT, INC., W12006 Emer Road, Humbird, Wisconsin 54746.
Positions: Hospital transcriptionists work at home nationwide. Work is primarily ER dictation.
Requirements: Minimum three years as a transcriptionist in any specialty. Need to have Word 98 or higher plus HIPAA compliant computer firewall. Must have high speed or cable modem.
Provisions: Company provides Lanier NextWAV Player on a "rental basis" for qualified candidates. Pays 10 cents per 62 character line including spaces plus incentive and holiday bonus pay.

ACCUTRAN, 3480 N. CR 1100 W., Royal Center, IN 46978; www.accutran.net.
Positions: Medical transcriptionists work part-time at home nationwide.
Requirements: Minimum two years experience as a transcriptionist. Need MS Word FTP software, WAV pedal, and e-mail.
Provisions: Pays per 65 character line with spaces.

ACCUTRANZ MEDICAL TRANSCRIPTION SERVICES, INC., 2822 Eagle Point Road, Middleburg, FL 32068; www.accutranzmedical.com.
Positions: Medical transcriptionists work from home nationwide doing hospital transcription in all specialties. Full-time acute care MTs transcribe H&Ps, discharge summaries, consultations, and operative reports.
Requirements: Minimum five years experience as a transcriptionist. Need WP5.1/Corel

or Word-based software plus high speed Internet access.
Positions: Competitive gross-line rate in WP51 with volume incentive bonuses available.

ACCU-WRITE TRANSCRIPTIONS, Cowpens, South Carolina 29330.
Positions: Digital medical transcriptionists and proofreaders work from home nationwide.
Requirements: Minimum five years experience required. Must be skilled in MS Word and have high speed Internet access. Send resume
Provisions: Pays twice monthly.

ACCUWRITE WORD PROCESSING SERVICE, 63124 Alderton Rd., Flushing, NY 11374.
Positions: Medical transcription, legal transcription, and word processing.
Requirements: Medical transcription requires accuracy and experience as well as the ability to understand different accents. Requires an IBM compatible with Word Perfect and micro/standard transcribing machine. Legal transcription requires experience with depositions and hearings. Word processing is for manuscripts such as books and technical articles, mailing lists and personalized letters. Must have strong Word Perfect experience and skill in addition to own equipment. Must be from surrounding area to get to the office for pick-up and drop-off. Send resume.

ACTION TRANSLATION & INTERPRETATION BUREAU, 7825 W. 101 St., Palos Hills, IL 60465.
Positions: Foreign language translators work in all languages and subjects.
Requirements: Thorough knowledge of both foreign language and English is required. Some particular area of expertise is also necessary. Residents in Northern Illinois only. Submit resume and references.

ADEPT WORD MANAGEMENT, P.O. Box 710438, Houston, TX 77271.
Positions: Legal and medical transcription. All specialties available.
Requirements: Must have experience or have completed the SUM program. Knowledge of Word Perfect required. Local residents only.
Provisions: Pays by the line.

AD-EX WORLDWIDE, 1733 Woodside Rd., # 115, Redwood City, CA 94061.
Positions: Translators and some technical writers for translation of technical, sales, and legal documents, as well as literature, into any major language, or from other language into English. Word processors and typesetters also used, but only those with foreign language expertise. Work is sent via the U.S. mail, Federal Express, or electronically.
Requirements: Only experienced, skilled professionals will be considered. Must be versed in one or more industrial, scientific, technical, military, or bio-med fields. Knowledge of foreign language is secondary, but must be thorough. Need word processor. Send resume and work sample.
Provisions: Payment methods vary. 90% of staff works at home. Average 10 to 40 workers a day.

ADVANCE LANGUAGE STUDIOS, 500 N Michigan Ave., #538, Chicago, IL 60610.
Positions: Translators and typesetters with foreign language expertise work in all languages and subjects.
Requirements: Experienced local translators only. Submit resume and references.

ALDERSON REPORTING, 1111 14th St. NW, Suite 400, Washington, DC 20005.
Positions: Scopist proofreaders (legal transcribers) working from audiotape cassettes to written transcripts.
Requirements: Must type 80 wpm minimum or 15 pages per hour. Need excellent vocabulary and spelling skills in variety of industries, including legal, educational, medical, and government. Solid PC skills, attention to detail, accuracy, and ability to meet deadlines required. Experience preferred. Local residents send resume.
Provisions: Part-time or full-time hours available with flexible day or evening shifts.

ALL AMERICAN MT, www.all-americanmt.com.
Positions: Medical transcriptionists work from home offices nationwide. The work mostly involves doing acute-care or multi-specialty clinic transcription full-time.
Requirements: Minimum three years of verifiable experience. Must have excellent grammar and proofreading skills, up-to-date PC system, MS Word 2000 or higher, a WAV player, high-speed Internet connection (Cable or DSL), FTP software, line counting software, e-mail, and knowledge of HIPAA and compliance. Tests will be given. Next-business-day turn-around-time required. Visit Web site for current openings.
Provisions: Pays up to 8 cents/65-character line (spaces included) semimonthly. There is also a two year training program for those who can demonstrate the skills necessary to become an excellent medical transcriptionist.

ALL COUNTY PROCESS SERVICE, INC., Bowling Green Station, P.O. Box 1759, New York, New York 10274; www.allcountyps.com.
Positions: Process servers in New York City area.
Requirements: Experience required and licensed preferred. Must have knowledge of NYC and State Court system and legal terminology.
Provisions: Part-time or full-time positions available. Salary plus expenses negotiable. For more information on company visit Web site.

ALL PURPOSE TYPING SERVICE, 1550 McDonald Ave. #202, Brooklyn, NY 11230.
Positions: Word processing on Word Perfect module (not character set) in Russian, Hebrew, and Arabic. Work is on reports, theses, etc.
Requirements: Must know database Paradox. Experience and skill required. Send resume.
Provisions: Offers sizable contracts (over 100 pages).

ALL TYPE, INC., 2202 Route 130, North Brunswick, NJ 08902; www.alltype.net.
Positions: Medical transcriptionists work from home nationwide doing work for hospitals, clinics, and doctors' offices.
Requirements: Minimum four years experience required. Must have broadband Internet access. Visit Web site and fill out online application.
Provisions: Pays up to $40,000 per year plus comprehensive benefits package for the full-time employees. Equipment is provided along with 24/7 technical support. Training is provided remotely and in NJ office with hourly training fee plus travel.

ALLMERICA FINANCIAL, 333 West Pierce Road, Suite 300, Itasca, IL 60143.
Positions: Insurance claim adjusters.
Requirements: One to three years experience adjusting homeowners' and small commercial property losses required. Must live in Chicago metro area.
Provisions: Pays salary plus benefits.

ALLIED INTERPRETING & TRANSLATING SERVICE, 320 N. Alta Vista Blvd., Los Angeles, CA 90036.
Positions: Foreign language translation of legal and medical documents. All languages.
Requirements: Certification required. Los Angeles residents only. Apply with resume.

ALL-LANGUAGE SERVICES, INC., 77 W 55th St., New York, NY 10017.
Positions: Translators handle legal, technical, financial, medical and engineering documents.
Requirements: Prefers native language translators. Prefers New York residents because some projects require coming into headquarters. Resume and references required.
Provisions: Pay methods vary according to assignment.

AMERICAN FAMILY INSURANCE, Resume Processing Center, PO Box 3600, Nogales, AZ 85628.
Positions: Full-time property claims analysts for major casualty insurance company.
Requirements: Minimum 2 years experience in property claim settlements. Must be able to conduct investigations, document information accurately and thoroughly, make valid decisions, and conduct negotiations. Prefer someone with construction estimating knowledge. People skills a definite must. Send resume only if qualified.
Provisions: Offers great salary and benefit package.

AQUARICON, Seattle, WA; http://aquaricon.com.
Positions: Data entry. Job involves purchasing used books (using company money) at thrift stores and book sales, enter data about the books into database, and ship them to buyers daily. Everything is paid for, no investment is required.
Requirements: Live in any large city. Need computer, printer and Internet connection. Data entry speed and accuracy test will be given. Must be available 20 hours per week during weekdays. Must purchase at least 150 books per week.
Provisions: You are paid a fee of $1.00 for each book purchased, and 50 cents for each book shipped, as an independent contractor. This translates into approximately $15 to $20 per hour depending on your data entry and organizational skills. No need to report to an office, all work is done at home or in stores. Visit Web site for more information.

AT-HOME PROFESSIONS, 2001 Lowe Street, Fort Collins, CO 80525; (800) 347-7899.
Positions: At-Home Professions is a unique institution established in 1981. It develops and provides career education specifically for the types of jobs that are commonly performed at home. The courses utilize home study methods and can be done at the student's own pace. Some of the courses include: medical transcription, medical coding, medical claims and billing, massage, legal transcription, bookkeeping, paralegal, wedding and event planning, accounting services, veterinary assisting, day care and introduction to computers.
Requirements: Admission standards vary somewhat for each course, but generally an applicant must be a high school graduate, hold a GED, or pass an admissions test. Tuition also varies and can be paid as-you-go with no interest.
Provisions: In addition to providing top quality training programs and course materials, this organization also includes great follow-up services. At-Home Professions provides placement services, promotion of graduates through advertising and events such as trade shows, continuing employment instruction and advice, and personal counseling in job-search techniques. At-Home Professions is accredited by the Accrediting Commission of the Distance Education and Training Council.

CLOSEUP: At-Home Professions

As you look through this chapter, it's obvious there is a great need for medical transcribers. You'll also notice this job requires knowledge and skill.

So how do you take advantage of such a large, growing opportunity? One option is by learning at home with At-Home Professions. The home study course was designed by people experienced in the field and can be completed in about four months. At-Home Professions boasts a successful at-home job placement service, but graduates say the service is unnecessary because once your skills are in place getting the work is easy.

Several years ago, Rochelle Wexler decided she wanted to have more flexibility in her schedule. Working in Manhattan for a publisher from nine to five had lost its appeal. She went looking for something that would have a demand in the future, something interesting. "I don't want to be bored to death," she says. "I have a problem with that. And what I didn't have was a burning desire to go back to school."

After seeing an ad for At-Home Professions in a magazine, Rochelle investigated the field of medical transcribing and found it met all her criteria.

The company checked out clean with the Better Business Bureau, still, it took a big leap of faith to go from a secure job to something totally new. "I depended on At-Home Professions to keep feeding me information and telling me 'you can do this.' I kept working in my job, studying the course in the evenings and on weekends."

Within a month of graduation, Rochelle had her first two clients (doctors). "When I started out I didn't want to say I had experience when I didn't so when I got uncomfortable I offered to do something for no charge." That technique worked well, and it wasn't long before Rochelle was working at home full-time. She does all of her own pick-up and delivery, but says she never has to leave the neighborhood. ("Doctors are everywhere!") The doctors give her the tapes that document their every action and Rochelle returns the transcribed copies within a few days.

Rochelle feels anyone could do this. "I was never a typist and had no interest in being a secretary. But now I have a computer and transcription machine and I make my living doing this. The work is piecework so the faster I type the more I make."

ATI-AMERICAN TRANSLATORS INTERNATIONAL, INC., 145 Addison Ave., Palo Alto, CA 94301.
Positions: ATI is a leading international translation and interpretation service. Foreign language opportunities involve legal and technical fields. English word processing, transcription, and telemarketing opportunities also exist.
Requirements: Word processing and transcribing positions require ownership of an IBM-compatible computer, WordPerfect, fax machine, and modem. Telemarketers must have at least one year of full-time experience. Translators and interpreters must have at least five years of professional, full-time experience, and must focus on a specific industry.
Provisions: Word processors, transcriptionists, and interpreters are paid on an hourly basis. Telemarketers are paid by commission. Translators are paid on a cents-per-word basis.

201

BECKER AND ASSOCIATES, P.O. Box 607, 6801 Fair Oaks Blvd # G, Carmichael, CA 95609.
Positions: Administrative assistants, marketing assistants, and appointment setters needed by this business consulting firm. Job tasks include research, setting appointments by phone, setting up meetings, and generally developing business relationships.
Requirements: The most important requirement is thorough knowledge of the Internet and e-mail.
Provisions: Hours are available for both part-time and full-time work. Pays up to $15 per hour plus bonuses. Can live anywhere in the U.S.

BERLITZ TRANSLATION SERVICE, 180 Montgomery Street, #1580, San Francisco, CA 94104.
Positions: Berlitz is a huge translation bureau with offices all over the country and in 23 foreign countries as well. Freelance translators in all languages work in all subject areas.
Requirements: Thorough knowledge of foreign language and English required. Only experienced translators are considered. Can live anywhere, but for those not near a Berlitz office, a computer and modem are required. Make note of equipment type on resume.
Provisions: Pays by the word.

BLESSING HOSPITAL, 1005 Broadway, Quincy, IL 62301.
Positions: Medical transcribers.
Requirements: Minimum three years experience required. Must have own equipment. Local residents only may apply.

BLUE RIDGE TEA AND HERB LTD., 22 Woodhull St., Brooklyn, NY 11231.
Positions: Stuffing envelopes.
Requirements: Need intelligent (common-sense) people to stuff envelopes of different classifications for shows and conventions. Must report in daily. Vehicle necessary for loading of boxes.
Requirements: Needs and work changes (envelopes, data entry, packing teas and herbs) with different stages of business. Local residents only send resume.

BON TEMPS, 15 Maiden Lane, New York, NY 10038; www.bontempsny.com.
Positions: This is a temporary placement agency that occasionally places homebased word processors, paralegals, proofreaders, and other clerical support workers in the legal industry. Serves New York City and the surrounding area. Visit the Web site to check current needs.

CARONDELET HEALTH NETWORK, ST. MARY'S HOSPITAL, 1601 W. St. Mary's Road, Tucson, AZ 85745.
Positions: Medical transcription.
Requirements: Must live in Tucson area. Apply in person.
Provisions: Full-time and part-time opportunities exist for both highly trained transcribers and entry level applicants with desires to get into the health care field on the ground floor. For the latter, there is training available (this is highly unusual!). Income potential up to $40,000 per year.

CENTRAL DATA PROCESSING, 603 Twinridge Lane, Richmond, VA 23235.
Positions: Data entry for permanent part-time.

Requirements: PC operators must be able to enter data on a tight time schedule (24-48 hours turn-around). Must be able to give 25-35 hours per week, be responsible for 4 to 5 hours per day unsupervised, and be able to do weekend work. Keyboarding speed must be a minimum of 60 wpm. Need home phone, car and be flexible to pick up and take work home (10 - 11:30 am, 2 to 5 times per week). Must live within 20 to 25 minutes of office.
Provisions: Pays $8 per hour. Will train in office, so no experience is necessary. PC is furnished or you can use your own if it is DOS compatible.

CERTIFIED TRANSLATION BUREAU, INC., 2778 E. Gage Ave., Huntington Park, CA 90255.
Positions: Foreign language translators for all subjects.
Requirements: Experienced translators only; any language. Apply with resume and references.

CHILDREN'S HOSPITAL, 4800 Sand Point Way NE, Seattle, WA 98105.
Positions: Medical transcribing of dictated medical and surgical reports from all specialty clinics and hospital service for the permanent hospital medical record.
Requirements: Must have multi-specialty hospital transcription experience, and advanced, highly accurate, and rapid typing skills. Excellent knowledge of spelling, grammar, and medical terminology, as well as a good working knowledge of Word Perfect, MS Word, and the use of electronic communications are required. A high level of attention to detail is also necessary. Local, qualified applicants should send resume and cover letter.

CHRONICLE TRANSCRIPTS, INC., 815 West Avenue J, Lancaster, CA 93534; www.CTiMed.com.
Positions: Medical transcriptionist needed nationwide.
Requirements: Minimum five years experience as a transcriptionist.
Provisions: Full-time positions available. Competitive pay based on 65 cpl including spaces. Health and PTO benefits for full-time employees. Pay is by direct deposit. Visit our website to complete online application and send resume.

CLAIM NET, INC., 9 Corporate Park, Irvine, CA 92606.
Positions: Claim Net is a temporary employment agency specializing in placing medical claims personnel since 1983.
Requirements: Two years minimum experience processing medicals is required. Local residents submit resume.
Provisions: Full-time and part-time positions available.

CLERICAL PLUS, 273 Derby Ave., Derby, CT 06418.
Positions: Data entry, word processing, and transcription.
Requirements: Must own IBM compatible and have and be adept at WordPerfect, Word, MultiMate, and MS Word. Transcription work is usually medical. For that, you will need a micro tape transcriber and experience. Must be local resident. Submit resume.

COMPUTER SECRETARY, 300 W. Peachtree NW, Suite 11H, Atlanta, GA 30308.
Positions: Word processing, legal and medical transcription.
Requirements: Must own DOS computer or Mac with Word Perfect and Lotus 1,2,3. Experience and good skills required. Local residents send resume.

CONTINENTAL TRANSLATION SERVICE, INC., 501 5th Ave. # 1400, New York, NY 10017.
Positions: Freelance translators handle technical manuals, legal documentation, marketing projects, and medical transcription in most foreign languages.
Requirements: Thorough knowledge of foreign language and English required. Must have expertise in one of the areas mentioned above. Submit resume. Prefers New York residents.
Provisions: Pay methods vary.

DAVID C. COOK PUBLISHING COMPANY, 850 North Grove Avenue, Elgin, IL 60601.
Positions: Manuscript typing and related clerical work.
Requirements: Must own word processing equipment and have good skills. Must be local resident. Must obtain home worker certificate from State Department of Labor.

CORLESS & ASSOCIATES, 1904 West Cass Street, Tampa FL 33606; www.corlessassociates.com.
Positions: Attorneys in State and Federal litigation fields deal with disputes over construction law, personal injury, insurance coverage, mold, and products liability. Work in virtual office environment.
Requirements: Three to five years experience preferred, with scientific and medical background a plus. Tampa residents only.
Positions: Pays $35 to $65 per hour.

COSMOPOLITAN TRANSLATION BUREAU, INC., 53 W. Jackson Blvd., Suite 1260, Chicago, IL 60604.
Positions: Cosmopolitan is a very old translation bureau that handles all languages and subjects.
Requirements: Native translators are preferred, but will consider translators with absolute knowledge of a foreign language and good English skills. Must have a particular area of expertise for the terminology of that field (such as legal or medical). Chicago translators only. Submit resume and references.

CPR TECHNOLOGIES TRANSCRIPTION SERVICE, 25129 The Old Road #303, Stevenson Ranch, CA 91381.
Positions: Medical transcription.
Requirements: Prefers local residents. Must have minimum 3 years acute care experience and do quality work. Send resume as an attached MS Word document or as formatted e-mail text to: employment@cpr-tech.com.

CPS MEDTEXT, 58 Sprucewood Dr., Levittown, NY 11756.
Positions: Medical transcribers.
Requirements: Must be a well-seasoned pro with own equipment. Local residents only mail resume.

CYMED, 4450 Belden Village St., NW #506, Canton, OH 44718.
Positions: Medical transcription.
Requirements: Equipment and experience required. Local residents only send resume.

THE CYBER TRANSCRIBER, 1883 Verano Brisa Drive, Olivenhain, CA 92024.
Positions: Many types of transcription available nationwide.

Requirements: Minimum two years as a transcriptionist in any specialty. Must have MS Word, Bytescribe's Doc Shuttle, and FTP software.
Provisions: Pays 7-9 cents a line.

CYBERSECRETARIES, PO Box 1570, Whitefish, MT 59937; www.youdictate.com.
Positions: Legal and general transcriptionists and word processors work from their home offices throughout the U.S. and Canada via the Internet.
Requirements: Must have extensive experience in word processing using Word 2000. Must be an expert at grammar, including punctuation and have extensive experience at generating documents in proper form. Must be detail-oriented and be able to proofread your own work quickly and accurately. Minimum accurate typing speed of 75 wpm required.
Provisions: Visit Web site for more information.

DALE TYPING SERVICE, 8700 Old Harford Rd. #207, Parkville, MD 21234.
Positions: Medical transcribers.
Requirements: Local residents only. Minimum three years experience and equipment required.

DOMENICHELLI BUSINESS SERVICES, 302 Ventura Street, Ludlow, MA 01056; www.moderndayscribe.com.
Positions: Hires medical, legal, and general transcriptions nationwide. All work is done via virtual network.
Requirements: High school education, two years of transcription experience, and strong virtual communications skills. Must be able to complete (transcribe and self-proof) a minimum of one hour of audio daily. Only candidates with proficiency in MS Word and whose home offices are equipped with Start-Stop or WAV pedal digital transcription systems AND standard-size tape transcribers will be considered. FTP capabilities are also required. Forward resume and/or visit Web site.

DTS AMERICA, INC., 1916 Patterson St., Nashville, TN 37203.
Positions: Medical transcription and proof reading.
Requirements: Only local applicants with a minimum of three years experience as transcriptionists will be considered. Send resume.

DWH OFFICE SERVICES, 101 Brightside Ave., Pikesville, MD 21208.
Positions: Word processors and transcribers.
Requirements: Must own DOS computer with Word Perfect plus standard and micro transcribing equipment. Skills and experienced required. Only local residents will be considered. Mail resume.

EASTERN MAIL DATA, 3253 Route 112, Medford, NY 11763.
Positions: Data entry.
Requirements: Must have production quality work. Need IBM compatible with at least 20 Meg minimum hard drive and floppy disc drive. Must be highly qualified and test for 10,000 keystrokes with alpha and numeric experience. Local residents only send resume.
Provisions: Company provides software and training for three days only. Turnaround time for finished work will be between 24 and 72 hours.

EASTERN CONNECTICUT HEALTH NETWORK, INC., 71 Haynes St.

Manchester, CT 06040.
Positions: Medical transcription.
Requirements: Previous medical transcription experienced required. Strong knowledge of anatomy, physiology, and medical terminology required. CMT preferred. Area residents only send resume.
Provisions: Various full-time and part-time shifts available. Offers salary with benefits package.

EDiX CORPORATION, 4445 Eastgate Mall, San Diego, CA 92121.
Positions: Medical transcription.
Requirements: Minimum three years acute care hospital transcription experience required. Also need a commitment to quality work and an extensive medical terminology background. Apply with resume.
Provisions: Pays competitive salary and excellent benefits.

EDS, 111 10th St, Des Moines, IA 50309.
Positions: Data entry operators.
Requirements: Must live in Des Moines, Urbandale, Norwalk, Winterset, West Des Moines, Clive, Johnston, Ankeny, Altoona, or Indianola. Must type 50wpm or more, have a ground level entrance to your home, not be employed elsewhere in a full time job, and have local phone access.
Provisions: Flexible scheduling, delivery of work to your door, and cash incentives for productivity.

ELMHURST MEMORIAL HEALTHCARE, 855 N. Church Rd., Elmhurst, IL 60126.
Positions: Full and part-time medical transcribers.
Requirements: Experience is required and specific experience working in radiology is preferred. Local applicants only send resume.
Provisions: To work at home, you must be qualified to work without supervision.

EMPLOYEE BENEFIT SERVICES, INC., 6235 Morrison Boulevard, Charlotte, NC 28211.
Positions: Claims processors.
Requirements: Experience is preferred, but not required. Send resume and salary requirements. Local residents only.

EVERETT CLINIC, 3901 Hoyt Avenue, Everett, WA 98201.
Positions: Medical transcription.
Requirements: Minimum two years experience in a multispecialty or hospital environment required. Local residents send resume.
Provisions: Offers 40 hours per week, flexible shifts, telecommuting, with daily tape pickup at main campus in Everett.

EXCELLENCE TRANSLATION SERVICE, P.O. Box 5863, Presidio of Monterey, Monterey, CA 93940.
Positions: Foreign language translators for general and technical documentation. All languages.
Requirements: Thorough knowledge of foreign language and English required. Can live anywhere in California. Submit resume and references.

EXECUTIVE OFFICE SERVICES, 120 Bannon Ave., Buchanan, NY 10511.
Positions: Word processors, data entry, and medical transcribers.
Requirements: Need DOS computer with Word Perfect for word processing, plus database for data entry and for medical transcription, a micro/standard transcribing machine. Skills and experience is required for any position. Must be local resident. Send resume.

FEDERATION OF THE HANDICAPPED, 52 Duane St. # 26, New York, NY 10014.
Positions: The Federation operates the Home Employment Program (HEP) for homebound disabled workers only. Within HEP there is a typing/transcription department.
Requirements: All positions here require evaluation through lengthy interviews and personal counseling. All workers must live in New York City.
Provisions: The workshop provides training plus any extra help necessary to overcome any unusual problems an individual might have. Pick up and delivery of supplies and finished work is provided regularly. Necessary equipment is provided. Pays piece rates. Disability insurance counseling is provided.

FRANKLIN RESOURCE CENTER, 1205 Franklin Ave., Garden City, NY 11530.
Positions: Medical and legal transcribing.
Requirements: Must know Word Perfect, type 75 wpm, and Dictaphone usage. Local residents send resume.
Provisions: Pay $12 to $13 per hour.

GARRETT TRANSCRIPTION SERVICE, 8460 Rippled Creek Court, Springfield, VA 22153.
Positions: Medical transcription.
Requirements: Experienced transcribers only with expertise on Word Perfect. Springfield residents only. Send resume.

GLOBAL LANGUAGE SERVICES, 2027 Las Lunas, Pasadena, CA 91107.
Positions: Foreign language translators of general and technical documents. All languages.
Requirements: Prefers native language translators, but will consider certified translators Some special area of expertise is required. Submit resume.

GUARD INSURANCE GROUP, 16 South River St., Wilkes-Barre, PA 18703.
Positions: Claims representative for Worker's Compensation carrier. Job entails performing investigations, gathering information and handling litigation files.
Requirements: Minimum 4 years experience working on Worker's Compensation claims in the state of Pennsylvania specifically. Local, qualified applicants send resume and cover letter.
Provisions: Pays salary plus full benefits.

HART SYSTEMS, INC., 60 Plant Ave., Hauppauge, NY.
Positions: Data entry.
Requirements: Must be local for daily drop-off. Call for interview.
Provisions: Training program provided.

HEALTHSCRIBE, INC., 21670 Ridgetop Cir. # 100, Sterling, VA 20164.
Positions: HealthScribe is a national medical transcription company.
Requirements: Minimum three years medical transcription experience. Apply with resume.
Provisions: Pays excellent salary with full benefits.

HIGHLAND PARK HOSPITAL, 718 Glenview Ave., Highland, IL 60035.
Positions: Medical transcribers. This is a new and small operation and opportunities are limited.
Requirements: Minimum three years experience required. Must have proper equipment. Local residents only.

HIRECHECK, 805 Executive Center Drive West, Suite 300, St. Petersburg, FL 33702; www.hirecheck.com.
Positions: Background checkers for employment screening service. These are non-criminal searches. Job involves calling past employers, maintaining paperwork and documentation, data entry, and processing of information.
Requirements: Requires previous customer service experience, typing speed of 45 wpm, computer and Internet skills, and above average telephone skills. You will also need to have a total of three separate phone lines, a computer with modem, high speed Internet access, a fax machine, and a telephone with voice mail. Must be able to perform 20 searches a day. Applicants will need to come to the St. Petersburg office for one week of unpaid training.
Provisions: Pays $2.50 for each completed search.

HORIZON CONSULTING, INC., 7700 Leesburg Pike, Suite 402, Falls Church, VA 22043.
Positions: Loan reviewer/underwriter. Job entails performing technical reviews of FHA loan files.
Requirements: Minimum 3 years underwriting experience and 1 year FHA recent underwriting experience. Must have unlimited Internet access required.
Provisions: Pays good salary and provides full benefits package.

JOHN HANCOCK MUTUAL LIFE INSURANCE CO., P.O. Box 111 Boston, MA 92117.
Positions: Underwriting.
Requirements: Qualifications include nursing/medical background, minimum two years underwriting experience, ability to meet high productivity standards, with superior communication, organizational, and analytical skills, attention to detail, flexibility, motivation, and ability to adapt to dynamic environment. Proficiency in computer software is essential. Send resume.

ILLINOIS HOSPITAL JOINT VENTURES, 1151 Warrenville, Naperville, Illinois 60601.
Positions: Medical transcribers.
Requirements: Must be local resident. Extensive experience is required. Must own necessary equipment.
Provisions: Pays piece rates.

INLINGUA TRANSLATION SERVICE, 8950 Villa La Jolla Dr., #2110, La Jolla, CA 92037.

Positions: Inlingua is a major translation bureau with more than 200 offices all over the world. Freelance translators handle legal, business, and medical documentation in all languages.
Requirements: A thorough knowledge of foreign language and English is required. Submit resume and note special areas of expertise.
Provisions: Pays by the word.

INTERNATIONAL LANGUAGE & COMMUNICATIONS CENTERS, INC., 79 W. Monroe, Suite 1310, Chicago, Il 60603.
Positions: Freelance translators handle business documents.
Requirements: Must be expert in a foreign language and English. Experience working with business documents is required. Requires translators with own computers. Must live in the Chicago area. Submit resume and references.

INTERNATIONAL TRANSLATION BUREAU, 125 West Fourth, Los Angeles, CA 90013.
Positions: Foreign language translators for general documentation. All major languages.
Requirements: Experienced translators only. Prefers to work with Los Angeles area residents. Submit resume and references.

INVESTORS TITLE INSURANCE COMPANY, P.O. Drawer 2687, Chapel Hill, North Carolina 27514.
Positions: Title loan underwriter support.
Requirements: Minimum 4 years underwriting and banking or lending experience. Although the job is home based, there is extensive travel involved. Must be able to work effectively with management level people and conduct agency audits. You will need to be organized and thoroughly computer literate. Qualified individuals living in the New York tri-state area send resume and cover letter.
Provisions: Pays excellent salary and benefits.

IRVINE LABS, INC., Huntington Beach, CA. www.irvinelabs.com.
Positions: Medical transcription.
Requirements: Minimum 3 years in any specialty. Excellent, verifiable references are a must. Must have own PC and transcription equipment.
Provisions: Scheduling is available around the clock, part-time or full-time.

JONES, HALL & ASSOCIATES, 521 E. Joppa Road, Towson, MD 21286.
Positions: Accounting.
Requirements: Minimum two years public accounting experience. Knowledge of Windows based accounting, tax, and office programs. Local qualified applicants submit resume.
Provisions: Offers full benefits and telecommuting option.

KAISER PERMANENTE MEDICAL GROUP, 27400 Hesperian Blvd., Hayward, CA 94545.
Positions: Financial analysts.
Requirements: College degree in business administration, economics, health care administration, operations research or public health administration. An MBA would be ideal. Minimum 4 years experience as a financial analyst with at least 1 year in health care. Strong skills in the Microsoft Office environment is necessary and mainframe programming experience is preferred. Bay area residents only send resume.

Provisions: Pays salary plus excellent benefits.

KELLER'S MEDICAL TRANSCRIPTION SERVICE, 20430 Town Center Lane, Suite 5A, Cupertino, CA 95014.
Positions: Medical transcription.
Requirements: Clinic or hospital experience required. Local applicants send resume.
Provisions: Flexible scheduling.

LAKE REGIONAL HEALTH SYSTEM, 5816 Highway 54, Osage Beach, MO 65065.
Positions: Medical transcribers for not-for-profit healthcare institution.
Requirements: Typing speed of at least 60 wpm, medical transcription experience in large medical setting, thorough knowledge of medical terminology, and good communication and organizational skill. Must have word processing and dictation equipment. Local transcribers send resume.
Provisions: You can work at home after completing in-house training.

LAMONT TRANSCRIBING, 2701 LeJeune Rd., Suite 301, Coral Gables, FL 33134.
Positions: Word processing and court reporting transcription.
Requirements: Must own DOS computer. Transcription work requires strong background in court reporting and a standard tape-transcribing machine. Local residents only. Send resume.

LANGUAGES UNLIMITED, 11250 Roger Bacon Dr., Reston, VA 20190.
Positions: Freelance translators work in all languages on documentation for international businesses.
Requirements: Must be very experienced in foreign language translation and in working with business documents such as patents, taxes, or finance. Submit resume and references.

LEAPLAW, Velawcity Inc., 20B Milliston Road, Suite 169, Millis, Massachusetts 02054; www.leaplaw.com.
Positions: Independent homebased attorneys work in litigation, corporate, real estate, tax, environmental, employment, and immigration areas. Company is an emerging "knowledge service provider" to the legal industry, located in Metro Southwest Massachusetts. Visit Web site for more information.

LEE ENTERPRISES, 17111 S. Wallace, South Holland, IL 60473.
Positions: Clerical duties for mail advertising business.
Requirements: Must be local resident. Must obtain home worker certificate from Illinois Department of Labor.

LIBRARY OF CONGRESS, National Library Service for the Blind and Physically Handicapped, Washington, D.C. 20542.
Positions: Homebound disabled proofreaders in the Braille Development Section.
Provisions: A training program is available to teach blind people to proofread Braille materials. A certificate is awarded upon completion of the program. Work is farmed out to homebound workers from the Library's production department on a piece rate basis. Number of participants varies.

LEGAL AID OF AMERICA, INC.; www.legalaidofamerica.com.
Positions: Paralegals work part-time at home nationwide.
Requirements: Must be familiar with Family Law and/or Bankruptcy (Chapter 7). Litigation and research. A minimum of 3 years experience required in divorce, custody, child support, small claims, and/or expungements and responses. Must have access to legal forms and/or software to prepare documentation. Need fax machine, e-mail address, and Internet access. If interested, please forward a cover letter, resume and a sample of previous legal documentation that you have prepared through Web site.
Provisions: Pays $15 per hour.

M HAYES AND ASSOCIATES, 30 East Padonia Road, Suite 201, Lutherville, MD 21093.
Positions: Nursing case manager for disability and health care cost containment firm. Job entails working on the phone and in the field to review and investigate Worker's Compensation injury cases.
Requirements: Must be licensed RN in Maryland and have relevant experience. Must be comfortable working on PC. Qualified local applicants submit resume and cover letter.
Provisions: Offers excellent salary, benefits and upward mobility.

MAG MUTUAL HEALTHCARE SERVICES, INC., 3025 Breckenridge Blvd., #120, Duluth, GA 30096.
Positions: Internet medical transcription.
Requirements: Requires medical terminology including anatomy, physiology, disease processes, pharmacology, and laboratory studies. Must have minimum 2 years MT experience in one of the following: acute care, hospital medical records, emergency medicine, radiology, or multi-specialty clinic. CMT preferred, but not required. Apply online: http://magmutual.com/his/employment-opportunities.html.
Provisions: Pays good line rates plus production bonuses. Full benefits package offered.

MECHANICAL SECRETARY, 10816 72nd Ave., Forest Hills, NY 11375.
Positions: Word processors and transcribers. Work covers several areas: medical, legal, insurance, advertising and general business. Currently has 15 home workers and there is a very long waiting list.
Requirements: Must have good skills and own approved equipment; DOS with Word Perfect for word processing plus a Dictaphone for transcribing. Experience is required. Send resume. Must be resident of Manhattan, Brooklyn, or Queens.
Provisions: Pick up and delivery of supplies and finished work is provided. Pays

production rates. Full-time work only.

MEDCOMP, INC., 206 N Washington St. # B17, Alexandria, VA 22303.
Positions: Medical transcription.
Requirements: Must own computer, printer and phone line for call-in. Medical transcription experience required. Local residents send resume.
Provisions: Part-time hours available for work-at-home positions.

MEDIFAX, 12400 South Harlem Ave., #203, Palos Heights, IL 60463.
Positions: Medical transcription for emergency department, individual physicians, and hospitals.
Requirements: Looking only for high quality workers in the local area. Apply online: http://medifax.net/employ1.htm.
Provisions: Pays good rates and offers bonuses.

MED-TECH RESOURCE, INC., 2053 Franklin Way Southeast, Marietta, GA 30067.
Positions: Medical transcription.
Requirements: Experience required. Local applicants send resume.
Provisions: Work from home after training on company's system. Offers full benefits package.

MED/TEXT TRANSCRIPTION, 5116 99th St., SW, Mukilteo, WA 98275.
Positions: Medical transcription.
Requirements: Two years multi-specialty experience required. Local residents send resume.
Provisions: Full-time, flexible hours available.

MEDQUIST, INC.
Positions: Medical transcribers for all work types, including hospital overflow work; discharge summaries and operative reports. Currently has over 6,000 home workers and 90 offices nationwide, including Los Angeles, San Francisco, Sacramento, Denver, and Chicago. For job opportunities near you, check the Medquist website: www.medquist.com.
Requirements: Acute care experience is required. A test in medical terminology is given to all applicants.
Provisions: Choice of part-time or full-time hours is available. Equipment is provided on a rental basis if necessary. Pays production rates that vary depending on the part of the country where you're located. Inquiries are always welcome from qualified transcribers.

MEDSCRIBE, 3325 Hendricks Ave., Jacksonville, FL 32207.
Positions: Nationwide medical transcribing specializing in emergency departments.
Requirements: There is an online screening test and application at: http://www.medscribe.net/Applicants/?ContentFile=Apply.
Provisions: Can work anywhere in the continental U.S. Pays competitive line rates, offers weekly line commitments, and premium pay for weekends and holidays. Also provides for continuing education. Schedules can be flexible.

MED-TYPE, SunMark Professional Bldg., 417 Welshwood Dr., Suite 206, Nashville, TN 37210; www.Med-Type.com
Positions: Medical transcribers for individual, group multi-specialty practices, and

hospitals.
Requirements: Experience and proof of quality work is essential. Must be local resident.

MEDWARE, 2250 Lucien Way # 305, Maitland, FL 32751.
Positions: Medical transcription.
Requirements: Experience in emergency room transcription preferred. Minimum six months to one year of experience in transcription required. Commitment to quality work a must. CMT desired. Must be available for weekend work. Apply online: www.medware-inc.com/Employment/empOnLine.htm.
Provisions: Full and part-time positions available with multiple scheduling options available. Full benefits package offered to remote workers.

METROPOLITAN RESEARCH ASSOCIATES, LLC, 305 Madison Avenue, Suite 1240, New York, NY 10165.
Positions: Clinical scientists and researchers for supporting clinical trials for the pharmaceutical, biotech, and medical device industries. Jobs entail reviewing clinical trial protocols and providing summary reports with professional recommendations.
Requirements: A complete understanding of the entire clinical research process is first and foremost. Education and several relevant years of experience are required.
Provisions: These are long-term contract positions. Telecommuting is allowed, but only to local residents.

MOBILEWORD COMMUNICATIONS, 145 Huguenot St., New Rochelle, NY 10801.
Positions: Transcription operators.
Requirements: Experience is required. Must be able to type 80 wpm. Must have a Telephone Transcribe Unit (TTU) for online remote transcription. Send resume.

MODERN SECRETARIAL SERVICE, 1122 S. Robertson Blvd., #10, Los Angeles, CA 90035.
Positions: Typists and word processors. Company specializes in insurance policy typing, but does all types of legal and general work. "We're always looking for good people."
Requirements: Must have good equipment and skills. Test will be given. Los Angeles residents only.

NATION'S CARELINK, 5701 Shingle Creek Pkwy #400, Minneapolis, MN 55430.
Positions: Administrative assistants for nationwide health assessment company. Job entails conducting health interviews with clients who have applied for insurance. The work is done at home on a PC and on the phone during a 5-hour work shift. Work is performed primarily in the evening.
Requirements: Send resume with salary requirements.
Provisions: Training is provided. Weekly hours are 30+.

NATIONWIDE INSURANCE, One Nationwide Plaza, Columbus, OH 43215.
Positions: In-home care representatives. This is a full time job that involves traveling around the service area inspecting property inspections and dealing with small business commercial customers.
Requirements: College degree preferred. Must have a solid knowledge of construction standards and regulations, home building material and contents, and standard homeowner insurance coverages. Must complete specified Home Care core curriculum on claims,

loss control, and basic insurance principles. Minimum 2 years experience is required. Must meet physical requirements. Send resume.

NCR CORPORATION, 59 Maiden Lane New York, NY 10038.
Positions: Database specialist/researcher. Work entails recording of customer interactions, tracking leads and new contacts, monitoring customer contact coverage, and researching potential accounts through various means.
Requirements: Experience is required. Local residents preferred.
Provisions: This is a salaried position.

NETWORK REPORTING; www.networkreporting.com.
Positions: Transcription of depositions.
Requirements: Must live in the Detroit metro area. Requires accurate typing speed of 75 wpm plus computer and Word Perfect experience. Will consider training right candidates.
Provisions: Full-time positions. Comprehensive training and equipment provided. Earnings directly related to the quality and quantity of work.

NEWSBANK, INC., 58 Pine Street, New Canaan, CT 06840.
Positions: About 20 indexers and proofreaders produce current affairs references from their home offices. The work is part-time; each works from 20 to 25 hours per week.
Requirements: Must be local in order to pick up and drop off work twice a week and attend meetings.
Provisions: There is a three-month training period in-house for learning the company's indexing methods and how to use a personal computer. All equipment is provided.

NORTH AMERICAN CO. FOR LIFE & HEALTH INSURANCE, 222 S. Riverside Plaza, Chicago, IL 60606.
Positions: General office work.
Requirements: Must be local resident with office experience. Must obtain home worker certificate from Illinois Department of Labor.

NORTHERN ILLINOIS MEDICAL CENTER, 4201 Medical Center Drive, McHenry, IL 60601.
Positions: Medical transcription.
Requirements: Must be local resident with experience and equipment. Must obtain home worker certificate from Illinois Department of Labor.

NORWEGIAN CRUISE LINE, 7665 Northwest 19th Street, Miami, FL 33126.
Positions: Vacation planners.
Requirements: Must have high school diploma or equivalent, excellent communication skills, minimum 1 year experience in customer service or sales, scheduling flexibility, PC skills, and travel or e-commerce sales experience is preferred.
Provisions: Training is provided in Broward County, FL. Great travel perks, benefits, salary, and bonuses.

ODAY TRANSCRIPTION SERVICES, 9268 Litchfield Court, Elk Grove, CA 95624.
Positions: Transcriptionists work from home nationwide on medical and legal workers' compensation evaluations.
Requirements: Two years experience as a transcriptionist. Requires excellent English skills. Need MS Word, Corel, WAV file software pedal.

A CLOSER LOOK:
MEDQUIST, INC.

With over 6,000 home-based medical transcribers associated with 90 offices around the country, Medquist may be the largest home work organization in the U.S.

Founder and president Mark Forstein started the company in 1970, he says, "By happy accident." It is by no accident, however, that Medquist (formerly known as Transcriptions Limited) reached its present level of success.

The company is now headed by David Cohen, CEO, who says home workers are a tremendous resource in the work force. Aside from the cost savings to employers like himself, he claims home workers are fiercely loyal and supportive of the work-at-home movement and each other.

Some transcribers have been with the company for many years. "These are mostly women who start out with us when they have young children. After the family is older, some of them want to get out of the house and back into the office routine for social contact. These women have been loyal to us and we return the trust by offering them the opportunity to come to work in our offices."

The offices handle any overload that comes up. Since the transcribers are independent contractors, they can refuse work at any time, for any reason. This gives them some latitude (and greatly reduced stress) within the structure which requires a 24-hour turnaround time as a rule.

The company operates on a seven-day week, 24 hours a day. It is managed by key people on a management pyramid.

Inquiries from experienced transcribers are always welcome, but you should be prepared to prove your worth. Experience in acute care would be best and you will be given an extensive test in medical terminology.

The training session lasts only for a few hours—just long enough to get an overview of how things work and what is expected. "We do not offer the luxury of on-the-job training."

If you know your stuff, though, you can make good money. Pay is based on production and varies depending upon the part of the country you are in. In California, average pay is more than $13 an hour and in Chicago, one woman made $60,000 last year.

You don't even need to own a computer or a trascriber. You can also choose the option of working part-time or full-time hours.

These options are the result of Cohen's efforts over the years to comply with any and all aspects of using independent contractors. "Nothing," he says, "has been left to chance."

Provisions: Part-time and full-time positions available in all specialties. There are many types of transcription needed. Pays average $0.08/gross line.

OMNILINGUA, INC., 306 6th Avenue Southeast, Cedar Rapids, IA 52401.
Positions: Native-speaking translators for work in many different fields. All languages are eligible.
Requirements: Expertise in any area of business is necessary.
Provisions: Can live anywhere. Pay methods vary. Inquiries are welcome from qualified translators.

ORACLE TRANSCRIPTION, INC., 4007-B Norbeck Rd., Rockville, MD 20853.
Positions: Medical transcriptionists.
Requirements: Hires only the best MTs available. Requires a minimum 3 years of experience, with 3 to 5 years experience in medical records preferred. Must also have excellent medical terminology knowledge in a variety of medical specialties, knowledge of current drugs, excellent grammar and punctuation skills, an ability to meet tight turnarounds, and accuracy rate of 98%. Apply online: www.oracleti.com.
Provisions: Offers full-time (5,000 lines per week) or part-time (3,500 lines per week). Training is provided in your home over the phone.

OUTSOURCING LAW, Bierce & Kenerson, 400 Madison Avenue, 14th Floor, New York, New York 10017; www.outsourcing-law.com.
Positions: This is a U.S. national network of outsourcing attorneys, experienced in managed services contracting, strategic alliances, joint ventures, teaming agreements and similar corporate transactions.
Requirements: Must have at least 10 years' experience in corporate and technology law, with at least 5 years' experience in outsourcing transactions. Can live anywhere in U.S., but particularly interested in candidates in Washington, D.C., Boston, Chicago, Denver, St. Louis, Seattle and Florida. Visit Web site for more information.
Provisions: To $250,000 per year.

PAR EXCELLENCE, 621 Shrewsbury Ave., Shrewsbury, NJ 07702.
Positions: CAD operators for facilities engineering.
Requirements: Experience and equipment required. Local applicants send resume.
Provisions: Part-time or full-time.

THE PEAK ORGANIZATION, INC., 25 West 31st Street, Penthouse, New York, NY 10001; www.peakorg.com.
Positions: This is a professional staffing agency that occasionally places homebased paralegals in the New York area. Visit the Web site for more information and to see current opportunities.

THE PERMANENTE MEDICAL GROUP, INC., 3801 Howe Street, Oakland, CA 94611.
Positions: Financial analysts and consultants for the largest medical group in Northern California. Responsibilities include supporting budget allocation decisions, providing analytical support to management in the financial department, and providing stats.
Requirements: Must have a degree in business administration, economics, health care administration, operations research or public health administration. A Master's degree is preferred. Minimum 4 years experience is required, preferably in the health care field. Must be comfortable working with Microsoft Office. Programming experience

would be ideal.
Provisions: Telecommuting is available to the right candidates. Excellent salary and benefits.

PETERS SHORTHAND REPORTING CORPORATION, 3336 Bradshaw Rd., Sacramento, CA 95827.
Positions: Court reporting and transcribing.
Requirements: Must be local resident. Some travel is required. Experience is necessary.
Provisions: Pays hourly, plus piece rates, plus expenses.

POMONA VALLEY HOSPITAL MEDICAL CENTER, 1798 N. Garey Ave., Pomona, CA 91767.
Positions: Hires Level III medical transcribers.
Requirements: Requires experience in the Basic 4 with a minimum of 5 years on the job including 2 to 3 years acute care hospital experience. Must be production oriented and be DSL line qualified. Excellent spelling, grammar and knowledge of medical terminology and anatomy a must. Local residents only please.

PREFERRED BUSINESS CENTERS, 875 N. Michigan, Suite 3614, Chicago, IL 60601.
Positions: General transcription.
Requirements: Must be experienced and have necessary equipment. Local residents only.

PREMIER TRANSCRIPTION, 9620 Colerain Ave. #20, Cincinnati, OH 45251.
Positions: Medical transcription.
Requirements: Minimum two years hospital experience required. Local applicants send resume.
Provisions: Flexible schedule and top pay.

QT MEDICAL SERVICES, INC., 334 East Lake Rd., #308, Palm Harbor, FL 34685.
Positions: Medical transcription.
Requirements: Must be highly qualified with at least 3 years of hospital transcription experience. All medical specialties are needed. Apply online: http://qtmedical.com. Local residents only.

RAPID TRANSCRIPT, INC., 4311 Wilshire Blvd., #209, Los Angeles, CA 90010.
Positions: This is a well-established medical transcription company that provides services both locally and nationwide to hospitals, physician groups, and imaging centers. They are always looking for good transcriptionists to work part-time or full-time.
Requirements: Apply online at www.rapidtranscript.com/position.html and then complete a 25-minute transcription test. Requires 1 year as a working MT, preferably in acute care. Relies most heavily on test scores for hiring decisions.
Provisions: Pays .07 to .095 cents per 65-character line (includes spaces and enters). Also offers bonuses. This is one of the rare companies that encourages Newbies.

REALREPLY.COM, Tam Yam Inc., 1314 E. Las Olas Blvd., #142, Ft. Lauderdale, FL 33301.
Positions: Clerical work involving processing customer orders for computer software.
Requirements: Abilities in data entry, filing, and typing (40 wpm) as well as proficiency in Windows and MS Word. You will also need Internet knowledge and written

communication skills. Apply by sending e-mail to recruiter@realreply.com.
Provisions: Hours can be part-time or full-time.

ROSE RESNICK LIGHTHOUSE, 214 Van Ness Ave., San Francisco, CA 94102.
Positions: This agency is the largest of its kind in Northern California, providing services to the blind and visually impaired community since 1902. There is a constant need of certified literary Braille transcribers with knowledge of computer Braille code. The agency supports Braille production using Duxbury and/or MegaDots.
Requirements: If you meet the qualifications mentioned above, send your list of qualifications, rate list, and contact information to Damian Pickering either by mail or email: dpickering@lighthouse-sf.org.

RICHMOND REPORTING, 535 Broadhollow Rd., Melville, NY 11747.
Positions: Legal transcribers.
Requirements: Need people with law industry background and knowledge of legal depositions. Must be able to do 70 wpm with accuracy and be able to report to the office 2 to 3 times a week to drop off work. Must own or have access to a computer with laser printer and a Stenorette (a Dictaphone machine with a reel-to-reel spool tape, NOT a cassette pop-in). Stenorette must have a foot pedal. Work is based on individual contracts. Send resume.

RMS COMPUTER SERVICES, 11 Kilkea Ct., Baltimore, MD 21236.
Positions: Word processors and proofreaders.
Requirements: Must own DOS computer with Word Perfect. Skills and experienced required. Must live close by. Send resume.

MARION J. ROSLEY SECRETARIAL SERVICES, 41 Topland Rd., Hartsdale, NY 10530.
Positions: Word processors, all types of transcription, and graphic art.
Requirements: Need all levels of people for word processing using Macintosh, Word Perfect and Windows. Local residents mail resumes.

SANS CONSULTING SERVICES, INC., 90 John Street, Suite 313, New York, NY 10038; www.sans.com.
Positions: This is a technical and legal placement agency that sometimes places homebased paralegals, legal clerks, and legal proofreaders in the New York City area. Visit Web site for more information and to check current openings.

SCRIBES ONLINE, 1310 Beulah Rd., Pittsburgh, PA 15235.
Positions: Medical Language specialists. These are full-time positions for experienced transcriptionists.
Requirements: High productivity and experience with digital dictation systems. Two years of in-patient transcription experience working with a variety of reports and specialties. Prefers in-patient and surgical experience as well as knowledge of productivity enhancement tools. Must have familiarity with home PC, Internet protocols and electronic communications.
Provisions: Pays per line plus incentive bonus. This is a high volume service.

SECRETARY ON CALL, 307L Cuernavaca Dr., N., Austin, Texas 78733.
Positions: Legal secretaries.

Requirements: Minimum 5 years experience. Apply via e-mail to jobs@secretaryoncall.com.

SELECT TRANSCRIPTION, INC., 544 3rd St., Elk River, MN 55330.
Positions: This is a medical transcription company owned and operated by transcriptionists.
Requirements: Must have a minimum of two years medical transcription experience in either an acute care or clinic setting. Local applicants send resume.
Provisions: Pays excellent wages plus health benefits are available.

SETON HEALTH, Attn: Human Resources, 1300 Massachusetts Ave., Troy, NY 12180.
Positions: Medical transcribers.
Requirements: Experience working in medical records department of hospital is required. Local residents send resume.
Provisions: Pays good rates. Offers flexible scheduling.

SH3, INC., 5338 E. 115th St. Kansas City, MO 64137.
Positions: Freelance translators for this service bureau.
Requirements: Thorough knowledge of French, German, Italian, or Spanish. You must be experienced and able to provide telecommunications, IBM PC (or compatible) disks. Send resume.

SHERMAN HOSPITAL, 934 Center St., Elgin, IL.
Positions: Medical transcribing.
Requirements: Must be local resident. Equipment, good skills and a minimum five years experience are required.

STAT TRANSCRIPTION SERVICES, 6475 Camden Ave., #210, San Jose, CA 95120.
Positions: Medical transcription.
Requirements: Two years experience in radiology. Local applicants send resume.

STATISTICS MEDICAL RECORDS, INC., 135 Carroll St., Bronx, NY 10464.
Positions: Medical transcription.
Requirements: Five years active experience required. No medical secretaries. Local applicants (New York and Westchester) send resume.
Provisions: Part/full-time flexible schedules. Company supplies equipment.

TALK2TYPE TRANSCRIPTIONS, INC., 14101 Valleyheart Drive, Suite 101, Sherman Oaks, CA 91423; www.talk2type.net.
Positions: Transcribers.
Requirements: Minimum typing speed of 85+ words per minute. Especially want people who can work nights. Local residents only.
Provisions: Full and part-time positions available.

TEAM DOUBLE CLICK, W10530 Airport Road, Lodi, WI 53555; www.TeamDoubleClick.com.
Positions: Team Double Click is a service bureau that teams up homebased workers with employers. They have a database of over 1000 virtual workers in dozens of job capacities. One of their greatest needs is for administrative assistants, but all kinds of workers are needed to provide help with: mailings, marketing assistance, answering

phones, appointment setting, research, Web design, bookkeeping, graphic design, data entry, e-mail processing, customer support, telemarketing, writing, audio editing, data entry, and transcription.

Requirements: Visit the Web site and fill out the online application form. Workers can live anywhere but must have Internet access since all work is assigned and completed online.

Provisions: All workers are independent contractors. Typically pays within one week.

CLOSEUP: Team Double Click

There is a new kind of service bureau emerging thanks to the Internet and Web-based technology. It's known as a virtual staffing agency. Team Double Click is one such agency, based in tiny Lodi, Wisconsin. It is owned and operated by Gayle and Jim Buske. A mere year after hanging out their virtual shingle, the company already has over 1000 virtual workers in their database and over 150 clients around the world.

Team Double Click is able to provide clients as far away as Saudi Arabia with numerous administrative, creative and/or technical services. Gayle Buske says, "Our virtual assistants can do almost anything that an in-person staff member can do - except filing, of course." Team members are homebased professionals of all kinds including administrative assistants, data entry workers, writers, editors, graphic designers, marketing pros, Web designers, transcribers, telemarketers, and more.

The virtual professionals here are all freelancers. They join the team by filling out an extensive form online that outlines skills and experience. When a client calls looking for help, Team Double Click quickly searches the database and reviews resumes to see who might be a fit. Anyone who is a good candidate is contacted individually to discuss the project. Sometimes projects are unusual and it's difficult to find the right person easily. When that happens, the agency sends out a "group call" via e-mail, asking anyone who is capable and available to reply.

For team members, the agency offers flexibility, marketing, and good pay. For example, the pay for general administrative work is about $18 an hour. Other tasks pay more. Team Double Click gets a 15 percent cut. It's a good deal for freelancers who don't have the time or inclination to market their own services or deal with the headache of billing.

Virtual staffing is still in its infancy and there aren't many companies out there like Team Double Click - yet. But the technology is here and trends follow technology. For example, only two years ago most transcription service bureaus needed home workers to live nearby so that tapes and finished hard copies could be picked up and delivered every day. Now the technology has evolved to the point where all transcription can - and is - being done online. With high-speed Internet connections plus a new type of transcribing machine (WAV), transcribers can live anywhere including the most remote areas.

"At some point we'd like to see virtual help as a universal way of doing business," Gayle says. It's going to take some time to educate potential business clients on the benefits of hiring virtual assistants. But it will happen. Anyone who doesn't believe that should remember that only 15 years ago working at home in any capacity was considered odd. Now it's the accepted norm.

"Lately, we've noticed a trend with the new clients we're adding," says Gayle. "Many are actually hiring us to take work away from bricks-and-mortar assistants. It's not because they're unhappy with them or their work - they're giving it to us because they've learned that hiring virtually is much more convenient and economical for them. I find this so encouraging. Our world is moving that much closer to a new way of working and hiring - virtually! It's our mission to make virtual working and virtual hiring the thing to do."

TELETRANS, INC., 22471 N. 81st Ave., Peoria, AZ 85382.
Positions: Company needs medical transcribers in the Phoenix area. This is a fully digitalized service.
Requirements: Minimum 3 years transcription experience or graduate of medical transcription school and experience with MS Word. Must work on a 48 hour turnaround. To apply, send resume as an attached MS Word document or as a formatted e-mail text to: employment@teletransinc.com. Put "resume" on the subject line.
Provisions: Pays competitive line rate.

THOMAS TRANSCRIPTION SERVICES, INC., P. O. Box 26613, Jacksonville, Fl 32226; www.thomastx.com.
Positions: Medical transcriptionists are needed nationwide. "We are always looking for qualified medical transcriptionists to join our company."
Requirements: Minimum three years experience. Visit http://www.thomastx.com/Employment.htm for application form.

TRANSCEND SERVICES, INC., 945 E. Paces Ferry Rd., NE #1475, Atlanta, GA 30305.
Positions: Medical language transcriptionists.
Requirements: Minimum 3 years acute care transcription experience in full service hospital or clinic. Must work at least 35 hours per week. Local applicants only please.
Provisions: Supplies PC hardware and software configured to company requirements. Pays production rates exceeding $30k per year plus incentive and production bonuses and benefits.

TRANSCRIPTION SOLUTIONS, P.O. Box 57392, Des Moines, IA 50317.
Positions: Medical transcription.
Requirements: Must be local and experienced. Send resume.

TRICON GLOBAL RESTAURANTS, www.triconglobal.com.
Positions: Management recruiters for this company's group of fast food restaurants: KFC, Taco Bell, Pizza Hut, etc. Duties include conducting direct sourcing calls, conducting screening interviews by phone, and assisting with all other phases of the hiring process.
Requirements: Recruiting experience required. Apply online.

TUREK - VENTURE 2, P.O. Box 187, Catasauqua, PA 18032.
Positions: Medical transcribers.
Requirements: Experience required in all types of medicine and practices. Need own equipment including micro and standard tape transcribing machines. Local residents send resume.

24 HOUR SECRETARY, 1004 Reisterstown Road, Pikesville, MD 21208.
Positions: Medical and legal transcription.

Requirements: At least three years experience with certificate preferred. Must own DOS computer with Word Perfect and the ability to take all types of tapes. Must be from surrounding area and come to the office to pick up documents. Will work with modem, but still needs to be local. Send resume.

UMI/DATA COURIER, 620 S. Third St., Louisville, KY 40202.
Positions: About 30 abstracters work at home as independent contractors. Home workers have been used here since 1976.
Requirements: Must live nearby in order to pick up the publications that you will be abstracting once a week. Reasonable good communication skills are needed. Send resume.
Provisions: Computers are necessary for the job and the company does provide them.

UPDATE LEGAL, www.updatelegal.com.
Positions: This is a legal placement agency with offices in San Francisco, Boston, New York, Houston, Newark, and Philadelphia. They place attorneys, paralegals and practice support staff with law firms and corporate legal departments. They occasionally have opportunities that permit part-time work from home.
Requirements: Must be highly qualified and experienced. Visit Web site to check current opportunities.
Provisions: Pays competitive rates.

VERDICTS.COM; www.verdicts.com.
Positions: Paralegals work at home in the Eastern and Central U.S. This firm publishes jury verdict summaries and uses legal researchers for case summaries. Each case takes about 1 to 2 hours to complete.
Requirements: Must have legal or casualty claims background. Requires a good understanding of the basics of personal injury litigation and the ability to write a coherent story that accurately reflects the essential issues of a specific jury trial. Must have computer with high speed Internet access.
Provisions: Full-time and part-time hours available. Pays a flat rate of $20 per completed summary plus telephone expenses. Most researchers here complete 500 to 800 case summaries annually.

VERNA MEDICAL TRANSCRIPTIONS, 156 Smithwood Avenue, Milpitas, CA 95035.
Positions: Medical transcribers for all types of medical records.
Requirements: Experience is necessary. Must own good typewriter and transcribing machine with either standard or micro cassettes. Must be local resident in order to pick up and deliver supplies and finished work.
Provisions: Pays piece rates. Part-time or full-time work is available.

VIDEO MONITORING SERVICE, 185 Berry St. #1400, San Francisco, CA 94107.
Positions: News monitors for national broadcast news retrieval service.
Requirements: Reliability, attention to detail, and good writing skills required. Need PC with modem. Openings are in Sacramento area. Submit resume.

WEBMERGERS.COM; www.webmergers.com.
Positions: Mergers & acquisitions research and indexing for financial research and publishing company. Half the job is data entry.
Requirements: Must have high speed Internet access. Must commit to at least 20 hours

per week. Excellent writing skills required. A good financial background (basic understanding of how to read company financial statements or SEC filings) is also highly desirable. Data entry and/or company research experience required. Visit Web site for more information.
Provisions: Pays $12 to $18 an hour.

THE WILMINGTON GROUP, 7040 Wrightsville Ave., Wilmington NC 28403.
Positions: Clinical research associates for global pharmaceutical development firm.
Requirements: Minimum 2 years experience site monitoring. This is a full-time home-based job.
Provisions: Salary of $65K, performance bonuses, sign-on bonus, and plenty of upward mobility.

WORD EXPRESS, 250 W. 54th St., Room 606, New York, NY 10019.
Positions: Word-processing of long manuscripts, screenplays, and address list.
Requirements: Must have DOS, Word Perfect, and Mac file transfer software. Requires good skills. Local residents only mail resume.
Provisions: Pays per page or per address.

WORD OF MOUTH, 2131 1/2 N. Gower St., Los Angeles, CA 90068.
Positions: Medical transcription.
Requirements: Must be experienced. Must have computer with modem and Dictaphone. Local residents send resume.

WORD PROCESSING UNLIMITED, 6404 Crestwood Rd., Baltimore, MD 21239.
Positions: Transcribing, data entry, and desktop publishing.
Requirements: Looking for people with higher skill levels and equipment. Strong Word Perfect, tape transcription, and knowledge of database packages required. For desktop publishing, a familiarity with Mac and a strong background required. Local residents only should send resumes including cover letter and statement of monies required.

WORDMASTERS, 1222 O'Berry Hoover Rd., Orlando, FL 32825.
Positions: Straight text typing and chiropractic transcription. Also writing and typing resumes.
Requirements: Must own and have experience on Word Perfect 5.1, Windows, and Lotus. Work on 24-hour turnover. Local residents mail resume.

WORDNET, 30 Nagog Park, PO Box 976, Acton, MA 01720.
Positions: Professional freelancers translate technical manuals and documentation in and out of all major languages.
Requirements: Must be experienced and skilled both in languages, technical verbiage, and computers. Because translation projects are transmitted electronically all over the world, a computer and modem is required. Send resume.

WORDS, ETC., 5500 Madison Avenue, Antelope, California 95843.
Positions: Transcription work in any specialty available nationwide.
Requirements: Minimum three years as a transcriptionist. Need MS Word, Word Perfect, Lanier recording equipment, and HyperTerminal or ProCom Plus.
Provisions: Pays weekly, .09 to .11 per line.

WORDSMART, 250 5th Ave., Suite 202, New York, NY 10001.
Positions: Transcribers.
Requirements: Need only top transcriptionists (70 - 75 wpm) with WordPerfect and standard cassette equipment. Much of the work is from phone conversation tapes; familiarity with banking terminology required.
Provisions: Pays $5 per single space page.

WORDTRONICS DIRECT MAIL SERVICE BUREAU, 190 East Post Rd., White Plains, NY 10601.
Positions: Data entry and letter shop services.
Requirements: For data entry, must own PC for creating mailing lists. Must be quick and efficient. Also experienced people stuffing, sealing, and bulk-rate letter shop services. Local residents only mail resumes.
Provisions: Earn $8 to $12 per hour on a per-piece payment.

WORLD WIDE, P.O. Box 2266, Culver City, CA 90231.
Positions: Medical transcribers for home work out of three Los Angeles offices. Currently has over 100 home workers.
Requirements: Must have experience and knowledge of medical terminology. Work will be for hospitals, clinics, doctors, and government. Must have good typewriter and transcribing machine. Los Angeles residents only.
Provisions: Specific training is provided. Pick up and delivery of supplies and finished work will be provided if necessary. Pays piece rates equal to about $12 an hour. Part time or full-time hours available. Inquiries are welcome.

WORLDWIDE TRANSLATION AGENCY, 1680 North Vine, Suite 610, Hollywood, CA 90028.
Positions: Foreign language translators work on a wide variety of documents.
Requirements: Los Angeles residents only. Must be experienced professional translator with resume and references.
Provisions: Pays by the word.

OPPORTUNITIES
WORKING WITH PEOPLE

In this section you will find a lot of jobs that have one basic requirement in common —the ability to work well with people. Both at-home and from-home jobs are included. Such jobs include telephone surveying, customer service, fund raising, recruiting, and staffing coordination.

Telephone surveying involves calling consumers to ask specific questions about their buying habits, or more weighty questions of social significance. The names and numbers are supplied and the surveyor is paid for each call. The work is not usually steady; it tends to come and go. This can be good for someone who cannot make a permanent commitment. If you want steady surveying work you should sign up with several companies in order to insure back-to-back assignments.

Customer service is a profession that is finally coming into its own. American companies are starting to realize the importance of listening to their customers and trying to satisfy their needs. A customer service representative is basically a problem-solver. The job requires an ability to listen and record customers' comments accurately.

Fund raising can also be an easy job. It doesn't pay as well as surveying, usually only minimum wage plus a small bonus for bringing in so much in donations. It is, however, very easy work to get and it can be good experience leading to more sophisticated and higher-paying phone work.

Staffing coordination is a fairly new opportunity for home workers. This work is found most often in the burgeoning health-care field. Agencies are used to fill the staffing needs of hospitals, nursing homes, and outpatients. Calls come in day and night, but most agencies don't keep their doors open 24 hours a day. After 5:00 on weekdays and on weekends, calls are forwarded to a staffing coordinator's home. It is the coordinator's job to dispatch nurses and home health care workers, as they are needed during those hours. Most coordinators have electronic pagers, so they need not be completely homebound.

Field surveying is a job that is custom-made for someone with an outgoing personality. The word "field" indicates that most of the work is done outside- which may mean in a mall, at a movie theatre, or door-to-door. The surveyor collects answers to survey questions in the field and then returns home to fill out the paperwork. It is perfect for the person that needs the flexibility that working from home offers, but who doesn't want to be stuck inside all the time. Field surveyors work for market research firms and opinion pollers.

There are also several types of jobs listed here that do require extensive education and/or experience. Recruiters (headhunters), lawyers, and telephone triage nurses are among these.

A BRIGGS PASSPORT & VISA EXPEDITORS, 1054 31st St NW Suite 270, Washington, DC 20007; www.abriggs.com.
Positions: Answering customer calls on Friday nights and weekends, total of about 150 calls.
Requirements: Must have constant Internet connection and have separate phone line. Need voice mail system to pick up calls that come in while you are talking to customers. You must be within local calling range of Washington, DC.
Provisions: Training provided in Georgetown office for two or three days, and the job begins when you are trained and can take calls at home. The pay is $100 per weekend. You must work every weekend. Visit site for more information.

ADVANCEMENT GROUP, 2819 Crow Canyon Road Suite 219E, San Ramon, CA 94583; www.advancementgroup.com.
Positions: Recruiters for management recruiting firm.
Requirements: Must live in the Bay Area. Recruiting and/or sales experience is required. Must be comfortable with continually developing new business by cold calling.
Provisions: Flexible work schedule and the opportunity to telecommute. Pays commission only with the potential of earning six figures within the first year. Provides health benefits package. Visit Web site for more information.

AIS MARKET RESEARCH, 1320 E Shaw Ave.#100, Fresno, CA 93704.
Positions: Field surveyors in the San Joaquin Valley.
Requirements: Must be resident of either Fresno or Modesto. Market research or similar experience required. Send for application.
Provisions: Work is part-time and sporadic. Pays by the survey.

ALL STAR PERSONNEL, INC., 2647 Ramsay Rd., Cleveland, OH 44122.
Positions: Recruiters identify and source applicants, phone screen and interview candidates by analyzing qualifications and matching hiring criteria.
Requirements: Three years of non-exempt and exempt level recruiting and hiring required. Work is full-time. Local area residents send resume.

AMERICAN RED CROSS, 2700 Wilshire Blvd., Los Angeles, CA 90057.
Positions: Telephone recruiters locate potential blood donors.
Requirements: Two years telemarketing experience required. Must be available Sunday through Thursday. Excellent communications skills necessary. Los Angeles residents only. Send resume.
Provisions: Pays hourly rate.

AMERICAN THRIFT STORE, 401 W. Jefferson Blvd., Dallas, TX 75208.
Positions: Telemarketers call for donations.
Requirements: Local residents only.

AMVETS, 2840 Lafayette Rd., Indianapolis, IN 46203.
Positions: Fundraisers call for donations of clothing and household articles.
Requirements: Must live in Indianapolis.
Provisions: Pays hourly wage plus bonus plan.

ARTHRITIS FOUNDATION, 657 Mission St. # 603, San Francisco, CA 94109.
Positions: Telephone recruiters find volunteers to go door-to-door for donations. This program repeats every fall and spring for about two months each time.

Requirements: Must live in the Bay area. Experience is not required, but the director says this work is very difficult and may not be suitable for newcomers. Must be available to work (call) during the evening hours of 6 to 9:30 pm.
Provisions: Pays per recruitment.

ATC HEALTHCARE SERVICES, INC., 5151 E Broadway Blvd Suite 530, Tucson, AZ 85712.
Positions: Weekend staffing coordinator for temporary agency.
Requirements: Must be local, organized, and people-oriented. Strong organizational skills also needed. Phone skills are a must.

ATLANTA MARKETING RESEARCH CENTER, 5600 Roswell Rd. NE, #N300, Atlanta, GA 30342.
Positions: Field surveyors and occasionally, telephone interviewers.
Requirements: Atlanta residents only. Experience preferred.
Provisions: Pays by the survey.

AWEBER SYSTEMS, INC., 2865 S. Eagle Rd. #338, Newtown, PA 18940; www.aweber.com.
Positions: Customer service reps for prescription business.
Requirements: Can live anywhere. Visit site and e-mail for more information.
Provisions: Competitive pay, excellent benefits, full training and support.

CALIFORNIA COUNCIL FOR THE BLIND, 3919 W Magnolia Blvd., Burbank, CA 91505.
Positions: Fundraisers telephone for donations of household discards.
Requirements: Must be resident of greater Los Angeles area. Good phone manner necessary.
Provisions: Pays hourly plus bonus plan.

CAMBRIDGE HOME HEALTHCARE, 737 Southgate Pkwy, Cambridge, OH 44256.
Positions: On call staffing for nursing agency.
Requirements: Need to be available evenings and weekends. Local applicants send resume.

CANADIAN DIABETES ASSOCIATION, National Life Building, 400-522 University Ave, Toronto ON M5G 2R5; www.diabetes.ca.
Positions: Recruiting people in the St Margaret's Bay, Prospect, Herring Cove, Timberlea and the Hammonds Plains areas to canvas for door to door campaign.
Requirements: Must live in Halifax, Nova Scotia. Must have excellent organizational and communication skills.
Provisions: This is part-time work paying $7 an hour.

CAREMORE IN-HOME SERVICE, 189 Lakeview Commons #100, Gibbsboro, NJ 08026.
Positions: On-call coordinator.
Requirements: RN with maturity, good judgment, problem solving and ability to work effectively with full-time RN care managers. Local applicants send resume.

CAR-LENE RESEARCH, 2127 Northbrook Ct., Northbrook, IL 60062.
Positions: Field surveyors and telephone interviewers for market research assignments.

Requirements: Must live in Deerfield, IL; Pomona, CA; Santa Fe Springs, CA; Northbrook, IL; Hanover, MA; Dallas, TX; or Richardson, TX. Market research experience is required.
Provisions: Pays by the survey.

CATALINA IN-HOME SERVICES, 1602 E. Fort Lowell Rd., Tucson, AZ 85719.
Positions: On-call scheduler for evenings.
Requirements: Scheduling experience required. Must be computer proficient and be willing to make long-term commitment. Local applicants send resume.

CENTURY 21 RANDOCK, 14525 Newport Hwy., Mead, WA 99021.
Positions: This Century 21 office is the first full service real estate company to offer real agents the opportunity to sell via the Internet.
Provisions: Technical training is available.

CERTIFIED MARKETING SERVICES, INC., 7 Hudson St., Kinderhook, NY 12106.
Positions: Market Research surveys are conducted nationwide by independent, part-time field workers.
Requirements: Must be over 18 years of age. No experience is required, but good organization and communication skills are helpful. Write for information.
Provisions: Hourly wage, travel expenses and reimbursables.

CH MORTGAGE, 5670 Greenwood Plaza Blvd., #420, Greenwood Village, CO 80111.
Positions: Appointment setters.
Requirements: Local residents only.
Provisions: Part-time hours available.

COMPUTER PARTNERS CORP. (CPC), P.O. Box 2071, 281 Norlynn Drive, Howell, MI 48843.
Positions: CPC provides its clients with varying levels of recruiting services. They are in particular need of technical recruiters.
Requirements: Minimum of one year experience, strong communication skills, an empathetic personality and must truly like working with people. Most of the work is performed off-site. Submit resume with salary requirements.

CONNECTICUT CHILDREN'S MEDICAL CENTER, 282 Washington St., Hartford, CT 06106.
Positions: Nursing for RN's Pediatric Advice Line. Provide telephone triage, communications to providers and data entry.
Requirements: Experience in ED, pedi ambulatory, pedi critical care or pedi homecare required. Need Connecticut RN license, strong communication skills, schedule flexibility, and ability to make autonomous decisions and be accountable. Local professionals send resume.
Provisions: Pays competitive salary plus benefits.

CONSUMER OPINION SEARCH, INC., 10403 Clayton Rd., St. Louis, MO 63131.
Positions: Field surveyors.
Requirements: St. Louis residents only. Good communication skills required.
Provisions: Pays by the survey.

CORPORATE APARTMENT SPECIALIST, 621 N Jackson St., Arlington, VA 22204.
Positions: Upscale provider of furnished temporary housing needs client support for Richmond territory.
Requirements: Experience in apartment leasing and/or relocation needed. Be available approximately 25 to 30 hours per week. Car required. Local applicants send resume.
Provisions: Pays salary plus benefits.

COVERED BRIDGE GIRL SCOUT COUNCIL, 1100 Girl Scout Lane, Terre Haute, IN 47807.
Positions: Membership specialists to expand membership within assigned communities.
Requirements: Prefers Bachelor's degree. Must be willing to work flexible hours. Send cover letter, resume and salary requirements.
Provisions: This is a 100% telecommute position.

CUSTOM HOME FOOD SERVICE, 2070 Attic Parkway NW, Kennesaw, GA 30152.
Positions: Telemarketing (no sales).
Requirements: Work at home in the Marietta area.
Provisions: Pays salary plus bonus.

DAVIS MARKET RESEARCH SERVICES, INC., 23801 Calabasas Rd., Calabasas, CA 91302.
Positions: Field surveyors.
Requirements: Local residents only. Experience working with the public required.

DEVON CONSULTING, 950 W. Valley Road, Suite 2602, Wayne, PA 19087; www.devonconsulting.com.
Positions: Technical recruiting. Duties include querying the company database and the Internet for qualified candidates, phone screening, interviewing, administering tech check skill testing, reference checking, attending job fairs and other strategic recruiting events, and various administrative duties.
Requirements: Must live near company headquarters. Ideal candidates should have excellent verbal communication skills, computer knowledge and the ability to handle multiple tasks. Minimum three years IT recruiting experience required. You will be required to come in to the company office occasionally. Send resume.
Provisions: Offers flexible schedule and advancement opportunities.

DISABLED AMERICAN VETERANS, 273 E. 800 South, Salt Lake City, UT 84111.
Positions: Telemarketers use the phone to ask for donations of household articles.
Requirements: No experience required. Must live in Salt Lake City.
Provisions: Pays minimum hourly wage plus bonus plan.

DISABLED AMERICAN VETERANS OF COLORADO, 8799 North Washington, Denver, CO 80229.
Positions: Fundraisers call for donations of household discards to be sold through thrift stores.
Requirements: Denver residents only. Must have good phone voice and self-discipline.
Provisions: Training provided. Pays small hourly wage plus bonus plan.

DMSI, PO Box 4460 Harrisburg, PA 17111.
Positions: Phone answering.
Requirements: Must be local resident. Need separate phone line and Internet access.

Provisions: Codes and scripts provided. Pays $.15 per minute.
E-mail: employment@dmsi.ccfreesohojobs

EDEN STAFFING, 420 Lexington Ave., # 2100, New York, NY 10016
Positions: Dispatchers for large staffing company. Work entails dispatching temporary workers and acting as liaison with clients.
Requirements: Must be articulate and quick thinking. Experience is preferred, but not required. Local residents only send resume. Must be available for midnight to 8 a.m. shift.

EDUCATIONAL PARTNERS ASSOCIATION; www.epa-cpr.com.
Positions: Phone survey clerk (no sales).
Requirements: Must be a resident of Ottawa, Ontario. Must be fluent in English. Computer skills are a plus. Knowledge of e-mail required.
Provisions: This is off-hours part-time employment. Pays $10 hourly for 12 to 30 hours per week.

EL CAMINO MEMORIAL PARK, 5600 Carol Canyon Rd., San Diego, CA 92121.
Positions: Telemarketers conduct surveys over the phone.
Requirements: Experience dealing with the public. Must live in San Diego.
Provisions: Training is provided. Pays salary plus bonus.

ELECTRONIC SEARCH, INC., 5105 Tollview Dr., # 245, Rolling Meadows, IL 60008.
Positions: Research recruiters, assistants, account executives, national account managers, and resume processors. Work entails name and resume sourcing, research, profiling, and Internet job posting.
Requirements: Must be motivated, organized, have excellent communication skills, and have a good home office setup.
Provisions: Full-time and part-time openings available. Training provided.

ENCORE UNLIMITED, PO Box 874, Superior, WI 54880.
Positions: Medical nursing case management.
Requirements: Experience is required in orthopedic and/or or neurological nursing, home health, or case management. Must have at least 5 years experience as an RN. Would prefer QRC. Local travel is required. Local qualified applicants should send resume and cover letter.
Provisions: Offers excellent salary and benefits package.

ETR TECHNOLOGY CENTER, 180 Oser Avenue, Suite 400, Hauppauge, NY 11788; www.etrtechcenter.com.
Positions: Pharmaceutical staffing and recruiting.
Requirements: Knowledge of the pharmaceutical marketplace. Experience in pharmaceutical staffing with a proven track record.. Must live in the New Jersey / New York area. Visit Web site and apply via e-mail.
Provisions: Provides excellent compensation package.

FACTS 'N FIGURES, 14550 Chase St., #78B, Panorama City, CA 91402.
Positions: Market research and public opinion surveys are conducted by field surveyors and telephone interviewers.

Requirements: Must be resident of greater Los Angeles. Interviewing experience is required.
Provisions: Pays by the survey.

FUTURO INFANTIL HISPANO, 2227 E Garvey Ave., N, West Covina, CA 91791.
Positions: Foster agency needs bilingual English/Spanish social workers for counseling or social psychology in the Pomona and Huntington Park areas.
Requirements: Must have MSW, MFCC, or Master degree in child counseling, child psychology or development.
Provisions: Offers salary plus excellent benefits plus telecommuting option.

GALLUP POLL, 47 Hulfish Street, 100 Palmer Square, Suite 200, P.O. Box 310, Princeton, NJ 08542. Attn: Field Dept.
Positions: Market researchers for field research. Across the country, there are 360 sampling areas. Market researchers conduct surveys in the field (usually door-to-door), returning home only to do the "paperwork." There are almost 2,000 of these home-based researchers around the U.S. This work is permanent part-time. It is conducted during weekends, approximately 1 - 2 weekends per month.
Requirements: No experience required and no age restriction for persons over 18. You need only to be able to read well, talk with people and have a dependable car. Send work experience, address and phone number with letter of interest.
Provisions: An applicant must complete sample work which is tested and graded before job begins. After a person is accepted as an interviewer, Gallup's techniques are self-taught using an Interviewer's Manual and by communicating with the Field Administrator in the Princeton Office. All workers are independent contractors and are expected to meet minimum quotas. Pays an hourly wage plus expenses. "We're always looking for responsible people, especially permanent part-timers."

GAVEL & GOWN SOFTWARE, INC., 184 Pearl St., Suite 304, Toronto, Ontario, Canada M5H 1L5.
Positions: This software manufacturer specializes in case management applications for the legal community with a market that encompasses all of North America. IT professionals wanting to become authorized resellers or certified consultants should forward resume.

GENERATION Z; www.generationz.com.
Positions: Recruiting IT professionals for this Internet development firm.
Requirements: Strong technical knowledge of recruiting. Familiarity with technologies such as OS, protocols, connectivity, various software applications, certifications and programming languages. Computer or technology degree or equivalent experience is required as well as a minimum 3 years in sales and management. E-mail your resume to development@generationz.com.
Provisions: Salary is over $100K.

LUANNE GLAZER ASSOCIATES, INC., 596 Glenbrook Rd. #10, Stamford, CT 06902.
Positions: Field surveyors and telephone interviewers for market research.
Requirements: Must be local resident. Excellent communication skills and ability to follow directions explicitly required.
Provisions: Training is provided. Pays by the survey.

RUTH GOLDER INTERVIEWING SERVICE, 1804 Jaybee Rd., Wilmington, DE 19803.
Positions: Field interviewers for market research.
Requirements: Interviewing experience required. Must live in Chester or Delaware County, Pennsylvania, or Salem County, New Jersey.

GOOD SAMARITAN COMMUNITY HEALTHCARE, 407 14th Ave., SE, Puyallup, WA 98371.
Positions: Medical professionals perform night telephone triage from 5 pm to 8 am with some home visitations possible.
Requirements: Local professionals send resume.
Provisions: Pays salary plus full benefits.

LOUIS HARRIS AND ASSOCIATES, 111 Fifth Ave., New York, NY 10020.
Positions: Market researchers and opinion surveyors are needed in the field.
Requirements: No experience is necessary. Louis Harris has "several hundred" sampling areas and it is necessary to live in one of them. Write and ask for an application, which will be kept on file. When something comes up, you will be called. If you are ready for work, you will receive your instructions over the phone. How you go about completing the assignment from there is up to you.
Provisions: Pays by the survey, about $15 to $50+ per survey.

HARVEY RESEARCH ORGANIZATION, INC., 600 Perinton Hills Office Park, Fairport, NY 14450.
Positions: Interviewers to work as independent contractors on continuing assignments. Work is available in all major cities. There are 50 to 100 interviewers in each sampling area. Most interviews are conducted in the field.
Requirements: Experience is necessary. Write a letter of interest. You will be sent an application, then a sample survey to complete before being hired permanently.
Provisions: Pays by the survey.

HAYES MARKETING RESEARCH, 7840 El Cajon Blvd., Suite 400, La Mesa, CA 92041.
Positions: Field surveyors and telephone interviewers for market research.
Requirements: Local area residents only. Experience required.
Provisions: Pays by the survey.

HEAKIN RESEARCH, INC., 3340 Mall Loop Dr. #1166, Joliet, IL 60431.
Positions: Field surveyors conduct market research survey in 15 areas.
Requirements: Experience is preferred. Must be resident of Los Angeles, Sacramento, San Francisco area, Chicago, Kansas City, Baltimore, Independence, Pittsburgh, Memphis, or Houston.

HEALTHCOR, 2480 W. 4th Ave., Unit 24, Denver, CO 80206.
Positions: Medical collections.
Requirements: Local applicants send resume.

HIGHLINE COMMUNITY HOSPITAL, 13030 Military Rd S, Tukwila, WA 98168.
Positions: On-call nursing, home infusion. Triage and respond to all calls making scheduled and unscheduled visits.
Requirements: Home care/infusion experience preferred. Local RNs submit resume.

HIRERIGHT, INC., 2100 Main Street Suite 400, Irvine, CA 92614; www.hireright.com.
Positions: Telephone researchers. This is a business to business Internet company that is currently focused on delivering pre-employment screening services that help employers rapidly hire the right person the first time. They now have over 3,800 researchers. The system is Internet-based.
Requirements: Must be energetic and enthusiastic phone researchers who can quickly and accurately complete employment and education verifications for company's clients. The ideal candidate should have experience working within a call center environment, processing high volume software-based transactions. Excellent written and verbal communications are essential. Must be familiar with e-commerce and the Internet and be comfortable with technology.
Provisions: This is a full-time job paying $10.00 to $12.00 per hour

HOSPICE OF SAN FRANCISCO, 225 - 30th, San Francisco, CA 94121.
Positions: Staffing coordinator for non-office hours.
Requirements: Experience in medical staffing required. Must live in San Francisco. Good phone manner important. Knowledge of medical terminology preferred.
Provisions: Pays hourly rates.

H/P TECHNOLOGIES, INC., 4545 N. 36th St. Suite 114, Phoenix, AZ 85018; www.hptechnologies.com.
Positions: Technical recruiters within the healthcare industry..
Requirements: Must be ambitious and possess industry experience, strong sales background and recruiting experience. Also need to have excellent computer, Internet searching, and technology skills.
Provisions: No cap on commissions. Recruiters here earn up to $100,000 per year.

HUMAN RESOURCES PROFESSIONAL GROUP (HRPG), PO Box 231276, Encinitas, CA 92033; www.hrpg.com.
Positions: Recruiting in the San Diego area for HR consulting firm serving small and mid-sized businesses. Company provides recruitment and staffing, audits and compliance, employee relations, training, on-site HR management and special projects.
Requirements: Must have minimum of two years recruiting experience, particularly in the areas of IT, biotech, medical device, pharmaceutical, and sales. Must be able and willing to travel all over SD County, have the ability to work onsite or from home, including access to the Internet.
Provisions: Positions are hourly and hours and assignments are flexible. Visit Web site and apply via e-mail with "Recruiter" in the subject line.

ILLINOIS AMVETS, 4711 W. 137th St., Crestwood, IL 60445.
Positions: Fundraisers phone for donations of household articles.
Requirements: There are 10 locations in Illinois; you must reside in one of them. No experience necessary outside of good speaking ability.
Provisions: Part-time hours are flexible. Pays commission for every pick-up; averages about $7.50 an hour.

INTEGRITY STAFFING, 30042 Mission Blvd., Suite 121-238, Hayward, CA 94544; www.integritystaffing.org.
Positions: Recruiting entry level to executive level positions such as office administration, management, sales, marketing, accounting, healthcare, or IT. Duties will include searching and recruiting quality candidates through use of Internet recruiting,

cold calling, and referrals; interviewing candidates via telephone and in person interviews as necessary; performing reference checks; and participating in review meetings with supervisor. Must have a fully functional home office.
Provisions: The salary is commission based.

INTERIM HEALTHCARE, 1601 Sawgrass Corporate Parkway, Sunrise, FL 33323.
Positions: This franchised agency (previously known as Medical Personnel Pool) is a nursing staff placement agency with offices coast to coast. In some areas where "satellite offices" operate in outlying area, home-based staffing coordinators are used to take incoming calls and dispatch nurses to work assignments. In some offices, this is done only at night and on weekends.
Requirements: Some phone experience is preferred. Staffing experience is also preferred, but not necessary. Must be self-directed. Write to find the office nearest to you or look it up in your local phone book.

J & R FIELD SERVICES, INC., 747 Caldwell Ave., North Woodmere, NY 11581.
Positions: Field surveyors.
Requirements: Market research experience is required. Must be local resident.

JACKSON ASSOCIATES, 1140 Hammond Dr., N.E. #H, Atlanta, GA 30328.
Positions: Field and telephone interviewers for market research surveys.
Requirements: Experience required. Must be local resident.
Provisions: Pays by the survey.

JOE COCHRAN AGENCY, 1032 Huffman St., Fort Wayne, IN 46808.
Positions: Appointment setters for insurance agency. Calls are made to select clients; no cold calls.
Requirements: Local residents only.

JOHNS HOPKINS HEALTH CARE, LCC, Human Resources, 6704 Curtis Court, Glen Burnie, MD 21060.
Positions: Specialty care coordinator for intensive care coordination and case management.
Requirements: Bachelor's degree in nursing with Master's preferred. Must be licensed as RN in Maryland and have 7 years of nursing experience including case management for at least 2 years. Although this job is home based, you will be traveling locally much of the time. Local qualified nurses, send resume and cover letter.
Provisions: Offers generous salary and benefits.

KELLY SERVICES, INC.
Positions: Staffing coordinators. Kelly relies on home-based staffing coordinators to take calls and dispatch temporary personnel during the night as a service to clients who operate on 24-hour shift rotations.
Requirements: Some experience in personnel placement is required. Write to locate the nearest office or find it in the phone book, then apply directly to that office.
Provisions: Positions are considered part-time only. Pays flat salary.

KENDA SYSTEMS, INC., One Stiles Road, Salem, NH 03079; www.kenda.com.
Positions: Technical recruiters with good connections and experience with successful IT placements.

Requirements: Proven record of success. Visit Web site, then e-mail resume.
Provisions: Payment is 100% commission.

THE KIDNEY FOUNDATION.
Positions: Fund raising on a local level. Work involves calling for donations of household items.
Provisions: Training provided. Pays hourly wage plus bonuses. The Kidney Foundation has branch offices in every city. Call the one nearest you for more information.

KINSHIP, 3210 Oliver Ave N, Minneapolis, MN 55412.
Positions: Local coordinators recruit and train volunteer mentors for youth.
Requirements: BA in social work or psychology required. Need reliable vehicle, experience with MS Word, knowledge of Dakota Co. Vol Management, public speaking, and experience with youth. Send resume.
Provisions: Offers flexible hours working from home. Pay includes benefits.

LOS ANGELES MARKETING RESEARCH ASSOCIATES, 5712 Lankershim Blvd., North Hollywood, CA 91601.
Positions: Field interviewers.
Requirements: Interviewing experience required.
Provisions: Pays by the survey.

MARY LUCAS MARKET RESEARCH, 4101 Rider Trl N # 100, Earth City, MO 63045.
Positions: Field surveyors and telephone interviewers.
Requirements: Market research experience is required. Must be resident of greater St. Louis area.

MAXIM HEALTHCARE SERVICES, 2250 N. Druid Hills Rd., NE, Atlanta, GA 30329.
Positions: Medical on-call coordinator for after hours and weekends.
Requirements: Prior staffing experience is necessary. Local applicants send resume.

MEDLINK OF OHIO, 1225 E. Waterloo Rd., Akron, OH 44306.
Positions: Homecare and staffing agency has need for part-time and weekend staffing coordinator to work from home with pager to respond and schedule service for clients.
Requirements: Local applicants send resume.

NATIONAL ANALYSTS, 1835 Market St., Philadelphia, PA 19103.
Positions: Opinion surveys are conducted in the field.
Requirements: Must live in one of the sampling areas. Experience is preferred.
Provisions: Training is provided. Pays by the survey.

NATIONAL OPINION RESEARCH CENTER, Social Science Research Center of the University of Chicago, 6030 South Ellis Avenue, Chicago, IL 60637.
Positions: Interviewers for long-term social science research projects. This nonprofit organization is the oldest research center in the country, founded in 1941. Research contracts come from government agencies and other institutional clients generally to study behavioral changes in specified areas of the population. There are 100 "area probability centers," plus studies are conducted in other locations specifically requested by the clients. All workers are considered part-time, temporary independent contractors

CLOSE UP: NORC

Founded in 1941, NORC is the oldest survey research organization established for non-commercial purposes. NORC is a not-for-profit organization affiliated with the University of Chicago.

Survey research is the collection of accurate, unbiased information from a carefully chosen sample of individuals.

Some organizations do opinion polls, asking people to rate the performance of public officials, for example. Others do market research, asking about such things as the products people use. NORC does social science research, asking about people's attitudes and behavior in areas of social concern, such as education, housing, employment (and unemployment), and health care.

NORC's clients include the American Cancer Society, Harvard University, the Rockefeller Foundation, the U.S. Dept. of Labor, and the Social Security Administration to name just a few. Nowhere will you find higher standards of quality in research of this kind.

To date, NORC has conducted more than 1,000 surveys. This may not sound like a lot considering the thousands that are conducted for companies like Gallup. Unlike Gallup, though, NORC's surveys are "longitudinal," meaning the same people are surveyed over long periods of time. Over 900 part-time NORC interviewers are located in cities,

towns, and rural areas throughout the United States. Many, but not all, are home-based. Each assignment is on a temporary, per-project basis. The average project lasts about 6 months. All interviewers must be available to work at least 20 hours a week. 40 hour weeks are common.

About half of the people working for NORC have been with the company at least 5 years. That's an outstanding record in an industry where rapid employee turnover is the norm. Nevertheless, NORC is constantly seeking more qualified interviewers--especially in hard-to-staff metropolitan areas such as New York, Chicago, Los Angeles and Miami.

Field Director Miriam Clarke says "We look for someone who is people-oriented, outgoing, and somewhat aggressive. Someone who does not like to be tied to a desk is a good candidate actually. Being able to follow instructions precisely is important, too."

An hour and a half of general training is provided at a central location. After that, project briefings are handled by mail and phone.

The pay range depends upon where you live, but the entry level base rate is $4.50 an hour and up, depending upon experience. Any particular qualifications, such as foreign languages, pay extra. Pay raises come once a year and are based on performance.

though projects often last up to 14 months. Most work is done face-to-face, some is done over the phone. Currently has over 700 interviewers and is actively seeking more, particularly in metropolitan areas.
Requirements: Must be available a minimum of 20 hours a week; some work 40 hours a week. Need to be people-oriented, independent, outgoing, somewhat aggressive, able to follow instructions precisely and pay attention to details. Send letter of interest.
Provisions: Training is provided; general training takes about a day and a half in the office. Project briefings are a combination of written materials and oral instructions over the phone. Pays minimum wage plus expenses. Pay goes up with experience or with particular qualifications that may be hard to find. Annual increases are based on performance.

NORWEGIAN CRUISE LINE, 7665 Northwest 19th Street, Miami, FL 33126.
Positions: Vacation planners (reservations agents) for major cruise line.
Requirements: A high school diploma or equivalent is required. Also required are good English communication skills, a minimum of one year of customer service or sales experience, PC skills, and the flexibility to work a variety of shifts. Send resume.

NORTHWEST CENTER FOR THE RETARDED, 1600 West Armory Way, Seattle, WA 98119.
Positions: Telemarketers to call for donations of household goods.
Requirements: Must be local resident.
Provisions: Training is provided. Pays hourly wage plus bonus plan.

OLSTEN HEALTH CARE SERVICES.
Positions: Staffing coordinators. Olsten now has over 300 offices nationwide in its health care services division. Each office has a minimum of two home-based staffing coordinators job sharing on a seven-days-on, seven-days-off routine. The job consists of taking calls during the day, at night, and on weekends to dispatch appropriate personnel for hospital and home health care positions.
Requirements: Some staffing experience or medical background is required. Write to locate the office nearest you, then apply directly to that office.
Provisions: Pays weekly salary plus placement bonuses.

OPINION RESEARCH CORPORATION, 755 College Road East, Princeton, NJ 08540.
Positions: Opinion surveyors conduct interviews in the field in New Jersey only.
Requirements: Ability to communicate effectively with people is a must. Send letter of interest.
Provisions: Pays by the survey.

ORION INTERNATIONAL CONSULTING, 5511 Capital Center Drive, Suite 216, Raleigh, NC 27606.
Positions: As a recruiter/E-cruiter, you place qualified, newly separated U.S. military technicians and veterans in various careers with this company's clients nationwide.
Requirements: Knowing and ability to use the Internet and in-depth knowledge of military life. A minimum of 3 years of recruiting experience with a retained search firm is required. You will also need strong skills in communications with candidates and clients, resume writing, interview preparation, and networking. Send resume.
Provisions: Pays $40,000 to $60,000 per year plus outstanding benefits including medical, dental, disability, profit sharing, and 401K.

PEDIACALL OF TEXAS, Grand Prairie, TX; www.pediacalloftexas.com.
Positions: Pediatric telephone triage nurses work from their homes in Dallas.
Requirements: Must be RN experienced with Barton Schmitt protocol knowledge.
Must be resident of Dallas, TX area. Must be professional and caring with great telephone
assessment skills. Excellent judgment required
Provisions: All necessary supplies provided. All shifts available including weeknights
and weekends..

PHYSICIANS LOCUM TENENS RECRUITERS, 1200 Abernathy Road, Suite 1700,
Atlanta, Georgia 30328; www.physicianslt.com.
Positions: Recruiters for agency that places physicians and other medical personnel.
Requirements: Must have physician or medical recruitment experience and be self-
motivated with the ability to properly manage yourself at home. Can live anywhere.
Send resume.
Provisions: This is a commission only independent contractor position.

PREVENT BLINDNESS OKLAHOMA, 4545 N.W. 16th St., Oklahoma City, OK
73127.
Positions: Fundraisers.
Requirements: Must have home phone available for use 15 hours per week, evenings.
Local residents only.
Provisions: Pays $10 per hour plus bonus.

PROSELECT, P.O. Box 72613, Marietta, GA 30007; www.proselectonline.com.
Positions: IT executive recruiters work with Account Managers in staffing existing job
openings.
Requirements: Must be experienced in locating and screening of IT personnel.
Provisions: Telecommuting and flexible working hours.

PRO STAFF, www.prostaff.com.
Positions: Executive recruiters. Pro Staff is one of the largest privately owned staffing
companies in the country.
Requirements: Qualified individuals will have a strong background in client sourcing
and development in addition to recruiting of executives and other high level professionals.
Strong presentation and negotiation skills are a must. Bachelors degree is preferred.
Must have at least five years recruiting experience. Proficiency in MS Office is necessary.
Only the most highly qualified candidates will be given home office consideration.
Provisions: The company has regional offices across the country. Visit the Web site and
click on the region you're interested in for more information.

PROVIDER SERVICES, 909 S. 336th, Suite 100, Federal Way, WA 98003.
Positions: Registered Nurse UR case manager.
Requirements: Must have broad clinical background, discharge planning and UR case
management experience, preferably in a managed care environment. Local applicants
send resumed which includes salary history.
Provisions: This is a flextime/telecommuting opportunity.

PUBLIC REACTION RESEARCH, One Dillon Rd., Kendall Park, NJ 08824.
Positions: Public opinion surveys are conducted in the field and over the phone.
Requirements: Some kind of interviewing experience is required. Must be resident of

greater Princeton area.
Provisions: Pays by the job.

PURPLE HEART SERVICE FOUNDATION.
Positions: Part-time telemarketers solicit for donations.
Requirements: Must work well with the public. Personal interview will be required.
Look for the office nearest you in your local phone book and contact that office directly.
Provisions: Hours are flexible. Pays commission of $10+ an hour.

READYNURSE STAFFING SERVICES, 2602 Highlands Blvd. North, Palm Harbor,
FL 34684; www.readynurse.com.
Positions: On-call staffing coordinator to handle phone calls after office hours.
Requirements: Staffing experience helpful. Customer service and phone skills required.
Provisions: Part-time hours.

REALTY EXECUTIVES OF DENVER, 7901 E Belleview Ave, Englewood, CO
80111.
Positions: Appointment setter for real estate company. (No sales.)
Requirements: Must be local resident with good phone skills.
Provisions: Pays salary plus bonus.

REMY CORPORATION, 1637 Wazee Street, 2nd Floor, Denver, Colorado 80202;
www.remycorp.com.
Positions: IT recruiters.
Requirements: Must have minimum three years of success in technical recruiting or
staffing. Record must be verifiable. Local Denver residents preferred, but not necessary
if qualified.
Provisions: Pays base salary plus commission totaling well into the six figures.

RESEARCH TRIANGLE INSTITUTE, Hanes Building, Research Triangle Park,
Raleigh, NC 27601.
Positions: Interviewers for opinion research surveys conducted primarily in the field.
Research Triangle is a nonprofit social research organization operating nationwide.
Requirements: Good communication skills needed. Send letter of interest.
Provisions: Pays hourly rate in some areas, pays by the survey in others. Training is
provided.

RESOURCE SPECTRUM, PO Box 2195, Grapevine, TX 76099;
www.spectrumm.com.
Positions: Recruiters. Resource Spectrum is a multi-million dollar staffing firm serving
companies throughout the world. Must live in one of the major markets.
Requirements: Experience recruiting in the IT, legal biotech, accounting, financial,
civil engineering, environmental engineering, construction, executive, marketing, or
healthcare fields.
Provisions: All recruiters work and start on commission only with no base salary.

ROBERTE VERIFICATIONS; www.roberteverifications.com.
Positions: Phone surveyors and mystery shoppers.
Requirements: Must be fluent in English, but French is an advantage. Must live in
Ottawa area. Experience in retail customer service required. Must have computer with

Windows. High school graduates only. Visit Web site for more information.
Provisions: Pays $10 per hour plus some benefits. This is very part-time work, on call.

THE ROPER ORGANIZATION, 566 Boston Post Road., Mamaroneck, NY 10543.
Positions: Opinion surveyors conduct research within sampling areas around the country. All research is conducted in the field.
Requirements: No opinion surveying experience is necessary, but experience involving some kind of public contact is preferred. Write and ask for name and address of nearest field supervisor.

S.A.I. STAFFING, Grosse Pointe Woods, MI 48236; www.saistaffing.com.
Positions: Personnel placement for professional and technical staffing firm.
Requirements: Must be knowledgeable and experienced recruiter (minimum five years). Applicants will go through a reference and security check. Need to live within driving distance of headquarters.
Provisions: Pays excellent commissions.

SALES CONSULTANTS OF BLOOMINGTON, INC., 707 N. East St., Suite 4, Bloomington, Illinois 61701; www.scbloomington.com.
Positions: This is a global search and recruiting firm with over 1,100 offices worldwide. Recruiters work at home.
Requirements: Must have sales experience, industry knowledge, and communication skills. College degree required. Previous recruiting experience is preferred but not required. You must be within driving distance of the Bloomington/Normal area. Must be PC literate and have virtual home office capabilities.
Provisions: Provides comprehensive training. Offers flexible hours and aggressive commission plan. Average earnings for full-time recruiters after one full year is $70,000.

SELECT COMFORT CORPORATION, 6105 Trenton Ln N., Minneapolis, MN 55442; www.selectcomfort.com.
Positions: Scheduling coordinator, customer service. This position includes working with customer 100% on the phone.
Requirements: Must be high school graduate (or GED), have excellent customer service and communication skills, have Windows computer experience including MS Word and Excel, and be a good problem solver with attention to detail and accuracy. Must live in Chicago. Some experience in scheduling, routing and customer service definitely preferred.
Provisions: Pays $11 to $13 per hour.

SETKA, INC., 3223 Crow Canyon Road, Suite 250, San Ramon, CA 94583; www.setka.com.
Positions: Technical recruiters/account managers.
Requirements: Experience in IT or professional staffing. Local residents only.
Provisions: Pays excellent commission. Offers long term opportunities to work either full-time or part-time.

SMYTH FIVENSON COMPANY, 8513 Irvington Avenue, Bethesda, MD 20817; www.smythfivenson.com.
Positions: Recruiters.
Requirements: Must have broad experience in human resources.
Provisions: Looking for part-time workers especially.

SNELLINGSEARCH, 80 Scenic, Freehold, NJ 07728.
Positions: Technical recruiters sought for personnel staffing. Snellingsearch is the technical and executive search division of Snelling Personnel Services, one of the world's largest providers of personnel staffing services for business and industry. They specialize in the recruitment and placement of information systems, computer/networking professionals in career/direct hire and temporary/contract positions.
Requirements: Qualified candidates must be able to attend weekly meetings at the Freehold, NJ office, have 5-15 years business experience with prior sales or technical recruiting experience, be computer literate, be self-motivated, and own a PC with modem.

SOFTPATH SYSTEM, 1945 Cliff Valley Way NE, Suite 312, Atlanta, GA 30329; www.softpath.net.
Positions: IT recruiters recruit, interview, refer, place and support qualified candidates.
Requirements: Must live in the metropolitan area of Washington D.C. Degree preferred but not required, but must have a minimum of two years experience in staffing industry OR three years in sales and/or in a technical arena with proven track record. Local market experience would be ideal.
Provisions: This is a full-time position.

SOFTWARE TESTING SERVICES, INC., 620 Cranbury Road Suite 202, East Brunswick, NJ 08816; www.stsv.com.
Positions: Technical recruiting in the East Brunswick, NJ area. The company is an established provider of quality assurance and software testing services to Fortune 1000 companies in the NY tristate area.
Requirements: Must have minimum 2-3 years of technical recruiting, consulting, telecommunications experience.
Provisions: Pays base salary of $40-$45K plus commissions.

STRATEGIC RESOURCE PARTNERS, INC., 111 N. Sepulveda Blvd Suite 250, Manhattan Beach, CA 90266; www.strategicrp.com.
Positions: IT recruiters.
Requirements: Bachelor's degree and at least three years successful IT recruiting experience. Local residents only.
Provisions: Pays $25 per hour.

SUMMIT HEALTH CARE, 1850 Lee Road, Winter Park, FL 32789.
Positions: Medical staffing coordinator.
Requirements: Prior staffing experience is required. Must be detail oriented, flexible, and self-motivated. Good communication skills a must. Local residents submit resume.
Provisions: Top pay. After-hours work only.

TEMPOSITIONS, Home Health Care Division, 140 Geary St # 4, San Francisco, CA 94104.
Positions: Staffing coordinator for evenings and weekends.
Requirements: Experience in medical staffing required. Must live in San Francisco.
Provisions: This is part-time work only.

THE THOR GROUP, 3601 Aviation Blvd. Suite 3900, Manhattan Beach, CA 90266; www.thorgroup.com.
Positions: Recruiters.

Requirements: Minimum two years recruiting experience. To see what areas are open, visit Web site.
Provisions: Pays $60k-$150k per year. Telecommuting is offered only after training is completed.

TIME ANSWERING, 877 Jefferson Ave., St. Paul, MN 55102.
Positions: Customer service for 24-year old inbound telemessaging center.
Requirements: Local residents write to request interview.
Provisions: Full-time shifts for both day and evening schedules available. Pays good monthly salary plus full benefits including medical, dental, retirement, and vacation.

UNIQUE COMPUTER INC., 27-08, 42nd Road, Long Island City, New York 11101; www.uciny.com.
Positions: Technical recruiters in New York and Washington D.C.
Requirements: Minimum four years experience as technical recruiter.
Provisions: Pays excellent commissions. Visit Web site and apply via e-mail.

UNITED CEREBRAL PALSY, 1217 Alhambra Blvd., Sacramento, CA 95816.
Positions: Fund raising by phone. Job consists of calling for donations of household discards for about four hours a day.
Requirements: Must live in Sacramento.
Provisions: Pays hourly wage plus bonus plan.

UNITED CEREBRAL PALSY, 29498 Mission Blvd., Hayward, CA 94544.
Positions: Fund raising by phone.
Requirements: Bay area residents only.
Provisions: Pays hourly rate plus bonus and vacation.

VETERANS' REHABILITATION CENTER, 9201 Pacific Avenue, Tacoma, WA 98444.
Positions: Fundraisers phone for donations of household items, clothing, etc.
Requirements: Must come to Tacoma for short training session. (Can live in Seattle.)
Provisions: Paid training is provided. Pays guaranteed hourly wage. Inquiries are welcome.

VISITING NURSE ASSOCIATION, 101 West Chestnut Street, Louisville, KY 40202.
Positions: Medical staffing coordinator.
Requirements: Medical background with staff/schedule experience required. Local applicants send resume.

OPPORTUNITIES IN SALES

The field of sales has long been a traditional from-home opportunity. Today, most salespeople have offices at home and some even conduct all their business from home.

Sales may be the only true opportunity to earn an executive level income with literally no educational requirements or experience. It is particularly good for women, who often report doubling or tripling their income after leaving other types of jobs. It also allows for a maximum amount of flexibility in terms of time spent and when it is spent.

What does it take to be a good salesperson? Good communications skills are at the top of the list. You must truly enjoy talking to people to make it in sales. You must be careful to listen to them as well. Assertiveness is also important. This does not mean you must be aggressive or go for the "hard sell," but shrinking violets aren't likely to make it in this field. The toughest part of this job is handling rejection. Nobody likes rejection; some people are traumatized by it. But, it goes with the territory. The professional salesperson knows that with each rejection, he/she is one step closer to a successfully closed sale.

Sales is a profession with its own set of rules, just like any other profession. The job basically consists of prospecting for customers, qualifying the prospect to make sure the potential customer is a viable prospect, making the presentation, overcoming objections, closing the sales, and getting referrals. A good company will teach you all you need to know about each of these steps. You can also find classes in salesmanship for both beginners and advanced students at community colleges and adult learning centers.

Many of the opportunities listed in this section have interesting ways of introducing the product. Home parties are especially fun and easy. Many home parties now seem more like classes than sales pitches with hands-on demonstrations in cooking, baking, needlework, and crafts. If you think you might be interested in a particular company, you can check it out first by hosting your own party. You'll not only be able to check out the company first hand, but you'll earn a bonus gift at the same time.

For those who want to be home all the time, telemarketing is the best bet. Telemarketing jobs rarely exceed four hours a day, but the pay can equal a full-time salary for a good communicator. For additional opportunities in telemarketing, look in your local newspaper "help wanted" ads.

ACCU-FIND, 196 W Moorestown Rd Route 512, Wind Gap, PA 18091.
Positions: Sales reps are responsible for creating new accounts and servicing established accounts.
Requirements: Must have sales experience, knowledge of Internet is helpful.
Provisions: Offers flexible hours, salary, good commissions plan, and health benefits availability.

ALCAS CUTLERY CORPORATION, 1116 East State Street, P.O. Box 810, Olean, NY 14760.
Positions: Alcas makes cutlery, cookware, and tableware. The products are sold with the aid of mail order catalogs.
Provisions: Catalogs and other supplies are provided. Pays commission.

ALLIED HOME MORTGAGE CAPITAL CORP., 700 State Highway 71, Sea Girt, NJ 08750.
Positions: Mortgage loan reps.
Requirements: Motivated personality a must. Local residents send resume.
Provisions: Offers training and pays commission.

ALOE MAGIC, 4553 Allisonville Rd. Bldg B, Indianapolis, IN 46205.
Positions: Aloe Magic has an extensive line of aloe-based cosmetics and health and skin care products. Reps use a variety of direct sales methods.
Provisions: Pays commission.

ALOETTE COSMETICS, INC., 4900 Highlands Pkwy SE, Smyrna, GA 30082.
Positions: Direct sales of skin care cosmetics.

AMERICAN BARTER EXCHANGE, INC, 20 Broadhollow Rd. # 3011A, Melville, NY 11747.
Positions: Telemarketing.
Requirements: Home-based telemarketers are trained to make appointments for outside salespeople to explain company's barter association and benefits. Must be articulate and capable of dealing with business people. Local residents only.
Provisions: Pays base salary plus commission and phone bill.

AMERITRUST CYBER TECHNOLOGIES, 900 Jorie Blvd., Suite 11, Oak Brook, Il 60523.
Positions: Inside business-to-business advertising sales via telephone.
Requirements: Prefers prior phone sales experience selling to business, those with excellent phone skills will be considered. Reliability and self discipline extremely important.
Provisions: Pays hourly rate plus bonus. Opportunities exist in Chicago, New York, and Los Angeles.

APARTMENTSTORES.COM; www.apartmentstores.com.
Positions: Telephone sales involving advertising sales to businesses within real estate and relocation.industries. ApartmentStores.com is a leading Internet-based real estate company and Web site for finding apartments for rent and moving companies.
Requirements: Must have proven sales experience and computer with broadband (high speed) Internet access.
Provisions: Can live anywhere in the U.S.

ARBONNE INTERNATIONAL, INC., 678 E Walnut Brook Dr Murray UT 84107.
Positions: Direct sales of European cosmetics and skin care products. Reps build customers bases using any direct sales methods that work for them.
Provisions: Training and ongoing managerial support is provided. Pays commission.

ART & SOUL, INC., 1229 Seitz Dr., Waukesha, WI 53186.
Positions: Direct sales of personalized products; watercolor and ink cartoon lithographs, magnets, key/bag tags, note pads, frames and designer t-shirts.
Requirements: Although optional, there is a standard business supply kit available for $100. It contains catalogs, advertising brochures, training booklets, personalizing equipment, etc.
Provisions: Prices, and therefore profits, are set by you.

ARTISTIC IMPRESSIONS, INC., 240 Cortland Ave., Lombard, IL 60148.
Positions: Direct sales of art works.

AUDI OF AMERICA, P.O. Box 556, Southfield, MI 48037.
Positions: Automobile parts specialist to help non-Volkswagen dealers with inventory. Duties include providing parts expertise, parts management, assistance with merchandising and administration of inventory.
Requirements: Must have thorough knowledge of automotive operations. Product knowledge of Volkswagen and/or Audi preferred, but not required. Qualified local residents send resume.
Provisions: Pays great salary plus offers full benefits.

AVON PRODUCTS, INC., www.avon.com. (800)FOR-AVON.
Positions: Avon, which is known for door-to-door sales, rarely uses this method anymore. Instead, its huge number of reps uses telemarketing methods to arrange home parties and make appointments for exclusive showings.
Requirements: Reps are required to buy samples, hostess thank-you gifts, and necessary paperwork.
Provisions: Pays commission. Management opportunities are available. You can now join the organization online.

BANKER'S LIFE & CASUALTY COMPANY, 1510 Newtown Pike, Suite 200, Lexington, KY 40511.
Positions: Sales managers and trainees for insurance company in Kentucky.
Requirements: You will need a Life and Health Insurance license.
Provisions: Company supplies leads, training, comprehensive benefits, excellent compensation, flexible daytime hours, great bonuses, and plenty of upward mobility. This is a great opportunity to be trained for a six-figure income job at home (anywhere).

BEAUTICONTROL, INC., 2121 Midway Road, Carrollton, TX 75006; www.beauticontrol.com.
Positions: BeautiControl primarily markets a cosmetic line that is tied into the "seasonal" method of color coordination. A secondary line of women's apparel is marketed in the same way. In 1985, the company topped $30 million in gross sales. BeautiControl does not use the party plan method of direct sales, but rather focuses on one-on-one sales. This is accomplished through intensive training, personal development, and corporate support of the consultants. A free color analysis is offered to potential customers; this

has proven to be the company's most powerful marketing tool.

Requirements: A one-time investment of $250 is required which includes over $900 worth of products, services, and training.

Provisions: Personal earnings are reported in the company's monthly in-house publication, "Achiever," and typically range from $12,000 down to $3,700 per month after being in the company for about two years. It is not unusual for new Consultants to earn $100 to $200 per day. There is opportunity to earn trips, diamond jewelry and a new Mustang convertible.

BEAUTY BY SPECTOR, 1 Spector Place, McKeesport, PA 15134.
Positions: Sales of hair goods and wigs for men and women.

BECKER AND ASSOCIATES, P.O. Box 607, 6801 Fair Oaks Blvd # G, Carmichael, CA 95609.
Positions: Marketers and prospecting assistants. Duties include contacting business owners and managers by phone, managing database programs of prospects, following up with prospects, setting and confirming appointments, and reporting on activity.
Requirements: These are nationwide opportunities. Send letter of interest.
Provisions: Pays $10-15 per hour.

BIZARRE PROMOTIONS, INC., 18708 Telegraph Rd, # C1, Romulus, MI 48174 .
Positions: Reselling of promotional products.
Requirements: $25 for start-up kit is rebated with $300 in sales.
Provisions: Offers access to over 500,000 promotional products imprinted with your customers' information.

BLUE ZEBRA USA, 25 Pequot Avenue, Suite A, Port Washington, NY 11050; www.bluezebrausa.com
Positions: This is a professional appointment setting company. Team members schedule appointments with businesses.
Requirements: Must be experienced, highly motivated, and professional. Requires five years of business-to-business sales experience and three years of experience cold calling businesses. Visit the Web site and resume via e-mail.
Provisions: Hours are hours per day for a total of 20-40 hours per week minimum. Pays commission per contract. Advancement opportunities.

BROWN BAG GOURMET GOODIES. http://brownbaggourmet.com.
Positions: Direct sales of gourmet coffees, teas, cocoas, cappuccinos, biscotti, cookies, chocolate spoons, and flavored stir sticks.
Provisions: Plenty of company support and a free Web site provided by the company.

BUSINESS EDGE, 1040 Avenue of the Americas, 24th Floor, New York, NY 10018; www.business-edge.com.
Positions: Telemarketing.
Requirements: Positions available only in Manhattan and Connecticut.
Provisions: Starting out the job is commission only, but can move up to salary plus commission.

BXI INTERNATIONAL, INC., 348 Albany Ave., Brooklyn, NY 11213.
Positions: Telemarketing for a 30-year-old barter association to network businesses. Example: Get a pet food company to sign for a minimum contract of $495 with BXI;

you receive 50% in cash or barter on that contract ($495 = $250 yours plus $245 is BXI's). If they give $250 cash plus $250 in pet food trade, you get $125 for BXI to use on balance of barter trade accumulation. There are 800#'s to call locally and internationally for restaurant use and trip information on such participating barter places as the Caribbean and Mexico. Example: Accumulate trade for a free vacation or just to write a check in a participating restaurant for a meal.

CALL DEPOT, 100 Biscayne Blvd., Miami, FL 33132.
Positions: Telemarketing of software in the $1,000 range.
Requirements: Sales experience required.
Provisions: Pays 25% commission.

CALLSNQUE; www.callsnque.com.
Positions: Business-to-business sales reps to bring in new clients for this customer relations outsourcing firm.
Requirements: Must be disciplined, organized, and results oriented. Requires minimum one years experience in sales.
Provisions: Can live anywhere. Apply online.

CAMERON FINANCIAL GROUP, INC., 1065 Higuera St., #102, San Luis Obispo, CA 93401.
Positions: Mortgage banking loan underwriters.
Requirements: Minimum 2 years in-house experience and DRE license. Send resume with references.
Provisions: Pays high commissions.

CASEPOST INC., 101 Pacifica, Irvine, CA 92612; www.casepost.com.
Positions: Telemarketers set appointments over the phone for client development specialists to meet with attorneys. Casepoint is a new client development service for the legal profession.
Requirements: Proven record of calling on professionals required.
Provisions: Pay is negotiable.

CASINO & BINGO INFO, PO Box 391, Magalia, CA 95954; www.casino-bingo-info.com/helpwanted.html
Positions: The work being offered is selling magazine advertising space to any business (other than adult material).
Requirements: Prefers sales experience, particularly in ad sales.
Provisions: Complete training and the necessary materials provided. Choose full or part time schedule. Pays weekly commissions.

CHARMELLE, INC., 101 Townsend Street, Ste 303, San Francisco, CA 94107.
Positions: Selling jewelry for this European owned company that supplies high-quality European designed costume jewelry at affordable prices to the U.S. market. The collection includes jewelry and accessories for both women and men. Each piece in the collection has been hand finished and plated with thick gold, rhodium or silver plating to ensure the highest possible quality. Sells through party plan and direct.
Provisions: Excellent training is provided. Pays commission.

CINTAS CORPORATION, 218 S. 14th St., Hopewell, VA 23860.
Positions: Telemarketing for uniform company.

Requirements: Need exceptional verbal and organizational skills. Apply in person.
Provisions: Set your own schedule, approximately 25 hours per week during school hours. Benefits include medical, dental, retirement, and profit sharing.

COMPASS FINANCIAL CORP., 4601 DTC Blvd, Denver, CO 80237.
Positions: Mortgage loan officer. Company offers FHA and VA approved loans.
Requirements: Pays 85/15 split or 100% for small monthly fee.

CONCEPT NOW COSMETICS, 12020 Mora Dr. # 9, Santa Fe Springs, CA 90670.
Positions: This 17-year-old company has been selling an extensive line of skin care products primarily though party plan sales. Reps operate through the U.S., Mexico, Canada, Puerto Rico, and the Virgin Islands.
Requirements: A start-up kit with $325 requires a $65 investment.
Provisions: No set territories. Training is available and includes tapes, manual, presentation outline and company support. Car allowance is provided along with specified promotions. Pays commission only for reps and override for managers.

COX COMMUNICATIONS CORP; www.coxmedia.com.
Positions: Part-time reps.
Requirements: Basic computer skills required along with a PC and Internet access. Prefers someone with experience in public relations or sales.
Provisions: Cox Media has offices in 35 cities. Visit the Web site to find opportunities near you.

COZY PLACES, Attn: Human Resources, 1658 E. Capitol Expressway, Suite 520, San Jose, CA 95121; www.cozyplaces.com.
Positions: Telemarketers to promote and sell advertising on Cozyplaces.com, a comprehensive online nationwide directory for Bed and Breakfast inns.
Requirements: Must be experienced telemarketer with 2-3 years direct telesales experience. Must be comfortable with cold calling.
Provisions: Can live anywhere in U.S.

CREATIVE MEMORIES, 2815 Clearwater Road, St. Cloud, MN 56301.
Positions: Party-plan sales of books, hobby products, photo albums, and photography products.

CRESTCOM INTERNATIONAL, LTD., 6900 E Belleview Ave., Englewood, CO 80111-1619.
Positions: Professional phone marketers book seminars for well-known speaker and management trainer.
Requirements: Local professionals send resume indicating experience.
Provisions: Work 25 hours per week. Pays base salary plus commission and bonus program.

D. J. ARDORE, INC., PO 188, Mountain Lakes, NJ 07046; www.djardore.com.
Positions: Telemarketers set appointments and also handle some data entry. This company produces a restaurant/dining guide. The appointments are for sales reps to meet with restaurants and sell advertising space.
Requirements: Must live within driving distance of company headquarters. Need PC with Internet access. Apply via e-mail with resume.
Provisions: Pay equals $10 - $12 an hour plus bonus incentives.

Homeworker Profile: Nancy Maynard

Nancy Maynard's work has changed in ways she never expected since graduating from Berkeley with two degrees. Her work life started in the impersonal corporate world of Xerox.

"I found there was pressure to slow down, to do just what you're supposed to do. There was no encouragement to do more to earn more. Raises were the same for everyone; they came along once a year no matter what. After six years, I asked myself why I should work hard for another $10 a week—especially since I'd get it regardless of my accomplishments."

Shortly before leaving Xerox, Nancy started working with Oriflame, selling their European skin care system. The initial intent was to make a little extra cash. Much to her surprise, she matched her corporate salary within six months. In another six months she became assistant manager and was well on her way to earning her present $40,000 a year salary, plus bonus gifts.

"In direct sales, a person is in control. I can say, 'I need a car. I'll buy it and work an extra four hours a week to pay for it.' She adds, "Of course, I don't need to do that. I've earned a gold Mercedes through Oriflame's incentive bonus plan!"

Nancy believes direct sales is an ideal choice for women who want to combine working and homemaking. It gives them control over their earning power and greater flexibility in their daily schedules.

For Nancy, that means spending time with her husband, who also works at home, and with their five year old daughter. "We both like to take time out of the day when we want to go to the park, have lunch together, or maybe just go for a walk. It allows us to give our daughter a better sense of us as people. What could be better than that?"

DATA CRITICAL CORP., 19820 N Creek Pkwy # 100, Bothell, WA 98011.
Positions: Sales reps and regional managers direct the sales activity for company's wireless telemedicine products to hospital accounts.
Requirements: Must be detail oriented and possess excellent communications and follow-through skills. Three to seven years of telemarketing experience required. Apply with resume.
Provisions: Company supplies PC, printer, fax, and scanner. Offers excellent compensation, benefits, retirement plan, and generous stock options.

DESKTOP AUTHOR, POB 875, Strawberry Hills NSW 2012 Australia; www.catalogstudio.com.
Positions: Ad sales. This Australian company is looking for reps anywhere in the U.S. to sell its inexpensive applications software to businesses of all sizes. Visit Web site for sample demo.
Requirements: Prefers experienced sales reps who have contacts within the advertising and business community.
Provisions: Pays commission only; 30% on every software sale and 20% on the production services. Software sells for $105 and production services is about $500 for typical turn-key production. Go to Web site to apply.

DISCOVERY TOYS, INC., 2530 Arnold Dr., Suite 400, Martinez, CA 94553. www.discoverytoysinc.com.
Positions: Discovery Toys was started as a home-based business in 1982. The company markets a line of educationally sound toys and accessories through home parties. Home party demonstrators and their supervisors are all home-based.
Requirements: Send letter of interest.
Provisions: Complete training is provided. Pays commission and override. Can live anywhere. You can now register to work with the organization online.

DONCASTER, 581 Rock Road, Rutherfordton, NC 28139; www.doncaster.com.
Positions: Doncaster trains women to be fashion consultants, "Selling the art of dressing well." Fashion Consultants present the Doncaster collection in private showing in their own homes four times a year. These fashions are considered to be investment quality and are designed primarily for career women.
Provisions: Training is provided. Pays commission. Management opportunities are available.

THE DOYLE GROUP, LTD., 3948 Ridgewood Rd., York, PA 17402; www.doylegroupltd.com.
Positions: Marketing and sales positions for business Web site development firm.
Requirements: No experience necessary if you are motivated and a self starter. You will need a computer and Internet access.
Provisions: Support staff will help by closing sales for those new to sales. You keep the commission on those sales. Flexible hours. Pays commission only, up to $1850 per sale. Live anywhere.

DUDLEY PRODUCTS AND PUBLICATIONS, 1080 Old Greensboro Rd., Kernersville, NC 27284.
Positions: Direct sales of cosmetics using home parties as primary sales method.
Provisions: Training is provided. Pays commission and override for managers.

EAST COAST DRIVING SCHOOL, 475 Wall St., Princeton, NJ 08540.
Positions: Telemarketing.
Requirements: Telephone support needed for evenings and weekends in the Princeton/ Trenton area. Script, leads provided.

ELECTRIC MOBILITY CORPORATION, Number 1 Mobility Plaza, Sewell, NJ 08080.
Positions: This manufacturer of electric mobility three-wheelers uses a national network of independent reps to demonstrate and sell their products. All reps are home-based, but must travel to demonstrate the products to interested buyers because they are either elderly or handicapped.
Requirements: This is not hard sell; reps must be easy going, caring, efficient and very organized. Apply with resume.
Provisions: Leads are generated through national advertising and are prequalified by telemarketers before being sent to reps. Territories are assigned by zip codes. Commissions are about $300 per sale.

ELECTROLUX CORP., 5956 Sherry Ln #1500, Dallas, TX 75225.
Positions: Direct sales of vacuum cleaners, floor polishers, and attachments.

ENCYCLOPAEDIA BRITTANICA, INC., Brittanica Centre, 310 South Michigan Ave, Chicago, IL 60604.
Positions: This is the largest company of its kind in the world. It also has a reputation for having the highest paid direct sales reps of any industry. Britannica is now sold through a variety of means, very little door-to-door effort is used.
Provisions: A two-week training session is provided. In most areas, write-in leads are provided. Pays highest commission in the industry, plus override for managers.

EXCLUSIVE DOMAINS, INC., 641 W. Lake Street, Suite 100, Chicago, IL 60661; www.xoffers.com.
Positions: Business-to-business telemarketing sales. Product is Internet advertising and online marketing services.
Requirements: Telemarketing experience. Also requires good phone demeanor, strong communication and organizational skills, solid work ethic, and self-motivation. You will be expected to make 50 to 100 calls per day and close 5 to 10 sales per week.
Provisions: Pays commission equal to $95-$295 per sale. Visit Web site, then email resume.

EXECUTIVE CAREER MANAGEMENT GROUP, 450 North Brand Blvd. Suite 600, Glendale, CA 91203; http://executivecareermanagementgroup.com.
Positions: Appointment setting, sales, and marketing for a public relations and executive career management firm.
Requirements: Because this company works with very high level clients, the requirements to work here are stringent. Must have appointment setting background plus a solid professional sales and/or marketing and PR background. Definitely prefers those with public relations background. Cold calling experience is also required. Must also have experience telecommuting. You will need a good home office setup with a computer and a flat rate long distance phone service. This is not a job for beginners.
Provisions: Can live anywhere in the U.S. Advancement opportunities after six months Full benefits provided after you have proven yourself.

EXTERIOR HOME CENTER, 14001C Saint Germain Dr. #225, Centerville, VA 20121.
Positions: Telemarketers/appointment setters for home improvement company in the Maryland, Virginia, DC area.
Provisions: Potential of $15 per hour plus bonuses.

FASHION TWO TWENTY, INC., 250 Coventry Dr., Painesville, OH 44077.
Positions: Direct sales of extensive line of quality cosmetics. Reps start by conducting home parties. After building an established clientele, home parties are usually replaced with prearranged personal consultations.
Requirements: There is usually a $15 fee to cover the cost of the manual and data processing. A new rep must also purchase the standard Show-Case kit. New consultants are expected to submit at least $150 retail orders per month.
Provisions: Pays commission. Management opportunities exist.

FINELLE COSMETICS, 480 Lowell St., Andover, MA 01810; www.finelle.com.
Positions: Direct sales of cosmetics and skin care products.

FLETCHER CONSULTING, INC., 6475 Perimeter Drive, #114, Dublin OH 43016; www.fcon.com/appt.
Positions: Appointment setter. The job involves contacting schools, churches, youth sports organizations and large employers in specific areas around the country. You will not be asking for money at any point - and you are not really "selling" anything.
Requirements: Must be a good communicator. Experience is a plus but is not required. You will need Internet access and e-mail. You must be willing to work at least 15 hours per week during normal business hours.
Provisions: Training provided. Pays per appointment on a sliding scale - the more appointments you set in a week, the more you are paid for each. Earnings typically amount to $15-$25 per hour and more is possible. Visit Web site for more information and to see what area is open.

FRIENDS LIFE CARE AT HOME, INC., 1777 Sentry Parkway West, 210 Dublin Hall, Blue Bell, PA 19422.
Positions: This is a unique Quaker-based long-term care program that needs sales/marketing reps in New Castle County, Delaware and Chester County, Pennsylvania.
Requirements: Need minimum of two years experience in sales/marketing to seniors with an understanding of long term care issues, and knowledge of the region. Must have demonstrated ability to work independently. Send resume and salary history.

GOLDEN PRIDE, INC., 1501 Northpoint Parkway, Suite 100, West Palm Beach, FL 33407.
Positions: Direct sales of health and beauty aids.

THE GOOD NATURE CO., INC., Oxford, Michigan. email: info@thegoodnatureco.com.
Positions: Party plan sales of lawn and garden ornaments, garden tools and accessories, bird houses and feeders.
Requirements: You must choose one of two business kits; both are affordable.
Provisions: Flexible hours, commission plan with monthly bonuses and other incentives.

GREEN LAKE CHIROPRACTIC, 1408 N. 80th St., Seattle, WA 98103.

Positions: Telemarketers.
Requirements: Must be experienced and be local resident.
Provisions: Pays $8 per hour to start plus bonuses. Offers choice of day or evening hours.

GROLIER INCORPORATED, 90 Sherman Turnpike, Danbury, CT 06816.
Positions: Grolier is best known for publishing Encyclopedia Americana and has expanded into other educational publishing (such as the Disney series and Mr. Light).
Provisions: Training is provided in one-week classroom sessions. No leads, no territories. Sales are direct and usually accomplished by setting appointments by phone in advance of the presentation. Pays commission (about 23%) to reps plus override to managers. Some expenses such as phone and car are reimbursed on an individual arrangement with management.

GUPTA TECHNOLOGIES, 975 Island Drive, Redwood Shores, CA 94065; http://guptaworldwide.com.
Positions: Software sales agents sell company's SQLBase database and team developer rapid application development tool directly to end users and resellers.
Requirements: At least three years experience selling software products. Prefer those with contacts that can be converted into sales.
Provisions: Has territories available throughout North America. Pays commission only.

HANOVER SHOE CO., INC., 118 Carlisle St., Hanover, PA 17331.
Positions: Hanover is over 50 years old and still markets its shoes primarily through the use of independent reps. Reps sell direct through any method they choose, usually by starting with friends and neighbors and building up an established pool of customers through referrals.
Provisions: A portion of the retail price is returned to the rep.

HEALTH ADMINISTRATION SYSTEMS, INC., 10270 Old Columbia Road, Suite 110, Columbia, MD 21046; http://has.com.
Positions: Marketing specialists develop sales leads, enhance publicity, and target products and services. The goal is to increase company's local, regional, and national presence.
Requirements: Marketing experience is required. E-mail resume.
Provisions: Part-time or full-time positions available.

HERBALIFE INTERNATIONAL, 1800 Century Park E , Los Angeles, CA 90067.
Positions: Direct sales of weight control food products.

HOME AND GARDEN PARTY, 2938 Brown Rd., Marshall, Texas, 75672; www.homeandgardenparty.com.
Positions: This is a home based party plan business featuring home decor items such as hand-turned stoneware pottery, framed prints, terracotta pottery, figurines, brass accessories, etc.
Requirements: There is an initial start-up cost of $150, which covers the cost of a sample kit with a retail value of more than $300. You could recover your total investment in less than two months and the company guarantees a one-year buy-back option if you leave. You are not required to carry inventory.
Provisions: Offers generous commission schedule plus override commissions, sponsor bonuses and possible infinity bonuses.

HOME & GROUNDS, 1020, 29th St. NW, Washington, DC 20007; www.homeandgrounds.com.
Positions: Telemarketing for this a "business to business" and "consumer based" advertising company that focuses on the home improvement, home plans, service contractor, interior design, home furnishings, real estate, art, antiques, nurseries and landscape markets.
Requirements: Telemarketing experience is preferred but not necessary.
Provisions: Can live anywhere in the U.S. Pays aggressive commissions and "stock options bonuses". Apply with resume.

HOME INTERIORS & GIFTS, INC., 2828 Trade Center, Carrollton, TX 75007.
Positions: Direct sales of pictures, figurines, shelves, foliage, and other home accents. Reps set up exclusive shows that include about 35 pieces of merchandise. After the show, the rep offers individual service and decorating advice to the customers.
Requirements: Reps must order, deliver, and collect.
Provisions: Training is provided in the form of ongoing sales classes, weekly meetings and monthly decorating workshops. The average rep presents about three shows a week and works about 25 hours a week.

HOUSE OF LLOYD, 11901 Grandview Road, Grandview, MO 64030.
Positions: Home party sales reps and supervisors. Product line includes toys and gifts.
Provisions: Training and start-up supplies are provided with no investment. Commission equals approximately $9 an hour. Can live anywhere.

THE HUTTON GROUP, 1650 N 42nd Circle, Vero Beach, FL 32963.
Positions: E-medical account executives. The job consists of demonstrating products to physician practices, seminars, and trade shows. Duties include managing sales and marketing activities, working with existing customers to tract their activities, and produce reports.
Requirements: Must have working knowledge of Microsoft software and be available to work 5 to 8 business days each month. Send resume.

HY CITE CORPORATION, ROYAL PRESTIGE, 333 Holtzman Rd., Madison, WI 53713.
Positions: Home party sales of cookware, china, crystal, tableware and stoneware.
Provisions: Training is provided. Pays commission. The company's marketing division provides all of the product literature, sales tools, and field assistance needed. All supplied are training manuals, presentation aids, and videotape and cassette training programs. Reps benefit from national advertising and customer promotion campaigns.

IDAHO STATESMAN, 1200 N Curtis Rd., Boise, ID 83706.
Positions: Independent sales representative for The Idaho Statesman. Job entails contacting former subscribers by phone.
Requirements: Must be self-motivated and able to overcome objections. Apply to circulation sales/marketing manager.
Provisions: Offers flexible schedule to suit your availability.

IMS TECHNOLOGY TELESALES, 317 La Mesa Avenue, Encinitas, CA 92024; www.telesalesspecialists.com.
Positions: Business to business telemarketing and prospecting for high technology clients. In addition to calls, job entails mailing follow-up, lead generation, inquiry

qualification, database development, list cleaning, product sales, surveys, marketing research.
Requirements: This is a job for professionals only. College graduates only. Requires business-to-business or corporate sales experience or previous high tech experience. You will need a fully equipped home office with PC. You will be required to work a minimum of 15 hours per week on a flexible basis.
Provisions: Part-time or full-time schedule available. Work schedule is flexible, typically 10-35 hours per week. Pays $15 per hour plus commission.

INFINITY INSURANCE COMPANY, P.O. Box 444, Birmingham, AL 35201.
Positions: Business development representatives for insurance company.
Requirements: Must be willing to travel daily within your territory. Some overnight travel will also be required. You will need a college degree and 2 years of successful sales experience. Apply with resume.
Provisions: Pays salary plus benefits and offers performance incentives, laptop, company vehicle, and a comprehensive training program.

INTENTIA, 10255 W. Higgins Rd., Suite 200, Rosemont, IL 60018.
Positions: Intentia is the maker of resource management software with over 4,000 manufacturing and distribution sites worldwide. Opportunities exist for industry-savvy pros in sales management, pre-sales, and post sales, and field sales.
Requirements: Three to seven years relevant (and successful) experience is required. Apply with resume.
Provisions: A flexible work environment that may include telecommuting.

INTREP, INC., 5178 Marks Court, New Albany OH 43054; www.intrep.com.
Positions: Telemarketing for progressive outsourcing company.
Requirements: Must have solid business background and be comfortable communicating at all management levels. Inside sales experience required as well as computer and software knowledge. Must have customer service orientation. You will need a well equipped home office with computer system and broadband Internet access.
Provisions: All geographical areas are open. Apply online.

ITXTEND, 5490 McGinnis Village Place, Suite 208, Alpharetta, GA 30005; www.itxtend.com.
Positions: Telemarketers for this software development and IT Services company. Company has a strong focus in healthcare.
Requirements: Must be organized and able to make cold calls. Need telemarketing and/or sales experience.
Provisions: Flexible schedule. Pays $10 to $12 depending on experience. Atlanta only.

JAFRA COSMETICS, INC., P.O. Box 5026, Westlake Village, CA 91359.
Positions: Jafra makes high quality, "natural" cosmetics and skin care products. Reps sell the products through the party plan and by offering free facials to participants.
Provisions: Pays commission.

KAIRO CORP., 5646 Waterbury Way #D-100, Salt Lake City, UT 84121; http://kairoscorp.com.
Positions: Telemarketing and sales to generate leads for business software.
Requirements: Positions are available in Salt Lake City only. Must be computer savvy

and have excellent communication skills. Apply with resume.

Provisions: Part-time or full-time positions available. Telemarketers are paid $8-$10 hourly plus bonus and sales reps potentially earn over $200k per year.

THE KIRBY CORPORATION, 1920 W. 114 St., Cleveland, OH 44102. www.kirby.com.

Positions: Kirby has been selling its vacuum cleaners door-to-door for many years. Now, reps use telemarketing methods to prearrange demonstrations.

Provisions: Some write-in leads are provided. Pays commissions.

KITCHEN-A-FAIR, 900 North 400 West Suite #15, North Salt Lake, Utah 84054. www.kitchenafair.com.

Positions: Kitchen-A-Fair is a 20-year-old maker of cookware, kitchen accessories, and home decorative items. All products are sold in home demonstrations. There is no ordering, packing, or shipping merchandise and no collection by the consultants.

Provisions: Training is provided. Regional advertising is provided by the company and the resulting inquires are passed along to the area consultants. The initial kit is free. Pays commission to consultants and up to 7% override to managers.

LINCOLN FINANCIAL ADVISORS, 200 E. Berry St., Ft. Wayne, IN 46802.

Positions: Insurance retirement consultant in the Indianapolis area. Job entails enrolling and servicing employees.

Requirements: Must be self-motivated and capable of working independently from home. Knowledge of insurance products, mutual funds, securities, and distribution systems is a must. Series 6 is required along with excellent oral and written skills and the ability to travel. Bachelor's degree preferred. Apply with resume.

LONGABERGER MARKETING, INC., 1360 E. Main St., Dresden, OH 43821.

Positions: Longaberger markets maple wood baskets that are handmade in America. Each basket is signed by the weaver. Longaberger consultants sell the baskets though home parties.

Requirements: The initial investment of $300 covers the cost of sample baskets, catalogs, invitations, a handbook, and enough materials to hold several shows.

Provisions: Training is provided not only for sales techniques but for learning how to best decorate and display the baskets. Pays commissions starting at 25% plus overrides for managers. Three levels of management opportunities exist. Managers are provided with special management award baskets, mailings, meetings, training sessions, incentives, and other awards.

LUCKY HEART COSMETICS, INC., 138 Huling Ave., Memphis, TN 38103.

Positions: Lucky Heart is a line of cosmetics for black women. The products are sold direct by independent distributors in any way they choose.

Requirements: A one-time $10 start-up fee is required.

Provisions: Color catalogs, samples and testers are provided. Pays commission plus bonuses. Management opportunities exist.

MACKE WATER SYSTEMS, INC., 190 Shepard Ave. Suite A, P.O. Box 545 Wheeling, Illinois 60090; www.mackewater.com.

Positions: Appointment setters. Macke Water Systems is a national provider of "bottle-less" water coolers, purification systems, and national coffee service. This is business-to-business appointment setting for sales reps in your local area or you can call nationwide, which should increase your earning potential.

Requirements: Minimum two years sales and/or telemarketing experience. Need computer with Internet access and a separate phone line.

Provisions: Leads are provided by logging into the company's online database. Pays per appointment set. Training provided. Can live anywhere.

MANAGEMENT RECRUITERS OF SACRAMENTO, 2316 Bell Executive Lane, Suite 100, Sacramento, CA 95825; www.mrsacramento.com.

Positions: Healthcare accounts managers. Job involves selling long-term energy contracts in the national healthcare vertical market.

Requirements: Must have experience dealing with Fortune 1000 level executives and energy departments. Must be free to travel extensively to customer locations and trade shows. College graduates only. Although no energy industry experience is required, you must have at least five years of sales experience in the healthcare field with a proven track record of success.

Provisions: Can work from your home office anywhere in the continental U.S.

MARY KAY COSMETICS, INC., 8787 Stemmons Freeway, Dallas, TX 75247. www.marykay.com.

Positions: Beauty consultants and sales directors. Mary Kay started this cosmetics empire on her kitchen table in 1963. In 1984 there were 151,615 consultants and 4,500 sales directors producing over $300 million in sales. All of these people worked from their homes.

Requirements: An investment of $100 is required to start.

Provisions: Pays commission up to 12%. Offers incentives such as jewelry, furs, cars and trips through special promotions and contests. Consultants can earn over $30,000 annually, generally averaging over $10 an hour after taxes. Directors average over $100,000 a year. Can live anywhere.

MASON SHOE MANUFACTURING COMPANY, 1251 First Avenue, Chippewa Falls, WI 54729.

Positions: Mason is a 35-year-old family business with an extensive line of American made, quality shoes. All shoes are guaranteed for quality and fit and can be easily exchanged or refunded.

Provisions: Reps are provided with catalogs and all necessary supplies. Incentive bonus plans several times a year. Portion of the retail price is taken out by the rep before placing the order with the company.

MATRIX TECHNOLOGY GROUP, 120 Wood Avenue South, Suite # 300, Iselin , NJ 08830; www.matrixonweb.com.

Positions: Lead generation and sales of Internet software for business applications.

Requirements: Must have strong cold calling skills and actually love to close a sale. Some computer experience is necessary. Should be able and willing to make at least 200 calls each day to generate leads. Go to Web site to apply.

Provisions: This is a full time position that pays well, over $40,000 per year.

MELALEUCA, INC., 3910 S. Yellowstone Hwy, Idaho Falls, ID 83402.

Positions: This is a well-established company that's been around since 1985. It offers a line of natural and unique everyday products that are highly effective yet pleasant and safe to have in the home. All products are marketed through a network of sales consultants. Send for information.

THE MEMORY TRAINING INSTITUTE, Attn: Carl Messina, Personnel Dept., 1062 Portland-Cobalt Road, Portland, CT 06480; www.mtilink.com.
Positions: Telemarketers set appointments with upper level management.
Requirements: Must be available weekends only, no weekends. Must enjoy phone work, be a self-starter, have successful telemarketing experience, be able to work without supervision, and be able to produce 8 appointments each week.
Provisions: Will train using a proven system. Pays well. Live anywhere in U.S.

MIDWAY PUBLISHING, INC., 700 N Bird St. #104, Alpine, TX 79830; www.midwaypublishing.com.
Positions: Sales reps for Web development company. Job includes locating prospective clients for Web sites. Presentations are made via Web, phone, or in person.
Requirements: Experience in sales or marketing.
Provisions: Can live anywhere in U.S. Pays commission only.

MIRACLE MAID, 8383 158th Ave., NE, Redmond, WA 98052.
Positions: Miracle Maid cookware is sold through pre-arranged product demonstrations in customers' homes.
Provisions: Training is provided. Pays commission.

MOONWOLF ENTERPRISES, 5303 Quintana St., Riverdale, MD 20737.
Positions: Selling Web hosting, design, and other services.
Requirements: Must be motivated and self-starting. Knowledge of technical aspects of the Internet is a definite advantage, but is not required.
Provisions: This is a 100% telecommute position. Pays commission.

MOUNTAINWEB.COM, Lakewood, CO.
Positions: Account executive to renew ski resort accounts.
Requirements: Working knowledge of the outdoor industry preferred. Must possess strong closing, negotiation, and communication skills. Ability to handle large client load a must. Apply by sending resume to chuck@mountainweb.com.
Provisions: Pays 20% commission (average sale is $200).

NATIONAL LOCATING SERVICE, INC., www.nationallocating.com.
Positions: Telemarketers to place vending machines for charities.
Requirements: Must have phone and Internet access.
Provisions: Can live anywhere. Visit Web site and apply via e-mail.

NATIONAL SAFETY ASSOCIATES, INC., 4260 E. Raines Rd., Memphis, TN 38118.
Positions: Direct sales of water treatment systems. NSA offers a proven program for part-time sales opportunities wherein a person can work 8-12 hours per week and earn up to $10,000 a year.
Requirements: New distributors of NSA products must first be sponsored by someone who is already a distributor. If one cannot be located, then the interested person must attend a regional training class. A schedule will be provided upon request.
Provisions: Training is provided. NSA products are sold through a trial use approach. A customer is given the opportunity to try the product for a few days, and then make the decision whether or not to purchase. Because of this method of selling, NSA recommends

that distributors have 4-5 units on hand for this purpose. NSA provides a credit line so that the new distributor has no purchase requirements to get started. Pays commission plus bonuses through the company-sponsored rebate program.

NATURE'S SUNSHINE PRODUCTS, INC., 1655 N Main, Spanish Fork, UT 84660.
Positions: Direct sales of herbs, vitamins, and personal care products.
Requirements: New distributors must attend a one-week training session at company headquarters at their own expense. Reps are trained to sell the products through network marketing.
Provisions: Commissions start at 8% and go up to 30%. Managers receive generous override commissions. Participating managers receive health and dental insurance, new car allowance, and a retirement program. Sales aids and incentive programs are provided to everyone.

NEAR & ASSOCIATES, 5955 Carnegie Blvd., Suite 300, Charlotte, NC 28209; www.nearassociates.com.
Positions: Sales reps develop new business for this outsourcing firm.
Requirements: Proven track record of at least seven years selling outsourcing services and/or executive placement services.
Provisions: Pays base salary plus commission.

NEO-LIFE DIAMITE INTL, 3500 Gateway Blvd., Fremont, CA 94538.
Positions: Direct sales of household products, vitamins, minerals, and some food products. Multilevel techniques are used.
Requirements: A small investment is required.
Provisions: Pays commission on a sliding scale.

NOEVIR, INC., 1095 S.E. Main St., Irvine, CA 92714.
Positions: Direct sales of cosmetics manufactured by Noevir, all of which are completely natural and herbal. Noevir has over 15,000 operators currently serving the U.S. The company is an affiliate of a larger Japanese company, and also has an office in Canada. Noevir is a wholly owned subsidiary of Noevir, Co., Ltd., the second largest direct selling company in Japan.
Requirements: The initial investment in Noevir is $30 for registration in addition to the purchase of one starter kit. These kits contain products, training information, and samples for the new operator. The kits, (choice of 2) are $150. There is also an option "C" which is a "build-your-own" kit. The minimum purchase for this kit is $50.
Provisions: Noevir offers a generous compensation package in addition to very high quality products.

NORTH SHORE LEASING & FUNDING CORP., P.O. Box 307, Kings Park, NY 11754; ww.nslf.com.
Positions: Telemarketing for national equipment finance company. This is business-to-business sales, calling companies to see if they need capital to acquire or replace existing equipment.
Requirements: Should possess outgoing personality, good telephone skills, and be an independent thinker. Need phone and fax.
Provisions: Can live anywhere.

OFFSHORE DATA ENTRY, a subsidiary of High Tech Exports, Gujarat, India; www.offshoredataentry.com.

Positions: This company has openings for highly skilled marketing consultants to sell marketing data entry services to businesses. This is a global company with opportunities to work anywhere in the world - USA, Canada, Europe, Australia etc.
Requirements: Minimum 4-5 years of marketing and 1-2 years of experience in data entry field. Must be IT savvy.
Provisions: Pays very high commissions. Can choose to work on exclusive or non-exclusive basis. Visit Web site, then e-mail resume.

KENNETH OLSON & ASSOCIATES, 399 Main St., Los Altos, CA 94022.
Positions: Telemarketers for business-to-business insurance sales.
Requirements: Must be local resident. Prefers experience in business-to-business dealings.
Provisions: Specific training is provided. Leads are also provided. No high pressure selling involved. Part-time hours only. Pays salary plus "substantial" commission.

ORIFLAME INTERNATIONAL, P.O. Box 977, Waxhaw, NC 28173. www.oriflame.com.
Positions: Direct sales reps for European cosmetics line. Oriflame International is a high-quality cosmetic line that has gained a reputation for being "the largest, most prestigious direct sales company in Europe." Company has been expanding throughout the U.S. for about five years. Advisors are trained as skin consultants. Business does not usually consist of door-to-door or party style sales. More often, advisors act as make-up artists and customers come to their home offices by appointment only. Opportunity also for part-time sales leadership positions. Significant "groundfloor" opportunity for Group Directors.
Provisions: Complete training is provided. Commissions are reportedly the highest in the U.S. for a direct sales company.

OUR WEDDING VENDORS; OurWeddingVendors.com.
Positions: Regional sales of online advertising for wedding services.
Requirements: Minimum three years experience in online ad sales. Must have excellent communications and phone skills. Will need a home office with phone, voice mail, fax, computer, e-mail and Internet access.
Provisions: Can live anywhere in the U.S. to apply, but must live within the region assigned. Check the Web site to see which regions are currently available. Industry and sales training is provided. Pays commission.

PAMPERED CHEF, 350 South Rohlwing Road, Addison, IL 60101; www.pamperedchef.com.
Positions: Hosting home parties called Kitchen Shows, where you'll demonstrate how Pampered Chef products can be used to easily and quickly prepare gourmet meals.
Provisions: Pays commission. There is plenty of room for advancement into management positions. This company offers a lot of support, particularly for working mothers.

PARTYLITE GIFTS, 59 Armstrong Rd. #A, Plymouth, MA 02360.
Positions: Home party sales of decorative accessories and giftware for the home.
Provisions: Pays commission plus bonuses. Management opportunities available.

PETRA FASHIONS, INC., 35 Cherry Hill Drive, Danvers, MA 01923; www.petrafashions.com.
Positions: Direct sales of lingerie and sleepwear. All items are under $30. Petra

consultants demonstrate the lingerie collection in private home parties. Consultants test show guests' "romance ratings" and offer fashion advice on garment style and fit. They do not collect money, take inventory or make deliveries. Petra accepts Mastercard and VISA and all show orders are shipped C.O.D. by UPS directly to the party hostess.
Requirements: No investment or experience is necessary. Petra offers a free starter kit of sample garments and paperwork that is valued at more than $500. There are no quotas or sales territories.
Provisions: Petra provides free training, hostess incentives, profit per show in excess of $75, advancement opportunities, overrides, awards, and recognition.

POLA, U.S.A., INC., 251 East Victoria Avenue, Carson, CA 90746; www.pola.com.
Positions: Home party sales of cosmetics.
Requirements: A start-up kit requires an investment.
Provisions: Pays commission.

POWERGY, INC., 111 Chestnut St., Providence, RI 02903.
Positions: Sales reps for power quality/energy conservation device.
Requirements: There is a refundable $75 deposit required for a sales kit.

PRIMERICA, 391 Gamble Oak Ct., Millersville, MD 21108.
Positions: Auto and home insurance sales for top national company.
Provisions: Regional center does all paper work and service.

PRINCESS HOUSE, INC., 470 Myles Standish Blvd., Taunton, MA 02780; www.princesshouse.com.
Positions: Home party sales of crystal products.
Provisions: Pays commission plus override for managers. Training is provided.

PROCARD INTERNATIONAL, 6709 West 119th Street, #501, Overland Park, Kansas 66209; www.procardinternational.com.
Positions: Marketing associates. Company represents over 300,000 dentists, doctors, and attorneys, over 1/2 of all hospitals, 83% of all pharmacies, and over 10,000 vision centers nationwide. Job involves activating accounts for people who have already requested dental, vision, prescription drug, and legal services.
Requirements: No sales experience is necessary for this job.
Provisions: Permanent or part-time positions available. Can live anywhere. Free leads provided.

PROCUREMENT PROFESSIONALS, 2400 E. Devon Ave., #210, Des Plaines, IL 60018.
Positions: This staffing service specializes in placing purchasing department personnel in Chicago. Opportunities exist for aggressive sales people to provide sales and marketing.
Requirements: The ideal candidate has prior experience in sales, self-motivated and independent. Send resume.

QUALITY LOGIC, 5401 Tech Circle, Moorpark, CA 93021; www.qualitylogic.com.
Positions: Account managers for high tech sales to large enterprise accounts.
Requirements: Must have at least seven years experience selling software business solutions above the $500,000 price point. College graduates only. Proven ability to telecommute without supervision. No travel is required.
Provisions: Full time positions only. Can be anywhere in the U.S.

QUICK PRACTICE, 500 N Broadway, Ste 256, Jericho, NY 11753; www.quickpractice.com.
Positions: Sales of medical software. Home telemarketers give away this company's product for free to qualified healthcare professionals.
Requirements: Previous telemarketing experience required. Internet a plus. Send resume.
Provisions: Pays $4.50 per qualified lead, plus 5% commission on sales that close from your leads. Average sale is $1200.00.

REGAL WARE, INC., 1675 Reigle Dr., Kewaskum, WI 53040. www.regalware.com.
Positions: Direct sales of cookware, usually through home parties.
Provisions: Training is provided. Pays commission.

RELIV DISTRIBUTORS, 136 Chesterfield Ind. Blvd., Chesterfield, MO 63005; www.relivonline.com.
Positions: Nutritional products that combine the ingredients from science and nature in targeted, well balanced, easy to use formulas.
Provisions: Weekly local meetings and training sessions, national conference calls, 24-hour story call lines, conferences and simple to use sales tools.

REXAIR, INC., P.O. Box 3610, 3221 W Big Beaver Rd # 200, Troy, MI 48007.
Positions: Direct sales of rainbow vacuum cleaners, AquaMate, and related products.

RICH PLAN CORP., 4981 Commercial Dr., Yorkville, NY 13495.
Positions: Direct sales of food, beverage products, and home appliances.

R3X.NET, INC., 709 West Huron St., Ann Arbor, Michigan 48103; www.r3x.net.
Positions: This company is in the business of very high level business consulting. Executive sales professionals here call on high level decision makers and corporate CEOs. Only those with this kind of experience will be considered.
Requirements: Must have a proven track record of exceeding quotas. Only the most qualified will be hired. Hours will average 35 to 40 per week.
Provisions: Those who qualify receive a free computer and high speed Internet access. The income potential here is huge, but it will be well earned. This is not an opportunity for amateurs. For complete information on this opportunity, visit the company Web site.

SALADMASTER, INC., 912 113th St., Arlington, TX 76011; www.saladmaster.com.
Positions: Home party sales of cookware and tableware.
Provisions: Training is available. Pays commission plus bonus plan.

SAN FRANCISCO CHRONICLE, Circulation Department, 925 Mission, San Francisco, CA 94103.
Positions: Telemarketers sell subscriptions. Work is part-time.
Requirements: Some previous telemarketing experience is required.
Provisions: Can live anywhere in Northern California. Training is provided. Some leads are supplied. Pays commission and bonuses.

SCHOOL CALENDAR, 1135 W. Morris Blvd., Morristown, TN 37813.
Positions: Account executives sell advertising space. Company is a 30-year-old publishing firm.

Requirements: Must be bondable.
Provisions: A protected territory is assigned. Training and accounts are provided. Pays commission and bonuses.

SECURE COMMUNICATION, INC., 150 W 28th St, , New York, NY 10003.
Positions: This company, Ergotron SCI, offers computer solutions and flat pane monitors to the hospital, manufacturing, and financial markets. They seek computer literate individuals capable of operating independently to introduce hot new products to major organizations.
Requirements: Need experience calling Fortune 1000 companies and hospitals.
Provisions: Training, excellent compensation, and benefits are offered along with telecommuting option.

SHAKLEE CORPORATON, Shaklee Terraces, 444 Market Street #3600, San Francisco, CA 94111.
Positions: Shaklee's line of products includes "natural" cosmetics, health care products, household products, and now some services as well. All of Shaklee's products are sold by independent distributors.
Requirements: Distributors must stock inventory in all basic products, which does require a cash investment.
Provisions: Pays commission.

SILHOUETTE MARKETING, 27350 SW 95th Ave., Wilsonville, OR 97070.
Positions: This merchandise demonstration service needs schedulers and field managers in major West Coast cities.
Requirements: Schedulers need to be experienced, able to manage people, possess organizational skills, and be able to work flexible hours from home. Field managers also need to be available to work flexible hours, have a car, and be able to interview and hire reliable people. Send resume.

SKYLIGHT TRAINING AND PUBLISHING, INC., 2626 S. Clearbrook Dr., Arlington Heights, IL 60005.
Positions: SkyLight is the educational training and publishing division of Simon &

Schuster. They need national accounts reps to sell to school personnel.
Requirements: Must have a Bachelor's degree (Master's degree preferred); excellent verbal and written communication skills; computer skills in word processing, database, presentation software, and contact manager; and a commitment to service. Sales experience should be in maintaining and managing territories, developing new leads through cold calling, and group presentations. Teaching or administrative experience in a school setting is important. Apply with resume and include salary requirements.

SMART AGE MEDIA, 271 Buchanan Ct, Troy, MO 63379; www.smartagemedia.com.
Positions: Appointment setters, no cold calling.
Requirements: Must have proven telesales experience. Should be available and willing to work 15 to 20 hours per week on the phone.
Provisions: Can live anywhere. Warm leads are provided. Pays commission only to start, but those who are successful may be offered salary plus commission after a trial period. Earnings amount to $100-$175 per sale that result from the appointments you set.

SMITH MARKETING GROUP, 1608 West Campbell Avenue, # 196, Campbell, CA 95008; www.smithmarketinggroup.com.
Positions: This is a full-service marketing and public relations agency offfering part-time, full-time, temporary, and long-term sales positions in business development.
Requirements: Must be a business development professional capable of identifying new prospects and generating new business for the firm. Would prefer those with experience doing business development for a marketing, communications, graphic design, public relations, or temporary staffing agency. Send resume or apply online.
Provisions: Set your own flexible schedule. Pays commission only.

SOUTHERN LIVING AT HOME, P. O. Box 830951, Birmingham, AL 35283.
Positions: Selling products that mirror the lifestyle found in Southern Living magazine through home parties.
Requirements: Purchase of a basic starter kit for $199. The kit has approximately a $500 value in product and business supplies, all the supplies needed to begin, catalogs, order forms, a Consultant Handbook with video, etc.

SPINS, 118 2nd Street, 3rd Floor, San Francisco, CA 94105; www.spins.com.
Positions: Regional sales and account management. Company provides marketing information to the natural products industry. This is a rapidly expanding market with many new opportunities.
Requirements: Requires the highest level of interpersonal and selling skills, strong analytical skills, and a technical aptitude. Prefers applicants with two or more years of experience in sales and also working with syndicated data. College graduates only. Knowledge or a keen interest in natural products. Must be proficient in the use of Windows, MS Office, and Excel.
Provisions: Provides competitive salary and bonus package with full benefits and stock options. Submit resume via e-mail.

SPIRIT PLUS, 315 3rd Ave. S., Nashville, TN 37201.
Positions: Direct sales of personally designed T-shirts.

STAMPIN' UP!, 9350 S 150 East, Sandy, UT 84070.
Positions: Innovative products for creative stamping ideas, offering the latest in designs

and techniques as well as hundreds of stamps and accessories. All products are sold via direct sales.

THE STORY TELLER. www.thestoryteller.com.
Positions: Direct sales of educational products based on story telling.
Requirements: Must purchase a starter kit. A complete kit costs $100, but there is a "mini-supply kit" for only $30.
Provisions: Pays from 20% to 35% profits, plus additional bonuses. There are also plenty of marketing tools available to help you.

SUCCESS MOTIVATION INSTITUTE, INC., P.O. Box 2508, Waco, TX 76702.
Positions: SMI is the world leader in personal and professional development. Their products help businesses and sales organizations improve results.
Requirements: Must fill out application and be accepted by the company. $100 for a sales kit is the only cost.
Provisions: Sales training kit includes a cassette tape, full-color visual, two videotapes, starter supply of forms, and a "Success Guide."

SUMMIT VIEWS, 540 N. Santa Cruz Ave #260, Los Gatos, CA 95030; www.summitviews.com.
Positions: Independent sales reps follow up on sales of products to natural food stores and hotels. The product is a densified wood firelog that is environmentally friendly, called Goodwood.
Requirements: Requires flexibility, great phone abilities, sense of humor, and interest in the environment.
Provisions: Flexible part time (10-20 hours per week). Pays hourly plus commission.

SUNLAND INTERNATIONAL, 6280-P San Ignacio Avenue, San Jose, CA 95119; www.sunland-intl.com.
Positions: Telemarketing sales reps for a leading supplier of DVD and CD drives, recordable media, external storage products, digital video recording peripherals and software.
Requirements: Strong phone and customer services skills required.
Provisions: Part-time and full-time positions available. Can live anywhere.

SVI AMERICA CORPORATION, 15800 John J Delaney Dr., Charlotte, NC 28210.
Positions: Sales reps for the metro New York/New Jersey and New England territories.
Requirements: At least five years experience selling services to businesses. Need to be computer literate, have excellent multi-tasking and time management skills, and be able to set up and work in a telecommuting environment with little direct supervision.

TALENT WORLD MAGAZINE, 38 West 32nd St. #805, New York, NY 10001; www.talentworld.biz.
Positions: Part-time telemarketers for ad space sales.
Requirements: Must live in Manhattan. Prefers those with proven phone sales. Ad sales experience a plus. Inexperienced may apply.
Provisions: Leads provided. Salary dependent on experience, plus commision. Training provided.

TASTEFULLY SIMPLE, 615 Nokomis St. # 500, Alexandria, MN 56308.
Positions: Tastefully Simple offers gourmet quality food that takes only minutes to

prepare. Consultants market over 30 upscale, convenience-driven gourmet foods through taste testing parties by providing recipes, meal ideas, and entertaining suggestions.

TAYLOR ENTERPRISES, 204 LightHouse Way, Little Elm, TX 75068.
Positions: Sales of digital imaging services.
Requirements: Experience and skill in all facets of sales from prospecting to presentations and servicing.
Provisions: Unlimited earning potential with the first year averaging $65,000 to $120,000.

THOMSON POLK DIRECTORIES, 4709 Golf Rd. # 600, Skokie, IL 60076; www.citydirectory.com/polk/index.htm.
Positions: Thomson Polk has been the leading publisher of city directories and CD-Rom products since 1870. They are looking for sales reps and account executives to market city and statewide directories and other sales lead products to businesses in their local areas.
Requirements: Must have 2 years of college with marketing education, business-to-business sales experience, and strong communication skills.
Provisions: Pays base salary starting the mid $20K range plus unlimited bonus potential.

TIME-LIFE BOOKS, 2000 Duke St., Alexandria, VA 22314.
Positions: Direct sales of educational publications.

TRI-CHEM, INC., 681 Main Street #24, Belleville, NJ 07109. www.tri-chem.com.
Positions: Tri-Chem has manufactured craft products since 1948 and the complete line is now sold in more than 40 countries around the world. The leading product in their line is a liquid embroidery paint. Reps conduct craft classes to show potential customers how to use the products.
Requirements: To become a Tri-Chem instructor, you must hostess an introductory class, book at least 4 more classes for your first two weeks, and pay a small registration fee.
Provisions: Training is provided. Pays commission starting at 25% and going up to 50% with volume. Tri-Chem offers new instructors a consultant kit worth up to $260 and bonus coupons for free products worth up to $234. Bonus programs provide additional earnings, vacation trips plus special seminars and conventions to enhance training. Management opportunities are available.

TUPPERWARE HOME PARTIES, P.O. Box 2353, Orlando, FL 32802.
Positions: Direct sales of plastic food storage containers, cookware, and children's toys.

TYNDALE HOUSE PUBLISHERS, INC., 351 Executive Dr., Carol Stream, IL 60188.
Positions: Home-based telemarketers.
Requirements: Must be local resident. Experience required.

UNION TRIBUNE, 4069 - 30th Street, Suite 9, San Diego, CA 92104-2631.
Positions: Telemarketers sell subscriptions.
Requirements: Must live in the San Diego area. Self-discipline is important.
Provisions: Training is provided. Some leads are supplied. Pays commission plus bonus.

USA TODAY, 1000 Wilson Blvd., Circulation Dept., Arlington, VA 22234.
Positions: Telemarketers solicit subscriptions. Work is distributed to home workers on a local basis only through USA Today's distributors. Distributors can be found in the phone book, or you can contact the main office to locate the distributor in your area.

USANA, 3838 W Parkway Blvd, West Valley City, UT 84120.
Positions: Direct sales of a science based health and nutrition line. Products include nutrition, weight loss, and personal care.
Provisions: Pays commission plus bonuses.

USBORNE BOOKS AT HOME, P.O. Box 470663, Tulsa, OK 74147.
Positions: Usborne's award-winning children's books have been sold worldwide since 1973. The books are all four color, lavishly illustrated, information packed books that children love to read. There is a wide range of subjects covering hobbies, science, nature guides and more. Beginning in 1981, Usborne books have been successfully sold through home party plans in Australia, Hong Kong, Singapore, England and now the United States. The home business division sells over 600 Usborne titles with new publications being announced semi-annually. It also offers four methods of selling: home parties, fundraisers, book fairs, and direct sales. Usborne Books at Home is also a member of the Direct Selling Association.
Provisions: No experience necessary, training materials provided, no territories, no inventory to maintain, and no collections or product delivery. The investment of $69.95 or $159.95 includes all training materials, supplies and the base kit or mini-kit of Usborne books. The start-up kit includes training materials and supplies for only $25.00.

VITA CRAFT CORPORATION, 11100 West 58 Street, Shawnee, KS 66203.
Positions: Home party sales of cookware, china, crystal, tableware and cutlery.
Provisions: Pays commission and bonuses. Training is provided.

VIVA WEB SITES, 3 Presidio, Montgomery, TX 77356; www.viva-websites.com.
Positions: Telemarketing to book sales appointments for Web development firm.
Requirements: This is an entry level position.
Provisions: Opportunities are in Houston, Texas and Tucson, Arizona only. Work is part-time, 20 hours per week. Pays hourly wage plus commission equaling $600-$6,000 per month.

WATER RESOURCES INTERNATIONAL, INC., 2800 East Chambers St., Phoenix, AZ 85040.
Positions: Direct sales of water conditioning and purification systems.

WATKINS INCORPORATED, P.O. Box 5570, Winona, MN 55987.
Positions: Watkins is a well-established company that uses independent reps to sell its extensive line of household goods including food, health products, and cleaning items.
Requirements: A small start-up investment is required.
Provisions: Pays commission.

WCNET; www.wcnet.org.
Positions: Appointment setters to set qualified appointments for sales managers. This is business-to-business calling during normal business hours.
Requirements: Must be self-motivated and have experience in sales or telemarketing. Visit Web site and apply via e-mail.

Provisions: Pays weekly and reimburses cost of phone.

WEDDING SOLUTIONS, 6347 Caminito Tenedor, San Diego, CA 92120; www.weddingsolutions.com.
Positions: Regional advertising sales managers for the largest publisher of wedding planning books in U.S.
Requirements: Must be seasoned sales professional with three to five years of experience selling online and/or print advertising. Must have proven advertising sales experience and closing ability, excellent writing, intermediate to advanced computer skills, Internet experience, communication and interpersonal skills.
Provisions: Offers $50,000 to $120,000 salary. Provides comprehensive sales support include all online marketing material; Web based CRM software, targeted leads in assigned territories, company 800 number, personal voicemail and e-mail. There are over 50 territories in US; visit Web site to see which are open.

WELCOME WAGON, Welcome Wagon Bldg., 145 Court Ave., Memphis, TN 38103; www.Welcomewagon.com.
Positions: Welcome Wagon is a personalized advertising service. Individuals in all areas work from home to represent local businesses in the homes of brides-to-be, new parents, and newcomers.
Requirements: Outgoing personality, articulate, past-business or community experience. Car is a necessity.
Provisions: Training is provided. Flexible scheduling; part-time or full-time. Pays commission.

THE WEST BEND CO., Premiere Cookware Division, 400 Washington St., West Bend, WI 53095. www.westbend.com.
Positions: Direct sales of cookware and electrical appliances. The company started in 1911 and has been a member of the Direct Selling Association since 1927. West Bend has a deep respect for the direct selling industry because of the success of their other company, Tupperware.
Provisions: Training is provided through the use of Zig Ziglar training programs. In addition to commission, reps earn bonuses and can advance to management.

WORKSHOPS OF GERALD E. HENN, 3672 Silliman St., New Waterford, OH 44445.
Positions: This is a party-plan direct selling company that markets 19th century decorative products. They manufacture the products in Ohio and take great pride in their quality. The company has nearly tripled in size during the past two years and currently has approximately 2,000 independent contractors that work out of their homes as sales representatives. Over 90% are working part-time and nearly 100% are female.
Provisions: New people start at a commission rate of 25% and ship products directly to the Hostess.

WORLD BOOK, INC., 510 Merchandise Mart Plaza, Chicago, IL 60654.
Positions: World Book, the encyclopedia publisher, sells its products through the use of direct sales reps.
Provisions: Training is provided. Some leads are provided. Pays commission. Sales kit costs $55. Management opportunities are available

X-RITE, INC, 3100 44th Street SW, Grandville, MI 49418.

Positions: Graphic art sales for this developer and manufacturer of instrument and software for color measurement and control. The products are sold into the graphic design, digital imaging, photographic, medical, plastics, and paints and coatings industries, among others. Positions are in the Boston area and reps will solicit orders in the Northeast territory.

Requirements: Need five years minimum professional selling experience in the graphic arts industry. Need proven organizational skills, BA/BS in graphic arts, motivation to work at home, and a willingness to travel overnight 25-50%.

Provisions: Offers competitive compensation, benefits including sales incentives, stock purchase, tuition reimbursement, and retirement plan.

YELLOW FREIGHT SYSTEMS, INC., 2627 State Road, Bensalem, PA 19020.

Positions: Account sales for Yellow Freight, the largest LTL carrier in the U.S.

Requirements: This opportunity is in Philadelphia. Must have college degree and 3 to 5 years sales executive experience in a service industry. Related industry experience is a plus.

Provisions: Pays competitive base salary plus incentives and a full range of flexible benefits.

ZONDERVAN BOOK OF LIFE, P.O. Box 6130, Grand Rapids, MI 49506.

Positions: The Book of Life is a set of books based on the parables of the Bible. The company was established in 1923 and has always used direct salespeople to market the product.

Requirements: A refundable $20 deposit is required.

Provisions: The deposit buys a sales kit, which includes all necessary training materials. Pays commission on a sliding scale, which increases with volume. Cash bonuses and promotions are available. Also available are credit union membership, company-paid insurance, and a deferred retirement compensation plan.

ZA CONSULTING, 541 N Fairbanks Ct. # 2740, Chicago, IL 60611; www.zaconsulting.com.

Positions: Business-to-business sales, selling management consulting services to physicians, group practices, hospitals, and other health system providers.

Requirements: The reason this job is homebased is because there is a great deal of travel involved and therefore, being near company headquarters is irrelevant. This job requires a person who is highly professional, a college graduate with a degree in healthcare administration, accounting, or finance. Must have strong presentation and public speaking skills. Need a thorough understanding of physician practices, strategic planning approaches, client relations, and management. Minimum five years experience in management required. Send complete resume.

Provisions: Pays salary and full benefits.

ALPHABETICAL INDEX-ALL COMPANIES

JOB BANK LOCATION INDEX

State Index

National and/or Multi-Regional Companies